MAX

Social and Economic Organization

MAX WEBER: The Theory of Social and Economic Organization o o TRANSLATED BY

A. M. HENDERSON AND TALCOTT PARSONS

EDITED WITH AN INTRODUCTION BY TALCOTT PARSONS

THE FREE PRESS, *New York*
COLLIER-MACMILLAN LIMITED, *London*

Collier-Macmillan Canada, Ltd., Toronto, Ontario

FIRST FREE PRESS PAPERBACK EDITION 1964

printing number
    8   9   10

Preface

THE volume herewith presented to the English-speaking public is a translation of Part I of Max Weber's *Wirtschaft und Gesellschaft,* which was in turn originally published as Volume III of the collaborative work *Grundriss der Sozialoekonomik,* in the planning of which Weber played a major role. Its relation to Weber's work as a whole is explained in the editor's Introduction. It is, however, relatively self-contained so as to appear suitable for separate publication in translation. The choice of an English title, for which the editor is wholly responsible, is meant to designate this independent significance.

The project for publication of this translation antedates the war. Its origin lay in a draft translation of Chapters I and II which was made by Mr. A. M. Henderson for Messrs. William Hodge & Co. Ltd. of London and Edinburgh. The present editor undertook, at the publisher's request, to revise and edit this draft. It was originally planned that Mr. Henderson would submit drafts also of Chapters III and IV, but his war service prevented this. Hence the present translation of the first two chapters is a rather free revision of Mr. Henderson's draft; the translation of the third and fourth chapters is wholly the editor's. Mr. Henderson has had no opportunity to see the final version, so entire responsibility for departures from his draft must be taken by the editor.

Publication has been long delayed by difficulties created by the war. I can only express my admiration for the persistence of the English publishers in continuing to adhere to the enterprise in spite of these difficulties and in bringing it to final fruition, and for their tolerance in publishing a fundamental work by an enemy national at such a time. We can, however, agree that the universality of science transcends even the conflict of war. The American edition has been reprinted from the page proofs of the English.

Besides the aid given by Mr. Henderson's draft, I should like to acknowledge the help derived from a draft translation of Chapter I, Section 1, by Alexander von Schelting and Edward Shils, which the authors kindly put at my disposal. A number of my professional colleagues, notably the late Professor Edwin F. Gay and Professor Robert K. Merton, made valuable criticisms of the manuscript translation and the Introduction at different stages. I should like also to acknowledge the assistance of Mr. Bernard Barber and Mr. and Mrs. Sherwood Dean Fox in preparation of the index, and of Mr. Ozzie G. Simmons in correction of the proof.

Finally I should like to record my gratification that this translation does not stand alone in bringing to the English reader some of the more comprehensive and fundamental works of Max Weber. There has also recently appeared, published by the Oxford University Press, a volume of selections from Weber's most important sociological writings translated and edited by Hans Gerth and C. Wright Mills.

TALCOTT PARSONS

Cambridge, Massachusetts
24 March 1947

Contents

PREFACE, v

INTRODUCTION

I. The Author and His Career, 3
II. Weber's Methodology of Social Science, 8
III. Weber's 'Economic Sociology,' 30
IV. The Institutionalization of Authority, 56
V. The Modern Western Institutional System, 78

I. THE FUNDAMENTAL CONCEPTS OF SOCIOLOGY, 87
    1. The Definitions of Sociology and of Social Action, 88
    2. The Types of Social Action, 115
    3. The Concept of Social Relationship, 118
    4. Modes of Orientation of Social Action, 120
    5. The Concept of Legitimate Order, 124
    6. The Types of Legitimate Order, 126
    7. The Bases of Legitimacy of an Order, 130
    8. The Concept of Conflict, 132
    9. Types of Solidary Social Relationships, 136
    10. Open and Closed Relationships, 139
    11. Representation and Responsibility, 143
    12. The Concept of 'Corporate Group' and Its Types, 145
    13. Types of Order in Corporate Groups, 148
    14. Types of Order Governing Action in Corporate Groups, 150
    15. Types of Organization and of Corporate Groups, 151
    16. Power, Authority, and Imperative Control, 152
    17. Political and Religious Corporate Groups, 154

II. SOCIOLOGICAL CATEGORIES OF ECONOMIC ACTION, 158
    1. The Concept of Economic Action, 158
    2. The Concept of Utility, 164
    3. Modes of the Economic Orientation of Action, 166
    4. Typical Measures of Rational Economic Action. 168
    5. Types of Economic Corporate Groups, 171

6. Media of Exchange, Means of Payment, Money, 173
7. The Primary Consequences of the Use of Money. Credit, 179
8. The Market, 181
9. The Formal and Substantive Rationality of Economic Action, 184
10. The Rationality of Monetary Accounting. Management and Budgeting, 186
11. The Concept and Types of Profit Making. The Role of Capital, 191
12. Calculations in Kind, 202
13. The Formal and Substantive Rationality of a Money Economy, 211
14. Market Economies and Planned Economies, 212
15. Types of Economic 'Division of Labour,' 218
16. Types of the Technical Division of Labour, 225
17. Types of the Technical Division of Labour (*cont.*), 227
18. Social Aspects of the Division of Labour, 228
19. Social Aspects of the Division of Labour (*cont.*), 233
20. Social Aspects of the Division of Labour (*cont.*), 238
21. Social Aspects of the Division of Labour (*concluded*), 245
22. The Expropriation of Workers from the Means of Production, 246
23. The Expropriation of Workers from the Means of Production (*cont.*), 248
24. The Concept of Occupation and Types of Occupational Structure, 250
24A. The Principal Forms of Appropriation and of Market Relationship, 254
25. Conditions Underlying the Calculability of the Productivity of Labour, 261
26. Types of Communal Organization of Labour, 265
27. Capital Goods and Capital Accounting, 267
28. The Concept of Commerce and Its Principal Forms, 268
29. The Concept of Commerce and Its Principal Forms (*cont.*), 270
29A. The Concept of Commerce and Its Principal Forms (*concluded*), 272
30. The Conditions of Maximum Formal Rationality of Capital Accounting, 275
31. The Principal Modes of Capitalistic Orientation of Profit Making, 278
32. The Monetary System of the Modern State and the Different Kinds of Money, 280
33. Restricted Money, 289
34. Paper Money, 291
35. The Formal and Material Value of Money, 292
36. Methods and Aims of Monetary Policy, 294
36A. Critical Note on the 'State Theory of Money,' 299
37. The Non-Monetary Significance of Political Bodies for the Economic Order, 309

38. The Financing of Political Bodies, 310
39. Repercussions of Financing on Private Economic Activity, 315
40. The Influence of Economic Factors on the Organization of Corporate Groups, 318
41. Motives of Economic Activity, 319

III. The Types of Authority and Imperative Co-ordination, 324

i. The Basis of Legitimacy, 324

1. The Definition, Conditions, and Types of Imperative Control, 324
2. The Three Pure Types of Legitimate Authority, 328

ii. Legal Authority with a Bureaucratic Administrative Staff, 329

3. Legal Authority: The Pure Type with Employment of a Bureaucratic Administrative Staff, 329
4. Legal Authority: The Pure Type with Employment of a Bureaucratic Administrative Staff (cont.), 333
5. The Monocratic Type of Bureaucratic Administration, 337

iii. Traditional Authority, 341

6. Traditional Authority, 341
7. Traditional Authority (cont.), 342
7A. Gerontocracy, Patriarchalism, and Patrimonialism, 346
8. Modes of Support of the Patrimonial Retainer, 351
9. Decentralized Patrimonial Authority, 352
9A. The Relations of Traditional Authority and the Economic Order, 354

iv. Charismatic Authority, 358

10. The Principal Characteristics of Charismatic Authority and Its Relation to Forms of Communal Organization, 358

v. The Routinization of Charisma, 363

11. The Routinization of Charisma and Its Consequences, 363
12. The Routinization of Charisma and Its Consequences (cont.), 367
12A. The Routinization of Charisma and Its Consequences (concluded), 369
12B. Feudalism, 373
12C. Feudalism Based on Benefices and Other Types, 378
13. Combinations of the Different Types of Authority, 382

vi. The Transformation of Charisma in an Anti-Authoritarian Direction, 386

14. The Transformation of Charisma in an Anti-Authoritarian Direction, 386

CONTENTS

vii. Collegiality and the Separation of Powers, 392

15. Collegiality and the Separation of Powers, 392
16. The Functionally Specific Separation of Powers, 404
17. The Relations of the Political Separation of Powers to the Economic Situation, 406

viii. Parties

18. The Concept of Parties and Their Features, 407

ix. Types of Government of Corporate Groups Which Minimize Imperative Powers; the Role of Representation, 412

19. Anti-Authoritarian Forms of Government, 412
20. 'Amateurs' or 'Non-Professional' Types of Administrative Personnel, 413

x. Representation, 416

21. The Principal Forms and Characteristics of Representation, 416
22. Representation by the Agents of Interest Groups, 421

IV. Social Stratification and Class Structure, 424

i. Concepts, 424

1. The Concepts of Class and Class Status, 424
2. The Significance of Acquisition Classes, 426
3. Social Strata and Their Status, 428

Index, 431

MAX WEBER: The Theory of
Social and Economic Organization

Introduction

I. The Author and His Career

THOUGH an increasing number of scholars in the English-speaking world have in recent years come to know Max Weber's work in the original German editions, the part of it which has heretofore been available in English translation has formed a wholly inadequate basis on which to understand the general character of his contributions to social science. *The Protestant Ethic and the Spirit of Capitalism*[1] is probably still his best-known work. This is an empirical historical essay which, in spite of its crucial significance to its author's work as a whole, is only a fragment even of his work on historical materials, and gives only an exceedingly partial idea of the analytical scheme upon which, to a very large extent, the interpretation of its significance depends. The *General Economic History*[2] is far broader in scope but a mere sketch in development. It was put together from students' notes of the last series of lectures Weber gave and cannot be considered an adequate statement of the results of his researches in economic or institutional history, to say nothing of sociological theory and the methodology of social science.[3]

Weber's was the type of mind which was continually developing throughout his intellectually productive life. He explicitly repudiated the desire to set up a 'system' of scientific theory, and never completed a systematic work. There are, however, exceedingly important systematic elements in his thought, and the volume herewith presented to the world of English-speaking scholarship has been selected for translation precisely because it contains the nearest approach to a comprehensive statement of these elements of all his published works. It contains both

---

[1] Translated by Talcott Parsons from vol. i of *Gesammelte Aufsätze zur Religionssoziologie*. Published, with a foreword by R. H. Tawney, by George Allen & Unwin, Ltd., London, 1930.

[2] Translated by Frank H. Knight from the volume entitled in German *Wirtschaftsgeschichte*. Published by George Allen & Unwin, Ltd., London, 1927.

[3] A major addition to the English translations of Weber's works has recently been made by the publication of *From Max Weber: Essays in Sociology,* translated and edited by Hans Gerth and C. Wright Mills, Oxford University Press, New York, Inc., 1946.

a greatly condensed statement of the methodological foundations of his
empirical and theoretical work, most of which had been more fully
discussed in his earlier methodological essays, and the systematic development not of all, but of a very important part, of a comprehensive,
logically integrated scheme of 'ideal types' of social action and relationships.

But this system of 'sociological theory' was not meant by Weber to
stand alone. It was conceived rather as the 'introduction' to an enormously ambitious comparative historical study of the sociological and
institutional foundations of the modern economic and social order. It
has been published, in the German, as Part 1 of the much larger work,
Wirtschaft und Gesellschaft. This work, even in Part 1, but still more
so in the later parts, was left seriously incomplete at its author's pre-
mature death, so that the editors did not even have an authoritative table
of contents in terms of which to decide on the arrangement of the existing manuscript material. Though a 'fragment' it is still an exceedingly
comprehensive one, and gives a better conception than does any other
single work of its author's extraordinary erudition, scope of interest, and
analytical power.

Before entering upon the discussion of some of the more important
technical questions of social science methodology, theory, and empirical
generalization which are raised by the work here translated, it will be
well to give the reader a brief sketch of the author and of the more
general character and setting of his work.

Max Weber[4] was born in 1864 and died in 1920. He came from the
most highly cultured portion of the German upper middle class, his
father being prominent in the politics of the National Liberal Party in
the Bismarckian era, and for many years a member of the *Reichstag*.
Max was brought up in Berlin and entered on the study of law, receiving
an appointment as *Privatdozent* at the University of Berlin. He became
diverted from the legal field at a relatively early stage, however, in that
he accepted an appointment as Professor of Economics at the University
of Freiburg, which he soon left to become the successor of Karl Knies
in the chair of economics at Heidelberg. After only a brief tenure in this
position, however, he suffered a severe breakdown of health which forced
his resignation from his professorship and kept him out of productive

[4] For Weber's biography, including a great deal of discussion of his work, see Marianne
Weber's excellent *Max Weber, Ein Lebensbild*. This also contains a complete bibliography
of his writings. See also the introduction to the volume translated by Gerth and Mills, cited
above in note 3.

work for about four years. After that, during the most fruitful years of his life, he lived as a private scholar in a state of semi-invalidism in Heidelberg. During the latter part of World War I, however, he accepted a temporary teaching appointment at the University of Vienna, and finally, in 1919, a regular appointment to the Chair of Economics at Munich. He died suddenly of pneumonia in the second semester of his incumbency there, at the height of his intellectual powers.

Though Weber's formal career was mainly confined to the academic sphere, his interest never was. From an early age he took a passionate interest in political affairs. For many years he was on terms of intimacy with politically important persons, and gave them considerable advice behind the scenes. He was among the first to develop strong opposition to the regime of Wilhelm II, though by no means mainly from the point of view of the ordinary 'left' parties. During the War he submitted several memoranda to the Government, and in the latter part of it began writing articles on current events for the *Frankfurter Zeitung*. He was a member of the Commission which drew up the memorandum on German war guilt for the Peace Conference, and of the Commission which submitted the first draft of the Weimar Constitution. It is not impossible that, had he lived, he would have occupied a prominent place in the politics of post-war Germany. There is a sense in which, throughout his life, he was torn between the life of the scholar and the urge to play an active part in the political arena.[5]

Weber's intellectual career and the process by which his thought developed are intimately connected with the intellectual situation and movements in Germany in his time. He first entered upon the study of law, under the aegis of the historical school, which was then in the ascendancy in the Universities, and his early views stood in conscious reaction against the 'formalism' of the Neo-Kantian philosophy of law, which was most prominently represented by Stammler. This antithesis led his interest beyond the mere interest in the history of legal institutions as such, to the study of their social and economic setting. His earlier studies in this field, notably his essay on the Decline of the Roman Empire, and his economic history of the Ancient World,[6] strongly emphasized the dependence of law on its economic and technological background. Hence the

[5] This conflict is documented in his two remarkable essays: *Wissenschaft als Beruf* and *Politik als Beruf*, both translated by Gerth and Mills.

[6] Both reprinted in the volume *Gesammelte Aufsätze zur Sozial und Wirtschaftsgeschichte*.

step from historical jurisprudence to historical economics was not a difficult one.

Weber was not, however, satisfied for long with this phase of his thinking. He was insistent on the observance of rigorous canons of factual objectivity in historical research, and could not tolerate the metaphysical 'cloudiness' of idealistic philosophers of history who saw everything readily explained by the process of unfolding of a *Volksgeist*. But neither could he be satisfied with the exclusive attention to questions of detailed historical fact which was so prominent in the work of the historical schools of his time. His was a mind which eagerly sought after broad generalization, however rigorous his standards of detailed scholarship, and early in his career he became absorbed in empirical problems of such scope as to be inaccessible to such methods alone. Part of the outcome of these dissatisfactions was the methodological reorientation, the starting point of which was a devastating critique of the logical foundations of the historical school of economics.[7]

Both in the emphasis on economic rather than formal legal factors, and in the statement of his empirical problems as revolving about the genesis of 'capitalism' in the Western World, Weber's earlier development took a course which brought him into close contact with the Marxian position. But he soon recoiled from this, becoming convinced of the indispensability of an important role of 'ideas' in the explanation of great historical processes. The first document of this new conviction was the study of the Protestant Ethic as an element in the genesis of modern capitalism. This was not, however, a final work but became the starting point of a long series of comparative empirical studies of the relations of religious movements and the economic order, which, though incomplete, have been brought together in the three volumes of his *Gesammelte Aufsätze zur Religionssoziologie*.

It may perhaps be said that it is out of his insight into and conviction of the inadequacy both of German Historical Economics and Jurisprudence and of Marxism to solve the problems he had become interested

[7] Weber never wrote a connected study of methodology. His various essays in the field have been collected since his death in the volume *Gesammelte Aufsätze zur Wissenschaftslehre*. The most important for his early polemical orientation are *Roscher und Knies und die logischen Probleme der historischen Nationalökonomie* and *R. Stammlers Überwindung der materialistischen Geschichtsauffassung*. For his own positive position see in particular *Die Objektivität sozialwissenschaftlicher und sozialpolitischer Erkenntnis, Der Sinn der 'Wertfreiheit' der soziologischen und ökonomischen Wissenschaften*, and *Methodische Grundlagen der Soziologie* (chap. i, sec. 1 of the present volume).

in that Weber launched on the development of an independent line of broad theoretical analysis in the social field, in particular into the development of a science of 'sociology.' It is in essentials the theoretical result of this intellectual development, so far as he stated it systematically at all, which is contained in the present volume. It stands in marked contrast to most of the main line of German social thought of his time, but is none the less understandable only in terms of the problems inherent in the German intellectual movements of the day. It is, in view of its almost purely German genesis, all the more remarkable that the major part of the theoretical structure Weber developed should with remarkable exactitude have converged with the work, done at about the same time, of various other scholars in other countries, notably that of Emile Durkheim in France and Vilfredo Pareto in Switzerland.[8] The theoretical scheme of *Wirtschaft und Gesellschaft* was very closely bound to the problems growing out of specifically German movements of thought. Its author specifically disclaimed any idea of putting forward a system of social or sociological theory. Finally, in many respects its statement and organization show that the process of systematic development and of methodological clarification were, even according to the standards which can now be applied, seriously incomplete. But in spite of these limitations this work must be regarded as one of the very few most fundamental contributions to the modern theoretical social sciences. Though he 'hid his light under a bushel' its author will unquestionably rank among the select few who have in a scientific sense been genuinely eminent theorists in the social field.[9]

[8] See the editor's *Structure of Social Action* for a detailed analysis of this process of convergence.

[9] *The Structure of Social Action*, especially chaps. xvi and xvii, contains a considerably more detailed critical analysis of Weber's theory and methodology than is possible in the present introductory essay.

II. Weber's Methodology of Social Science

It is perhaps one of the most important canons of critical work, that the critic should attempt so far as possible to see the work of an author in the perspective of the intellectual situation and tradition out of which it has developed. This is one of the best protections against the common fallacy of allowing superficial interpretation of verbal formulae to mislead one into unfair interpretations of ideas and inadequate formulations of problems.

The most essential background of Weber's methodological work was the 'historical' tradition of German thought. Back of this, in turn, lay the process by which there developed a radical dualism in the types of intellectual discipline dealing with empirical subjects, and a corresponding dichotomy of the types of method appropriate to the two, the 'natural' and the 'socio-cultural' sciences. The following is a highly schematic outline of what seems to be the most essential development.

It is convenient to take the work of Kant as the point at which to study a set of 'preconceptions' which, though for the most part long tacitly taken for granted, seems to have played an important part in the formulation of problems and possible directions for their solution in scientific methodology. According to this view, the world of 'nature' was the world of human experience in so far as it was accessible to understanding in terms of the 'natural sciences,' which came in the end to mean the conceptual scheme of the classical mechanics. But this realm, Kant's 'phenomenal world,' tended to be treated not only logically, but also empirically, as a closed system. From this tendency, above all, seems to be derived the tacit assumption, sometimes explicitly stated, that *only* phenomena of nature in this specific sense were capable of being grasped in terms of a generalized analytical conceptual scheme.

The tendency of 'Western' positivistic thought was to identify this 'order of nature' with ontological reality as a whole. But this was not true of the tradition in which Weber was brought up. In Germany, rather, Kant's conception of the world of 'spirit'[1] developed into a great tradition of intellectual disciplines dealing with human culture and behaviour. A main pattern of thinking there throughout the nineteenth century was the conception that human knowledge fell into these two radically different categories, the natural sciences and the studies of culture and social behaviour.[2]

Though both were conceived as consisting of systematic empirical knowledge, subject to canons of accuracy of observation and logical precision and consistency, the tendency in Germany has been to emphasize the depth of the contrast, to hold that the methodological canons most characteristic of the natural sciences were in the nature of the case not applicable to the social-cultural and vice versa. This is particularly true of the role of generalized conceptual schemes, of theory, and this is the point at which Weber chose to make his principal attack.

On the positive side was the emphasis on the necessity, for the sciences of human behaviour and culture, of the 'subjective' point of view of *Verstehen* in the technical sense of the term in the works of such writers as Dilthey, Rickert, and Weber. But in the predominant tradition this was couched in terms of the view that explanation of human phenomena must take place in 'historical' terms, in terms of genetic sequences as such. The tendency was to regard each genetic sequence as unique and incapable of comparison with any other; in particular radically to deny the relevance of generalized theoretical categories.

Weber's essential starting point is an acceptance of the subjective point of view, combined with a critical attack on the 'historical' position. His basic thesis in this connexion is that generalized theoretical categories are as essential to the proof of causal relationships in the human and cultural field as they are in the natural sciences.

At the same time he found it necessary to attack another very common methodological misconception, that either the aim or the actual result of scientific investigation in any field can be to attain a complete picture of the ontological reality of the phenomena. Over against this he set the view that all empirical knowledge is in the nature of the case abstract. It never includes 'all the facts,' even that can easily be ascertained, but only those which are relevant to certain interests of the investigator. There is, in this selectivity of facts, both for the formulation of problems

[1] Usually *Geist* in the German literature.
[2] *Naturwissenschaften* and *Geistewissenschaften* or *Kulturwissenschaften*.

and for the content of conceptualization, a very important element of relativity in all science, natural or social. Weber, however, maintained that this fact, which he not merely conceded but insisted upon, did not destroy the reliability or objectivity of propositions either in the social field, or in the natural. He held that the question of the grounds of validity of a proposition, once enunciated, is logically distinct from that of explaining the empirical process by which interest in it came about. This element of relativity touches the question of validity only at the point of calling for limitation of the relevance of the propositions concerned, and hence of the order of generalization or inference from them which is legitimate.

All this Weber developed in earlier essays [3] and takes for granted in the methodological discussion of the present translation, where he proceeds directly to discuss some of the foundations of a systematic science of *verstehende Soziologie,* a system of sociological categories couched in terms of the subjective point of view, that is of the meaning of persons, things, ideas, normative patterns, and motives from the point of view of the persons whose action is being studied. Certain aspects of this background are, however, essential to the understanding of Weber's treatment of a number of problems in this work, particularly the nature of the kind of generalized theoretical concept to which he paid the most attention, the 'ideal type,' and certain closely related problems connected with his treatment of rationality, and of the relations of sociology and psychology.

The impasse from which Weber took his departure was as follows: One tendency of the thought of his time was to attempt to assimilate the sciences of human behaviour as closely as possible to the natural sciences. Interpreting the later overwhelmingly in an 'empiricist' manner, the result was to squeeze out all that was most distinctive in the traditional and common-sense treatment of human problems, notably the use of subjective categories. If, on the other hand, the attempt was made to use these modes of approach it was thought that it had to be in a set of terms which excluded the principal *logical* characteristics of the natural sciences, notably the use of generalized theoretical categories and their integration in logically articulated theoretical systems. What Weber did was to take an enormous step in the direction of bridging the gap between the two types of science, and to make possible the treatment of

---

[3] Notably *Roscher und Knies und die logischen Probleme der historischen National-ökonomie* and *Die Objektivität sozialwissenschaftlicher Erkenntnis.*

social material in a systematic scientific manner rather than as an art. But he failed to complete the process, and the nature of the half-way point at which he stopped helps to account for many of the difficulties of his position.

Weber laid great emphasis in his earlier methodological work on the fact that proof of causal relationship in any scientific field, involved reference, explicitly or implicitly, to the same logical schema of proof.[4] The most important features of this schema are, perhaps, three: (1) The description of the phenomenon to be explained in terms of a conceptual scheme, a frame of reference which was inherently abstractive and selective with respect to the facts treated as relevant and their mode of statement; (2) the subsumption of the detailed statements of fact involved under generalized theoretical categories which would make comparison and generalization possible; (3) the comparison of the state of affairs thus described and analysed with one or more others, real or hypothetical, in which the detailed facts are different but the generalized categories the same. With respect to the problem of imputation of causal significance to a 'factor' in the antecedent state of a system, it is logically necessary to show, by application of generalized knowledge to the comparison of states, that if the facts of the antecedent state had been different, the later state of the system, the facts to be explained, would also have been different in specific ways. Weber's problem was to define the kinds of generalized categories which met the logical requirements of this schema and at the same time embodied the point of view peculiar to the historical-cultural sciences, the use of subjective categories.

In this connexion Weber's polemical orientation was directed against a methodological position according to which such categories could only be used to formulate individually unique complexes of meaning and sequences of motivation. Weber fully agreed with the proponents of this position that concrete phenomena were individually unique, but disputed the relevance of this fact to his problems. Scientific conceptualization is, he said, in the nature of the case abstract and never fully exhausts or reflects concrete reality. This seems to be the logical pattern underlying his statement at the very beginning, that 'meaning' may be of two kinds, the 'actually existing' meaning to a concrete individual actor or, on the other hand, the 'theoretically conceived pure type of subjective mean-

---

[4] Cf. *Structure of Social Action*, chap. xvi, where this schema is more elaborately analysed.

ing.'[5] This pure type, which is generally known as the 'ideal type,' was
the first and most obvious level of generalized abstract concept which
Weber's analysis encountered, the concept which, while meeting the
logical requirements of the schema of proof, was closest to the concrete
individual reality.

But two other circumstances seem to be importantly involved in the
direction which his methodological formulations took. As the editor
has shown in previous works,[6] it is inherent in the frame of reference of
'action' which is basic to Weber's whole methodology, that it is 'normatively oriented.' The actor is treated not merely as responding to stimuli,
but as making an 'effort' to conform with certain 'ideal,' rather than
actual, patterns of conduct with the probability that his efforts will be
only partially successful, and there will be elements of deviation. The
ideal type, then, is not merely an abstraction, but a particular kind of
abstraction. It states the case where a normative or ideal pattern is perfectly complied with.[7] Thus Weber says:

the construction of a purely rational course of action . . . serves the sociologist
as a type. . . By comparison with this it is possible to understand the ways
in which actual action is influenced by irrational factors of all sorts, . . . in
that they account for the deviation from the line of conduct which would be
expected on the hypothesis that the action were purely rational.[8]

On one plane this would be true of an ideal type which was formulated
in terms of any kind of normative pattern. The special place which
Weber gives to patterns of rationality involves other considerations. Part
of it is a matter of the relativity in the direction of interest of the social
scientist on which Weber so constantly insisted. He felt that the development and role of certain patterns of rationality constituted the most important problems of our time in the Western World, and deliberately
formulated his conceptual scheme to throw them into high relief. But
there is probably still a further relevant consideration. It has already been
noted that Weber emphasized particularly the role of abstract generalized
concepts in science. Throughout his work it is notable how intimately
he associates the methodological problems of science with the substantive
problems of rationality of action.[9] The rational ideal type thus probably

[5] See chap. i, sec. 1, para. 1, p. 89.
[6] See notably the *Structure of Social Action*, especially chap. ii, note A.
[7] Conceived, of course, as 'ideal' from the point of view of the actor, not of the observer.
[8] P. 92.
[9] Cf. *Structure of Social Action*, p. 586.

appealed to him precisely because the normative patterns of rationality, since they were defined by the role of scientifically verifiable knowledge, directly embodied this element of generality in the determinants of action. This is clearly brought out in his invoking, against Knies' use of the idea of freedom of the will, the argument that in those types of action which we treated as most highly rational, there was both a high sense of freedom and a maximum of predictability and understandability in generalized terms. Thus it was that Weber, in his formulations of systematic theory, concentrated overwhelmingly on rational ideal types.

Discounting its confusion in some of Weber's work with other kinds of concept,[10] there is no doubt that the rational ideal type is an authentic generalized theoretical concept, and on one level adequately met the requirements of his methodological problems. At the same time, however, he apparently failed to place it adequately in relation to certain other possibilities, thus neglecting alternative formulations and falling into certain biases on the higher levels of generalization.

The ideal type as Weber used it is both abstract and general. It does not describe a concrete course of action, but a normatively ideal course, assuming certain ends and modes of normative orientation as 'binding' on the actors. It does not describe an individual course of action, but a 'typical' one—it is a generalized rubric within which an indefinite number of particular cases may be classified. But it does describe what Weber called an 'objectively possible' course of action. It contains, within the logical requirements of the relevant frame of reference, all the necessary properties or features of a concrete act or complex of action. The importance of this lies in the fact that the different logically distinct elements which are essential to the formulation of this type may be, indeed generally are, independently variable. The ideal type contains no particular statements of fact. But it does, logically, involve a fixed relation between the values of the various variable elements involved. If analysis is confined to its use, certain possibilities of variation on other levels are arbitrarily excluded from consideration. This is not, of course, to say in any simple sense that it is 'wrong,' but only that it is limited in certain respects.

Weber begins the process of systematic conceptualization by setting up a classification of four types of action.[11] This procedure itself makes it difficult to interpret his position at a great many points because he

---

[10] Cf. A. von Schelting, *Max Weber's logische Theorie der historischen Kulturwissenschaften, Archiv für Sozialwissenschaft*, vol. xlix.

[11] Pp. 115 ff.

neglected to inquire systematically on a comparable level into the structure of total social systems of action. Indeed such a conception of generalized structure would be a logically necessary prerequisite of a complete classification of types. Failing this, the classification of types is unsatisfactory in various respects. It takes its starting point from the concept of rationality and the distinction of two different kinds of ultimate-end system and the corresponding relation of ultimate ends to the choice of means. In the case of *Wertrationalität* the choice of means is oriented to the realization of a single absolute value without reference to considerations of cost. In that of *Zweckrationalität,* on the other hand, it is oriented to a plurality of values in such a way that devotion to any one is limited by the possibility of its entailing excessive cost in the form of sacrifice of the others.[12] By contrast with these rational types he then formulates what are essentially two different residual categories. The one, the 'affectual' type, does not distinguish what may be called biologically inherited emotional tendencies from value-attitudes which are not formulated in logically determinate fashion, hence not involved in the rational types. The other category, 'traditional' action, is on quite a different level. It is of great significance to Weber's empirical research, but does not fit directly with the others in the same classification.

Having set up these four types of action Weber proceeds immediately to another structural level and deals with ideal types of social relationships.[13] His systematic conceptual scheme is essentially a system of such logically inter-related ideal types of social relationship. The concept of a generalized system on the action level, however, though he did not develop it explicitly, is implicit in the logical framework in terms of which he develops the classification of relationship types.

This system is a remarkable structure. In the care and precision with which it is formulated, in its comprehensiveness, and above all in the closeness of its relevance to Weber's empirical research interests, it is probably unique in the literature. Furthermore it involves a kind of conceptualization which is essential at some point in the development of systematic sociological theory. The perspective in which Weber develops it, however, leads to certain serious difficulties which will be noted presently.

It has been pointed out that, in formulating his classification of the four types of action, Weber neglected to develop the analysis of the struc-

---

[12] For a fuller discussion see *Structure of Social Action,* chap. xvii.
[13] Pp. 118 ff.

ture of a total social system which is a logically necessary prerequisite of such a classification. Essentially the same is true, on a somewhat different level, of Weber's types of social relationship. In each case the question is not raised of how this particular type, and the conceptual elements which make it up, fit into the conception of a total functioning social system of action or of relationships, as the case may be. Combined with this is the fact that the use of the ideal type concentrates attention on extreme or polar types. In the nature of the case the only kind of total system into which they would fit is the limiting type of system which is least likely to be found in reality even in at all close approximation.[14] The result is to throw attention away from such conceptions as that of a system as a balance of forces in equilibrium, of relative degrees of integration and disorganization. It also leads to a kind of 'type atomism' one aspect of which is to minimize the elements which link the type in question with other elements of the structure of the same system. Some of these difficulties can best be brought out in relation to some particular problems which play a prominent part in Weber's methodological discussion.

The first is the problem of rationality. As has been pointed out, Weber chooses to deal predominantly with rational ideal types and to treat elements other than the rational as accounting for the deviations of the actual course of action from the prescriptions of the constructed type. This seems to be the principal source of a marked tendency for Weber's thought to move in terms of the dichotomy of rational and irrational. Thus he says [15] that after having constructed a rational ideal type, 'it is then possible to introduce the irrational components as accounting for the observed deviations from this hypothetical course.' And further on 'by comparison with this (i.e. the ideal type) it is possible to understand the ways in which actual action is influenced by irrational factors of all sorts, such as affects and errors, in that they account for the deviation. . .'

There is, of course, no objection as such to the *classification* of concrete actions in terms of their conformity with and deviation from a particular type, nor to the labelling of the case of conformity as 'rational' and of

14 This does not of course exclude the possibility of a critically important range of variation in actual social structures. Indeed his awareness of this is one of Weber's most important insights. But the actual range of variation corresponds only roughly to a classification of logically extreme 'pure' ideal types.

15 P. 92.

deviation as 'irrational.' It depends how this simple starting point is used. Now the term rationality is used as pointing to certain specific criteria distinguishing some kinds of action from others. Weber unfortunately does not give us an explicit statement of these criteria, but they can be inferred from his discussion. An act is rational in so far as (a) it is oriented to a clearly formulated unambiguous goal, or to a set of values which are clearly formulated and logically consistent; (b) the means chosen are, according to the best available knowledge, adapted to the realization of the goal. The question of efficiency, a very important one in defining rationality, is not introduced by Weber at all until Chapter II and then only in a very limited context. But these criteria do not, even within the frame of reference of action, give an adequate description of any concrete act. They do not, for instance, specify the content of an end or goal, but only the character of its formulation. They do not describe the situation in which it is carried out, but only certain modes of relation between this situation and the end. They describe only part of the criteria by which choices of means can be determined.

But these other elements, though not included in the criteria of rationality, are none the less present in the acts, even the ideal types of acts. Thus even a theoretical limiting case of a particle in a mechanical system must have *all* the properties required by the frame of reference for a determinate description. All other elements, if explicitly formulated at all, however, are treated by Weber as elements of deviation from the rational type. All the important problems of a system of action which arise in connexion with Pareto's category of that part of *non*-logical action which is not *il*logical, are obscured by Weber's mode of approach.

Partly, this is simply an error of omission. Certain elements, the presence of which is logically implied, are ignored. But this is not all. Since the basic dichotomy of Weber's analysis is that of the rational and the irrational, and since the latter elements are treated as elements of *deviation,* the tendency is to create a false, theoretically unwarranted antithesis. Elements which may well in some empirical cases be integrated with the rational elements in a system, are pushed into conflict with it. Thus ultimate values tend to be treated as an absolutely 'irrational' force. In a closely connected sense affect is also treated as irrational. Weber again and again, in these methodological remarks, refers to it in these terms.[16]

When the problem of rationality is approached in terms of the concep-

[16] Cf. for instance p. 92.

tion of the human individual as actor, as a total functioning system, a very different view emerges. The first fundamental point is that the criteria by which rational types are distinguished are not adequate to describe even a total unit act, to say nothing of a system of action. In this sense (as opposed to that of the maximization of these elements) a 'purely rational' act or system is a contradiction in terms—it is not 'objectively possible.' Speaking of a system rather than a unit act, these criteria above all fail to include the following: (a) The empirical facts of the external non-social situation; (b) the outline of the structure of the individual personality as it is relevant to ordering the actor's orientation, not only to other actors, but to himself. Included in this is the fact that we treat people as having 'goals,' 'interests,' 'emotions,' etc.; (c) the basic value-orientations which individuals have and which are institutionalized in the society of which they are a part. These, and perhaps other elements, are not 'rational,' but neither does it make sense to speak of them as 'irrational.' They are essential to complete an 'objectively possible' description of a system to which the criteria of rationality apply. Certain particular 'values' of these generalized categories may be relevant in interpreting particular cases of deviation from the types Weber treats as rational, may hence be sources of irrationality in these cases, but this whole question lies on a radically different level from that of defining the elements of a generalized system of action. Weber, in fact, never does this explicitly at all. But these problems are logically involved in his procedure.

Irrationality, as Weber himself defines it, namely deviation from rational types, is thus not a matter of the presence of generalized elements other than those included in the criteria of rationality, but is much more complex than that. It is a problem which cannot be satisfactorily treated in terms of conformity with and deviation from an isolated ideal type. It involves at many points considerations touching the integration and malintegration of total social systems of action. In the absence of systematic analysis of these considerations, Weber falls into what is not so much a naive 'rationalistic bias'—an interpretation against which he justifiably protests [17]—but rather a question of thinking in terms of a certain kind of abstract dichotomy in a far too limited theoretical context. In ways not possible to analyze in this introductory essay, this difficulty plays an important part in some of Weber's broadest empirical generalizations, notably those touching the 'process of rationalization.' [18]

[17] P. 92.
[18] See *Structure of Social Action*, chap. xvii.

It has been stated that the basic source of difficulty lies in Weber's failure to carry through a systematic functional analysis of a generalized social system of action. Was he aware of the possibility of doing this and its possible significance? It is probable that he was not, as is illuminatingly brought out by the way in which he discussed the 'functional' method without really bringing out this possible line of analysis.

After his general discussion of *Verstehen* and the definition of a motive, Weber introduces the topic [19] in a characteristic way by stating that subjective categories can be applied *only* to the action of *individual* persons. For cognitive purposes other than the sociological it may well be useful to consider the individual as an aggregate of cells or some other elementary units or, conversely, to employ 'collective' concepts which treat pluralities of individuals as units. But however useful these latter concepts may be, for instance in a legal context, for sociology they must always be redefined as dealing *only* with certain kinds of uniformities in the action of the relevant individuals. Such concepts may also serve as norms to which the action of individuals is oriented.

From these considerations Weber arrives at a treatment of the methods of so-called 'organic' sociology. However much this kind of analysis of the relation of 'parts' to a 'whole' may have to remain the goal of other sciences, for sociology, as he understands it, it can be only of preliminary significance. In the first place, it serves for initial orientation and in this connexion is useful and necessary though also, if it leads to illegitimate reification, dangerous.[20] In the second place it serves to direct attention to the problems of substantive analysis which are most important. But then he goes on to say that precisely in the field of action it is not necessary to stop with this, but it is possible to proceed with something no natural science is capable of, the subjective understanding of the behaviour of the individual component, which, in the case of cells, is out of the question.

In discussing the use of a functional approach for preliminary orientation and statement of problems Weber makes a number of references to the bearing of a phenomenon on the 'survival' of the system, organism or society, under consideration.[21] This suggests that one of the sources of Weber's failure to think explicitly in terms of a theoretically general-

[19] Cf. pp. 101 ff.

[20] Weber refers here particularly to the work of Othmar Spann, whose 'universalism' he interprets as involving a functional method in this sense. Cf. p. 106.

[21] Cf. p. 105.

ized social system lies in certain features of the biological thought of his time—which, though perhaps responsible for subtle biases in biology,[22] are much more harmful when taken over into the social field.[23]

The important feature of this thought for present purposes is the tendency to attempt to simplify dynamic problems by attributing as many as possible of the features of the organism to the necessities imposed upon it by the environment if it or its species is to survive. This has tended to divert attention from the functional analysis of the organism as a going concern to the external conditions of the survival of organisms. To a certain extent it is a result of the preoccupation in biological theory with problems of evolution rather than of physiology. But from the latter point of view the basic conceptual scheme of an organism functioning in an environment contains the germs of a generalized system of functional theory. Since all physiological process involves interchange with the environment, the existence and properties of the latter cannot be ignored. But there is no question of attempting to 'reduce' the organism to environmental terms except for its own propensity to survive. Indeed from this point of view the basic structural facts about the organism are treated, within the framework of the generalized theoretical system, as given in observation.

This source of difficulty is accentuated by another peculiar to the study of human society. The 'functional' approach has, in the history of thought, been predominantly associated with biology. Its use in other fields has hence not unnaturally been associated with a tendency to attempt to reduce the subject-matter of those fields to biological terms. In the social field this has taken two primary forms. In the first of these a social system is treated as a plurality of biological organisms and functional problems are formulated in terms of their functional needs and survival as organisms. In so doing a possibility of fundamental importance is overlooked—namely, that the functional approach could be used in terms of a different frame of reference, namely that of 'action'—or actor-situation rather than organism-environment. If this is done biological considerations become primarily conditional to the main, explicitly considered factors. The second possibility is to treat the social system as if it were itself an organism. The logical difficulties involved in this procedure are sufficiently familiar to make it unnecessary to go into them here. Weber

[22] Cf. Kurt Goldstein, *The Organism.*

[23] To be sure he does at one point qualify this by inserting 'survival and above all the maintenance of a cultural type,' p. 107.

is quite right that this precludes any exploitation of the possibilities of analysis of individual action in terms of subjective categories. The biological version of this view shades off into another type of 'organism,' one in which a culturally specific whole which dominates its parts takes the place of the organism. In the form of the *Volksgeist* and other concepts this view has played an important part in the historical schools and in idealistic social thought.

Apparently Weber understood a functional approach to mean one of these things, either an individualistic form of biological orientation which precluded the use of subjective categories, or the illegitimate reification of collectivities as organisms or as cultural totalities. He did not perceive that starting from the frame of reference of subjectively interpreted individual action—which he himself used so extensively—it was possible by functional analysis to develop a generalized outline of social systems of action. As has been remarked, such an outline was in fact to a large extent implicit in the structure of his own system of ideal types.

Weber's fundamental reason for being suspicious of too much emphasis upon a functional approach to social science lay in his strong conviction of the indispensability, in order to attain the level of knowledge he considered possible and essential, of careful detailed analysis of the motivation of the individual. To him, departure from the 'whole' smacked of a kind of mysticism by which it was possible to derive far-reaching conclusions without adequate empirical basis, to pull scientific rabbits out of the functional hat. Given the kind of treatment of the whole prevalent in his day, he was right. But he failed to see the possibility of developing his own type of theory further into a system which could be treated functionally in such a way as to articulate directly with his analysis of motivation. The difficulty lay in his unwarranted antithesis of the 'functional' approach and analysis of the motives of the individual. This calls for a few comments.

On the common-sense 'historical' level of analysis referred to above, the situation in which the individual whose motivation is to be analysed has to act, and the accepted 'definitions' (in Thomas'[24] sense) of that situation, are treated descriptively only, as concretely given in the individual case. Of course this description, like any other, logically implies a coherent system of generalized categories. But whatever these may be, they are not subjected to critical examination. As is the case with so many

[24] See W. I. Thomas, *The Unadjusted Girl*, Introduction.

of the categories essential to the analysis of human behaviour, they are so familiar on a certain level that any critical analysis seems superfluous.

Weber does not remain on a fully concrete 'historical' level in this sense. His analysis of motivation is couched in terms of ideal type concepts which generalize beyond any particular individual case, and are hence also abstract. They contain references to basic generalized categories of orientation of action, as in the distinction between *Wert-* and *Zweck-rationalität,* and to generalized descriptions of situationally significant fact, as in the role of territoriality in his discussion of political organization, in the concept of *Gebietsverband.* Also he gives reference in a generalized form to aspects of the integration of human relationships in a social system of such references. What there is of such a system is implicit in his order of treatment, and in the logical interrelations of his types.

Now on the level of the total social system as a whole there are certain basic aspects of its structure which can be differentiated out when the system as a whole is treated from a functional point of view. The subject is far too complex to enter into fully here, but a few essential points may be stated. It would seem to be a fundamental fact, crucial to the functional approach, that the primary modes of differentiation in the structure of a system are related to its functional needs in such a way that some differentiated parts are particularly important and effective in contributing to one or a related group of functional needs. Thus in biology we speak of the alimentary system, the sense organs, etc. as functionally differentiated structures.

There can be no doubt that the same applies in general terms to social systems. The primary differentiated units in this case are component individuals and their roles and actions. The latter is more important to Weber since it is immediately to the act that a motive in his sense corresponds. Two primary functional contexts are most conspicuously related to the structure of social systems. On the one hand such a system must meet the exigencies of its external situation, both human and non-human, and on the other must be integrated so that its parts function in a certain degree of harmony. Both sets of functions must be carried on in such a way that they are compatible with the biological and psychological needs of at least a sufficient proportion of the component human individuals.

In the first case, situational facts become related to social structure in terms of their direct relevance to human interests, for instance the economically significant scarcity and technologically significant properties of the physical means for meeting human needs, or a territorial area as a sphere within which certain uniformities of human action and relationships are maintained, by political authority and otherwise. In the second case authority, for instance, is a mode of structuring human relationships which can be functionally related to the necessity of integrating the activities of many people, both by preventing disruptive activities and by co-ordinating actions in the interest of goals which could not be achieved by individuals acting independently. In each case there is a limited number of particularly crucial categories of situational fact and of integratively significant aspects of human relationships.

Systematic investigation of the relations of human activity to the external situation and to other persons would reveal, on this level, a coherent system of such generalized categories. These, along with the basic modes of orientation of actors, are fundamental to the conception of a generalized system of action and relationships on the social level. And the systematic ordering of these categories is not possible without the 'functional' point of view; it provides the integrating principles in terms of which such categories constitute a generalized system rather than an *ad hoc* collection of disconnected concepts. It is fundamental to this approach that these are *generalized* categories. But it is precisely in terms of them that even a coherent descriptive account of the ranges of variability of concrete social structures becomes a possibility. Without at least the implicit outline of such a system, a sense of variability would be possible, to be sure, but it would be random variability. It would be impossible to use such a scheme to work out systematically determinate uniformities in social change and process.

It is fundamental to the understanding of Weber's relation to this problem to realize that the situational and relational categories which constitute the parts of a generalized social system inevitably enter directly into the formulation of his specific ideal type concepts. But to each of these in turn corresponds directly a complex of typical motivation in Weber's sense. Hence the 'subjective' point of view is as essential to the description of social structure as it is to the action of the individual. Weber's motives are not, as he himself clearly saw, 'psychological' entities. Their concreteness relative to the psychological level is precisely defined by the fact that they include socially structural definitions of the situation, and hence articulate directly with the structural-functional analysis of social systems, which means of the *variability* of social systems.

This is precisely the reason for the fruitfulness of Weber's ideal type analysis on the level of institutional behaviour and change, as contrasted with all the many attempts to explain such social phenomena in 'psychological' terms such as instinct, drives, conditioned reflexes.

The underlying problem under discussion here involves some fundamental considerations touching the role of 'theory' in empirical science. There are a variety of different levels on which 'explanation' of an individual fact or event may be attempted. On the common sense level this is usually a matter of showing the presence of certain conditions without which the phenomenon could not have happened. The conditions are usually treated as 'given' independently of the phenomena on which attention is centered. It may be said, however, that science becomes theoretically sophisticated in so far as it is able to treat a variety of interrelated phenomena simultaneously in terms of their interdependence. To do this without error involves the use—the more complex the system the more so—of a complex generalized conceptual scheme.

In the social field the fundamental problem is as follows. It is not difficult, knowing an individual's 'motives' in Weber's sense, and knowing the situation in which he is placed, to achieve a fairly satisfactory understanding of a particular act of his. That situation is, however, compounded of the actions, past, present, and prospective, of a large number of individuals whose action is interdependent, 'mutually oriented,' as Weber puts one aspect of it. Though it is thus not difficult, knowing the situation, to understand the action of any one individual, it is an entirely different matter to grasp the behaviour of the system of action as a whole, when the concrete situation of each component individual is a varying function of the action of the others. This requires a dynamic analysis which, in turn, is only possible through the use of a generalized conceptual scheme.

It would seem that in the history of science only two types of conceptual scheme have appeared which are logically capable of performing this function of making the dynamic treatment of systems as a whole possible. By far the more efficient of these is an analytical system of dynamically interrelated variables, a particular set of the values of which, taken together, is adequate to the description of a given state of an empirical system. In the classical case of analytical mechanics this makes possible, through mathematical manipulation, the direct solution of dynamic problems. Besides the values of variables as such, only the basic properties of the units of the system and the constants of its 'environment' are empirically needed. The feasibility of such analysis, however, depends on very specific conditions, with respect to the nature of the variables and their logical interrelations, and to the operations required to ascertain their values. Only within very narrow limits, if at all, are these conditions fulfilled in the fields of the biological and the social sciences.

There is, however, a second type, which, though technically far less perfect than an analytical system of dynamic equations, is far better than nothing. This is what may be called a generalized structural-functional system. The fundamental logical difference from the analytical type lies in the involvement of the structure of the empirical system as an essential element in the solution of dynamic problems. In analytical mechanics the structure of an empirical system at any given moment can always be *derived* from the basic data with the aid of the equations of the theoretical system. The necessity of structural categories in the other type of theory is an indication that the dynamic problems are too complex to admit of determinate solution without them, because there are too many variables involved, or because their nature and logical interrelations are not adequately known or are such as not to admit of the application of the requisite mathematical techniques of manipulation. The structure of the system, from the point of view of the logic of analysis, treats certain features of the empirical system as constant for the purposes in hand. They are thus removed from involvement in the dynamic problem, which is in so far simplified.

There is, however, an obvious interest in widening the area of dynamic treatment and of legitimate inference from it as much as possible. For this to be possible, the categories in terms of which structure is described must, logically, be part of the same system as those used in dynamic analysis. The essential link is supplied by the concept of function. The processes which are dynamically analysed are those which are 'functionally' related, in the given situation, to the maintenance of a level of functional performance by the system, as a whole, as a 'going concern.' Only in so far as they can thus be related do they become significant to the understanding of the behaviour of the system as a whole. And only, in turn, in so far as problems involving the behaviour of total systems are tackled can certain levels of empirical generalization be attained.

Weber's fundamental empirical interests lay in problems of institutional change. He was absorbed in problems of the structural peculiarities of modern Western society, of the conditions on which it was dependent, and of its stability and tendencies of change. It was precisely in its differences from other social systems, in its alterations during its development, and in its possible alterations in the future, as an institutionally organized system of action, that Weber was interested. In tackling these problems he had two basic alternatives. He could dissociate the behaviour of the whole from the understanding of action on the individual level altogether, and attempt to grasp the 'laws' of its total behaviour. This is precisely what many idealistic and other philosophies of history have attempted to do, and what Weber protested against. He felt strongly, and rightly, that only through relating the problems of the dynamics of the whole to the motives of individuals could he achieve a genuinely scientific level of explanation. But to do this he *had* to employ a functional method. The only trouble was that he did not do it rigorously and systematically enough.

In practice, however, he went quite far in its use. If he had not, his ideal type theory would have been nothing but formal classification. He could have pinned labels on various types of social structure and relationship, but he never could have achieved dynamic results. But the empirical material to be discussed below shows that he did achieve dynamic results on an impressive scale. This was fundamentally possible because he did treat motivation 'functionally' in terms of the significance of the action of the individual for the functioning of the system as a whole.

This same situation helps to explain Weber's attitude toward psychology and its relations to sociology. He insisted emphatically that his form of motive-interpretation was not psychology. He tended to regard psychology as no more relevant to sociology than any other science which dealt with factors conditional to human behaviour, like physics, geology, etc.[25] He does not anywhere discuss in detail just what he meant by the term psychology, but there was a tendency to think of it primarily in the context of natural science and hence not accessible to the application of subjective categories. He does, to be sure, mention in passing a branch of *verstehende* psychology which would be more closely related to sociology, but does not elaborate on it.

It must be remembered that Weber was particularly concerned with the variability of human societies, and the attendant behaviour, on the institutional level. Generally speaking, and considerably more so in Weber's time than now, psychological approaches to human behaviour have been specifically blind to the importance of institutional variability. They have tended to relegate it to the status of secondary or contingent

[25] See pp. 94, 100.

fortuitous 'circumstances' and to lay the principal emphasis on universal traits or tendencies of 'human nature' like instincts. This type of concept Weber found of no use for his purposes, as is shown by his critique of an instinct of 'acquisition' in the face of the complexity of explaining various types of 'acquisitive' behaviour on the institutional level.[26] Weber's *Sinnzusammenhänge* were not psychological entities precisely because they included situational elements which were variable on the level of the situation and of the definition of the situation. Hence Weber tended not to be interested in psychology and to repudiate its relevance to his problems.

In this, it seems, through misunderstanding of the methodological situation, he went too far. If, in order to clarify many of his problems, it is necessary to place the structural elements implied in his formulations of ideal types in their context of a generalized system of social structure, it is by the same logic necessary to clarify the nature of the unit of reference, the 'actor.' It cannot be true that the conceptual scheme in terms of which this unit is treated is no more closely relevant to sociology than any other dealing with the conditions of action. For the actor is the unit of systems of action, and the frame of reference and other categories, in terms of which this unit is treated, are inherently part of the same theoretical system as categories on the level of types of action or social structure. Hence in some sense, a 'psychology' is an essential *part of* (not, note, 'basis' or 'set of assumptions for') a theory of social action.

In explaining Weber's failure to inquire systematically into this field, two circumstances are perhaps of primary importance. His own empirical interests, which were so strongly on the level of the broadest institutional variation, did not force this range of problems immediately upon him. His 'psychology' in matters of detailed particular insight may be said to have been, on a common-sense basis, on the whole excellent. What was lacking was systematization and, given his immediate interests, this was a relatively less urgent problem than many others. He could, and did, go far without it.

Secondly, he got little help from the psychology of his own time. Psychologists as a whole have, overwhelmingly until recently, and even now to a considerable extent, been guilty of a rather gross form of the fallacy of misplaced concreteness. They have attempted to reason directly from considerations of the nature of the human individual as a unit to

---

[26] Remarks on this problem are scattered throughout Weber's work. One important discussion is in chap. i of *The Protestant Ethic*.

the social level of generalization,[27] with results which, to a man of the scope of empirical knowledge of a Weber, must have seemed hardly less than grotesque. It was, in the state of knowledge of the time, a task which Weber would, for the most part, have had to undertake independently.

But just as psychology is an essential part of a complete system, it is indispensable that it in turn be treated as part of the system. Psychologists as a group have not treated the individual as a unit *in* a functioning social system, but rather as the concrete human being who was then conceived as proceeding to form social systems. They have thus not adequately taken account of the peculiar sense in which their categories are abstract. The categories of psychology in the motivational field, for instance, are not concrete motives, but *elements in* motivation, describing such aspects as its affectual tone. Weber was fundamentally right that the adequate concrete motive *always* involves the situational elements which are specifically non-psychological. By doing, however, what Weber failed to do, taking a concrete, in a sense institutional, starting point, and then using the resources of modern psychology to complete the analysis on its psychological side, it is undoubtedly possible to develop a far more adequate analysis of concrete motivation than either psychology or the social sciences have, for the most part, previously commanded.

Weber, however, got into serious trouble which could have been greatly mitigated had he extended his systematic theory into a more careful analysis in the direction of psychology. This is notably true of his treatment of rationality as that has been discussed above. The isolation of rationality and the treatment of affect as *only* a factor of deviation from rational norms is clearly incompatible with the findings of modern psychology, which rather point definitely to the integration of affective and rationally cognitive elements in the same action. Much the same is true of Weber's tendency to confine ideal type analysis to the rational case and the related tendency to confine, in his methodological formulations

[27] A notable example in this field is to be found in the history of Freudian theory. Freud himself, in spite of his acute psychological insight, took little cognizance of the variability of social structures on the institutional level and attempted to spin out a complete scheme of social evolution from the concepts and facts of his psychology alone. This of course had implicit 'institutional' assumptions, but these were treated as constant rather than variable, contrary to the immense weight of established fact. His 'orthodox' followers have if anything greatly increased the sterile rigidity of this scheme. But a most important movement within psychoanalysis has developed which recognizes the necessity of integrating the specific contributions of psychoanalytic psychology with an institutional sociology derived largely from anthropological sources.

at least, the applicability of subjective categories to consciously intended motives. In questions like these Weber shows a vacillating uncertainty which could largely be cleared up by better psychological analysis.

The trouble has been taken to expose some of the more conspicuous deficiencies in Weber's development of systematic theory precisely because he himself was such an eminent theorist. Without the added critical perspective which has now become possible there is danger that the difficulties inherent in the state in which Weber left his theory may play into the hands of those inclined to repudiate systematic theory altogether. Without denying their seriousness, however, these difficulties can and should be met by constructive criticism and further development rather than by regression to a scientifically more primitive level.

Explicitly, Weber's methodological consideration of generalized theory was confined to the level of ideal types. He even went so far, on occasion, as to state that in the action field theory was possible only [28] on this level, a statement which his own practice, though largely implicitly, refutes.

Ideal type theory is, however, perhaps the most difficult level on which to develop a coherent generalized system. Type concepts can readily be formulated *ad hoc* for innumerable specific purposes and can have a limited usefulness in this way. This does not, however, suffice for a generalized system. For this purpose they must be arranged and classified in a definite order of relationship. Only then will they have highly generalized significance on either a theoretical or an empirical level. Such systematization cannot, however, be developed on an *ad hoc* empirical basis. Logically it involves reference both to considerations of extremely broad empirical scope and to comprehensive theoretical categories.

It may be surmised that in Weber's case the primary pressure for a higher level of theoretical systematization came from the very great comprehensiveness of the empirical problems he attempted to throw light on, combined with the very high level of his methodological insight into the logical requirements of his procedures. In any case there is implicit in the organization of his type-system the outline of a systematized general theory on another level, that of the structure of systems of social action. This system has been analysed fully in the editor's *Structure of Social Action* and need not be gone into here.

It is, however, largely confined to the 'action' level. Further development from Weber's starting points would lead to a generalized scheme of the structure of social relationships and groups which is logically

[28] Pp. 92, III.

an indispensable immediate background for a typological classification of the possibilities of variation within each basic structural category.

Along with his inadequate attention to psychological problems the absence of this forms perhaps the most serious gap in Weber's systematic theory. Had he developed it he could hardly have failed to see that the most fruitful mode of use of generalized theory in the social field lies in 'functional' analysis. For only when the motives of individuals are seen in their significance for a more comprehensive functioning system does motive interpretation achieve a truly sociological level. Much of this is implicit in Weber's empirical work. But it would have saved him much difficulty if it could have been made clearly explicit and its consequences systematically taken into account.

III. Weber's 'Economic Sociology'

THE whole of the present volume in a sense constitutes the elaboration —although far from complete—of a system of ideal type theory. What may be called the key outline is, however, given in Chapter I. In Chapters II and III Weber turns to the elaboration of his analysis in two primary sectors of social life, what would ordinarily be called the economic and the political respectively. What he is essentially concerned with in both cases is a typological analysis of the institutional structuring of economic interests and activity, on the one hand, of political authority and its modes of exercise on the other.[1]

As compared with the first chapter these two are much closer to specific empirical problems. Since some of the principal methodological issues raised by Weber's procedure have already been discussed, attention may now be turned to the more empirical aspects of his work.

Undoubtedly by far the most systematic and comprehensive empirical investigation which Weber undertook was that of the relations of religious ideas and attitudes to economic activities and organization, the incomplete results of which are published in his three volumes on the Sociology of Religion. These studies, although of enormous comparative scope, were, however, specifically oriented to the problems of understanding certain of the crucial aspects of the social and economic order of the modern Western World.

In the course of these studies Weber had occasion to go very fully into the economic and political organization of the societies he was studying at their various stages of historical development. Moreover, he did not entirely confine himself to the aspects most immediately relevant to the problems of the role of religion. From this and other sources he had accumulated a vast store of factual knowledge and interpretations bear-

[1] Chap. iv constitutes a fragmentary beginning of a similar analysis of social stratification. It is, however, too fragmentary to justify extended critical comments.

ing on the economic and political development of the Western World which in his later years became ripe for systematization.

It should be remembered that the empirical material presented by Weber in these chapters was meant to be illustrative of the conceptual development, not a connected empirical analysis as such. This was reserved for the later part of the total work and was realized only in fragmentary fashion. There is, nevertheless, sufficient empirical discussion here to give a better conception of Weber's approach to and treatment of comparative institutions and the understanding of modern Western society than any other of his works available in English, perhaps than any other of his works at all except *Wirtschaft und Gesellschaft* taken as a whole.

Weber begins the chapter by stating emphatically that what he is about to present is not in any sense 'economic theory.' [2] In this he is undoubtedly correct—at no point does he attempt to develop an analysis of the process of price determination nor of the distribution of income through the play of market forces. What he presents is rather an account of the social, or perhaps better the institutional, structure of systems of economic activity and *above all* the ranges of variation to which this structure is subject. Economic theory as such is notably lacking in interest in the variability of institutional structure. It is, however, a fact of considerable importance that Weber, unlike many historical and institutional economists, shows a high level of comprehension of the nature of economic theory. His scheme is not, like that, for instance, of Veblen, meant to replace what has ordinarily been called economic theory, but to supplement it, to provide an account of certain ranges of the institutional data essential to it.

Weber's whole treatment is dominated, as is all his work, by two deep underlying convictions which need to be brought out explicitly as they have much to do with the empirical fruitfulness of his analysis. Both contrast with the dominant tone of much of 'economic' thought.

The first is the conviction of the fundamental variability of social institutions. To him the institutional system of the modern Western World is not a 'natural order' which has come about by the mere process of removal of obstacles. It represents, in every fundamental respect, only one of several possible lines of social development. Other radically different structures, such as those found in the great oriental civilizations, are not 'arrested stages' in a development leading in the same direction, but are simply different. It follows that, at least in many of its principal

[2] P. 158.

aspects, our own situation is not to be explained by the operation of the most general factors common to the situation of all men, but by quite specific combinations of circumstances.

The second closely related conviction is that of the inherent instability of social structures. For Weber human society, and underlying that, the situation of human action and the character of humanly possible responses to that situation, are shot through with deep-seated tensions which make the maintenance of any given state of affairs precarious. This is particularly true of what for Weber would undoubtedly be among the 'higher' structures, those displaying a high level of rationalization. 'Traditionalism' represented for him by far the most stable social situation, but one which was undoubtedly thought of as 'primitive' or backward.[3] This emphasis of Weber's thought also contributes to lending his work a very different character from that most prominent in the work of the more orthodox traditions of economic thought.

In the present discussion it is out of the question to attempt to comment on the many detailed questions of particular concepts and empirical interpretation raised in this chapter, fascinating though many of these are—attention must rather be confined to the broadest lines.

Seen in these terms the chapter may, in addition to its directly theoretical character, be considered an analysis of the modern Western economic order seen in comparative perspective. The comparative perspective is used in the first place descriptively and structurally to bring out the distinctive features of our economy more sharply and to show its structural relations to others through various lines of continuity of variation. But Weber does not stop at the structural level. He goes on to analyse certain specific points of instability and strain and the corresponding tendencies to change in the structure—tendencies to transform it in the direction of quite different structural types—with the possibility of extremely far-reaching social and cultural consequences.

In dealing with the modern economy in this way Weber takes certain conditions, which are much more fully analysed in other parts of his work, for granted, or discusses them only incidentally. The first is that, to a high degree, it is a 'rationalized' economy in which its bearers orient their decisions to the rational weighing of utilities and costs in a context of relatively wide scope. Closely related to this is the assumption of a 'mentality,' a set of attitudes to economic activity relatively favourable

---

[3] Cf. especially his Introduction to the whole series on the Sociology of Religion, translated in the same volume as the *Protestant Ethic*.

to the functioning of such an economy. This consists, in a very broad sense, in the 'spirit of capitalism' which is so prominent in his sociology of religion. In part this involves a particularly favourable attitude toward, and ethical sanction of, acquisitive activity. But it must be strongly emphasized that this is only part of the picture. Besides that, and in fields of activity other than the acquisitive, it involves above all rationality— a receptive attitude toward new solutions of problems by contrast with traditionalism—the devotion to a task for its own sake without ulterior motives—what Weber calls the attitude of a 'calling'—and readiness to fit into functionally specialized roles and be governed by universalistic standards.

Thirdly, there is the existence of a political organization and legal order of a particular type, namely the modern rational-legal state and a universalistic impartial legal system. These Weber discusses explicitly here more than the other factors. They will be mentioned here, but more fully discussed in relation to Weber's 'political sociology' in the next section. Finally, there is a vaguer factor, which Weber does not discuss specifically very fully anywhere in his works. It is partly implied in his treatment of rationality and of the spirit of capitalism. This consists in the relative weakness, in the modern Western World, of such social ties as would seriously interfere with the mobility of resources (above all, human) which is essential to our economy. This is above all true of the more extended kinship ties found in so many societies, and of the solidarity of local communities and of various kinds of social status groups. These do not admit either of personally following out openings for occupational or economic opportunity, or of being treated, under pressure of circumstances or of authority, as an 'instrument' of such goals by others.

With these assumed conditions Weber centres his explicit analysis primarily upon two interdependent strategic sectors of the social structure of the modern economy, those impinging on the use of money and the structure of markets and relation of economic units to them on the one hand, those connected with the relations of 'appropriation,' that is of property, on the other.

Weber attributes enormous significance to the role of money. There are, in his treatment, three primary aspects of this importance. In the first place it obviously makes possible an enormous extension of the range of possible exchange relationships in that any particular transaction need involve only purchase of a good, service, or other economic advantage with money or its sale for money. 'Indirect exchange' is the basic phenomenon. The kind of economic system Weber is interested in can develop only in direct proportion to the extension of the area of possible money transactions. Exchange in kind, because of the necessity of finding a direct user for or supplier of the specific utility offered or desired is inherently extremely limited in scope.

Secondly, however, money not only facilitates exchange generally, but it in proportion even more strongly facilitates the 'acquisitive' orientation of economic activity. For without it acquisitive orientation is limited either to the things the actor desires for his own consumption, or for which he can secure a taker through barter exchange. Above all, orientation to the increase of money resources as an immediate goal of acquisitive activity introduces, as perhaps Aristotle was the first clearly to formulate, a qualitatively different factor into the situation. It is further important that money can become a measure of the success of acquisitive activity and a symbol of prestige.

Third, finally, the use of money has the extremely important consequence of introducing, into the qualitative heterogeneity of concrete, economically significant goods, services, and other advantages, a common denominator which makes it possible to compare them systematically and measure their economic significance. Above all it is a numerically quantitative common denominator, so that economic activity can become in general oriented to arithmetical calculation. This possibility enormously broadens the scope of rational planning in economic connexions. A 'budget' need no longer consist alone in the allocation of concrete resources, but can be based on a single money income. The varied activities and interests of a profit-making enterprise can be oriented to the single criterion of successful operation, the money balance of profit and loss during accounting periods. Perhaps this possibility of money accounting is the most decisive of the three consequences of the use of money for Weber's particular interests.[4]

Closely related to the use of money, though not logically dependent on it, is Weber's distinction of two fundamentally different modes of orientation of rational economic action.[5] One is to the rational allocation of available resources as between the various uses to which they may be put by an individual or any sort of collectivity. This he calls 'budgetary management' (*Haushalten*). The other is the exploitation of opportunities for profit, that is of the increase of available resources, directly in

[4] Cf. sec. 7, pp. 179 ff.
[5] Cf. secs. 10 and 11.

exchange or through production for exchange. Though inherent in the structure of economic activity as such, this distinction becomes of great empirical importance only with the widespread use of money. To be sure, money makes a far higher degree of rationality in budgetary activity possible. But without it the difficulties in the way of 'profit-making' activity are so formidable that this can scarcely be said to be of important structural significance except in economies with widespread use of money and markets. Not only, however, is the development of profit-making dependent on the use of money, but one may say that a highly developed market system, along with the other institutional conditions that favour it, will almost inevitably give rise to a considerable development of profit-making enterprise.

This, it should be noted, Weber does not in the least attribute to any inherent propensity of human nature such as the 'self-interest' of many of the orthodox economists. Whatever the relevant elements of motivation on a psychological level, the factors Weber is interested in are on a different level, they are 'structural.' Throughout his work he continually emphasizes that the modern business man is not in the least exceptionally 'acquisitively minded,' that profit-making appears wherever the objective opportunity for it is given. What is characteristic of the modern economy is not in this particular connexion the attitudes, but the extent and peculiar character, of the opportunity. Furthermore, the people involved in many specifically non-capitalistic structures, such as the Indian village economy, are not a whit less 'acquisitive' than Western business men.

It is at this point that Weber introduces one of the fundamental elements of tension in the modern economy, what he calls the tension between the 'formal' and 'substantive' (*materiel*) rationality of the economy.[6] By the unfamiliar term formal rationality he means the extent to which it is possible to carry through accurate rational calculation of the quantities involved in economic orientation of either of the above types, and hence to act upon the results of such calculation. By substantive rationality, on the other hand, he means the extent to which it is possible to secure what, according to a given system of values, is an adequate provision of a population with goods and services, and in the process remain in accord with the ethical requirements of the system of norms.

The tension arises from the fact that a high level of formal rationality can be attained only under certain specific substantive conditions, which

[6] Cf. sec. 9, pp. 184 ff.

are always in some important ways in conflict with the interests and moral sentiments implied in a high level of substantive rationality. Of these conditions Weber mentions three principal ones. In the first place, high formal rationality is dependent on a wide extension of market competition between autonomous economic units. The prices which are an essential basis of rational accounting are, as he says, not so much 'claims to unspecified utilities' without relation to the conflict relations of human beings, as they are 'estimates of the chances of success' in a situation of the conflict of interest with other competitors. The outcome of such a competitive conflict can never be guaranteed to be strictly in accord with the standards of substantive rationality.

Secondly, because of its enormous simplification of the goals and standards of success of economic activity, the highest degree of formal rationality takes the form of *capital* accounting. The thing Weber emphasizes immediately is the dependence of this in turn on the highest possible degree of 'market freedom,' that is of the absence of impingement on the market of economically irrational interests or influences, or of economically rational ones, which, like monopolies, by restricting market freedom interfere with the access of others to the conditions of high calculability. In addition, capital accounting implies, Weber notes, a high level and stability of discipline in the functioning of the enterprise, and stable relations of appropriation of all the important elements in the situation, materials, premises, equipment, labour, legal rights, and privileges, etc.[7]

Finally, third, it is not 'need' or 'desire' as such which influences the production and marketing of goods, but 'effective demand.' There is in the first place no guarantee that any given distribution of purchasing power is in accord with the standards of substantive rationality. This is true not only as between individuals but also between impersonally organized interests. For instance, so far as higher education and research are dependent on private support through gifts and endowment there would seem to be no reason to suppose that the relative funds available to institutions for this purpose at all accurately reflected the valuation of the goals in the society at large. Too many fortuitous circumstances influence their income. Furthermore there is reason to believe that the processes of a competitive market economy themselves influence the distribution of income in ways contrary to any given set of substantive standards, notably through the cumulative tendency to increasing inequality which operates

[7] Cf. sec. 30, pp. 275 ff.

unless control of it is more stringent than there seems any realistic possibility of attainment.

The tension operates reciprocally. The process of extension of formal rationality, and of the conditions underlying it, creates situations and stimulates types of action which in various ways come into conflict with whatever substantive norms there are in the society and the sentiments and symbols associated with them. As a result of this conflict there are at various points tendencies to 'interference' with the operation of the free market economy. Under relatively stable conditions these forces may be held in a state of relative balance, even though it be precarious, but under other conditions it is quite possible for the interfering tendencies to enter upon a cumulative development such as to lead to a far-reaching process of change, undermining many of the essential conditions of the market economy.

The specific tendency of this character, with which Weber seemed to be most preoccupied, was that of restriction of the area of autonomous market relations, with the corresponding system of competitively determined prices. Though it by no means stood alone in his thinking Weber tended to concentrate, in this connexion, on the implications of socialism in the technical economic connexion of proposals for a complete rationally planned economy. In this connexion it is important to distinguish between two levels of analysis which enter into Weber's argument. He raises, on the most abstract economic level, the question of the theoretical possibility of fully rational allocation of the resources of a complex community by centralized planning, and comes to the conclusion that this is intrinsically impossible [8] for two reasons. On the one hand, it could not be based on money calculations because a system of 'assigned' prices could not, for theoretical reasons, take the place of prices determined by actual market competition. They would have to be too highly arbitrary to base rational calculation upon. On the other hand, without an extensive system of money prices, calculation would have to be 'in kind' and there is no possibility of rational results in a complex economy because it involves reducing qualitatively heterogeneous elements to a common denominator, which could only be done by making arbitrary assumptions.

Weber wrote on this subject when analysis of this technical problem was in its beginnings, and the weight of the best contemporary opinion seems to be against him. But even if it were granted that he was wrong

[8] Cf. sec. 12, especially pp. 207 ff.

on this level, the theoretical possibility of rational allocation is far from being an empirical probability. It could become such only if certain very specific conditions were fulfilled, and Weber adduces much evidence to show that this is extremely unlikely.

It should be remembered that Weber held that the relatively high development of a market economy was precarious anyway. Hence even apart from the theoretical possibility of rational centralized allocation, it is quite reasonable to suppose that the absence of spontaneously determined (not necessarily 'perfectly competitive' in the technical sense) prices might well be enough to shift the balance of forces sufficiently to lead to quite other forms of economic organization. Weber felt this to be particularly true since the pressure of other tensions in the economy and the social system at large tend to work in the same direction.

These more 'empirical' difficulties in a rational planned economy may be summed up as follows: Perhaps the least important is the question of adequacy of knowledge in the hands of the planning authority. Undoubtedly in the 'capitalistic' economy many decisions have to be made on the basis of nothing more than shrewd guesses as to the state of affairs and probable consequences of projected action. But the provision of adequate information for such an authority is an enormous task. A more serious question concerns the adherence of the planning authority to fidelity to the standards of substantive rationality which are supposed to guide their decisions. Weber says it would have to be a standard of ultimate values. But in a complex society, which is necessarily also a changing society, there is *never available,* except for an extreme authoritarian form of crystallization which would have repercussions of its own, a completely consistent unambiguous formulation of these values which would be agreed to by everyone in the society. There are many different nuances and emphases which, moreover, always tend to get caught up in the many tensions and conflicts inherent in a complex society, which only a utopian would expect to be eliminated entirely under socialism. Hence the planning authority would be under important pressure in two respects: Their own personal sentiments, through the operation of the conflicting currents upon them, could very well deviate importantly from those of other groups, or of the main trend, and they would be subject to pressures which, in despite of their personal sentiments, they were politically compelled to take account of. Furthermore any failure of important groups to be fully satisfied with their actions would lead to repercussions intensifying the conflict, and perhaps the deviation.

A third important field of limitation lies in the question of adequate enforceability of decisions once made. Under modern conditions this involves command over a highly complex administrative machinery, notably a bureaucratic organization. Bureaucratic organization, a subject to which Weber devoted much attention,[9] is just as much a peculiar feature of modern Western society as is an extensive system of market prices, and depends on as unstable conditions, many of which are probably closely linked with those underlying the latter. But even with the highest standards of bureaucratic efficiency known, the question of its adequacy cannot be lightly dismissed. And the indirect repercussions of a great, and especially a relatively sudden, extension of its scale and scope may be of great importance.

Finally, the requisite calculability of human behaviour, all the way from the supreme authority down through the social structure, depends on many complex conditions, among them above all the relations of appropriation, and a relatively stable equilibrium in the important tensions of the society. The maintenance of property relations and of labour discipline cannot be taken for granted.

The main reason both for Weber's and for the present editor's raising the problem of socialistic economic planning is not to deliver a critique of socialism. It is rather a way of illuminating the fact that in Weber's analysis a system of spontaneously determined prices has an important functional significance to the economy, and is in a certain sense, so long as it functions fairly well, a stabilizing factor. This is because competitive prices form a relatively fixed point of orientation for a wide variety of activities. They narrow the scope necessary for certain rational decisions all through the society while at the same time allowing a high degree of flexibility and freedom from traditionalistic fixation. This narrowing of the scope which it is necessary to include in rational calculations eases the pressure on rational action of the many 'irrational' forces which necessarily impinge upon it. But the structure which has this functional significance is itself relatively unstable. It is both subject to a great many relatively precarious conditions and itself a factor, in its relatively autonomous development, in intensifying certain of the tensions of the social situation. Weber on the whole accepts the views of the functions of a competitive price system current in 'orthodox' economic theory. But on this side of the problem he extends the perspective into considerations of considerably broader scope. The price system is one of the important foci

[9] Cf. chap. iii, secs. 3-5. Also *Wirtschaft und Gesellschaft*, part iii, chap. vi.

of orientation for one of the prime characteristics of the modern Western social system as a whole, its 'rationality.' A serious disturbance of the conditions facilitating rational orientation in this area would have repercussions all through the complex system of rational activity in our society, in science, technology, law, and administration.

At the same time that Weber goes beyond the orthodox economists in analysing the functional significance of a price system, he also goes much farther in the analysis of the conditions on which it depends and in the exposure of points of instability inherent in those conditions.[10, 11]

The second primary focus of Weber's empirical attention in this chapter is on what he calls the conditions of 'appropriation' or in more usual terms the 'property' system. This constitutes a sociological rather than a legal analysis of property which, so far as the editor's knowledge goes, is unique in the literature, both for its analytical penetration and its empirical significance.

In Chapter I [12] Weber defined the basic concept of 'appropriation.' Appropriation he treats as an aspect of the 'closure' of a social relationship, that is the exclusion of individuals from it, or their admission only

[10] One of those conditions to which Weber devotes considerable attention which has not been taken up here, is a stable rational monetary system. The modern monetary system is to him as distinctive of our society as the other features discussed. But in his analysis of it Weber brings out the same underlying elements of instability that he does in the other connexions. See secs. 32-37 of chap. ii.

[11] It would be interesting to compare Weber's analysis of the instabilities of the modern capitalistic economy with that of a common Anglo-Saxon type of 'heterodox' economics in the United States, particularly Veblen. Veblen undoubtedly lays his finger on *some* of the factors of instability in the modern 'business' economy, in his analysis of business relationships as a process of jockeying for strategic position, etc. In so doing he, with considerable success, pricks the bubble of the utopian optimism of the existing order so common among orthodox economists, especially of the past generation. But as compared with Weber his analysis even of elements of instability is exceedingly narrow. Quite adequate comprehension of all Veblen's real contributions can be found in Weber's work—many of them he took for granted as too obvious to need demonstration. Weber, however, was able to understand the positive functional significance of the modern price system, more broadly the business economy, in a way which was entirely inaccessible to Veblen. Furthermore, though he is at least as effective in deflating 'individualistic' utopianism, he is singularly free from anything corresponding to the counterutopianism of Veblen, his idealization of 'technology.' The conclusion seems inescapable that Veblen was a highly unsophisticated person who demonstrates the typical reaction of a disillusioned idealist in his scientific work. Weber, who it should be remembered was a close contemporary, was on a totally different level of scientific and cultural sophistication. The fact that a Veblen rather than a Weber gathers a school of ardent disciples around him bears witness to the great importance of factors other than the sheer weight of evidence and analysis in the formation of 'schools' of social thought.

[12] Sec. 10, pp. 139 ff.

upon specific conditions. A relationship is, on the other hand, 'open' when it is accessible to any individual who wishes to participate and who is factually in a position to do so.

One primary aspect of the closure of relationships in turn is the monopolization' of 'advantages' (*Chancen*), that is of anything which is valued. Monopolization, however, is meaningless unless the advantages in question are in some sense and to some degree transferable, that is can constitute 'possessions,' the enjoyment of which might be given over to or appropriated by another. Such monopolized advantages may be freely accessible to the participants in the closed relationship, they may be made accessible subject to various forms of regulation or rationing and, finally they may be 'appropriated' by the participants, as individuals or as members of a participating unit.

As Weber treats it, a social relationship is closed only by virtue of the content of an 'order' to which the corresponding action is held subject, in the most important cases a legitimate order. The specific feature of appropriation as opposed to the other modes of access to advantages is that, according to the binding order, the individual (or other unit) has 'rights' of access which other members and the governing authority of the closed group must respect, so that rights thus recognized cannot be interfered with except under definite conditions.

Weber reserves the term 'property' for a particular class of appropriated rights, namely those which survive the individual lifetime, and are inheritable by a particular individual heir or other social unit, whether by testament, or by an automatic rule of succession. If alienable they constitute 'free property.'

It should be noted that Weber does not approach the subject in terms of a classification of objects or things. The concrete content of appropriated rights may be anything, tangible or intangible, for which the individual or unit has one or more 'uses,' which has 'utility.' Moreover, it is not the concrete object, the 'thing' as such, tangible or intangible, which is the basis of the interest in appropriation, but the 'use' to which it can be put. Correspondingly it is not the 'things' which are appropriated, but *rights in* them. It is by no means impossible for a number of different individuals or units to have appropriated rights in the *same* concrete thing, such as a certain tract of land, at the same time.

A functional classification of the content of appropriated rights is, however, essential to Weber's analysis. Economic utilities are, he says, of three classes, goods, services, and a residual category of objects of rights not fitting either of the other classes. This includes such intangibles as 'good will' and the advantages of participating in all manner of social relationships so far as these can be the object of economic orientation. Goods are physical objects of economic significance, and services the actions of human beings in the same context. Corresponding to this is a classification of objects of appropriated rights. The most important distinction Weber makes is that between the non-human and the human 'means of production' or, more broadly, sources of economic utility. Human means are sub-classified into two types, labour services and managerial functions. The concept of labour turns on the fulfilment of the specifications of others, that of managerial function on the co-ordination of the activities of others. Non-human means are classified roughly as natural resources, raw materials, premises, implements, saleable or consumable products, money funds, and a residual category of valuable rights and privileges. In all this there is nothing original, as Weber would be the first to admit.

With respect to all these classes, however, there is a range of possible variation in degree of appropriation relative to freedom of access and in the specific forms of appropriation found. Certain of these variations are of critical significance in terms of relative favourableness or unfavourableness to the functional needs of a free-market economy such as that of the modern Western World. The optimum combination from this point of view is given by Weber in the formula, the maximum full appropriation of rights over the non-human means of production by owners, and the complete lack of appropriation of rights over the human agents of production, that is 'formally free' labour.[13] In so far as production is carried on in complex organizations, and not by isolated individuals, this implies the 'expropriation' of the workers from control of the means of production. It is interesting that Weber here points out that the 'corporate' system of recent times carries this out more fully than the classical individualistic capitalism of the nineteenth century in that it has gone far to abolish the appropriation of managerial functions by individual owners of the enterprise. Management tends to be appointed to a considerable extent on grounds of ability and competence.

This is, according to Weber, the essence of the modern property system, and a close approach to it is essential to a high degree of formal rationality of economic activity. Even to-day, however, there are a good many restrictions on it, and it is in a high degree of approach a very exceptional rather

[13] Cf. sec. 30, pp. 275 ff.

than a common combination. There are, to be sure, certain formal respects in which a system of unrestricted slave labour could be considered more favourable to high economic rationality and hence productivity than the present system. On empirical grounds, however, Weber argues that under almost all conditions this is not actually the case. These grounds include the additional investment of capital in human resources through purchase and maintenance of slaves, the exposure of slave property to all manner of economically irrational influences, the peculiar instability of the slave market, and uncertainty of recruitment of a slave labour force. A second class of factors concerns the relation of slave labour to particularistic *Gemeinschaft* ties, notably family ties. The permission of family relationships to slaves has greatly increased the cost of their use because their families have to be maintained, and has decreased mobility. Hence 'the most complete exploitation of slave labour has been possible only when they were separated from family relationships and subjected to a ruthless discipline.' [14] Finally, Weber notes that it is impossible, with slave labour, to exercise stringent selection according to efficiency, and to dismiss according to the fluctuations of the business situation. This would be theoretically possible if a perfectly mobile slave market existed, but there has never been any very close approach to such a condition. Weber's conclusion is that the possibilities of a high level of economic rationality with the employment of slave labour are empirically very narrowly limited, far more so than is the case with the modern system of free labour.

There is a further aspect of the modern property system which is clearly implied in Weber's treatment, but which he does not bring out explicitly nearly so clearly as these others. That is the separation of the economically significant aspect of the concrete objects of appropriation, goods, human means of production and others, from their other aspects. This is by no means generally the case. For instance under feudalism it was impossible simply to 'own' land in the modern sense. The holder of a fief was, in the German terms, not merely a *Grundbesitzer* but necessarily also a *Grundherr*. That is to say, what we treat as property rights, and political jurisdiction (in certain respects) were inseparable. It was impossible to have the one without the other. Perhaps the clearest point at which this important consideration comes out in Weber's analysis is in his discussion, in a slightly different context, of the separation, in the modern economy, of the enterprise from the budgetary units of the owner or of

[14] P. 276.

others involved in its functioning.[15] The profit-making enterprise is primarily of economic significance. A budgetary unit may be, but this is generally not the case. If it is a unit of final consumption (exclusively or in addition to productive functions) it is never the case, since by definition consumption cannot be carried on as such for economic ends. In general then, the budgetary unit is one in which its economic aspects tend to be inseparably bound up with elements, hence modes of orientation, other than the economic. Many of these are, as Weber points out, 'irrational' from the point of view of economic orientation, that is of rational economic calculation, and are hence disturbing elements in the economy. But this separation, which is functionally so important to the economy, cannot be carried out on a grand scale without institutional foundations in the definitions of the content of property rights, that is the legitimation of separate treatment of different aspects of human relations to the *same* concrete objects of appropriation. Among many other sources of its importance, a very important element of the essential mobility of the means of production depends on this separation being carried through to a high degree.[16]

In all three of these respects the modern system of appropriation is relatively unstable. Perhaps the most familiar tendencies in conflict with it are those in the direction of introducing limitations on the control and disposal of resources on the part of those responsible for their economic exploitation. One of the most familiar cases is that of land. Probably the commonest case is for land to be 'tied up' through mandatory hereditary succession in the hands of kinship groups or of village or other communities which are continuous from generation to generation. This means above all that land is inalienable, and this generally goes with traditional modes of use such that its use for other purposes encounters serious obstacles. One of the best-known examples was the necessity, in England in the eighteenth century, for something like the enclosure movement to break up the 'open field system' before a thoroughgoing reform of the technical procedures of agriculture could become possible.

In the clearest cases these limitations on the optimum economic use of a resource consist in a system of appropriated rights of others in the same resource. We think of the 'vested interests' of owners in the modern sense as a serious obstacle to changing the use to which resources are put —for instance to putting them in the service of socially more important

---

[15] Cf. especially p. 200.

[16] Cf. the editor's article 'The Professions and Social Structure,' *Social Forces*, May 1939.

ends. But even here through such procedures as eminent domain these resistances can relatively easily be broken down. But it is safe to say that a complex of appropriated rights, such as the feudal institutions of control of the land and its use, would present far more serious obstacles. Indeed any considerable weakening of the relative absoluteness of centralized control over resources given by modern ownership would with high probability result in a greatly increased rigidity of the economic system, and would favour traditional stereotyping of the modes of exploitation of resources.

There are many classes of persons and rights which may potentially challenge the fullness of control of 'owners' as those primarily responsible for economic use, over resources. Only one of these, but one particularly important for the present situation, consists in the workers involved in the same organized process of production. Weber has no difficulty in showing that, unlike the handicrafts and small peasant agriculture, the technical conditions of production in large organized units completely preclude the appropriation of the principal means of production by the individual worker. Centralized control over the process as a whole is functionally essential to efficiency, and this control cannot exist without what we consider property rights.[17] But there is another possibility, namely that appropriation should be in the hands of an association of the workers. This would point to the system of 'producers' co-operation.' Weber notes the fact that historically this is an exceedingly rare phenomenon. That is not to say that 'communal' appropriation by working groups as groups is unknown. Far from it—indeed this is the commonest form of agricultural village economy the world over. But these groups are not functionally specialized economic groups—they are all-inclusive covering all the most important areas of social interest. The social control system in one of these areas dovetails with that in others to give a strength to the structure as a whole which is out of the question in an economic group in the modern sense. Weber sees little possibility of producers' co-operatives successfully taking over the functions of modern industrial management and control—an opinion with which the great majority of economists would agree.

Nevertheless there are, as Weber points out, important tendencies in

[17] This does not preclude the existence of 'rights' which are contingent on maintenance of the worker's status within the organization. Thus there may be 'his' machine and 'his' stock of materials which no other worker, without something like 'cause,' can interfere with or even the management. But a full property right would make this independent of a controlled status in the organization.

the present situation for workers' groups to appropriate important elements of control over the means of production. This above all touches the conditions of the contract of employment, and hence the power of selection in the hands of management. Weber felt that this tendency had serious potentialities of replacing selection on the basis of productive efficiency by essentially different criteria, such as loyalty to the union or usefulness to it as an organization. Undoubtedly the power of hiring and firing in the hands of management has often been used 'arbitrarily' according to criteria other than the productive efficiency of the worker. But it does not follow that limitations on this power imposed by workers' organizations will predominantly limit only this 'arbitrary' area leaving the concern with productive efficiency essentially free of 'abuses.' By its reduction of the mobility of labour resources, and limiting of the area of free choice open to management, it can readily work in the direction of traditional stereotyping. The most essential thing here for Weber was the tendency he thought he saw to treat occupancy of the particular job, or group of jobs, as an appropriated right of the individual worker, or of the union.[18]

The converse of the tendency to appropriation of the non-human means of production by the workers is that to the appropriation of human means of production by 'owners.' The extreme is of course full slavery, but as is too well known to need comment, short of this there are very many different kinds and degrees of 'unfreedom' in the status of labour forces, and some form of unfree labour is, especially in the 'higher' civilizations, at least almost as much the rule as the exception. That it is not altogether incompatible with some of the variants of Western civilization in a broad

[18] It does not follow that the growth of unionism is as such undesirable, or anything other than inevitable. It seems probable that the ideal type of complete 'expropriation' of the workers from the right to jobs and to access without management's consent to the means of production, generates social tensions of such magnitude that its maintenance is not in the long run possible. (Of course the most important tensions probably do not lie at the exact points formulated in the explicit 'grievances' talked of by the vocal spokesmen of labour.) Hence it is probable that considerable modification of this ideal type situation is essential to a stable functioning of the organization of industrial labour. But admitting this, as Weber at least in part would readily have done, does not justify the conclusion that the greater the limitation placed on control by management the better. Optimum efficiency is a matter of delicate balance of these tendencies, not of maximization of one or the other.

Weber had little to say about any important tendency to extension of appropriation by the workers beyond the 'job' to the material means of production. Since he wrote, however, there has appeared the phenomenon of the 'sit-down strike.' Though this is as yet far from being recognized as an institutionalized right, if it should be, it is in the logic

sense is shown by its role in our own history, from the slavery of classical Antiquity through the various forms of medieval serfdom to the slavery of the more modern era in colonial areas and in the Southern United States. To be sure personal unfreedom, perhaps particularly in the labour relationship, is deeply repugnant to the moral sentiments of at least the 'liberal' part of modern Western society. But its possibility, which ought to be evident from its role in our history, has been dramatically brought to the fore again as a possibility of deliberate public policy in the treatment of 'subject peoples' by National Socialist Germany.

Quite apart from deliberate public policy, however, Weber's analysis shows that the possibility is not as remote as many of us think. Perhaps his most important insight is that there is both a similarity of effect and an instrinsic connexion between appropriation of the means of production by workers and appropriation of workers by owners.[19] As to effect, both tend to break down the mobility of economic resources, human and non-human, and to open the door to traditionalistic stereotyping of economic structures.

But any strong tendency to the one also creates conditions favourable to the development of the other. Perhaps the most fundamental reasons for this may be stated as follows: If the rights of control over non-human resources could be abstracted from social relationships of dependency it would be different. Thus if the worker works entirely or largely independently and has stable unproblematical marketing channels for his product there is no problem. But large-scale organization and the necessity for a wide market subject him necessarily to authority in the organization of production and to dependency on those who control access to

of the measure that it implies a claim on the part of the workers in a plant, to something like a property right in their premises of work—not of course necessarily full 'ownership.'

In this whole connexion it should be noted that the vital problem is that of the relation of the worker to 'management,' that is to the persons who have authority over him, over his employment or dismissal and over the discipline of the work process. Whether management in this sense is that of a capitalistic enterprise or some other sort of unit such as an organ of government is for many purposes secondary. Full socialization would not, *ipso facto*, destroy the 'expropriation' of the workers unless one were to consider the socialistic state as one enormous producers' co-operative. But even if it were such in principle the average individual would be so remote from the points of controlling decision that he could hardly have a much greater sense of personal participation in the decisions than he does in those of his present 'capitalistic' employers. One wonders how far the decisions of the Soviet planning commission are felt to be those of the 'workers' by most Soviet workers.

[19] P. 237.

markets. These two types of dependency are compatible with personal freedom only so far as they are associated with relatively stable expectancies, and are rather strictly limited in the scope of interests involved. Thus typically in our society it touches only the discipline of the working functions, and the conditions of the labour contract—wages, etc. But appropriation in important degree of rights to his job on the part of the worker increases the scope of his 'stake' in the job. Above all it is part of a more general tendency to rigidity in the system, and just as this appropriation makes it more difficult for the employer to deprive him of his status, it at the same time binds him more tightly to it—since it is more difficult to find other jobs.[20]

Again, this would work to the 'advantage' of the worker if it were not for the continuing intrinsic significance of the two relations of dependency in which he stands. But with the continuance of a more permanent stable relation to his status, and a broader scope of interests bound up with it, there also grows a different order of obligations, which seen from another point of view tend to become rights in the hands of those upon whom he is dependent. Above all, if the employer cannot dismiss him except on very onerous conditions, it is likely to develop that the worker cannot leave except under more or less equally onerous conditions. In so far then as the 'employer' gains rights over the worker's 'personal freedom' which are outside the limits of individual contract, the latter has fallen into an 'unfree' status, a stereotyped institutionalized dependency in place of the more or less definite factual dependency of being a formally free 'wage slave.'

The only escape from this consequence would seem to lie either in a strength of the moral sentiments opposed to personal unfreedom which, apart from congruence with the realistic balance of social forces, is extremely unlikely to be maintained in the long run, or in the maintenance of a favourable balance of power on the worker's side. But it would seem to be certain that this latter is possible only through the intervention of large-scale workers' organizations, and probability then favours the development of dependent status within the organization and, probably, some kind of coalescence between the leadership of the workers' organization and management. It does not solve the dilemma of the individual worker.

Though subject of course to quantitative differences of judgment, the essential point of Weber's analysis of this problem is that too great depar-

[20] Since they are appropriated by other workers.

ture from the combination of relatively unrestricted rights to non-human property in the hands of those responsible for the organization of production, with relatively unrestricted personal freedom (i.e. exemption from being an object of property rights) on the part of the human factors in production, would, whatever end it started from, tend to lead to a state of affairs where restrictions on the 'freedom of property' would be likely to be combined with restrictions on personal freedom, with some form of system of unfree labour. What he envisaged was undoubtedly a traditionally stereotyped kind of economy where authority in the management of production was, as compared with the present, greatly restricted through traditional barriers, especially those arising from fusion of this authority with social interests of other than economic significance. At the same time, largely as a result of the same sort of fusions with non-economic elements, authority and conversely dependency, would be extended into areas which are now specifically exempted by our institutional patterns. Of course these tendencies are greatly strengthened by their relation to the strains inherent in a free market economy which have been discussed above.

The only essentially non-economic social structure with the impingement of which on the modern economic order Weber deals at all fully in this chapter is the political authority.[21] A brief summary of the important problems he takes up here is in order. In the first place, as has been noted above, he lays great emphasis on the importance for a free market economy of a rational monetary system. As with all the other institutional prerequisites he discusses he shows that this is not something to be taken for granted. It is both shown by comparative study to be highly exceptional in history, and functionally to be dependent on relatively precarious conditions. Above all, writing in 1919 before the catastrophic stage of the German inflation was reached, Weber warned strongly that the pressures working toward an inflationary breakdown of the monetary system were exceedingly strong, far stronger than many of the monetary experts of the day, like G. F. Knapp, realized. These pressures he analysed primarily in terms of the interrelations of the state with the market economy.

The second factor on which Weber lays emphasis is that of a system of law which favours optimum calculability in economic relationships, both in the relations of economic enterprise to the state, and in the relations of private economic actors to each other, in commodity, money

[21] Cf. secs. 32-6 on money, 37-9.

and labour markets, and in the general support of the sanctity of contracts. The analysis, however, of the factors on which such a legal system depends is not developed in this chapter, but is partly deferred to the next chapter, and still more to his treatment of the Sociology of Law.[22]

The third phase of the impingement of the political structure on the economic which Weber takes up is the provision of such bodies with the economic means necessary to carry on their activities, what he calls 'financing.' Here again we find the same basic themes. The modern system of money taxation is highly exceptional in history. It is both dependent on a high development of a market economy, and has an important influence upon it. It is most appropriate to a type of organization of the state in which those who 'make their living' out of the activities of the state are primarily remunerated in the form of money salaries and where there is the same kind of separation between the sphere of 'office' and of private life that there is in 'capitalistic' economic organization. This implies the absence of appropriation, by the holders of political authority, of any rights to such authority independently of legitimate election or appointment. But such appropriation is exceedingly common historically and with it generally goes a quite different system of financing, by 'benefices.' These, according to Weber, are appropriated sources of income which the incumbent of the political status enjoys as a right. The tendency under this system is to attempt to secure the maximum control over these sources of income (in money or in kind) with the result of drastic restriction of the area of free market relationships. It is one of the main paths to the combination of economic with other aspects of a concrete system of action which leads to relations of personal dependency and the traditional stereotyping of the economic order.

Toward the end of the chapter [23] Weber sums up the principal institutional conditions of maximum 'formal rationality' of capital accounting, hence, with some qualification of rationalized economic systems generally. The most important are as follows: (1) Complete appropriation of all non-human means of production by owners and absence of formal appropriation of opportunities for profit in the market; (2) autonomy in the selection of management by owners; (3) absence of appropriation of jobs by workers and conversely absence of appropriation of workers by

---

[22] *Rechtssoziologie,* part ii, chap. vii of *Wirtschaft und Gesellschaft.* This is not included in the present translation. A separate translation, however, is to appear under the auspices of the Association of American Law Schools.

[23] Sec. 30, pp. 275 ff.

owners; (4) absence of substantive regulation of consumption, production, prices, i.e. substantive freedom of contract; (5) calculability of technical conditions of the productive process (including labour discipline); (6) calculability of functioning of public administration and the legal order, with a legal guarantee of contracts; (7) separation of the enterprise from the budgetary unit; (8) a formally rational monetary system.

There has been much discussion, in connexion with Weber's work and elsewhere, of the concept of 'modern capitalism.' Any critical treatment of that question should keep in mind the whole background of Weber's analysis in this chapter, and the considerations brought to the fore in the above discussion of it. In one essential point, however, he gives a particularly clear statement toward the end of the chapter. For him a fundamental phenomenon is the development of profit-making enterprises rationally oriented to 'capital accounting' that is to the goal of increase of money resources at the command of the enterprise. It is this phenomenon, as such, in terms of which he defines the general concept 'capitalism.' There are, however, a variety of different possibilities within this, only some of which are typical of or particularly highly developed in the modern business economy. Weber makes the following distinctions between types of capitalistic orientation: (1) A continuous process of purchase and sale on a free market or a continuous productive enterprise with capital accounting; (2) trading and speculation in money funds and various forms of indebtedness and the extension of credit; (3) the exploitation of opportunities for 'booty' through influence with political groups or persons with political power; (4) the exploitation of sources of profit through domination by force or under special protection of political authority ('colonial capitalism,' etc.); (5) the exploitation of unusual transactions with political bodies, such as financing wars, etc.; (6) speculation in commodities and securities, the promotional financing of enterprises, and the profitable regulation of market situations.

He goes on to say [24]

Types 1 and 6 are to a large extent peculiar to the modern Western World. The other types have been common all over the world for thousands of years where the possibilities of exchange, money economy, and money financing have been present. In the Western World they have not had such a dominant importance as modes of profit-making as they had in Antiquity, except in restricted areas and for relatively brief periods, particularly in times of war. . . It is only in the modern Western World that rational capitalistic enterprises with fixed capital, free labour, the rational specialization and combination of functions, and the allocation of productive functions on the basis of capitalistic enterprises, bound together in a market economy, are to be found. . . This difference calls for an explanation and the explanation cannot be given on economic grounds alone.

The other four types of orientation Weber classifies together as constituting 'politically oriented capitalism.' Thus among the various phenomena which, in the most elementary sense, can be called 'capitalistic' it is by their uneven differential incidence at least as much as by the quantitative development of capitalism as such that Weber characterizes the modern economy. To what extent the institutional structure of the modern world as a whole, including its 'economic' aspect, is best characterized as 'capitalism' as Weber himself tended to do, is a question which, in terms of Weber's own analysis and its possible extension, will be briefly taken up in the final section of this introduction.

A few remarks may be made about Weber's approach to the fundamental problem of economic motivation. As may perhaps be expected his treatment is fragmentary. The section with that title [25] does not really deal with it, but consists rather in a schematic classification of the sources of income.[26] Scattered through the chapter are, however, a good many remarks on various aspects of the problem. The first thing to be said is that Weber, with his strong emphasis on institutional variability, was almost completely free of the grosser biases involved in the received economic doctrine of 'rational self-interest.' He was aware of the complexity of the motivational forces underlying economic activity, particularly in giving weight to the more or less direct expression of value-attitudes in the idea of the calling, and showing a realization of the importance of social prestige. Above all his institutional relativism and his functional analysis of the instabilities of an economic system, particularly the modern market economy, opens up the problem of motivation on an entirely new level from that of the traditional economics. But in accordance with his defective treatment of psychological problems, as noted above, there is relatively little of connected motivational analysis to take the place of the older doctrines.

There is, however, one train of thought which is worthy of calling attention to, as its further development would lead far into the problems

[25] Sec. 41.
[26] It may be suspected that the section is incomplete, that Weber classified sources of income as a preliminary to an analysis of motivation.

of the relation of institutions and individual motivation. Weber is strong in his insistence on the distinction between 'routine' economic arrangements and certain forms which play a part outside settled routine conditions. Of these, two particularly important ones are the systematic organization of the use of force in military structures, and the direct expression in the profane world of other worldly religious attitudes.[27] Both tend to forms of 'communistic' provision for economic requirements, and both generate strong tensions where they impinge upon the workaday world. In his very definition of the concept of economic activity Weber insists on excluding the use of force from the category of 'economic means' saying that it follows radically different laws from the peaceful processes of provision for needs and acquisition.[28] War is always to him an unsettling element in an economic situation, and the influence of groups primarily oriented to military values is in general economically 'irrational.' For somewhat different reasons the same is true of religious orientations: 'take no thought for the morrow, God will provide,' Weber cites as a typical example of the uneconomic orientation of religious sentiment.

The specific connexion of economic rationality with settled routine conditions points to a peculiar connexion between institutional patterns, backed by moral sentiments, and the 'self-interest' of the mass of individual persons. In a sense in which it is not true of these other cases, in a settled economy interests are harnessed into conformity with an established institutionalized order. Weber's many remarks about the importance of 'vested interests' are indicative of this. This points strongly to a theory of economic motivation in an integrated institutional system which is closely related to that of Durkheim, and of such anthropologists as Malinowski.[29] But this lay on the periphery of Weber's interests, and, so far as his own analytical scheme had developed, his competence. Its further development is, however, one of the most important tasks of social science in completing the work Weber began.

Even though it is in a certain sense incidental to his main theoretical purpose, this chapter constitutes what is in many ways the framework of a unique kind of analysis of the modern economic order. It is unique in that it starts from all the main definitions of the facts which have been current in economic science, but brings to bear upon them a totally dif-

---

[27] Sec. 26, pp. 265 ff.

[28] Pp. 159-160.

[29] Cf. *De la division du travail social* and *L'Education morale* and Malinowski's *Coral Gardens and their Magic*, vol. i.

ferent perspective and a quite new institutional kind of analysis. The result is a kind of orientation to a great many of the most crucial empirical problems very different from almost any other to be found in the literature. It is probably, especially when taken in connexion with the other relevant parts of Weber's works, the most comprehensive and all things considered the most successful essay into the field of 'economic sociology' which has yet been attempted.

It is to be expected that anything so comprehensive would, with the perspective of time, show inadequacies and one-sidedness in certain connexions. Here, in conclusion, one such 'bias' may be singled out for comment. Weber seems to be very particularly concerned with the modern economy as a system of *market* relationships. It is true that he had a great deal to say about the organization of productive enterprise but, in spite of his emphasis on bureaucracy, perhaps not as much as might have been expected. Along with this he was especially interested in the impingement on the economy of the political power system of the modern state, and of value-attitudes associated with the religious and cultural tradition.

It may at least be suspected, if not more, that a somewhat different perspective would have emerged if he had put greater stress on a different mode of approach which has come to be well established in more recent sociology. He might, that is, have thought of a society more as a system of differentiated and co-operating *roles,* which are subject to the same order of institutional variability in structure as the elements Weber considered. Then his attention would presumably have become more strongly focused on the fundamental structure of 'occupational' roles which characterized the modern Western World and which, in its basic structural uniformities, cuts across the distinctions between economic, political and other 'spheres' of social life. It is noteworthy that Weber introduces the concept of occupation very briefly and only at the *end* of his discussion of the 'division of labour,' not at the beginning.[30] It is probable that Weber's own analysis of value-attitudes applies even better to occupational roles than it does to 'economic activities' as such. This emphasis on the economic rather than the occupational perhaps tends to account for one of Weber's conspicuous blind spots in this field, his failure to bring out the structural peculiarities of the modern professions and to differentiate between the organization of professional services and what may be called the 'administrative hierarchy' of occupational structure types. His 'bureaucracy' is a composite of both. This tendency of his

[30] Sec. 24, pp. 250 ff.

in turn probably has its roots in 'Marxian' modes of thought in that, though polemically attacking the Marxian theory of history, Weber tended to take the Marxian form of statement of the problems implicitly for granted and treated the 'economic system' as a more autonomous entity, functioning according to laws of its own, than it really is. It is interesting to raise the question whether a systematic reworking of Weber's problems taking these considerations into account might not somewhat alter his sense of the tragic dilemma, of the dependence of the whole modern institutional order on a peculiarly unstable system of competitively determined prices in a free market economy. At most, however, it would probably lead to a difference of emphasis, not a 'refutation' of Weber's views.

IV. The Institutionalization of Authority

A CERTAIN 'utopianism' which tends to minimize the significance of authority, coercive power, and physical force in human affairs has been a conspicuous feature of a large part of modern social and perhaps particularly economic thought. One of the most striking features of Weber's sociological work is his continual and intensive concern with the problems of this field. Never does he treat an empirical problem without explicit inquiry into the bearing of power and authority factors on it. Indeed this constitutes one of the few major axes of this whole treatment of social phenomena.

The foundations of his treatment of authority are laid near the beginning of the logical unfolding of his conceptual scheme. After developing the broadest outline of his analysis, with the orientation of action to normative order, the basic types of relationship, etc., when he comes to the treatment of organized groups by far the most prominent place is given to a type to which an element of authority is fundamental, the *Verband*,[1] or 'corporate group' as that difficult term has here been translated. Whatever the content of its interests, the distinguishing feature of the *Verband* for Weber is an internal differentiation of roles with respect to authority. In a sense this derives from the very nature of the orientation of co-ordinated action to an 'order,' the terms of the order must be carried out and enforced, which in turn requires a responsible agency of administration and enforcement. Thus from the ordinary 'members' of a group Weber distinguishes those who carry responsibility and authority in this connexion. These in turn he subdivides into a 'chief' (*Leiter*) with the highest authority, and those who, though in certain respects under the authority of the chief, nevertheless at the same time exercise authority over the ordinary members, the 'administrative staff' (*Verwaltungsstab*). It is safe to hold that Weber considered this basic structure to be normal for groups of any size and complexity in all fields of routine human

[1] Chap. i, sec. 12, pp. 145 ff.

action. Departures from it were to him limiting cases which could only obtain under exceptional circumstances and, once realized, would tend to be particularly unstable. Perhaps the principal exception is the replacement in the status of 'chief' of an individual by a 'collegial' body of equals, such as a 'board' or committee. But even here there is a very strong tendency for one individual to become at least the *primus inter pares* if not the actual chief. Thus in the British system of cabinet government there has been a steady process of increase in the power of the Prime Minister so that in recent times he has far overshadowed the other members of the cabinet and had full powers of appointment and dismissal over them.

This basic uniformity in the structure of groups, however, is not incompatible with a fundamental range of variation in the character of the structure of authority within it. In developing the concept of *Verband* Weber lays particular stress on the importance of the relation of action within it to an order. It is hence not surprising that in differentiating types of organization of authority he takes as his point of departure variation in the nature of the claim to legitimacy which is necessarily involved in an institutionalized status for the chief and his staff, and which depends in turn on the character of the order to which they as well as the members are in some sense subject.

From this starting point Weber opens his analysis with the introduction of a classification of three basic types [2] which, with their analytical development and empirical use, must count as one of Weber's few most important contributions to social science. As in other connexions, he is here particularly concerned with illuminating the character of authority in the modern Western World, and hence makes the type most conspicuous in our society his point of reference, defining and characterizing the others in terms of their specific contrasts with it.

This first type is what Weber calls 'rational-legal authority.' [3] The order in question then consists in a body of generalized rules, in the type case logically consistent and claiming to cover all possible 'cases' of conduct within the jurisdiction of the *Verband* as well as to define the limits of that jurisdiction. These rules are universalistic in that they apply impartially to all persons meeting the logically formulated criteria of their

[2] The classification is given in sec. 2, pp. 328-9. This scheme has been very little discussed in the literature in English. The fullest discussion is in Goldhamer and Shils, 'Types of Power and Status,' *American Journal of Sociology*, September 1939.

[3] Secs. 3-5, pp. 329 ff.

definitions, and impersonal in that the status and qualities of individuals are treated as a function of the application of the generalized rules to them and so far as they do not fall within them must be treated as irrelevant. The fundamental source of authority in this type is the authority of the impersonal order itself. It extends to individuals only in so far as they occupy a specifically legitimized status under the rules, an 'office,' and even then their powers are limited to a 'sphere of competence' as defined in the order. Outside this sphere they are treated as 'private individuals' with no more authority than anybody else. There is thus in principle a separation of the sphere of office and that of private affairs, corresponding closely to that between the enterprise and the budgetary unit in the economic sphere. Where authority includes, as it very generally does, command over the use of property, there is clear segregation between the property of the *Verband,* over which the incumbent of office has certain powers by virtue of his office, and his personal possessions which are controlled according to entirely different criteria. Often this extends to segregation of the premises of work from those of private life.

Where rational-legal authority involves an organized administrative staff, according to Weber it takes the form of a 'bureaucratic' structure. Here each member of the staff occupies an office with a specific delimitation of powers and a sharp segregation of the sphere of office from his private affairs. Remuneration is, in the type case, in the form of a fixed salary, preferably in money form. The different offices are organized in terms of a stringent hierarchy of higher and lower levels of authority in such a way that each lower level is subject to control and supervision by the one immediately above it. This control and supervision above all includes the power of appointment, promotion, demotion, and dismissal over the incumbents of lower offices. Fitness for an office is typically determined by technical competence, which in turn may be tested by such rational procedures as examination and very generally involves a long period of formalized training as a condition of eligibility. Bureaucracy in this sense, Weber says, is by far the most efficient instrument of large-scale administration which has ever been developed and the modern social order in many different spheres has become overwhelmingly dependent upon it.[4]

---

[4] Weber's formulation of the characteristics of bureaucratic organization, which has become a classic, raises some serious analytical difficulties in the treatment of social structure. It is the present writer's opinion that he has thrown together two essentially different types which, though often shading into each other, are analytically separate. Taking account of

The second main type which Weber takes up is what he calls 'traditional authority.' [5] The term is not altogether happy since its traditional-

this distinction would considerably alter the perspective of Weber's analysis on a number of empirical problems.

The problem may be approached by noting the importance Weber attaches to technical competence (p. 335) as a basis of bureaucratic efficiency, and his statements that bureaucratic administration is 'essentially control by means of knowledge' (p. 337). Now the terms 'knowledge' and 'technical competence' immediately suggest the 'professional' expert such, for instance, as the modern physician. But it is furthermore suggestive that Weber nowhere calls attention to the fact that medical practice like various other professional functions in the Western World has not been predominantly organized in bureaucratic form, but rather, at least to a large extent, in that of 'private practice.' In private practice the physician does, to be sure, exercise a kind of authority, he issues, as we often say, 'orders' to his patients, and there is a rather high probability in most cases that these orders will be followed. This authority rests, fundamentally, on the belief on the part of the patient that the physician has and will employ for his benefit a technical competence adequate to help him in his illness. That is he has knowledge and skill which the patient does not have, and cannot criticize in detail so that the patient must take his doctor's advice or orders 'on authority.'

It is true also that this position of authority is not a matter wholly of the individual impression made by the particular physician, but is institutionalized. Its possessor is socially categorized through such instrumentalities as formal training, the M.D. degree, a license to practice, etc. But the distinctive thing is that this institutionalization does not carry with it coercive powers and the physician does not occupy an office in Weber's sense. His getting his orders obeyed depends entirely on securing the voluntary consent of his patient to submit to them.

Weber, however, started from the organization of authority within a corporate group. The fundamental model he had in mind was that of legal 'powers,' particularly powers of coercion in case of recalcitrance. The position of the exerciser of authority of this sort is legitimized by his incumbency of a legally defined office. It is not logically essential to it that its exerciser should have either superior knowledge or superior skill as compared to those subject to his orders. Thus the treasurer of a corporation is empowered to sign checks disbursing large funds. There is no implication in this 'power' that he is a more competent signer of checks than the bank clerks or tellers who cash or deposit them for the recipient. Legal 'competence' is a question of 'powers' in this sense, technical competence is of a different order.

Of course persons occupying positions of legal authority, the higher the more so, generally are in some important sense and degree 'superior' to those under them in respect to ability and achievement. They can successfully do things which the others, if the places were changed, could not in fact accomplish. But this is not logically essential to the definition of the type of structure, and holds of only a *part* of the actual functional content of office. Furthermore it does not follow that typically the superior ability and potentiality of achievement of the 'executive' is of the same order as the technical competence which is decisive in such fields as medicine or engineering. The differentiation of the two kinds of functional superiority, even only on an ideal type basis is, however, a difficult and subtle problem.

There can obviously be no such thing as the 'private practice' of the functions of bureaucratic office. But professional services are often, indeed increasingly, carried out in complex

---

[5] Secs. 6-9, pp. 341 ff.

ism is only one of a rather complex combination of criteria which Weber attributes to the type. In this respect, however, in contrast with the order involved in rational-legal authority which is legitimized by having been 'enacted' or 'imposed' by a legitimate agency and procedure, the system of order is treated as having always existed and been binding. Even actual innovations are justified by the fiction that they were once in force but had fallen into disuse and only now are brought back to their rightful position of authority. One of the important consequences, and symptoms, of the existence of traditional authority is that there can be no such thing as new 'legislation.'

There is, however, not only the difference that in the one case rules are enacted, in the other traditionally received. The order has a different kind of content. It contains two main elements. One is a body of concrete rules. There may be elements of generalizations in these, but there is a great difference of degree from the rational-legal case. Conformity with the abstract logical requirements of a rationalized system is not as such a criterion of legitimacy, and many concrete prescriptions are involved with no other justification than that they have always been held to be binding. But in addition to rules governing the conduct of the members, the order underlying a system of traditional authority always defines a system of statuses of persons who can legitimately exercise authority. Such a status is different from an 'office.' It does not involve

organizations rather than by independent individuals. There is, however, considerable evidence that when this is the case there are strong tendencies for them to develop a different sort of structure from that characteristic of the administrative hierarchy which Weber has, in most respects, classically described in his discussions of bureaucracy. Instead of a rigid hierarchy of status and authority there tends to be what is roughly, in formal status, a 'company of equals,' an equalization of status which ignores the inevitable gradation of distinction and achievement to be found in any considerable group of technically competent persons. Perhaps the best example of this tendency, which Weber curiously enough seems to have overlooked in its bearing on this problem, is to be found in the universities of the modern Western World. Much the same will, on close examination, be found to be true of the professional staffs of such organizations as hospitals or law firms.

It is probable that Weber's neglect to analyse professional authority is associated with a tendency to overemphasize the coercive aspect of authority and hierarchy in human relations in general, important as it is in particular cases. This was a healthy reaction against the common utopianism in these respects of so much of social thought. But working out the implications of this point would, as has been noted, considerably alter the perspective of many of Weber's empirical generalizations.

The above selects only one among several sources of difficulty in Weber's formulation. In fairness to him it should, however, be remembered that the exposition of his views in the text is highly schematic, neglecting many of the complications he himself called attention to.

specifically defined powers with the presumption that everything not legitimized in terms of the order is outside its scope. It is rather defined in terms of three things. There are, first, the concrete traditional prescriptions of the traditional order, which are held to be binding on the person in authority as well as the others. There is, secondly, the authority of other persons above the particular status in a hierarchy, or in different spheres—as when a king assumes judicial authority when he is personally present—and finally, so long as it does not conflict with either of these sets of limitation, there is a sphere of arbitrary free 'grace' open to the incumbent. In this sphere he is bound by no specific rules, but is free to make decisions according to considerations of utility or *raison d'état*, of substantive ethical 'justice,' or even of sheer personal whim.

So long as the incumbent of such a status does not act counter to the traditional order, or infringe upon the prerogatives of his hierarchical superiors, loyalty is due, not to the 'order' as such, but to him personally. He is not restricted to specified powers, but is in a position to claim the performance of unspecified obligations and services as his legitimate right. There is thus notably no clear-cut separation between the sphere of authority and the individual's private capacity apart from his authority. His status is a 'total' status so that his various roles must be far more stringently integrated than is the case with incumbency of an office.

Two implications of this situation are, perhaps, particularly important. Property tends not to be stringently distinguished as between the 'means of administration' which, in a rational-legal structure are strictly limited to use in an official capacity, and personal property which can be used for personal needs and desires. Furthermore the property aspect in either or both respects is far less likely to be segregated from other aspects of the individual's status. Above all the enjoyment of property rights over things or persons generally carries with it personal authority, usually with at least an element of political jurisdiction, notably over persons and land. So far then, as the 'means of production' are appropriated within a system of traditional authority there is a strong tendency for it to be accompanied by various forms and degrees of unfree personal status for the persons subject to authority. Secondly there is a strong tendency for the status of authority to be fused with other aspects of status which in a rational-legal system are normally treated as part of the individual's 'private' sphere. Perhaps the most important case of this is kinship. The result would be to treat status by kinship and in a system of authority as identical and hence inseparable. This involves, of course, the hereditary principle, which is always likely to develop in systems of traditional authority.

Weber presents a subclassification [6] of the different kinds of traditional authority in terms of variation in the development and role of the 'administrative staff.' His base line is given in the concepts of 'primary' gerontocracy and patriarchalism where either a group or an individual as the case may be, occupy a position of authority but without a significant degree of independent control of an administrative staff. If they are called on for decisions they are dependent, for their enforcement, on the co-operation of persons whose status and functions are traditionally fixed, and do not to a significant degree fall within the scope of the 'arbitrary' grace of the incumbent of authority. One might say that the holder of authority is more of a 'sage' or wise man than an 'executive.' This case tends to be the one which is most stringently bound to the fulfilment of concrete traditional prescriptions and gives little scope for the large-scale development of power systems.

The sphere of arbitrary free choice, however, contains the seeds of a possible development. Where this is used to develop a complex administrative staff under the personal control of the chief, and not involved in a system of traditionally stereotyped statuses with which he cannot interfere, Weber speaks of 'patrimonialism.' There are, of course, indefinite gradations of degree. Weber lays stress on two crucial points of transition. One touches the recruitment of the administrative staff, the shift from the recruitment from 'patrimonial' sources, that is persons otherwise in a state of dependency on the chief through kinship, serfdom, a client relationship, etc., to recruitment of persons otherwise altogether independent of him. This of course greatly widens the sphere of arbitrary power since the chief is not bound in controlling them by the prescriptions of their independent traditional status. The other range of variation involves the attitude toward persons subject to authority. In one case the person in authority acts 'on behalf' of the collectivity and the typical individual is a 'member' of the collectivity with definite traditional rights and expectations, which define limitations on arbitrary will. The other case is that where they are treated as 'subjects' and the chief tends to treat his position of authority as a personal prerogative, almost as his private property, and the subjects hence as instruments in carrying out whatever projects he may have in hand. The extreme type case of this personal absolutism on a traditional basis of legitimation Weber calls 'Sultanism.'

[6] Sec. 7 (a), pp. 346 ff.

The effect of the transition from patriarchalism in the direction of patrimonialism is to emancipate an important part of the structure of authority from the direct control of tradition. The position of authority as such is still traditionally legitimized, but not the detailed structure of carrying it out which is, on the contrary, a 'right' of the chief to do what he will within his sphere of personal prerogative. One effect of such emancipation from detailed traditionalism is of course immensely to widen the area of free individual action and planning. But another in many respects equally fundamental consequence is to unloose a potential struggle for power which under 'primary' traditionalism could have no possibility of developing. The aspect of this struggle to which Weber pays particular attention is that between the chief and the members of the administrative staff. It is not common for a very high level of personal absolutism to be maintained for a long period. The rule is for important limitations on the chief's power to be imposed through pressures exerted by the administrative staff.

This is usually a matter of a struggle for the control of 'advantages' the most important of which are power as such, the 'means of administration' as Weber calls them, and remuneration. In a traditional framework this tends to take the form of a determination of the total status of the individual concerned, not merely of his office. If the imposition of a limitation on the chief is successful there is a strong tendency for it to become traditionalized as an established, even appropriated, right of the incumbent of a status in the structure of authority. Under most conditions appropriation will tend to extend beyond the lifetime of the particular incumbent, to become hereditary, and thus to fuse the structure of authority with the class structure. Under other conditions, as in China, the right established may be that of the members of a class with a well-integrated cultural tradition, but without individual appropriation beyond the period of office.

Under traditional conditions the tendency is for all three elements of advantage to be fused in the perquisites of a single status, and all together to be either under the control of the chief, or in various ways and degrees kept beyond his control. There are, however, two main types which, with reference to the property interests involved, Weber calls 'benefices' and 'fiefs' respectively.[7] A benefice is a bundle of rights granted to the individual on a 'personal' basis, that is without hereditary succession, and as a free grant of the chief. A 'fief' on the other hand is granted

[7] Sec. 8, pp. 351 ff.

formally by virtue of a contract, which implies specific reciprocal obligations on the part of the chief, and a standard of the honour of the holder
which the chief must respect. A feudal contract is, as Weber points out,
peculiar in that it involves a total status and diffuse mutual obligations
of loyalty. It is thus not like a modern business contract.[8]

The contrast between rational-legal and traditional authority is associated for Weber with that between formal and substantive rationality.
A system of rational-legal authority is highly favourable to the development of a formalized legal system, while that of traditional authority
favours two types of substantive ethical norms, the traditionally bound
embodied in concrete traditional precepts, and the free, exercised within
the sphere of arbitrary personal will of the chief. One of the obstacles to
the development and maintenance of rational-legal authority is the extent to which this legal formalism offends the sentiments of 'substantive
justice' in a population.

Another important connexion is that involving the status of money.
Command over money funds, both in the means of administration and
in remuneration, is the economic mode of provision most appropriate to
a system of rational-legal authority precisely because it is the most mobile
and because it is most easily dissociated from the individual's status in
the other, the 'private' respects. A system of provision by benefices or
fiefs in kind strongly favours the pattern of traditional authority.

Both the first two types of authority are, for Weber, modes of organization appropriate to a settled permanent social system. Though subject,
like all human arrangements, to change, they are of specifically 'routine'
character. The third, the 'charismatic' type, differs in precisely this respect. It is, by definition, a kind of claim to authority which is specifically
in conflict with the bases of legitimacy of an established, fully institutionalized order. The charismatic leader is always in some sense a revolutionary, setting himself in conscious opposition to some established aspects
of the society in which he works. Furthermore this *Ausseralltäglichkeit*,
this emancipation from routine, is a note which runs all through Weber's
treatment of charismatic authority[9] and its organization, notably with
respect to modes of provision with the means of administration and to
the status of members of the administrative staff.

The 'deviance' of the charismatic leader is not, however, by any means

[8] It is a *Statuskontrakt* not a *Zweckkontrakt*. See *Rechtssoziologie, Wirtschaft und Gesellschaft*, p. 413.
[9] Secs. 10-12, pp. 358 ff.

either mere eccentricity or the indulgence of purely personal wishes. He introduces, rather, a pattern of conduct conformity with which is treated as a definite duty. By virtue of it the leader claims moral authority and hence legitimacy for giving orders to his followers, or whoever falls within the scope of the pattern.

As Weber treats charisma in the context of authority, its bearer is always an individual 'leader.' His charismatic quality has to be 'proved' by being recognized as genuine by his followers. This is not, however, as Weber is careful to point out, the ordinary case of leadership by 'consent' of the led, in the usual democratic meaning. The authority of the leader does not express the 'will' of the followers, but rather their duty or obligation. Furthermore, in the event of conflict there can in principle be only one correct solution. Majorities, if employed at all, are given authority only because they are thought to have *the* correct solution, not because a greater number have as such a greater right to prevail. And the leader does not compromise with his followers in a utilitarian sense. Recognition by them is interpreted as an expression of the moral legitimacy of his claim to authority.

Above all this claim is one to impose obligations in conflict with ordinary routine roles and status. Hence the member of the administrative staff cannot occupy either an office in the rational-legal sense or a traditionalized status. He is usually a personal disciple, actuated by enthusiasm for the 'cause' and by personal loyalty to the leader or both. The leader usually attributes charismatic qualities to him, and assigns him particular *ad hoc* missions to perform. On the one hand he can have no established 'rights' in his status, particularly against the leader. On the other there can be no inherent limitations on the scope of his authority or functions such as are essential to the pattern of office. The limitations can only be defined by the leader, and are inherently unstable, being settled in terms of momentary exigencies.

Corresponding to the two great fields of charismatic activity for Weber, religious proselytizing and the use of force, there are two primary sources of support of charismatic movements, both for provision with the means of administration and for remuneration of the followers, namely formally free gifts and 'booty.' Both of these forms are specifically outside the range of routinized economic provision and can only become permanent and stable sources of income through a profound change in their character.[10]

[10] P. 362.

In Weber's treatment perhaps two points stand out about charisma besides the fact that it is a source of legitimate authority, namely that it is a revolutionary force, tending to upset the stability of institutionalized orders, and that in the nature of the case it cannot itself become the basis of a stabilized order without undergoing profound structural changes.[11] As a result of these changes it tends to become transformed into either the rational-legal or the traditional type.

The initial source of its revolutionary character lies in setting up the authority of an individual against the established order, the office or traditionalized status of those originally in authority. But if the 'movement' secures sufficient recognition to have the prospect of permanent organization the successors of the original leader cannot in the nature of the case base their claim to legitimacy on the same grounds. Hence the problem of succession,[12] both of who shall succeed and of the pattern of determination of the legitimacy of his status, is crucial for all charismatic movements. The functional problem is that of maintaining the authority of the original point of reference—as in a divine mission—and yet meeting the changed conditions. With respect to the pattern it may take the form of hereditary succession (*Gentilcharisma*), of succession in an office (*Amtscharisma*), or a succession by an unbound process of individual selection. There is an important functional interest in eliminating arbitrary elements so far as possible. In another connexion the leader himself may have the primary role in designating his successor and the pattern of succession, or in varying ways and degrees the decisions may be participated in by the members of the administrative staff or the total membership of the group of followers.

Though Weber does not analyse it in detail here,[13] of course the character of the system of ideas in terms of which the charismatic claims of the movement is formulated has an important influence on the way in which this routinization works out, especially on the pattern in which authority is held by succeeding individuals. Thus the fundamentally important development of the charisma of office in the Roman Catholic Church would hardly have been possible if grace, embodied in the sacramental authority of the priesthood through apostolic succession, had not been conceived as something impersonally separable from particular individuals or lines of descent. This objective character of sacramental au-

---

[11] Pp. 363 ff.
[12] Pp. 364 ff.
[13] This is a principal theme of the studies on the Sociology of Religion.

thority was an indispensable condition of the development of priesthood as an office rather than as an hereditary status. Similarly in the political sphere the Roman *imperium* was an objective *power* which could be transferred from one individual magistrate to another, it was not conceived as the prerogative of a status as such.

The same fundamental alternatives which arise in connexion with the problem of succession for the leader are involved all through the structure of authority. For Weber the fundamental question is whether the administrative staff will tend to take on more the character of a band of patrimonial retainers and hence lead in a traditional direction, or that of a group of officials in a rational-legal direction.

Another basic field of routinization is that involved in the relation of the movement to economic affairs, especially to provision with the means of administration and remuneration of the administrative staff.[14] Provision by free gifts is inherently unstable. To meet routine needs it must be regularized in the form of a system of obligations on the part of the donors which from being merely ethically obligatory become to a greater or less extent factually compulsory. Thus they tend to take on either the character of taxes, as in the established Christian churches, or of some kind of 'liturgies,' of compulsory payments or services. The need of insuring the regularity of such sources of income often exerts a pressure in the direction of limiting the personal freedom of the obligated groups.

Finally there is a fundamental need for regularizing the status of the members of the administrative staff—it cannot long continue just a group of persons who are from time to time assigned *ad hoc* missions by the chief. This takes the familiar directions of developing offices or of developing traditionalized statuses with benefices or fiefs as their mode of support. It should also be remembered that precisely because of the instability inherent in the position of a successful charismatic movement, the way is open for a struggle for power within the movement, and for the appropriation of important rights by the members of the administrative staff.

In the process of routinization the charismatic element does not necessarily disappear. It becomes, rather, dissociated from the person of the individual leader and embodied in an objective institutional structure, so that the new holders of authority exercise it at second remove as it were, by virtue of an institutionally legitimized status or office. This points to certain difficulties in Weber's analysis which will have to be briefly discussed later.

[14] Cf. especially sec. 12, pp. 367 ff.

What is, for Weber, characteristic of the modern institutional order, is the relative predominance of the pattern of rational-legal authority. This is above all true of the modern state. Only in Rome has there been an at all comparable development, and this was less fully elaborated in a number of respects. Furthermore, this predominance of rational-legal authority is not a fortuitous curiosity of modern Western civilization— it is one of its fundamental characteristics, closely interdependent with a great many others. The free market economy could not function without it on an at all comparable scale. Such fundamental things as personal freedom, and the most important liberties as of speech, scientific investigation, the press, are basically dependent upon it.

Moreover, as is true of all the main institutional characteristics of the modern order, rational-legal authority is relatively unstable. If there is one safe generalization of sociology it would seem to be that no structuralization of human relationships is 'foolproof' and immune to change. Such institutions exist only in the fantasies of utopian dreamers such as the heralds of the *Tausend jähriges Reich*. But to a considerable extent each particular institution has its own peculiar sources of instability and hence its specific tendencies to change into other specific forms. Of the two forms of 'routine' organization of authority Weber certainly considered the traditional to be the more stable, and that there was a basic tendency for the rational-legal form to break down into the traditional, either directly or through the intermediate influence of charismatic movements.

One approach to the analysis of this problem, for which there is much material in Weber's discussion and observations, starts with the fact that a system of rational-legal authority can only operate through imposing and enforcing with relative efficiency, seriously frustrating limits on many important human interests, interests which either operate, independently of particular institutions, in any society, or are generated by the strains inherent in the particular structure itself. One source of such strain is the segregation of roles, and of the corresponding authority to use influence over others and over non-human resources, which is inherent in the functionally limited sphere of office. There are always tendencies to stretch the sanctioned limits of official authority to take in ranges of otherwise 'personal' interests. In other words this form of institutionalization involves a kind of 'abstraction' of a part of the human individual from the concrete whole which is in a certain sense 'unreal' and hence can only be maintained by continual discipline. A particular case of this is the tendency of persons in authority to claim obedience, and for this claim to be recognized, on a personal basis, as John Jones, rather than on the basis of office as such. It is then not the impersonal order which is being obeyed, but the personal prestige of the incumbent. The segregation required by rational-legal authority is subtle and difficult to maintain.

In our society we distinguish sharply between 'personal' and 'official' capacities. Within a considerable area the personal sphere is to us one which is thought of as altogether uninstitutionalized. But this is by no means even predominantly the case. It also includes some elements of institutionalized status which, like those of kinship and marriage, are formally sanctioned in the law, but do not constitute incumbency of an office, or such other functionally specific roles as those of employee. But still more it includes a very wide area of 'informally' institutionalized status such as that of social class and ethnic origin in the United States. There is reason to believe that the scope of 'purely personal' behaviour in the uninstitutionalized sense is narrowly limited by the functional requirements of social systems, and that what we in Western society have of it, which is exceptionally broad, is to a considerable extent made possible only by the 'protection' of the individual by rational-legal norms. The tendency to break down the segregation between the official and the personal spheres will not, therefore, probably result mainly in the permanent increase of individualistic freedom, but rather in the increase of institutionalization of individual functions and status in the 'total' status form, in other words, of features Weber treats as typical of traditional authority.

A second fundamental consideration is that discipline and authority, probably always in any large-scale permanent system, generate various forms of resistance and resentment. It is naturally a condition of the continued existence of an institutionalized system of authority that it should, with relative efficiency, 'take care' of this resistance and prevent it from undermining the system of authority. But this control is probably always relatively precarious, and under favourable conditions the loopholes in the system present opportunities for cumulative change. A system of rational-legal authority is not, as the history of such things goes, necessarily particularly severe in its repressive measures—indeed it generally involves important mitigations of the severity of other forms. To some extent this is sometimes a source of strength in spite of the fact that it is deprived of otherwise effective instrumentalities of discipline. But at the same time it probably also in other directions generates tensions peculiar to itself. The very fact that its sphere of authority is functionally limited deprives it of the support of certain motives which contribute to the solidarity of other systems, notably motives of personally loyal attachment to particular individuals and *Gemeinschaft* groups. Above all, for a variety of reasons, it tends to generate widespread feelings of insecurity.

One immediate effect of this may well be to emancipate individuals or groups of them from the control of rational-legal structures.[15] There are certain possibilities that this emancipation may result in a more or less stable institutionalization of anti-authoritarian patterns which protect the freedom of the individual. But this is only one possibility and in most cases not the most likely. There are, as has just been pointed out, functional reasons why limitations on the sphere of personal freedom tend to become institutionalized, in terms of authority as well as other forms. The probability is then that a break-down of rational-legal authority through successful defiance of it on the part of its 'objects' will result in its gradual replacement by other forms, notably the traditional. This may take the form of a gradual change in the character of authority relationships within the *Verband,* or in the subjection of the individual to authority in a rival organization. Thus the industrial worker may escape the authority of his employer only to fall under that of union leaders.

This functional tendency undoubtedly is reinforced by important elements of motivation, which Weber did not directly analyse. One way to mitigate the anxiety associated with a state of psychological insecurity is to abdicate individual responsibility in favour of dependence on a source of authority. This is especially likely to be of the traditional type since on these deeper psychological levels the prototype of a state of security is that of dependence on the parent. A rational-legal officeholder is not likely to be an effective parent substitute. In general modern clinical psychology has taught us that attitudes toward authority may be deeply ambivalent. The same individual who in one context is notably rebellious against some forms of authority will often readily submit to even more stringent control if it occurs in a somewhat different context.

The direct transition to traditional patterns is not, however, the only path by which a system of rational-legal authority can change funda-

---

[15] The restriction of production in modern industry is an excellent example of this kind of resistance to authority. Though doubtless considerably increased by the deliberate policies of labour organizations, there is evidence that it goes considerably deeper than that and appears spontaneously where change imposed by rational measures from above upsets the settled routines and informal social relationships of a working group. See Roethlisberger and Dickson, *Management and the Worker.*

mentally—it can also give way to charismatic movements. Weber had relatively little to say directly about the conditions which favour the development of charismatic movements—he was more concerned with their character and consequences. But a good deal of evidence has accumulated on this subject which fits admirably into his analysis. Any situation where an established institutional order has to a considerable extent become disorganized, where established routines, expectations, and symbols are broken up or are under attack is a favourable situation for such a movement. This creates widespread psychological insecurity which in turn is susceptible of reintegration in terms of attachment to a charismatic movement. In addition to relatively generalized and diffuse 'anomie' [16] and insecurity, there are generally specifically structured sources of strain and frustration which may have much to do with the definition of the specific content of effective charismatic appeal.

There is reason to believe that a social order of which a system of rational-legal authority is an important part is considerably more subject to this kind of disorganization than is a highly traditionalized society. The rationalized structures are never exhaustive of the whole social structure, and there is often important strain between them and the parts which are predominantly traditionalized, a strain which seems to provide the principal basis in fact for the 'cultural lag' theory which has been so popular in recent years. 'Reason' is, as Weber several times [17] remarks, an inherently dynamic force subject to continual change, and hence has a strong tendency not to permit the development of settled routines and symbolic associations which would minimize psychological strain. At any rate there is ample empirical evidence of the susceptibility of our society to the type of movement which Weber describes, all the way from the prevalence of innumerable fads through the proliferation of many kinds of religious cults [18] to the Communist and National Socialist movements themselves which are grand scale movements involving charismatic authority in the political field.

The immediate result of a charismatic movement will be, so far as its influence extends, to undermine the stability of the prevailing institutional order, in this case of rational-legal authority. This is partly because its sources of legitimacy are challenged, partly because the movement itself requires forms of organization which are in conflict with the estab-

[16] A term used by Durkheim, especially in *Le Suicide*.
[17] Cf. for instance p. 363.
[18] For instance, Christian Science, Buchmanism, Father Divine, etc.

lished. But the charismatic basis of organization is inherently unstable and temporary. The question of its long-run effects will depend on whether the process of routinization takes the traditional or the rational-legal direction. This in turn depends on a complex variety of factors, but on general grounds it may be said that there is a presumption in favour of the path of traditionalization, both because it is in general more stable and because the specific strains generated in a rational-legal system would, by contrast, strengthen the forces biassed in that direction.

In the first instance there is the question of the ideal patterns involved in the sources of legitimacy of the charismatic movement. In this case, as between the two most important charismatic political movements of our time, there seems to be an important difference. Communism is, on the whole, in this respect a child of the rationalistic enlightenment of modern times—its basic values are associated with science, human equality, technology, and contain important elements of ethical universalism, and give indeed some basis for specificity of functional roles. National Socialism, on the other hand, represents to a far greater degree a 'fundamentalist reaction,' a reassertion in revolutionary form of precisely those traditional values which have been most injured and threatened by the development of the rational-legal institutional order itself in the first place. Hence its character would seem to point to a far greater likelihood of its leading in a traditionalistic direction.

But the character of the relevant ideal patterns does not stand alone. Above all there is the question of economic provision and of the status of the administrative staffs. In National Socialism, for instance, it is clear that provision was very largely in terms of 'booty,' for the first few years derived mainly from the expropriation of the established classes and organizations within Germany.[19] Since then the spoils of conquest played a tremendous part. It would seem altogether possible that, if the movement escapes collapse through military defeat, this may well develop into a system of benefices in the hands of the magnates of the party. Similarly, there is the question of what is to become of the vast organization of party functionaries.[20] There were several indications of a bitter struggle for power within the party—most dramatically in the blood purge of June 1934—even during the lifetime of the original charismatic leader.

[19] Not only the property of the 'rich' but, for instance, the funds of trade unions have been, formally or informally, expropriated.
[20] On the sociological structure of the Nazi party see Hans Gerth, 'The Nazi Party: Its Leadership and Composition,' *American Journal of Sociology*, January 1940.

The prevention of appropriation of important rights on the part of the administrative staff, especially after the problem of succession arises, would presuppose a unity and effectiveness of the highest central authorities which, considering the heterogeneity of its composition and the intensity of the personal rivalries known to exist, would seem most unlikely. Above all it is crucially important that some elements of this administrative staff have control over armed force more or less in their own right. The Gestapo and the SS might well turn out to play a role analogous to that historically of the Praetorian Guard or of the Janissaries. For the administrative staff to eventuate in a pure rational-legal bureaucracy would presuppose a continuity of central control which is most unlikely to be realized.

On the background of his general analysis of authority, Weber, though in fragmentary fashion, outlined a significant analysis of certain aspects of modern democracy.[21] In the first place he calls attention to the fact that two of the most important types of check on centralized authority, the separation of powers and the presence of collegial bodies in place of monocratic positions of authority, are primarily associated with aristocratic rather than democratic regimes. They have originated largely in the process of appropriation by groups in the administrative staff, of powers and rights in the course of a struggle with the chief. Thus above all, these famous features of the British constitution were the result of the ability of the nobility and gentry to put checks on the power of the Tudor and Stuart monarchies. In another field, the peculiar supremacy of law in England was, though partly the work of Parliament, also in no small measure a result of the influence of the organized legal profession—a specifically privileged group—in restraining the arbitrary action of the crown.

The development of rational-legal authority, with bureaucratic administration, is both dependent on the breakdown of traditionalized particularistic privileged groups and in turn itself has a levelling influence, in that it treats social class by birth and other privileged statuses as to a large degree irrelevant to status in the system of authority. Along with this levelling influence, both the struggle for power in the Western national states, and the pressure of certain of the ideological patterns have tended to weaken the control of a centralized authority over an administrative

[21] Cf. especially secs. 14 ff. Cf. also the essay *Politik als Beruf* in *Gesammelte politische Schriften*, and the editor's articles 'Max Weber and the Contemporary Political Crisis,' *Review of Politics*, January and April 1942.

machine. Above all, as Weber illustrates from the United States in particular, elective officials in the nature of the case cannot be subject to the
same order of discipline that appointive officials are. And the democratic
system has, through the spoils system, on occasion made great inroads on
bureaucratic organization even in the sphere of appointive administration.

But the combination of a relatively levelled undifferentiated mass upon
which to base political support, rather than groups with fixed and differentiated status, and the democratic principle of appeal to the electorate
for legitimation, has opened the way to the emergence of leaders with a
wide personal appeal. This in turn is associated with the party system.[22]
A party leader can, to a greater or less degree, approach the type of a
charismatic leader, and use of the methods of appeal and the forms of
organization of his power appropriate to that type. Though, for the most
part as in England and the United States, modern party leadership has
only in a minor degree taken a revolutionary charismatic form, elsewhere
it has done so pre-eminently. To Weber the demagogic party leader, once
he became genuinely charismatic with the implied denial of the legitimacy of the position of any rivals, either within or outside his party,
could readily become a dictator with a consequent shift in the character
of the authority system. This need not involve a drastic break with the
democratic reference of legitimacy. As Weber pointed out,[23] the plebiscite
could be used as a major symbol of the democratic legitimation of such
a leader, and would tend to be effective relatively regardless of its actual
genuineness as an expression of the popular will. Weber saw this already
happening in the case of the two Napoleons in France, and evidently
expected it to happen on a larger scale again. Though Weber died when
Hitler was no more than a recently demobilized and dissatisfied German
war veteran, he went far to predict the political pattern in which the
Nazi movement eventually developed out of the traditional patterns of
Western democracy. Indeed, it can scarcely be doubted that this link
with democratic sentiments, through continuity with the 'party' system
and even including the specific instrument of the plebiscite, was essential
to the elevation of the Fascist dictatorships to their position of power.
Up to the end Hitler liked to refer to the allegedly arbitrary interference
of the British with the 'self-determination' of the populations of Europe.
To incorporate the will of the German people is a claim which the Nazi
movement made with some plausibility—when it came to those of the

[22] Cf. sec. 18 ff., pp. 407 ff.
[23] Pp. 387-8.

occupied territories it requires a stretching of the meaning of categories which only a highly emotional devotion to the Nazi faith could make possible.

As in the case of his analysis of economic institutions, there are a number of points in the analysis of authority where difficult critical problems are raised. Perhaps the most general is the question of how far the several different variables involved in the differential criteria of the three types of authority in fact necessarily vary together to the extent implied in making this classification exhaustive of the major empirical possibilities. Thus the functional specificity of roles in rational-legal authority is contrasted with its diffuseness in the other two types. This criterion of distinction seems to be satisfactory but, as has been pointed out above, it is questionable whether functional specificity of roles is always associated with bureaucratic organization. Similarly it is questionable whether, in routine structures, diffuseness is necessarily associated with traditionalism or charisma. A non-traditional diffuseness seems to be a most important element of our patterns of friendship, marriage, and even other aspects of kinship. It is true that the pattern of romanic love has many charismatic features, but marriage is by no means exhausted by this pattern. In quite another connexion it seems questionable whether a charismatic appeal is necessarily associated with such particularistic patterns of loyalty to an individual leader as Weber tends to indicate. There seems to be an important distinction between the pattern of legitimacy and the individual bearer of authority under it, which Weber does not sufficiently work out and emphasize.

The concept of charisma in particular seems to involve important difficulties. In most of his explicit treatment of it Weber associates it most specifically with the claim to authority of an individual personal leader and treats it on this structural level, as a matter of the differentiation of roles of persons, not an element of the structure of systems of action.[24] In another connexion, however, where he attempts to systematize his categories for the generalized analysis of religious phenomena,[25] he treats charisma as a quality, not necessarily only of persons, but of non-empirical aspects of the situation of the action, of, in a special technical sense, a 'supernatural' order, recognition of which underlies the moral legitimacy of normative rules generally. The concept, that is, becomes exactly equi-

---

[24] In the relevant sections of the present volume and in *Wirtschaft und Gesellschaft*, part iii, chaps. ix and x.

[25] *Religionssoziologie, Wirtschaft und Gesellschaft*, part ii, chap. iv.

valent to Durkheim's 'sacred.' There are indications of this ambivalence [26] in Weber's treatment of charismatic authority in that in the routinization of charisma, the charisma of the original leader does not disappear, but becomes 'objectified' as a quality of the order developing from a charismatic origin, as the charisma of office or of a ruling house. What seems to have happened is that, in formulating the concept for the treatment of authority Weber mixed two different levels of analysis, one the concrete structure of a certain class of movements of social change, with special reference to the role of a type of person, the other, analytically the more basic level, of the analysis of systems of action, of the basic elements of orientation of the action of the individual to his situation and to the normative patterns governing his action. What on the first level is a characteristic *only* of certain specific types of leaders of specific kinds of movement, becomes on the second an element of *all* systems of action. From the second point of view all authority has a charismatic basis in some form. The special type Weber calls charismatic is then characterized by specific kinds of content, modes of embodiment and relation to the basis of legitimacy of the established institutional order in conflict with which it stands.

This suggests a further difficulty, parallel to that encountered in Weber's treatment of economic institutions. All of the most important theoretical elements of Weber's analysis of authority are of generalized significance for the whole field of social relationships. Yet he tends to treat the sphere of the organization of authority as *analytically* autonomous in a way which obscures this continuity of pattern throughout the social system as a whole. What Weber seems to have done is illegitimately to hypostatize a certain mode of structuring of social systems as an independent entity. To be sure he is continually calling attention to its complex interrelations with other structures, such as the economic, but still in such a way as to presuppose a *kind* (not necessarily a degree) of independence which is unreal. This is a particular example of the consequences of Weber's failure to employ systematically the concept of a generalized social system on all the main levels. A generalized account of the principal variables patterning social relationships is logically prior to the treatment of such relatively specialized structures as those of authority and of economic allocation. The analytical continuity which runs through them in Weber's treatment is not the outcome of such a

[26] The problem is more fully discussed in the editor's *Structure of Social Action*, chap. xvii.

careful systematic analysis, but rather of the *ad hoc* necessities of his empirical work.

These strictures should, however, in this case as in others, not be permitted to bias the perspective in which Weber's work is seen. If, along with many others equally possible, they were systematically taken account of, they might well lead to considerable refinement of Weber's analysis, to the elimination of a number of particular difficulties, and to some alteration of the perspective in which his empirical results were seen. This would, however, constitute going on from where Weber left off, not 'refuting' him and substituting another theory. Probably Weber's analysis of authority even as it stands constitutes the most highly developed and broadly applicable conceptual scheme in any comparable field which is available, not only in the specifically sociological literature, but in that of social science as a whole.

V. The Modern Western Institutional System

THROUGHOUT Weber's scientific career run two major threads of interest, in the methodology and theoretical formulation of social science, and in the understanding of the social structure and dynamics of modern Western civilization. Undoubtedly the latter was his dominant interest, the former being regarded as instrumental to it. In pursuing his interest in the society of his own time, to a degree unknown before, he made use of the comparative method, illuminating the subject of interest by contrast as well as by agreement and historical antecedent. It is this, with the orientation of his comparative analysis to generalized theory, which distinguishes his work most strikingly from all the historical schools of thought with their tendency, on the highest level of generalization, to issue in evolutionary philosophies of history.[1]

Though they were worked out in a long process of development involving varied particular projects of research, there is a sense in which Weber's main contributions to this problem came to focus in two primary parts of his work, his sociology of religion and his comparative institutional sociology as summarized in the present volume. At both points in his own mind to a very great though probably decreasing extent, and still more in that of his interpreters, Weber treated the modern order as that of 'capitalism.' His first contribution to the sociology of religion was the essay on *The Protestant Ethic and the Spirit of Capitalism* with its strong emphasis on finding adequate motivation for acquisitive activity in a system of market relationships. Similarly, in his treatment of the sociological foundations of economic activity in the present volume, Weber tended to centre his attention on the system of market relationships, the significance of money and money calculation, and property relationships, all with special reference to the functioning of profit-making enterprise.

[1] Marxian theory may, in this connexion, legitimately be classified as belonging to the Historical School.

But from the very beginning in both connections Weber was by no means concerned only with acquisitive activity in general. He distinguished explicitly the 'rational bourgeois capitalism' in which his primary interest lay from other forms which had been common to other civilizations, and which were dependent on quite different conditions. Only this was, he held, specific to the modern Occidental World. Thus from the very beginning of his work he was not merely attempting to contribute to the explanation of a phenomenon the essential descriptive features of which were clear to everyone and common ground for all competent scholars in the field. A great deal of the originality of Weber's contribution consists, rather, in bringing into the centre of attention aspects even of our own economic order, which have been obscured in a great deal of social and economic thought, and showing their very great importance for our society.[2]

But the very investigation of these aspects and their formulation in terms of comparative perspective tended to show more and more that they could not be treated as of merely economic significance in any simple sense. 'Capitalism' in the sense in which Weber meant it, must be regarded not as a form of economic organization alone, but as the distinctive pattern of a whole society. Terminologically this agreed with other schools of thought, notably the Marxian, of which Weber was acutely conscious. But the farther Weber's studies progressed, and the greater his knowledge of fact and the broader his comparative perspective became, the less did the ordinary criteria of capitalism seem adequate to characterize such a total institutional order. Weber never proposed any specific alternative, but there is nevertheless a strong basis in his work for changing the emphasis from the economic aspect as such to common elements which underlie both this and many other aspects of our society.

Seen in terms of Weber's sociology of religion there is peculiar to our society the relative predominance of a certain basic attitude or orientation toward world activity, the attitude which he treats as distinctive of 'ascetic Protestantism.'[3] Five components of this attitude are, perhaps, particularly significant. In the first place it is 'ascetic' in the sense that it has strong inhibitions against immersion in the most immediate worldly

[2] A notable example of failure to understand this is to be found in H. M. Robertson, *The Rise of Economic Individualism*, which has the sub-title 'A Criticism of Max Weber and His School.' See the editor's critical review 'H. M. Robertson on Max Weber and His School,' *Journal of Political Economy*, vol. xliii, 1935.

[3] See The Protestant Ethic, but also various other parts of the *Aufsätze zur Religionssoziologie*, especially the section *Konfuzianismus und Puritanismus* in vol. i.

interests and satisfactions for their own sake. In its original protestant form it had a definitely transcendental orientation to supernatural values, but even though now secularized, it still maintains a high level of tension between ideal and real.

The existence of such tension, which is to Weber typical of a transcendentally founded religious ethic, can, however, work out in either of two directions. The consequent relative devaluation of things worldly can lead to a negative reaction, to flight into mystical contemplation or otherworldly asceticism, or it can, on the other hand, lead to a drive for active mastery over worldly things and interests, to making over the world in the image of a transcendental ideal. This, above all as embodied in the Calvinistic conception of the Kingdom of God on Earth, is a crucial feature of ascetic Protestantism and the basic orientation again has survived in secularized form.

Third is 'rationality.' This concept is, as has been shown, a difficult one in Weber's work. What he means here includes above all two things. On the one hand tradition is radically devalued—nothing is sacred merely because it has become traditionally accepted and established, everything must be tested anew in terms of a universalistic standard. On the other hand it means the systematization of conduct according to rational norms. No single act can stand by itself or be valued on its own merits alone, but only in terms of its bearing on a whole system of rational conduct. The drive of ascetic Protestantism is not merely for mastery, but in this sense for rational mastery over the world.

Fourth is ethical universalism, the insistence on treatment of all men by the same generalized, impersonal standards. This is of course common to all branches of Christianity, but in combination with the active ascetic attitude becomes an obligation for the ordering of ordinary secular life which it has not been elsewhere.

Finally, to Weber the high functional differentiation and specialization of roles in our society was by no means to be taken for granted as the simple result of utilitarian 'division of labour.' In many societies there are deep-seated sentiments opposed to carrying such specialization too far, above all those which oppose treating a human being merely as an 'instrument' of impersonal ends. Particularly in a society which places an unprecedentedly high valuation on human life and personality as such, willingness to fit into specialized instrumental roles requires explanation. An element of this explanation Weber found in the protestant orientation in that in his process of active mastery over the world the individual was an instrument of a higher instance, of God's will, and was working in the service of an impersonal end beyond his own personal interests. At any rate the importance of this willingness for the modern occupational system can scarcely be doubted or overestimated.

It is primarily the combination of these five elements of orientation which Weber means by the concept of the 'calling.' It is the conception of an individual's 'business in life' as a calling in this sense, as a matter of moral obligation, which is to a comparable degree, distinctive of the modern world. It will be noted that acquisitiveness or a valuation of profit does not enter into this at all. Weber devoted a great deal of attention to the motivation of acquisitive activity in terms of the protestant ethic. But it is quite clear that this is a secondary problem.[4] It touches certain ranges of particular activity in particular situations within the broader general orientation. The pattern of the calling can be acted out in roles such as that of scientist, physician, civil servant, or even Christian minister which in our society are specifically defined as non-acquisitive roles in which the 'profit-motive' is not supposed to play any part. Indeed it is acquisitive orientation *only* in the context of the calling pattern which Weber treated as characteristic of modern 'rational bourgeois capitalism' as distinguished from other types.

Weber himself of course attributed a decisive influence in the development of this fundamental orientation to Protestantism, and the present writer thinks him, with a few qualifications, right in doing so. But it should not be forgotten that this historical question is logically distinct from that of whether he was right in placing the descriptive emphasis in characterizing the modern institutional order where he did, by contrast for instance with the Marxians for whom a system of profit-making enterprise as such and the consequent 'exploitation' are the essential things.

The attitude orientation characteristic of the modern world has been sketched because it is a primary clue to the generalized features of our institutional order which Weber brought out most sharply. The orientation to transcendental religious goals has, of course, to a large extent receded, but there are important elements of asceticism in our valuation of subjection to discipline in the interest of relatively remote and impersonal goals, and particularly in the valuation of rationally disciplined labour, at times almost as an end in itself. The active orientation to mas-

---

[4] Most critics of Weber seem entirely unaware of this fact. To them the 'spirit of capitalism' is purely and simply acquisitiveness. Cf. Robertson, op. cit.

tery is very clear in our valuation of technological achievement, and in our attitudes toward social reform and our unwillingness to tolerate 'evils.' These two elements of orientation supply a kind of pervasive framework rather than specific institutional patterns. The same is to some extent true of the third element, rationality, especially in a negative sense. One of the most important elements which Weber included under traditionalism in other societies was magic. One of the most striking fields is that of health. Modern scientific medicine is altogether unique in the extent to which it treats ill health as a problem of rational technique rather than of ritual healing. Only in Greco-Roman Antiquity has there been anything even remotely approaching it.

Universalism and functional specificity are much more readily recognizable as pattern principles underlying specific institutional forms. The first is particularly important in two fields, the patterns governing personal status and rights, and those governing the treatment of ability and achievement. The principal freedoms which we have come to value so highly, and the relative immunity from invidious discriminations on such grounds as birth, individual favouritisms, ethnic or class status, have their roots in this pattern. 'Equality before the law' is doubtless very far from being able to guarantee effective substantive equality for 'all sorts and conditions of men,' but that kind of particularistic discrimination is surely far less prominent in our society than in most others of a high degree of complexity. Secondly, the valuation, and its expression in recognition and status, of ability and achievement by such universalistic standards as technical competence has, particularly in the occupational field, a far wider scope in modern Western society than in most others. No other large-scale society has come so near universalizing 'equality of opportunity.' An important consequence of the universalistic pattern in these two fields is the very high degree of social mobility, of potentiality for each individual to 'find his own level' on the basis of his own abilities and achievements, or, within certain limits, of his own personal wishes rather than a compulsory traditional status.

Again there are perhaps two main fields in which functional specificity is of particular significance. On the one hand we are to a most unusual extent emancipated from the dependence of every act and interest on a 'total' status. To take one of the most conspicuous examples, the acquisition and uses of property both as instruments of all sorts of ends and for immediate consumption uses, is to a very high degree dissociated from personal status and immediate involvement in a system of political authority. This dissociation of the sphere of property is to a high degree essential to mobility and to the realization of universalistic standards. A second, closely related phenomenon is the freedom to enter into private agreements with limited content without involving the total status of the parties, but only specifically limited interests. What we think of as 'freedom of contract' would not be possible in an institutional system in which, as in the Middle Ages, all the principal elements of an individual's status were treated as bound together. The granting of a fief was, to be sure, in a sense a 'contract' but not a limited one in the modern sense. It involved property interests, a status in the system of political authority, and a fundamental reciprocal relation of personal loyalty 'for better or for worse' in whatever exigencies might arise between lord and vassal. The nearest modern analogy is that of the marriage 'contract.' But in the feudal case while the fiction of freedom was maintained, in fact both parties were usually bound to each other by the rule of heredity. It was thus more like marriage in a system of compulsory preferential mating.

More obvious than this is the differentiation of specifically delimited spheres of functional activity, in systems of authority in the concept of office, in others in spheres of technical competence, or of assigned function under authority. This is of course in part determined by the situational exigencies of efficient performance. But for the case of authority Weber has quite conclusively shown that there is much more to it than that, that it involves a specific discipline on the institutional level. In quite different contexts, as for instance that of the informal discipline governing such a non-bureaucratic function as medical practice, the same thing can be shown.[5]

The fact that these institutional patterns are, in a comparable degree of development, distinctive of the modern Western World, is brought out by Weber with peculiar sharpness and clarity by his systematic comparative analysis which demonstrates the radically different character, in the relevant respects, of the institutional structures of most of the other great civilizations. Weber commanded a knowledge of comparative institutions which is perhaps unique in the history of the social sciences. Perhaps his most impressive single demonstration of the radical contrast with things western is to be found in his analyses of the classical civilizations of China and India in his Sociology of Religion.[6]

[5] Cf. the editor's article already referred to, 'The Professions and Social Structure,' Social Forces, May 1940.

[6] Vol. i and ii.

But precisely this comparative perspective, while heightening his realization of the uniqueness of our social system, also heightened his sense of its precarious state of instability. The institutional features which preoccupied him are the ones which to a peculiar degree have made possible the distinctive achievements of Western history in science, in technology, in law and government, in the large-scale organization of administration, even in the arts and literature. But at the same time they are far more vulnerable to disruptive influences than other alternative forms. They themselves generate crucial internal strains which make a transition to different situations likely.[7]

It is perhaps in this context that one can best attempt to place Weber as an interpreter of the course of modern society. He came at a time when, perhaps particularly in the Anglo-Saxon world, most scholars were still under the spell of what has already proved to be an altogether unrealistic utopian optimism about the future. Everything would, we were told, continue indefinitely to become 'bigger and better' in the paths laid out by the development of the recent past. Weber was undoubtedly one of those who saw far deeper than this into the real balance of forces of his time. He is certainly not, however, to be regarded as one of a certain class of prophets of doom, for instance of the Spenglerian variety. There is little in his work of the idea of inevitable unrolling of the life cycle of a civilization. On the contrary he certainly believed that the course of history often hung precariously in the balance and could be crucially influenced by the actions of individuals and movements. His personal ethic was a Spartan ethic of 'responsibility' not one of contemplatively watching the inevitable process unfold.

But if not a prophet of inevitable doom, Weber was not an unrealistic optimist. He saw tendencies which he thought might well lead to a drastic alteration in the institutional foundations of our society.[8] He correctly diagnosed the period of World War I as one of deep crisis in our civilization as a whole. He died too soon after that war to have a clear conception of the shape of its aftermath as we are experiencing it now. It would be entirely out of character to set Weber up as a detailed prophet of the future. No one realized better than he the futility of trying

[7] A number of these strains have been discussed above. The list is by no means exhaustive, even of those to the understanding of which Weber contributed.

[8] See especially *Politik als Beruf*, op. cit. p. 449. 'Nicht das Blühen des Sommers liegt vor uns, sondern zunächst eine Polarnacht von Eisiger Finsternis und Härte, mag äusserlich jetzt siegen welche Gruppe auch immer.'

to predict detailed events long in advance. But, with the hindsight which so greatly simplifies our problem, we can see that, considering the blindness of most of his contemporaries, Weber on the whole saw the nature of the crisis, and the general direction of change very clearly. He did not predict Hitler or the Nazi movement, but he quite clearly saw that a large-scale charismatic movement in reaction against modern 'liberal' institutions but with certain 'democratic' elements was a very real possibility. He also saw various more direct tendencies for social structure to shift over toward the traditionalistic type.

It would probably be a legitimate extension of Weber's analysis to hold that the National Socialist movement has mobilized the forces antagonistic to the maintenance of these distinctive Western patterns more powerfully than this has ever happened before. According to Weber's analysis, the effect of its securing definite political predominance over the principal area of Western civilization would almost certainly be its gradual transformation into a traditionalized structure, a structure which in detail could not be foreseen, but which might well assume the form of some kind of feudalism. Such a transformation could not in the long run fail to choke off the most distinctive cultural products of our society, above all science and rational thinking, and to lead to a great revival of 'superstition' and mythology. But by the same token, such a consequence is not inevitable. We may well stand at one of those great crucial dividing points of history like the Persian Wars to which Weber devoted such a penetrating analysis. On the outcome of the present struggle may well depend whether Western civilization will have an opportunity to fulfill its as yet unsuspected potentialities, or revert to a rigidly fixed traditionalism.

This is a remarkable diagnosis of the situation of a great civilization, probably unique in its sober realism and its intellectually sophisticated allowance for the immense complexity of the problems, for its ability to draw clear and definite conclusions from such complex materials and yet not fall into dogmatic over-simplification. This intellectual achievement in no small measure owes its possibility to the fact that its author, in a certain sense against his own will, devoted himself to the problems of systematic theory in his field. What he achieved in the field of theory was far from perfect, indeed its improvement in several directions has already become possible. But as he forged it and used it, it was a powerful instrument of understanding in the attack on some of the most complex and baffling problems the human mind has ever attempted to solve. But such results do not come about automatically even given the instrument ready-made. To forge the instrument so largely himself and at the same time achieve such mastery in its use, is scientific achievement of a very high order.

TALCOTT PARSONS.

I. The Fundamental Concepts of Sociology

PREFATORY NOTE

An introductory discussion of concepts can hardly be dispensed with, in spite of the fact that it is unavoidably abstract and hence gives the impression of remoteness from reality. Its method, however, makes no claim to any kind of novelty. On the contrary it attempts only to formulate what all empirical sociology really means when it deals with the same problems, in what it is hoped is a more convenient and somewhat more exact terminology, even though on that account it may seem pedantic. This is true even where terms are used which are apparently new or unfamiliar. As compared to the author's essay in *Logos*,[1] the terminology has been simplified as far as possible and hence considerably changed in order to render it more easily understandable. Unfortunately the most precise formulation cannot always be reconciled with a form which can readily be popularized. In such cases the latter aim has had to be sacrificed.

On the concept of 'understanding'[2] compare the *Allgemeine Psycho-*

[1] Vol. iv (1913, pp. 253 ff.); reprinted in *Gesammelte Aufsätze zur Wissenschaftslehre*, pp. 403-450.

[2] The German term is *Verstehen*. As Weber uses it this is a technical term with a distinctly narrower meaning than either the German or the English in everyday usage. Its primary reference in this work is to the observation and theoretical interpretation of the subjective 'states of mind' of actors. But it also extends to the grasp of the meaning of logical and other systems of symbols, a meaning which is usually thought of as in some sense 'intended' by a mind or intelligent being of some sort. The most important point about this concept seems to the editor to be the fact that in so far as phenomena are 'understood' in this technical sense, the relevant facts are stated and analysed within a certain frame of reference, that of 'action.' For present purposes the most important feature of this frame of reference is its use of 'subjective categories.' The essential thing is the operational applicability of such categories, not the common sense empirical question of whether the actor is conscious of the meanings imputed to him or in the ordinary sense 'intended' a given course of action. For a further discussion of these problems, see Talcott Parsons, *The Structure of Social Action*, especially chaps. ii and xix.

It has not seemed advisable to attempt a rigorous use of a single English term whenever

pathologie of Karl Jaspers, also a few observations by Heinrich Rickert in the second edition of the *Grenzen der Naturwissenschaftlichen Begriffsbildung* and particularly some of Simmel's discussions in the *Probleme der Geschichtsphilosophie*. For certain methodological considerations the reader may here be referred, as often before in the author's writings, to the procedure of Friedrich Gottl in his work *Die Herrschaft des Wortes*. This book, to be sure, is written in a somewhat difficult style and its argument does not appear everywhere to have been thoroughly thought through. As regards content, reference may be made especially to the fine work of Ferdinand Tönnies, *Gemeinschaft und Gesellschaft*, and also to the gravely misleading book of Rudolph Stammler, *Wirtschaft und Recht*, which may be compared with my criticism in the *Archiv für Sozialwissenschaft* (vol. xxiv, 1907). This critical essay contains many of the fundamental ideas of the following exposition. The present work departs from Simmel's method (in the *Soziologie* and the *Philosophie des Geldes*) in drawing a sharp distinction between subjectively intended and objectively valid 'meanings'; two different things which Simmel not only fails to distinguish but often deliberately treats as belonging together.

I: The Definitions of Sociology and of Social Action

1. Sociology (in the sense in which this highly ambiguous word is used here) is a science which attempts the interpretive understanding of social action in order thereby to arrive at a causal explanation of its course and effects. In 'action' is included all human behaviour when and in so far as the acting individual attaches a subjective meaning to it. Action in this sense may be either overt or purely inward or subjective; it may consist of positive intervention in a situation, or of deliberately refraining from such intervention or passively acquiescing in the situation. Action is social in so far as, by virtue of the subjective meaning attached to it by the acting individual (or individuals), it takes account of the behaviour of others and is thereby oriented in its course.[3]

Weber employs *Verstehen*. 'Understanding' has been most commonly used. Other expressions such as 'subjectively understandable,' 'interpretation in subjective terms,' 'comprehension,' etc., have been used from time to time as the context seemed to demand.—ED.

[3] In this series of definitions Weber employs several important terms which need discussion. In addition to *Verstehen*, which has already been commented upon, there are four important ones: *Deuten*, *Sinn*, *Handeln*, and *Verhalten*. *Deuten* has generally been translated as 'interpret.' As used by Weber in this context it refers to the interpretation of subjective states of mind and the meanings which can be imputed as intended by an actor.

(a) *The Methodological Foundations of Sociology* [4]

1. 'Meaning' may be of two kinds. The term may refer first to the actual existing meaning in the given concrete case of a particular actor, or to the average or approximate meaning attributable to a given plurality of actors; or secondly to the theoretically conceived *pure type* [5] of subjective meaning attributed to the hypothetical actor or actors in a given type of action. In no case does it refer to an objectively 'correct' meaning or one which is 'true' in some metaphysical sense. It is this which distin-

Any other meaning of the word 'interpretation' is irrelevant to Weber's discussion. The term *Sinn* has generally been translated as 'meaning'; and its variations, particularly the corresponding adjectives, *sinnhaft, sinnvoll, sinnfremd,* have been dealt with by appropriately modifying the term meaning. The reference here again is always to features of the content of subjective states of mind or of symbolic systems which are ultimately referable to such states of mind.

The terms *Handeln* and *Verhalten* are directly related. *Verhalten* is the broader term referring to any mode of behaviour of human individuals, regardless of the frame of reference in terms of which it is analysed. 'Behaviour' has seemed to be the most appropriate English equivalent. *Handeln,* on the other hand, refers to the concrete phenomenon of human behaviour only in so far as it is capable of 'understanding,' in Weber's technical sense, in terms of subjective categories. The most appropriate English equivalent has seemed to be 'action.' This corresponds to the editor's usage in *The Structure of Social Action* and would seem to be fairly well established. 'Conduct' is also closely similar and has sometimes been used. *Deuten, Verstehen,* and *Sinn* are thus applicable to human behaviour only in so far as it constitutes action or conduct in this specific sense.—ED.

[4] Weber's text is organized in a somewhat unusual manner. He lays down certain fundamental definitions and then proceeds to comment upon them. The definitions themselves are in the original printed in large type, the subsidiary comments in smaller type. For the purposes of this translation it has not seemed best to make a distinction in type form, but the reader should be aware that the numbered paragraphs which follow a definition or group of them are in the nature of comments, rather than the continuous development of a general line of argument. This fact accounts for what is sometimes a relatively fragmentary character of the development and for the abrupt transition from one subject to another. Weber apparently did not intend this material to be 'read' in the ordinary sense, but rather to serve as a reference work for the clarification and systematization of theoretical concepts and their implications. While the comments under most of the definitions are relatively brief, under the definitions of Sociology and of Social Action, Weber wrote what is essentially a methodological essay. This makes sec. 1 out of proportion to the other sections of this and the following chapters. It has, however, seemed best to retain Weber's own plan for the subdivision of the material.—ED.

[5] Weber means by 'pure type' what he himself generally called and what has come to be known in the literature about his methodology as the 'ideal type.' The reader may be referred for general orientation to Weber's own Essay (to which he himself refers below), *Die Objektivität sozialwissenschaftlicher Erkenntnis;* to two works of Dr. Alexander von Schelting, 'Die logische Theorie der historischen Kulturwissenschaften von Max Weber' (*Archiv fuer Sozialwissenschaft,* vol. xlix), and *Max Webers Wissenschaftslehre;* and to the editor's *Structure of Social Action,* chap. xvi. A somewhat different interpretation is given in Theodore Abel, *Systematic Sociology in Germany,* chap. iv.—ED.

guishes the empirical sciences of action, such as sociology and history, from the dogmatic disciplines in that area, such as jurisprudence, logic, ethics, and esthetics, which seek to ascertain the 'true' and 'valid' meanings associated with the objects of their investigation.

2. The line between meaningful action and merely reactive behaviour to which no subjective meaning is attached, cannot be sharply drawn empirically. A very considerable part of all sociologically relevant behaviour, especially purely traditional behaviour, is marginal between the two. In the case of many psychophysical processes, meaningful, i.e. subjectively understandable, action is not to be found at all; in others it is discernible only by the expert psychologist. Many mystical experiences which cannot be adequately communicated in words are, for a person who is not susceptible to such experiences, not fully understandable. At the same time the ability to imagine one's self performing a similar action is not a necessary prerequisite to understanding; 'one need not have been Caesar in order to understand Caesar.' For the verifiable accuracy[6] of interpretation of the meaning of a phenomenon, it is a great help to be able to put one's self imaginatively in the place of the actor and thus sympathetically to participate in his experiences, but this is not an essential condition of meaningful interpretation. Understandable and non-understandable components of a process are often intermingled and bound up together.

3. All interpretation of meaning, like all scientific observation, strives for clarity and verifiable accuracy of insight and comprehension (*Evidenz*). The basis for certainty in understanding can be either rational, which can be further subdivided into logical and mathematical, or it can be of an emotionally empathic or artistically appreciative quality. In the

[6] This is an imperfect rendering of the German term *Evidenz*, for which, unfortunately, there is no good English equivalent. It has hence been rendered in a number of different ways, varying with the particular context in which it occurs. The primary meaning refers to the basis on which a scientist or thinker becomes satisfied of the certainty or acceptability of a proposition. As Weber himself points out, there are two primary aspects of this. On the one hand a conclusion can be 'seen' to follow from given premises by virtue of logical, mathematical, or possibly other modes of meaningful relation. In this sense one 'sees' the solution of an arithmetical problem or the correctness of the proof of a geometrical theorem. The other aspect is concerned with empirical observation. If an act of observation is competently performed, in a similar sense one 'sees' the truth of the relevant descriptive proposition. The term *Evidenz* does not refer to the process of observing, but to the quality of its result, by virtue of which the observer feels justified in affirming a given statement. Hence 'certainty' has seemed a suitable translation in some contexts, 'clarity' in others, 'accuracy' in still others. The term 'intuition' is not usable because it refers to the process rather than to the result.—ED.

sphere of action things are rationally evident chiefly when we attain a completely clear intellectual grasp of the action-elements in their intended context of meaning. Empathic or appreciative accuracy is attained when, through sympathetic participation, we can adequately grasp the emotional context in which the action took place. The highest degree of rational understanding is attained in cases involving the meanings of logically or mathematically related propositions; their meaning may be immediately and unambiguously intelligible. We have a perfectly clear understanding of what it means when somebody employs the proposition $2 \times 2 = 4$ or the Pythagorean theorem in reasoning or argument, or when someone correctly carries out a logical train of reasoning according to our accepted modes of thinking. In the same way we also understand what a person is doing when he tries to achieve certain ends by choosing appropriate means on the basis of the facts of the situation as experience has accustomed us to interpret them. Such an interpretation of this type of rationally purposeful action possesses, for the understanding of the choice of means, the highest degree of verifiable certainty. With a lower degree of certainty, which is, however, adequate for most purposes of explanation, we are able to understand errors, including confusion of problems of the sort that we ourselves are liable to, or the origin of which we can detect by sympathetic self-analysis.

On the other hand, many ultimate ends or values toward which experience shows that human action may be oriented, often cannot be understood completely, though sometimes we are able to grasp them intellectually. The more radically they differ from our own ultimate values, however, the more difficult it is for us to make them understandable by imaginatively participating in them. Depending upon the circumstances of the particular case we must be content either with a purely intellectual understanding of such values or when even that fails, sometimes we must simply accept them as given data. Then we can try to understand the action motivated by them on the basis of whatever opportunities for approximate emotional and intellectual interpretation seem to be available at different points in its course. These difficulties apply, for instance, for people not susceptible to the relevant values, to many unusual acts of religious and charitable zeal; also certain kinds of extreme rationalistic fanaticism of the type involved in some forms of the ideology of the 'rights of man' are in a similar position for people who radically repudiate such points of view.

The more we ourselves are susceptible to them the more readily can we imaginatively participate in such emotional reactions as anxiety, anger, ambition, envy, jealousy, love, enthusiasm, pride, vengefulness, loyalty, devotion, and appetites of all sorts, and thereby understand the irrational conduct which grows out of them. Such conduct is 'irrational,' that is, from the point of view of the rational pursuit of a given end. Even when such emotions are found in a degree of intensity of which the observer himself is completely incapable, he can still have a significant degree of emotional understanding of their meaning and can interpret intellectually their influence on the course of action and the selection of means.

For the purposes of a typological scientific analysis it is convenient to treat all irrational, affectually determined elements of behaviour as factors of deviation from a conceptually pure type of rational action. For example a panic on the stock exchange can be most conveniently analysed by attempting to determine first what the course of action would have been if it had not been influenced by irrational affects; it is then possible to introduce the irrational components as accounting for the observed deviations from this hypothetical course. Similarly, in analysing a political or military campaign it is convenient to determine in the first place what would have been a rational course, given the ends of the participants and adequate knowledge of all the circumstances. Only in this way is it possible to assess the causal significance of irrational factors as accounting for the deviations from this type. The construction of a purely rational course of action in such cases serves the sociologist as a type ('ideal type') which has the merit of clear understandability and lack of ambiguity. By comparison with this it is possible to understand the ways in which actual action is influenced by irrational factors of all sorts, such as affects [7] and errors, in that they account for the deviation from the line of conduct which would be expected on the hypothesis that the action were purely rational.

Only in this respect and for these reasons of methodological convenience, is the method of sociology 'rationalistic.' It is naturally not legitimate to interpret this procedure as involving a 'rationalistic bias' of sociology, but only as a methodological device. It certainly does not involve a belief in the actual predominance of rational elements in human life, for on the question of how far this predominance does or does not

[7] A term now much used in psychological literature, especially that of Psychoanalysis. It is roughly equivalent to 'emotion' but more precise.—ED.

exist, nothing whatever has been said. That there is, however, a danger of rationalistic interpretations where they are out of place naturally cannot be denied. All experience unfortunately confirms the existence of this danger.

4. In all the sciences of human action, account must be taken of processes and phenomena which are devoid of subjective meaning,[8] in the role of stimuli, results, favouring or hindering circumstances. To be devoid of meaning is not identical with being lifeless or non-human; every artifact, such as for example a machine, can be understood only in terms of the meaning which its production and use have had or will have for human action; a meaning which may derive from a relation to exceedingly various purposes. Without reference to this meaning such an object remains wholly unintelligible.[9] That which is intelligible or understandable about it is thus its relation to human action in the role either of means or of end; a relation of which the actor or actors can be said to have been aware and to which their action has been oriented. Only in terms of such categories is it possible to 'understand' objects of this kind. On the other hand processes or conditions, whether they are animate or inanimate, human or non-human, are in the present sense devoid of meaning in so far as they cannot be related to an intended purpose. That is to say they are devoid of meaning if they cannot be related to action in the role of means or ends but constitute only the stimulus, the favouring or hindering circumstances.[10] It may be that the incursion of the Dollart at the beginning of the twelfth century[11] had historical significance as a stimulus to the beginning of certain migrations of considerable importance. Human mortality, indeed the organic life cycle generally from the helplessness of infancy to that of old age, is naturally of the very greatest sociological importance through the various ways in

[8] The German term is *sinnfremd*. This should not be translated by 'meaningless,' but interpreted in the technical context of Weber's use of *Verstehen* and *Sinndeutung*. The essential criterion is the impossibility of placing the object in question in a complex of relations on the meaningful level.—Ed.

[9] *Unverstehbar.*

[10] Surely this passage states too narrow a conception of the scope of meaningful interpretation. It is certainly not *only* in terms such as those of the rational means-end schema, that it is possible to make action understandable in terms of subjective categories. This probably can actually be called a source of rationalistic bias in Weber's work. In practice he does not adhere at all rigorously to this methodological position. For certain possibilities in this broader field, see the editor's *Structure of Social Action*, chaps. vi and xi.—Ed.

[11] A gulf of the North Sea which broke through the Netherlands coast, flooding an area.—Ed.

which human action has been oriented to these facts. To still another category of facts devoid of meaning belong certain psychic or psychophysical phenomena such as fatigue, habituation, memory, etc.; also certain typical states of euphoria under some conditions of ascetic mortification; finally, typical variations in the reactions of individuals according to reaction-time, precision, and other modes. But in the last analysis the same principle applies to these as to other phenomena which are devoid of meaning. Both the actor and the sociologist must accept them as data to be taken into account.

It is altogether possible that future research may be able to discover non-understandable uniformities underlying what has appeared to be specifically meaningful action, though little has been accomplished in this direction thus far. Thus, for example, differences in hereditary biological constitution, as of 'races,' would have to be treated by sociology as given data in the same way as the physiological facts of the need of nutrition or the effect of senescence on action. This would be the case if, and in so far as, we had statistically conclusive proof of their influence on sociologically relevant behaviour. The recognition of the causal significance of such factors would naturally not in the least alter the specific task of sociological analysis or of that of the other sciences of action, which is the interpretation of action in terms of its subjective meaning. The effect would be only to introduce certain non-understandable data of the same order as others which, it has been noted above, are already present, into the complex of subjectively understandable motivation at certain points. Thus it may come to be known that there are typical relations between the frequency of certain types of teleological orientation of action or of the degree of certain kinds of rationality and the cephalic index or skin colour or any other biologically inherited characteristic.

5. Understanding may be of two kinds: the first is the direct observational understanding [12] of the subjective meaning of a given act as such, including verbal utterances. We thus understand by direct observation, in this sense, the meaning of the proposition $2 \times 2 = 4$ when we hear

---

[12] Weber here uses the term *aktuelles Verstehen*, which he contrasts with *erklärendes Verstehen*. The latter he also refers to as *motivationsmaessig*. 'Aktuell' in this context has been translated as 'observational.' It is clear from Weber's discussion that the primary criterion is the possibility of deriving the meaning of an act or symbolic expression from immediate observation without reference to any broader context. In *erklärendes Verstehen*, on the other hand, the particular act must be placed in a broader context of meaning involving facts which cannot be derived from immediate observation of a particular act or expression.—ED.

or read it. This is a case of the direct rational understanding of ideas. We also understand an outbreak of anger as manifested by facial expression, exclamations or irrational movements. This is direct observational understanding of irrational emotional reactions. We can understand in a similar observational way the action of a woodcutter or of somebody who reaches for the knob to shut a door or who aims a gun at an animal. This is rational observational understanding of actions.

Understanding may, however, be of another sort, namely explanatory understanding. Thus we understand in terms of *motive* the meaning an actor attaches to the proposition twice two equals four, when he states it or writes it down, in that we understand what makes him do this at precisely this moment and in these circumstances. Understanding in this sense is attained if we know that he is engaged in balancing a ledger or in making a scientific demonstration, or is engaged in some other task of which this particular act would be an appropriate part. This is rational understanding of motivation, which consists in placing the act in an intelligible and more inclusive context of meaning.[13] Thus we understand the chopping of wood or aiming of a gun in terms of motive in addition to direct observation if we know that the woodchopper is working for a wage or is chopping a supply of firewood for his own use or possibly is doing it for recreation. But he might also be 'working off' a fit of rage, an irrational case. Similarly we understand the motive of a person aiming a gun if we know that he has been commanded to shoot as a member of a firing squad, that he is fighting against an enemy, or that he is doing it for revenge. The last is affectually determined and thus in a certain sense irrational. Finally we have a motivational understanding of the outburst of anger if we know that it has been provoked by jealousy, injured pride, or an insult. The last examples are all affectually determined and hence derived from irrational motives. In all the above cases the particular act has been placed in an understandable sequence of motivation, the understanding of which can be treated as an explanation of the actual course of behaviour. Thus for a science which

13 The German term is *Sinnzusammenhang*. It refers to a plurality of elements which form a coherent whole on the level of meaning. There are several possible modes of meaningful relation between such elements, such as logical consistency, the esthetic harmony of a style, or the appropriateness of means to an end. In any case, however, a *Sinnzusammenhang* must be distinguished from a system of elements which are causally interdependent. There seems to be no single English term or phrase which is always adequate. According to variations in the context, 'context of meaning,' 'complex of meaning,' and sometimes 'meaningful system' have been employed.—ED.

is concerned with the subjective meaning of action, explanation requires a grasp of the complex of meaning in which an actual course of understandable action thus interpreted belongs.[14] In all such cases, even where the processes are largely affectual, the subjective meaning of the action, including that also of the relevant meaning complexes, will be called the 'intended' meaning.[15] This involves a departure from ordinary usage, which speaks of intention in this sense only in the case of rationally purposive action.

6. In all these cases understanding involves the interpretive grasp of the meaning present in one of the following contexts: (a) as in the historical approach, the actually intended meaning for concrete individual action; or (b) as in cases of sociological mass phenomena the average of, or an approximation to, the actually intended meaning; or (c) the meaning appropriate to a scientifically formulated pure type (an ideal type) of a common phenomenon. The concepts and 'laws' of pure economic theory are examples of this kind of ideal type. They state what course a given type of human action would take if it were strictly rational, unaffected by errors or emotional factors and if, furthermore, it were completely and unequivocally directed to a single end, the maximization of economic advantage. In reality, action takes exactly this course only in unusual cases, as sometimes on the stock exchange; and even then there is usually only an approximation to the ideal type.[16]

Every interpretation attempts to attain clarity and certainty, but no matter how clear an interpretation as such appears to be from the point of view of meaning, it cannot on this account alone claim to be the causally valid interpretation. On this level it must remain only a peculiarly

[14] On the significance of this type of explanation for causal relationship. See para. 6, pp. 96 ff. below in the present section.

[15] The German is *gemeinter Sinn*. Weber departs from ordinary usage not only in broadening the meaning of this conception. As he states at the end of the present methodological discussion, he does not restrict the use of this concept to cases where a clear self-conscious awareness of such meaning can be reasonably attributed to every individual actor. Essentially, what Weber is doing is to formulate an operational concept. The question is not whether in a sense obvious to the ordinary person such an intended meaning 'really exists,' but whether the concept is capable of providing a logical framework within which scientifically important observations can be made. The test of validity of the observations is not whether their object is immediately clear to common sense, but whether the results of these technical observations can be satisfactorily organized and related to those of others in a systematic body of knowledge.—ED.

[16] The scientific functions of such construction have been discussed in the author's article in the *Archiv für Sozialwissenschaft*, vol. xix, pp. 64 ff.

plausible hypothesis. In the first place the 'conscious motives' may well, even to the actor himself, conceal the various 'motives' and 'repressions' which constitute the real driving force of his action. Thus in such cases even subjectively honest self-analysis has only a relative value. Then it is the task of the sociologist to be aware of this motivational situation and to describe and analyse it, even though it has not actually been concretely part of the conscious 'intention' of the actor; possibly not at all, at least not fully. This is a borderline case of the interpretation of meaning. Secondly, processes of action which seem to an observer to be the same or similar may fit into exceedingly various complexes of motive in the case of the actual actor. Then even though the situations appear superficially to be very similar we must actually understand them or interpret them as very different, perhaps, in terms of meaning, directly opposed.[17] Third, the actors in any given situation are often subject to opposing and conflicting impulses, all of which we are able to understand. In a large number of cases we know from experience it is not possible to arrive at even an approximate estimate of the relative strength of conflicting motives and very often we cannot be certain of our interpretation. Only the actual outcome of the conflict gives a solid basis of judgment.

More generally, verification of subjective interpretation by comparison with the concrete course of events is, as in the case of all hypotheses, indispensable. Unfortunately this type of verification is feasible with relative accuracy only in the few very special cases susceptible of psychological experimentation. The approach to a satisfactory degree of accuracy is exceedingly various, even in the limited number of cases of mass phenomena which can be statistically described and unambiguously interpreted. For the rest there remains only the possibility of comparing the largest possible number of historical or contemporary processes which, while otherwise similar, differ in the one decisive point of their relation to the particular motive or factor the role of which is being investigated. This is a fundamental task of comparative sociology. Often, unfortunately, there is available only the dangerous and uncertain procedure of the 'imaginary experiment' which consists in thinking away certain elements of a chain of motivation and working out the course of action which would then probably ensue, thus arriving at a causal judgment.[18]

17 Simmel, in his *Probleme der Geschichtsphilosophie*, gives a number of examples.

18 The above passage is an exceedingly compact statement of Weber's theory of the logical conditions of proof of causal relationship. He developed this most fully in his essay

For example, the generalization called Gresham's Law is a rationally clear interpretation of human action under certain conditions and under the assumption that it will follow a purely rational course. How far any actual course of action corresponds to this can be verified only by the available statistical evidence for the actual disappearance of under-valued monetary units from circulation. In this case our information serves to demonstrate a high degree of accuracy. The facts of experience were known before the generalization, which was formulated afterwards; but without this successful interpretation our need for causal understanding would evidently be left unsatisfied. On the other hand, without the demonstration that what can here be assumed to be a theoretically adequate interpretation also is in some degree relevant to an actual course of action, a 'law,' no matter how fully demonstrated theoretically, would be worthless for the understanding of action in the real world. In this case the correspondence between the theoretical interpretation of motivation and its empirical verification is entirely satisfactory and the cases are numerous enough so that verification can be considered established. But to take another example, Eduard Meyer has advanced an ingenious theory of the causal significance of the battles of Marathon, Salamis, and Platea for the development of the cultural peculiarities of Greek, and hence, more generally, Western, civilization.[19] This is derived from a meaningful interpretation of certain symptomatic facts having to do with the attitudes of the Greek oracles and prophets towards the Persians. It can only be directly verified by reference to the examples of the conduct of the Persians in cases where they were victorious, as in Jerusalem, Egypt, and Asia Minor, and even this verification must necessarily remain unsatisfactory in certain respects. The striking rational plausibility of the hypothesis must here necessarily be relied on as a support. In very many cases of historical interpretation which seem highly plausible, however, there is not even a possibility of the order of verification which was feasible in this case. Where this is true the interpretation must necessarily remain a hypothesis.

7. A motive is a complex of subjective meaning which seems to the actor himself or to the observer an adequate ground for the conduct in

Die Objektivität sozialwissenschaftlicher Erkenntnis, op. cit. It is also discussed in certain of the other essays which have been collected in the volume, *Gesammelte Aufsätze zur Wissenschaftslehre*. The best and fullest secondary discussion is to be found in Von Schelting's book, *Max Webers Wissenschaftslehre*. There is a briefer discussion in chap. xvi of the editor's *Structure of Social Action.*—Ed.

[19] See Edvard Meyer, *Geschichte des Altertums*, Stuttgart, 1901, vol. iii, pp. 420, 444 ff.

question. We apply the term 'adequacy on the level of meaning'[20] to the subjective interpretation of a coherent course of conduct when and in so far as, according to our habitual modes of thought and feeling, its component parts taken in their mutual relation are recognized to constitute a 'typical' complex of meaning. It is more common to say 'correct.' The interpretation of a sequence of events will on the other hand be called *causally* adequate in so far as, according to established generalizations from experience, there is a probability that it will always actually occur in the same way. An example of adequacy on the level of meaning in this sense is what is, according to our current norms of calculation or thinking, the correct solution of an arithmetical problem. On the other hand, a causally adequate interpretation of the same phenomenon would concern the statistical probability that, according to verified generalizations from experience, there would be a correct or an erroneous solution of the same problem. This also refers to currently accepted norms but includes taking account of typical errors or of typical confusions. Thus causal explanation depends on being able to determine that there is a probability, which in the rare ideal case can be numerically stated, but is always in some sense calculable, that a given observable event (overt or subjective) will be followed or accompanied by another event.

A correct causal interpretation of a concrete course of action is arrived at when the overt action and the motives have both been correctly apprehended and at the same time their relation has become meaningfully comprehensible. A correct causal interpretation of typical action means that the process which is claimed to be typical is shown to be both adequately grasped on the level of meaning and at the same time the interpretation is to some degree causally adequate. If adequacy in respect to meaning is lacking, then no matter how high the degree of uniformity and how precisely its probability can be numerically determined, it is still an incomprehensible statistical probability, whether dealing with overt or subjective processes. On the other hand, even the most perfect adequacy on

20 The expression *sinnhafte Adäquanz* is one of the most difficult of Weber's technical terms to translate. In most places the cumbrous phrase 'adequacy on the level of meaning' has had to be employed. It should be clear from the progress of the discussion that what Weber refers to is a satisfying level of knowledge for the particular purposes of the subjective state of mind of the actor or actors. He is, however, careful to point out that *causal* adequacy involves in addition to this a satisfactory correspondence between the results of observations from the subjective point of view and from the objective; that is, observations of the overt course of action which can be described without reference to the state of mind of the actor. For a discussion of the methodological problem involved here, see *Structure of Social Action*, chaps. ii and v.—ED.

the level of meaning has causal significance from a sociological point of view only in so far as there is some kind of proof for the existence of a probability [21] that action in fact normally takes the course which has been held to be meaningful. For this there must be some degree of determinable frequency of approximation to an average or a pure type.

Statistical uniformities constitute understandable types of action in the sense of this discussion, and thus constitute 'sociological generalizations,' only when they can be regarded as manifestations of the understandable subjective meaning of a course of social action. Conversely, formulations of a rational course of subjectively understandable action constitute sociological types of empirical process only when they can be empirically observed with a significant degree of approximation. It is unfortunately by no means the case that the actual likelihood of the occurrence of a given course of overt action is always directly proportional to the clarity of subjective interpretation. There are statistics of processes devoid of meaning such as death rates, phenomena of fatigue, the production rate of machines, the amount of rainfall, in exactly the same sense as there are statistics of meaningful phenomena. But only when the phenomena are meaningful is it convenient to speak of sociological statistics. Examples are such cases as crime rates, occupational distributions, price statistics, and statistics of crop acreage. Naturally there are many cases where both components are involved, as in crop statistics.

8. Processes and uniformities which it has here seemed convenient not to designate as (in the present case) sociological phenomena or uniformities because they are not 'understandable,' are naturally not on that account any the less important. This is true even for sociology in the present sense which restricts it to subjectively understandable phenomena —a usage which there is no intention of attempting to impose on anyone else. Such phenomena, however important, are simply treated by a different method from the others; they become conditions, stimuli, furthering or hindering circumstances of action.

[21] This is the first occurrence in Weber's text of the term *Chance* which he uses very frequently. It is here translated by 'probability,' because he uses it as interchangeable with *Wahrscheinlichkeit*. As the term 'probability' is used in a technical mathematical and statistical sense, however, it implies the possibility of numerical statement. In most of the cases where Weber uses *Chance* this is out of the question. It is, however, possible to speak in terms of higher and lower degrees of probability. To avoid confusion with the technical mathematical concept, the term 'likelihood' will often be used in the translation. It is by means of this concept that Weber, in a highly ingenious way, has bridged the gap between the interpretation of meaning and the inevitably more complex facts of overt action. —Ed.

9. Action in the sense of a subjectively understandable orientation of behaviour exists only as the behaviour of one or more *individual* human beings. For other cognitive purposes it may be convenient or necessary to consider the individual, for instance, as a collection of cells, as a complex of bio-chemical reactions, or to conceive his 'psychic' life as made up of a variety of different elements, however these may be defined. Undoubtedly such procedures yield valuable knowledge of causal relationships. But the behaviour of these elements, as expressed in such uniformities, is not subjectively understandable. This is true even of psychic elements because the more precisely they are formulated from a point of view of natural science, the less they are accessible to subjective understanding. This is never the road to interpretation in terms of subjective meaning. On the contrary, both for sociology in the present sense, and for history, the object of cognition is the subjective meaning-complex of action. The behaviour of physiological entities such as cells, or of any sort of psychic elements may at least in principle be observed and an attempt made to derive uniformities from such observations. It is further possible to attempt, with their help, to obtain a causal explanation of individual phenomena, that is, to subsume them under uniformities. But the subjective understanding of action takes the same account of this type of fact and uniformity as of any others not capable of subjective interpretation. This is true, for example, of physical, astronomical, geological, meteorological, geographical, botanical, zoological, and anatomical facts and of such facts as those aspects of psycho-pathology which are devoid of subjective meaning or the facts of the natural conditions of technological processes.

For still other cognitive purposes as, for instance, juristic, or for practical ends, it may on the other hand be convenient or even indispensable to treat social collectivities, such as states, associations, business corporations, foundations, as if they were individual persons. Thus they may be treated as the subjects of rights and duties or as the performers of legally significant actions. But for the subjective interpretation of action in sociological work these collectivities must be treated as *solely* the resultants and modes of organization of the particular acts of individual persons, since these alone can be treated as agents in a course of subjectively understandable action. Nevertheless, the sociologist cannot for his purposes afford to ignore these collective concepts derived from other disciplines. For the subjective interpretation of action has at least two important relations to these concepts. In the first place it is often necessary to employ very similar collective concepts, indeed often using the same terms, in

order to obtain an understandable terminology. Thus both in legal terminology and in everyday speech the term 'state' is used both for the legal
concept of the state and for the phenomena of social action to which its
legal rules are relevant. For sociological purposes, however, the phenomenon 'the state' does not consist necessarily or even primarily of the
elements which are relevant to legal analysis; and for sociological purposes there is no such thing as a collective personality which 'acts.' When
reference is made in a sociological context to a 'state,' a 'nation,' a 'corporation,' a 'family,' or an 'army corps,' or to similar collectivities, what is
meant is, on the contrary, *only* a certain kind of development of actual
or possible social actions of individual persons. Both because of its precision and because it is established in general usage the juristic concept is
taken over, but is used in an entirely different meaning.

Secondly, the subjective interpretation of action must take account of
a fundamentally important fact. These concepts of collective entities
which are found both in common sense and in juristic and other technical forms of thought, have a meaning in the minds of individual persons, partly as of something actually existing, partly as something with
normative authority. This is true not only of judges and officials, but of
ordinary private individuals as well. Actors thus in part orient their action
to them, and in this role such ideas have a powerful, often a decisive,
causal influence on the course of action of real individuals. This is above
all true where the ideas concern a recognized positive or negative normative pattern.[22] Thus, for instance, one of the important aspects of the
'existence' of a modern state, precisely as a complex of social interaction of individual persons, consists in the fact that the action of
various individuals is oriented to the belief that it exists or should
exist, thus that its acts and laws are valid in the legal sense. This
will be further discussed below. Though extremely pedantic and cum-
bersome it would be possible, if purposes of sociological terminology
alone were involved, to eliminate such terms entirely, and substitute
newly-coined words. This would be possible even though the word 'state'
is used ordinarily not only to designate the legal concept but also the real
process of action. But in the above important connexion, at least, this
would naturally be impossible.

Thirdly, it is the method of the so-called 'organic' school of sociology [23]

---

[22] By a negative normative pattern, Weber means one which prohibits certain possible
modes of action.—Ed.

[23] A classical example is Schäffle's brilliant work, *Bau und Leben des sozialen Körpers*.

to attempt to understand social interaction by using as a point of departure the 'whole' within which the individual acts. His action and behaviour are then interpreted somewhat in the way that a physiologist would
treat the role of an organ of the body in the 'economy' of the organism,
that is from the point of view of the survival of the latter.[24] How far in
other disciplines this type of functional analysis of the relation of 'parts'
to a 'whole' can be regarded as definitive, cannot be discussed here; but
it is well known that the bio-chemical and bio-physical modes of analysis
of the organism are on principle opposed to stopping there. For purposes
of sociological analysis two things can be said. First this functional frame
of reference is convenient for purposes of practical illustration and for
provisional orientation. In these respects it is not only useful but indispensable. But at the same time if its cognitive value is overestimated and
its concepts illegitimately 'reified,'[25] it can be highly dangerous. Secondly,
in certain circumstances this is the only available way of determining
just what processes of social action it is important to understand in order
to explain a given phenomenon.[26] But this is only the beginning of
sociological analysis as here understood. In the case of social collectivities,
precisely as distinguished from organisms, we are in a position to go
beyond merely demonstrating functional relationships and uniformities.
We can accomplish something which is never attainable in the natural
sciences, namely the subjective understanding of the action of the component individuals. The natural sciences on the other hand cannot do
this, being limited to the formulation of causal uniformities in objects
and events and the explanation of individual facts by applying them. We

[24] One of the most illuminating treatments of physiological problems from such a functional point of view, which is readily understandable to the layman, is W. B. Cannon: *The
Wisdom of the Body,* second edition, 1938. The point of reference on this physiological
level is not primarily survival value to the species in the sense of the Darwinian theory of
evolution, but rather the maintenance of the individual organism as a 'going concern' in
carrying through its typical life cycle. What is the life cycle, is to the physiologist essentially a matter of empirical observation.—ED.

[25] The term 'reification' as used by Professor Morris Cohen in his book, *Reason and
Nature,* seems to fit Weber's meaning exactly. A concept or system of concepts, which critical analysis can show to be abstract, is 'reified' when it is used naively as though it provided an adequate total description of the concrete phenomenon in question. The fallacy
of 'reification' is virtually another name for what Professor Whitehead has called 'the
fallacy of misplaced concreteness.' See his *Science and the Modern World.*—ED.

[26] Compare the famous dictum of a well-known physiologist: 'sec. 10. The spleen. Of
the spleen, gentlemen, we know nothing. So much for the spleen.' Actually, of course, he
'knew' a good deal about the spleen—its position, size, shape, etc.; but he could say nothing about its function, and it was his inability to do this that he called 'ignorance.'

do not 'understand' the behaviour of cells, but can only observe the relevant functional relationships and generalize on the basis of these observations. This additional achievement of explanation by interpretive understanding, as distinguished from external observation, is of course attained only at a price—the more hypothetical and fragmentary character of its results. Nevertheless, subjective understanding is the specific characteristic of sociological knowledge.

It would lead too far afield even to attempt to discuss how far the behaviour of animals is subjectively understandable to us and vice versa; in both cases the meaning of the term understanding and its extent of application would be highly problematical. But in so far as such understanding existed it would be theoretically possible to formulate a sociology of the relations of men to animals, both domestic and wild. Thus many animals 'understand' commands, anger, love, hostility, and react to them in ways which are evidently often by no means purely instinctive and mechanical and in some sense both consciously meaningful and affected by experience. There is no *priori* reason to suppose that our ability to share the feelings of primitive men is very much greater.[27] Unfortunately we either do not have any reliable means of determining the subjective state of mind of an animal or what we have is at best very unsatisfactory. It is well known that the problems of animal psychology, however interesting, are very thorny ones. There are in particular various forms of social organization among animals: 'monogamous and polygamous families,' herds, flocks, and finally 'state,' with a functional division of labour. The extent of functional differentiation found in these animal societies is by no means, however, entirely a matter of the degree of organic or morphological differentiation of the individual members of

[27] The present state of anthropological research, which has advanced enormously since Weber wrote, would seem to throw considerable doubt on the validity of this statement. In making it, Weber apparently does not adequately take account of the fundamental fact that no non-human species has even a primitive form of language; whereas no human group is known without a 'fully-developed' one. The ability to use language is on the one hand a fundamental index of the state of development of the individual himself, so far as it is relevant to the theory of action. On the other hand, language is perhaps most crucially important source of evidence for subjective phenomena. What has seemed to so many 'civilized' men to be the strangeness and incomprehensibility of the behaviour and thought of primitive peoples, is apparently primarily a matter of the former's failure to submit the latter to an adequately thorough and rigorous investigation. It can be said with considerable confidence that a competently trained anthropological field worker is in a position to obtain a level of insight into the states of mind of a people whom he has carefully studied, which is quite comparable, if not superior, to that of the historian of a civilization at all widely different from his own.—ED.

the species. Thus, the functional differentiation found among the termites, and in consequence that of the products of their social activities, is much more advanced than in the case of the bees and ants. In this field it goes without saying that a purely functional point of view is often the best that can, at least for the present, be attained, and the investigator must be content with it. Thus it is possible to study the ways in which the species provides for its survival; that is, for nutrition, defence, reproduction, and reconstruction of the social units. As the principal bearers of these functions, differentiated types of individuals can be identified: 'kings,' 'queens,' 'workers,' 'soldiers,' 'drones,' 'propagators,' 'queen's substitutes,' and so on. Anything more than that was for a long time merely a matter of speculation or of an attempt to determine the extent to which heredity on the one hand and environment on the other would be involved in the development of these 'social' proclivities. This was particularly true of the controversies between Götte and Weisman. The latter's conception of the omnipotence of natural selection was largely based on wholly non-empirical deductions. But all serious authorities are naturally fully agreed that the limitation of analysis to the functional level is only a necessity imposed by our present ignorance which it is hoped will only be temporary.[28]

It is relatively easy to grasp the significance of the functions of these various differentiated types for survival. It is also not difficult to work out the bearing of the hypothesis of the inheritance of acquired characteristics or its reverse on the problem of explaining how these differentiations have come about and further what is the bearing of different variants of the theory of heredity. But this is not enough. We would like especially to know first what factors account for the original differentiation of specialized types from the still neutral undifferentiated species-type. Secondly, it would be important to know what leads the differentiated individual in the typical case to behave in a way which actually serves the survival value of the organized group. Wherever research has made any progress in the solution of these problems it has been through the experimental demonstration of the probability or possibility of the role of chemical stimuli or physiological processes, such as nutritional states, the effects of parasitic castration, etc., in the case of the individual organism. How far there is even a hope that the existence of 'subjective' or 'meaningful' orientation could be made experimentally probable, even

[28] See, for example, for an account of the state of knowledge of the termites, the study of Karl Escherich, *Die Ameise*, 1906.

the specialist to-day would hardly be in a position to say. A verifiable conception of the state of mind of these social animals accessible to meaningful understanding, would seem to be attainable even as an ideal goal only within narrow limits. However that may be, a contribution to the understanding of human social action is hardly to be expected from this quarter. On the contrary, in the field of animal psychology, human analogies are and must be continually employed. The most that can be hoped for is, then, that these biological analogies may some day be useful in suggesting significant problems. For instance they may throw light on the question of the relative role in the early stages of human social differentiation of mechanical and instinctive factors, as compared with that of the factors which are accessible to subjective interpretation generally, and more particularly to the role of consciously rational action. It is necessary for the sociologist to be thoroughly aware of the fact that in the early stages even of human development, the first set of factors is completely predominant. Even in the later stages he must take account of their continual interaction with the others in a role which is often of decisive importance. This is particularly true of all 'traditional' action [29] and of many aspects of charisma.[30] In the latter field of phenomena lie the seeds of certain types of psychic 'contagion' and it is thus the bearer of many dynamic tendencies of social processes. These types of action are very closely related to phenomena which are understandable either only in biological terms or are subject to interpretation in terms of subjective motives only in fragments and with an almost imperceptible transition to the biological. But all these facts do not discharge sociology from the obligation, in full awareness of the narrow limits to which it is confined, to accomplish what it alone can do.

The various works of Othmar Spann are often full of suggestive ideas though at the same time he is guilty of occasional misunderstandings and above all of arguing on the basis of pure value judgments which have no place in an empirical investigation. But he is undoubtedly correct in doing something to which, however, no one seriously objects, namely, emphasizing the sociological significance of the functional point of view for

[29] See sec. 2.

[30] Since the term 'charisma' was, in its sociological usage, introduced by Weber himself from a different field, no attempt has been made to find an English equivalent and it will be used directly throughout. Weber took it from the corresponding Greek which was used in the literature of early Christianity and means 'the gift of grace.' For further discussion of the concept, see below, chap. iii, especially secs. 2 and 10.—ED.

preliminary orientation to problems. This is what he calls the 'universalistic method.' We certainly need to know what kind of action is functionally necessary for 'survival,' but further and above all for the maintenance of a cultural type and the continuity of the corresponding modes of social action, before it is possible even to inquire how this action has come about and what motives determine it. It is necessary to know what a 'king,' an 'official,' an 'entrepreneur,' a 'procurer,' or a 'magician' does; that is, what kind of typical action, which justifies classifying an individual in one of these categories, is important and relevant for an analysis, before it is possible to undertake the analysis itself.[31] But it is only this analysis itself which can achieve the sociological understanding of the actions of typically differentiated human (and only human) individuals, and which hence constitutes the specific function of sociology. It is a monstrous misunderstanding to think that an 'individualistic' *method* should involve what is in any conceivable sense an individualistic system of *values*. It is as important to avoid this error as the related one which confuses the unavoidable tendency of sociological concepts to assume a rationalistic character with a belief in the predominance of rational motives, or even a positive valuation of 'rationalism.' Even a socialistic economy would have to be understood sociologically in exactly the same kind of 'individualistic' terms; that is, in terms of the action of individuals, the types of 'officials' found in it, as would be the case with a system of free exchange analysed in terms of the theory of marginal utility. It might be possible to find a better method, but in this respect it would be similar. The real empirical sociological investigation begins with the question: What motives determine and lead the individual members and participants in this socialistic community to behave in such a way that the community came into being in the first place and that it continues to exist? Any form of functional analysis which proceeds from the whole to the parts can accomplish only a preliminary preparation for this investigation—a preparation, the utility and indispensability of which, if properly carried out, is naturally beyond question.

10. It is customary to designate various sociological generalizations, as for example 'Gresham's Law,' as scientific 'laws.' These are in fact typical probabilities confirmed by observation to the effect that under certain given conditions an expected course of social action will occur, which is understandable in terms of the typical motives and typical subjective

---

[31] This is what Rickert means by *Wertbezogenheit*.

intentions of the actors.[32] These generalizations are both understandable and definite in the highest degree in so far as the typically observed course of action can be understood in terms of the purely rational pursuit of an end, or where for reasons of methodological convenience such a theoretical type can be heuristically employed. In such cases the relations of means and end will be clearly understandable on grounds of experience, particularly where the choice of means was 'inevitable.' In such cases it is legitimate to assert that in so far as the action was rigorously rational it could not have taken any other course because for technical reasons, given their clearly defined ends, no other means were available to the actors. This very case demonstrates how erroneous it is to regard any kind of 'psychology' as the ultimate foundation of the sociological interpretation of action. The term 'psychology,' to be sure, is to-day understood in a wide variety of senses. For certain quite specific methodological purposes the type of treatment which attempts to follow the procedures of the natural sciences employs a distinction between 'physical' and 'psychic' phenomena which is entirely foreign to the disciplines concerned with human action, at least in the present sense. The results of a type of psychological investigation which employs the methods of the natural sciences in any one of various possible ways may naturally, like the results of any other science, have, in specific contexts, outstanding significance for sociological problems; indeed this has often happened. But this use of the results of psychology is something quite different from the investigation of human behaviour in terms of its subjective meaning. Hence sociology has no closer logical relationship on a general analytical level to this type of psychology than to any other science. The

[32] It is desirable at this point to call attention to Weber's usage of the term 'law' in a scientific sense. In conformity with his strong emphasis upon the role of ideal types among possible kinds of generalized concepts in the social sciences, by 'law,' or a German expression he frequently uses, *generelle Erfahrungsregel,* he usually means what is perhaps most conveniently called a 'type generalization.' It is not an empirical generalization in the ordinary sense in that it does not adequately describe any particular concrete course of events but is abstract in the same sense as the ideal type. Where it is possible on the basis of ideal type analysis to construct not merely a structural form, but, under certain conditions, a course of events which can be predicted if certain conditions are given, it is possible to formulate such generalizations. These generalizations are, however, not methodologically equivalent to most of the laws of physics, especially of analytical mechanics. The latter do not generally formulate a concrete course of events, but rather a uniform relationship between the values of two or more variables. Weber does not even consider the possibility of formulating laws of this latter type, essentially because he does not develop social theory explicitly in the direction of setting up a system of inter-dependent variables, but confines it to the ideal type level.—ED.

source of error lies in the concept of the 'psychic.' It is held that every-thing which is not physical is *ipso facto* psychic, but that the *meaning* of a train of mathematical reasoning which a person carries out is not in the relevant sense 'psychic.' Similarly the rational deliberation of an actor as to whether the results of a given proposed course of action will or will not promote certain specific interests, and the corresponding decision, do not become one bit more understandable by taking 'psychological' considerations into account. But it is precisely on the basis of such rational assumptions that most of the laws of sociology, including those of eco-nomics, are built up. On the other hand, in explaining the irrationalities of action sociologically, that form of psychology which employs the method of subjective understanding undoubtedly can make decisively im-portant contributions. But this does not alter the fundamental meth-odological situation.

11. It has continually been assumed as obvious that the science of sociology seeks to formulate type concepts and generalized uniformi-ties of empirical process. This distinguishes it from history, which is oriented to the casual analysis and explanation of individual actions, structures, and personalities possessing cultural significance. The em-pirical material which underlies the concepts of sociology consists to a very large extent, though by no means exclusively, of the same concrete processes of action which are dealt with by historians. Among the various bases on which its concepts are formulated and its generalizations worked out, is an attempt to justify its important claim to be able to make a con-tribution to the casual explanation of some historically and culturally important phenomenon.[33] As in the case of every generalizing science the abstract character of the concepts of sociology is responsible for the fact that, compared with actual historical reality, they are relatively lack-ing in fullness of concrete content. To compensate for this disadvantage, sociological analysis can offer a greater precision of concepts. This preci-

[33] This is one of the most important problems with which Weber was concerned in his methodological studies. He insisted on the very great importance of the cultural significance of a problem for the values of the time in determining the direction of interest of the investigator. He formulated this relation in his important concept of the *Wertbeziehung* of social science concepts. But he went so far as to deny the legitimacy of the formulation of a generalized theoretical system as an aim of theoretical analysis in social science. This denial seems to rest on a failure on Weber's part to carry his criticism of certain aspects of German idealistic social thought through to its logical conclusion. For Weber's position, see *Die Objektivität sozialwissenschaftlicher Erkenntnis*, op. cit., and Von Schelting, *Max Webers Wissenschaftslehre*. For a criticism of Weber's position, see *Structure of Social Action*, chap. xvi.—ED.

sion is obtained by striving for the highest possible degree of adequacy on the level of meaning in accordance with the definition of that concept put forward above. It has already been repeatedly stressed that this aim can be realized in a particularly high degree in the case of concepts and generalizations which formulate rational processes. But sociological investigation attempts to include in its scope various irrational phenomena, as well as prophetic, mystic, and affectual modes of action, formulated in terms of theoretical concepts which are adequate on the level of meaning. In *all* cases, rational or irrational, sociological analysis both abstracts from reality and at the same time helps us to understand it, in that it shows with what degree of approximation a concrete historical phenomenon can be subsumed under one or more of these concepts. For example, the same historical phenomenon may be in one aspect 'feudal,' in another 'patrimonial,' in another 'bureaucratic,' and in still another 'charismatic.' In order to give a precise meaning to these terms, it is necessary for the sociologist to formulate pure ideal types of the corresponding forms of action which in each case involve the highest possible degree of logical integration by virtue of their complete adequacy on the level of meaning. But precisely because this is true, it is probably seldom if ever that a real phenomenon can be found which corresponds exactly to one of these ideally constructed pure types. The case is similar to a physical reaction which has been calculated on the assumption of an absolute vacuum. Theoretical analysis in the field of sociology is possible only in terms of such pure types.[34] It goes without saying that in addition it is convenient for the sociologist from time to time to employ average types of an empirical statistical character. There are concepts which do not require methodological discussion at this point. But when reference is made to 'typical' cases, the term should always be understood, unless otherwise stated, as meaning *ideal* types, which may in turn be rational or irrational as the case may be (thus in economic theory they are always rational), but in any case are always constructed with a view to adequacy on the level of meaning.

It is important to realize that in the sociological field as elsewhere, averages, and hence average types, can be formulated with a relative degree of precision only where they are concerned with differences of degree in respect to action which remains qualitatively the same. Such cases do occur, but in the majority of cases of action important to history

[34] The difficulty of maintaining the position Weber here takes has been discussed in the Introduction. See pp. 12 ff.—ED.

or sociology the motives which determine it are qualitatively heterogeneous. Then it is quite impossible to speak of an 'average' in the true sense. The ideal types of social action which for instance are used in economic theory are thus 'unrealistic' or abstract in that they always ask what course of action would take place if it were purely rational and oriented to economic ends alone. But this construction can be used to aid in the understanding of action not purely economically determined but which involve deviations arising from traditional restraints, affects, errors, and the intrusion of other than economic purposes or considerations. This can take place in two ways. First, in analysing the extent to which in the concrete case, or on the average for a class of cases, the action was in part economically determined along with the other factors. Secondly, by throwing the discrepancy between the actual course of events and the ideal type into relief, the analysis of the non-economic motives actually involved is facilitated. The procedure would be very similar in employing an ideal type of mystical orientation with its appropriate attitude of indifference to worldly things, as a tool for analysing its consequences for the actor's relation to ordinary life; for instance, to political or economic affairs. The more sharply and precisely the ideal type has been constructed, thus the more abstract and unrealistic in this sense it is, the better it is able to perform its methodological functions in formulating the clarification of terminology, and in the formulation of classifications, and of hypotheses. In working out a concrete causal explanation of individual events, the procedure of the historian is essentially the same. Thus in attempting to explain the campaign of 1866, it is indispensable both in the case of Moltke and of Benedek to attempt to construct imaginatively how each, given fully adequate knowledge both of his own situation and of that of his opponent, would have acted. Then it is possible to compare with this the actual course of action and to arrive at a causal explanation of the observed deviations, which will be attributed to such factors as misinformation, strategical errors, logical fallacies, personal temperament, or considerations outside the realm of strategy. Here, too, an ideal-typical construction of rational action is actually employed even though it is not made explicit.

The theoretical concepts of sociology are ideal types not only from the objective point of view, but also in their application to subjective processes. In the great majority of cases actual action goes on in a state of inarticulate half-consciousness or actual unconsciousness of its subjective meaning. The actor is more likely to 'be aware' of it in a vague sense than he is to 'know' what he is doing or be explicitly self-conscious about it. In most cases his action is governed by impulse or habit. Only occasionally and, in the uniform action of large numbers often only in the case of a few individuals, is the subjective meaning of the action, whether rational or irrational, brought clearly into consciousness. The ideal type of meaningful action where the meaning is fully conscious and explicit is a marginal case. Every sociological or historical investigation, in applying its analysis to the empirical facts, must take this fact into account. But the difficulty need not prevent the sociologist from systematizing his concepts by the classification of possible types of subjective meaning. That is, he may reason as if action actually proceeded on the basis of clearly self-conscious meaning. The resulting deviation from the concrete facts must continually be kept in mind whenever it is a question of this level of concreteness, and must be carefully studied with reference both to degree and kind. It is often necessary to choose between terms which are either clear or unclear. Those which are clear will, to be sure, have the abstractness of ideal types, but they are none the less preferable for scientific purposes.[35]

(b) *The Concept of Social Action* [36]

1. Social action, which includes both failure to act and passive acquiescence, may be oriented to the past, present, or expected future behaviour of others. Thus it may be motivated by revenge for a past attack, defence against present, or measures of defence against future aggression. The 'others' may be individual persons, and may be known to the actor as such, or may constitute an indefinite plurality and may be entirely unknown as individuals. Thus 'money' is a means of exchange which the actor accepts in payment because he orients his action to the expectation that a large but unknown number of individuals he is personally unacquainted with will be ready to accept it in exchange on some future occasion.

2. Not every kind of action, even of overt action, is 'social' in the sense of the present discussion. Overt action is non-social if it is oriented solely to the behaviour of inanimate objects. Subjective attitudes constitute social action only so far as they are oriented to the behaviour of others. For example, religious behaviour is not social if it is simply a matter of contemplation or of solitary prayer. The economic activity of an individual

---

[35] On all these questions see the author's article in *Archiv für Sozialwissenschaft*, vol. xix, op. cit. Reprinted in *Gesammelte Aufsätze zur Wissenschaftslehre*, pp. 176-214.

[36] The definition of social action has been given above. See p. 88.

is only social if, and then only in so far as, it takes account of the behaviour of someone else. Thus very generally in formal terms it becomes social in so far as the actor's actual control over economic goods is respected by others. Concretely it is social, for instance, if in relation to the actor's own consumption the future wants of others are taken into account and this becomes one consideration affecting the actor's own saving. Or, in another connexion, production may be oriented to the future wants of other people.

3. Not every type of contact of human beings has a social character; this is rather confined to cases where the actor's behaviour is meaningfully oriented to that of others. For example, a mere collision of two cyclists may be compared to a natural event. On the other hand, their attempt to avoid hitting each other, or whatever insults, blows, or friendly discussion might follow the collision, would constitute 'social action.'

4. Social action is not identical either with the similar actions of many persons or with action influenced by other persons. Thus, if at the beginning of a shower a number of people on the street put up their umbrellas at the same time, this would not ordinarily be a case of action mutually oriented to that of each other, but rather of all reacting in the same way to the like need of protection from the rain. It is well known that the actions of the individual are strongly influenced by the mere fact that he is a member of a crowd confined within a limited space. Thus, the subject matter of studies of 'crowd psychology,' such as those of Le Bon, will be called 'action conditioned by crowds.' It is also possible for large numbers, though dispersed, to be influenced simultaneously or successively by a source of influence operating similarly on all the individuals, as by means of the press. Here also the behaviour of an individual is influenced by his membership in the crowd and by the fact that he is aware of being a member. Some types of reaction are only made possible by the mere fact that the individual acts as part of a crowd. Others become more difficult under these conditions. Hence it is possible that a particular event or mode of human behaviour can give rise to the most diverse kinds of feeling—gaiety, anger, enthusiasm, despair, and passions of all sorts—in a crowd situation which would not occur at all or not nearly so readily if the individual were alone. But for this to happen there need not, at least in many cases, be any meaningful relation between the behaviour of the individual and the fact that he is a member of a crowd. It is not proposed in the present sense to call action 'social' when it is merely a result of the effect on the individual of the existence of a

crowd as such and the action is not oriented to that fact on the level of meaning. At the same time the borderline is naturally highly indefinite. In such cases as that of the influence of the demagogue, there may be a wide variation in the extent to which his mass clientele is affected by a meaningful reaction to the fact of its large numbers; and whatever this relation may be, it is open to varying interpretations.

But furthermore, mere 'imitation' of the action of others, such as that on which Tarde has rightly laid emphasis, will not be considered a case of specifically social action if it is purely reactive so that there is no meaningful orientation to the actor imitated. The borderline is, however, so indefinite that it is often hardly possible to discriminate. The mere fact that a person is found to employ some apparently useful procedure which he learned from someone else does not, however, constitute, in the present sense, social action. Action such as this is not oriented to the action of the other person, but the actor has, through observing the other, become acquainted with certain objective facts; and it is these to which his action is oriented. His action is then *causally* determined by the action of others, but not meaningfully. On the other hand, if the action of others is imitated because it is 'fashionable' or traditional or exemplary, or lends social distinction, or on similar grounds, it is meaningfully oriented either to the behaviour of the source of imitation or of third persons or of both. There are of course all manner of transitional cases between the two types of imitation. Both the phenomena discussed above, the behaviour of crowds and imitation, stand on the indefinite borderline of social action. The same is true, as will often appear, of traditionalism and charisma.[37] The reason for the indefiniteness of the line in these and other cases lies in the fact that both the orientation to the behaviour of others and the meaning which can be imputed to the actor himself, are by no means always capable of clear determination and are often altogether unconscious and seldom fully self-conscious. Mere 'influence' and meaningful orientation cannot therefore always be clearly differentiated on the empirical level. But conceptually it is essential to distinguish them, even though merely 'reactive' imitation may well have a degree of sociological importance at least equal to that of the type which can be called social action in the strict sense. Sociology, it goes without saying, is by no means confined to the study of 'social action'; this is only, at least for the kind of sociology being developed here, its central subject

[37] See sec. 2.

matter, that which may be said to be decisive for its status as a science. But this does not imply any judgment on the comparative importance of this and other factors.

2: The Types of Social Action

Social action, like other forms of action, may be classified in the following four types according to its mode of orientation: (1) in terms of rational orientation to a system of discrete individual ends (*zweckrational*), that is, through expectations as to the behaviour of objects in the external situation and of other human individuals, making use of these expectations as 'conditions' or 'means' for the successful attainment of the actor's own rationally chosen ends; (2) in terms of rational orientation to an absolute value (*wertrational*); involving a conscious belief in the absolute value of some ethical, aesthetic, religious, or other form of behaviour, entirely for its own sake and independently of any prospects of external success; (3) in terms of affectual orientation, especially emotional, determined by the specific affects and states of feeling of the actor; (4) traditionally oriented, through the habituation of long practice.[38]

[38] The two terms *zweckrational* and *wertrational* are of central significance to Weber's theory, but at the same time present one of the most difficult problems to the translator. Perhaps the keynote of the distinction lies in the absoluteness with which the values involved in *Wertrationalität* are held. The sole important consideration to the actor becomes the realization of the value. In so far as it involves ends, rational considerations, such as those of efficiency, are involved in the choice of means. But there is no question either of rational weighing of this end against others, nor is there a question of 'counting the cost' in the sense of taking account of possible results other than the attainment of the absolute end. In the case of *Zweckrationalität*, on the other hand, Weber conceives action as motivated by a plurality of relatively independent ends, none of which is absolute. Hence, rationality involves on the one hand the weighing of the relative importance of their realization, on the other hand, consideration of whether undesirable consequences would outweigh the benefits to be derived from the projected course of action. It has not seemed possible to find English terms which would express this distinction succinctly. Hence the attempt has been made to express the ideas as clearly as possible without specific terms.

It should also be pointed out that, as Weber's analysis proceeds, there is a tendency of the meaning of these terms to shift, so that *Wertrationalität* comes to refer to a system of ultimate ends, regardless of the degree of their absoluteness, while *Zweckrationalität* refers primarily to considerations respecting the choice of means and ends which are in turn means to further ends, such as money. What seems to have happened is that Weber shifted from a classification of ideal types of action to one of elements in the structure of action. In the latter context 'expediency' is often an adequate rendering of *Zweckrationalität*. This process has been analysed in the editor's *Structure of Social Action*, chap. xvi.

The other two terms *affektuell* and *traditional* do not present any difficulty of translation. The term affectual has come into English psychological usage from the German largely through the influence of psychoanalysis.

1. Strictly traditional behaviour, like the reactive type of imitation discussed above, lies very close to the borderline of what can justifiably be called meaningfully oriented action, and indeed often on the other side. For it is very often a matter of almost automatic reaction to habitual stimuli which guide behaviour in a course which has been repeatedly followed. The great bulk of all everyday action to which people have become habitually accustomed approaches this type. Hence, its place in a systematic classification is not merely that of a limiting case because, as will be shown later, attachment to habitual forms can be upheld with varying degrees of self-consciousness and in a variety of senses. In this case the type may shade over into number two (*Wertrationalität*).

2. Purely affectual behaviour also stands on the borderline of what can be considered 'meaningfully' oriented, and often it, too, goes over the line. It may, for instance, consist in an uncontrolled reaction to some exceptional stimulus. It is a case of sublimation when affectually determined action occurs in the form of conscious release of emotional tension. When this happens it is usually, though not always, well on the road to rationalization in one or the other or both of the above senses.

3. The orientation of action in terms of absolute value is distinguished from the affectual type by its clearly self-conscious formulation of the ultimate values governing the action and the consistently planned orientation of its detailed course to these values. At the same time the two types have a common element, namely that the meaning of the action does not lie in the achievement of a result ulterior to it, but in carrying out the specific type of action for its own sake. Examples of affectual action are the satisfaction of a direct impulse to revenge, to sensual gratification, to devote oneself to a person or ideal, to contemplative bliss, or, finally, toward the working off of emotional tensions. Such impulses belong in this category regardless of how sordid or sublime they may be.

Examples of pure rational orientation to absolute values would be the action of persons who, regardless of possible cost to themselves, act to put into practice their convictions of what seems to them to be required by duty, honour, the pursuit of beauty, a religious call, personal loyalty, or the importance of some 'cause' no matter in what it consists. For the purposes of this discussion, when action is oriented to absolute values, it always involves 'commands' or 'demands' to the fulfilment of which the actor feels obligated. It is only in cases where human action is motivated by the fulfilment of such unconditional demands that it will be described as oriented to absolute values. This is empirically the case in widely varying degrees, but for the most part only to a relatively slight extent. Nevertheless, it will be shown that the occurrence of this mode of action is important enough to justify its formulation as a distinct type; though it may be remarked that there is no intention here of attempting to formulate in any sense an exhaustive classification of types of action.

4. Action is rationally oriented to a system of discrete individual ends (*zweckrational*) when the end, the means, and the secondary results are all rationally taken into account and weighed. This involves rational consideration of alternative means to the end, of the relations of the end to other prospective results of employment of any given means, and finally of the relative importance of different possible ends. Determination of action, either in affectual or in traditional terms, is thus incompatible with this type. Choice between alternative and conflicting ends and results may well be determined by considerations of absolute value. In that case, action is rationally oriented to a system of discrete individual ends only in respect to the choice of means. On the other hand, the actor may, instead of deciding between alternative and conflicting ends in terms of a rational orientation to a system of values, simply take them as given subjective wants and arrange them in a scale of consciously assessed relative urgency. He may then orient his action to this scale in such a way that they are satisfied as far as possible in order of urgency, as formulated in the principle of 'marginal utility.' The orientation of action to absolute values may thus have various different modes of relation to the other type of rational action, in terms of a system of discrete individual ends. From the latter point of view, however, absolute values are always irrational. Indeed, the more the value to which action is oriented is elevated to the status of an absolute value, the more 'irrational' in this sense the corresponding action is. For, the more unconditionally the actor devotes himself to this value for its own sake, to pure sentiment or beauty, to absolute goodness or devotion to duty, the less is he influenced by considerations of the consequences of his action. The orientation of action wholly to the rational achievement of ends without relation to fundamental values is, to be sure, essentially only a limiting case.

5. It would be very unusual to find concrete cases of action, especially of social action, which were oriented *only* in one or another of these ways. Furthermore, this classification of the modes of orientation of action is in no sense meant to exhaust the possibilities of the field, but only to formulate in conceptually pure form certain sociologically important types, to which actual action is more or less closely approximated or, in

much the more common case, which constitute the elements combining to make it up. The usefulness of the classification for the purposes of this investigation can only be judged in terms of its results.

3: THE CONCEPT OF SOCIAL RELATIONSHIP

The term 'social relationship' will be used to denote the behaviour of a plurality of actors in so far as, in its meaningful content, the action of each takes account of that of the others and is oriented in these terms. The social relationship thus *consists* entirely and exclusively in the existence of a *probability* that there will be, in some meaningfully understandable sense, a course of social action. For purposes of definition there is no attempt to specify the basis of this probability.

1. Thus, as a defining criterion, it is essential that there should be at least a minimum of mutual orientation of the action of each to that of the others. Its content may be of the most varied nature; conflict, hostility, sexual attraction, friendship, loyalty, or economic exchange. It may involve the fulfilment, the evasion, or the denunciation of the terms of an agreement; economic, erotic, or some other form of 'competition'; common membership in national or class groups or those sharing a common tradition of status. In the latter cases mere group membership may or may not extend to include social action; this will be discussed later. The definition, furthermore, does not specify whether the relation of the actors is 'solidary' or the opposite.

2. The 'meaning' relevant in this context is always a case of the meaning imputed to the parties in a given concrete case, on the average or in a theoretically formulated pure type—it is never a normatively 'correct' or a metaphysically 'true' meaning. Even in cases of such forms of social organization as a state, church, association, or marriage, the social relationship consists exclusively in the fact that there has existed, exists, or will exist a probability of action in some definite way appropriate to this meaning. It is vital to be continually clear about this in order to avoid the 'reification' [39] of these concepts. A 'state,' for example, ceases to exist in a sociologically relevant sense whenever there is no longer a probability that certain kinds of meaningfully oriented social action will take place. This probability may be very high or it may be negligibly low. But in any case it is only in the sense and degree in which it does exist or can be estimated that the corresponding social relationship exists. It is im-

[39] See above, pp. 101-3.

possible to find any other clear meaning for the statement that, for instance, a given 'state' exists or has ceased to exist.

3. The subjective meaning need not necessarily be the same for all the parties who are mutually oriented in a given social relationship; there need not in this sense be 'reciprocity.' 'Friendship,' 'love,' 'loyalty,' 'fidelity to contracts,' 'patriotism,' on one side, may well be faced with an entirely different attitude on the other. In such cases the parties associate different meanings with their actions and the social relationship is in so far objectively 'asymmetrical' from the points of view of the two parties. It may nevertheless be a case of mutual orientation in so far as, even though partly or wholly erroneously, one party presumes a particular attitude toward him on the part of the other and orients his action to this expectation. This can, and usually will, have consequences for the course of action and the form of the relationship. A relationship is objectively symmetrical only as, according to the typical expectations of the parties, the meaning for one party is the same as that for the other. Thus the actual attitude of a child to its father may be at least approximately that which the father, in the individual case, on the average or typically, has come to expect. A social relationship in which the attitudes are completely and fully corresponding is in reality a limiting case. But the absence of reciprocity will, for terminological purposes, be held to exclude the existence of a social relationship only if it actually results in the absence of a mutual orientation of the action of the parties. Here as elsewhere all sorts of transitional cases are the rule rather than the exception.

4. A social relationship can be of a temporary character or of varying degrees of permanence. That is, it can be of such a kind that there is a probability of the repeated recurrence of the behaviour which corresponds to its subjective meaning, behaviour which is an understandable consequence of the meaning and hence is expected. In order to avoid fallacious impressions, let it be repeated and continually kept in mind, that it is *only* the existence of the probability that, corresponding to a given subjective meaning complex, a certain type of action will take place, which constitutes the 'existence' of the social relationship. Thus that a 'friendship' or a 'state' exists or has existed means this and only this: that we, the observers, judge that there is or has been a probability that on the basis of certain kinds of known subjective attitude of certain individuals there will result in the average sense a certain specific type of action.[40]

[40] Compare above, paras. 6 and 7 under 1.

For the purposes of legal reasoning it is essential to be able to decide whether a rule of law does or does not carry legal authority, hence whether a legal relationship does or does not 'exist.' This type of question is not, however, relevant to sociological problems.

5. The subjective meaning of a social relationship may change, thus a political relationship, once based on solidarity, may develop into a conflict of interests. In that case it is only a matter of terminological convenience and of the degree of continuity of the change whether we say that a new relationship has come into existence or that the old one continues but has acquired a new meaning. It is also possible for the meaning to be partly constant, partly changing.

6. The meaningful content which remains relatively constant in a social relationship is capable of formulation in terms of maxims which the parties concerned expect to be adhered to by their partners, on the average and approximately. The more rational in relation to values or to given ends the action is, the more is this likely to be the case. There is far less possibility of a rational formulation of subjective meaning in the case of a relation of erotic attraction or of personal loyalty or any other affectual type than, for example, in the case of a business contract.

7. The meaning of a social relationship may be agreed upon by mutual consent. This implies that the parties make promises covering their future behaviour, whether toward each other or toward third persons. In such cases each party then normally counts, so far as he acts rationally, in some degree on the fact that the other will orient his action to the meaning of the agreement as he (the first actor) understands it. In part, they orient their action rationally to these expectations as given facts with, to be sure, varying degrees of subjectively 'loyal' intention of doing their part. But in part also they are motivated each by the value to him of his 'duty' to adhere to the agreement in the sense in which he understands it. This much may be anticipated.[41]

4: Modes of Orientation of Social Action

It is possible in the field of social action to observe certain empirical uniformities. Certain types, that is, of action which correspond to a typically appropriate subjective meaning attributable to the same actors, are found to be wide-spread, being frequently repeated by the same individual or simultaneously performed by many different ones. Sociologi-

[41] For a further elaboration of this subject, see secs. 9 and 13 below.

cal investigation is concerned with these typical modes of action. Thereby it differs from history, the subject of which is rather the causal explanation of important individual events; important, that is, in having an influence on human destiny.

An actually existent probability of a uniformity in the orientation of social action will be called 'usage' (*Brauch*), if and in so far as the probability of its maintenance among a group of persons is determined entirely by its actual practice. Usage will be called 'custom' (*Sitte*) if the actual performance rests on long familiarity. On the other hand, a uniformity of action may be said to be 'determined by the exploitation of the opportunities of his situation in the self-interest of the actor.' This type of uniformity exists in so far as the probability of its empirical performance is determined by the purely rational (*zweckrational*) orientation of the actors to similar ulterior expectations.[42]

1. Usage also includes 'fashion' (*Mode*). As distinguished from custom and in direct contrast to it, usage will be called fashion so far as the mere fact of the novelty of the corresponding behaviour is the basis of the orientation of action. Its place is closely related to that of 'convention,'[43] since both of them usually spring from a desire for social prestige. It will not, however, be further discussed here.

2. As distinguished from both 'convention' and 'law,' 'custom' refers to rules devoid of any external sanction. The actor conforms with them of his own free will, whether his motivation lies in the fact that he merely fails to think about it, that it is more comfortable to conform, or what-

[42] In the above classification as well as in some of those which follow, the terminology is not standardized either in German or in English. Hence, just as there is a certain arbitrariness in Weber's definitions, the same is true of any corresponding set of definitions in English. It should be kept in mind that all of them are modes of orientation of action to patterns which contain a normative element. 'Usage' has seemed to be the most appropriate translation of *Brauch* since, according to Weber's own definition, the principal criterion is that 'it is done to conform with the pattern.' There would also seem to be good precedent for the translation of *Sitte* by 'custom.' The contrast with fashion, which Weber takes up in his first comment, is essentially the same in both languages. The term *Interessenlage* presents greater difficulty. It involves two components: the motivation in terms of self-interest and orientation to the opportunities presented by the situation. It has not seemed possible to use any single term to convey this meaning in English and hence, a more roundabout expression has had to be resorted to.—ED.

[43] The term 'convention' in Weber's usage is narrower than *Brauch*. The difference consists in the fact that a normative pattern to which action is oriented is conventional only in so far as it is regarded as part of a legitimate order, whereas the question of moral obligation to conformity which legitimacy implies is not involved in 'usage.' The distinction is closely related to that of W. G. Sumner between 'mores' and 'folkways.' It has seemed best to retain the English term closest to Weber's own.—ED.

ever else the reason may be. But always it is a justified expectation on the part of the members of the group that a customary rule will be adhered to. Thus custom is not 'valid' [44] in anything like the legal sense; conformity with it is not 'demanded' by anybody. Naturally, the transition from this to validly enforced convention and to law is gradual. Everywhere what has been traditionally handed down has been an important source of what has come to be enforced. To-day it is customary every morning to eat a breakfast which, within limits, conforms to a certain pattern. But there is no obligation to do so, except possibly for hotel guests ('American plan'), and it has not always been customary. On the other hand, the current mode of dress, even though it has partly originated in custom, is to-day very largely no longer customary alone, but conventional.[45]

3. Many of the especially notable uniformities in the course of social action are not determined by orientation to any sort of norm which is held to be valid, nor do they rest on custom, but entirely on the fact that the corresponding type of social action is in the nature of the case best adapted to the normal interests of the actors as they themselves are aware of them. This is above all true of economic action, for example, the uniformities of price determination in a 'free' market, but is by no means confined to such cases. The dealers in a market thus treat their own actions as means for obtaining the satisfaction of the ends defined by what they realize to be their own typical economic interests, and similarly treat as conditions the corresponding typical expectations as to the prospective behaviour of others. The more strictly rational their action is, the more will they tend to react similarly to the same situation. In this way there arise similarities, uniformities, and continuities in their attitudes and actions which are often far more stable than they would be if action were oriented to a system of norms and duties which were considered binding on the members of a group. This phenomenon—the fact that orientation to the situation in terms of the pure self-interest of the individual and of the others to whom he is related can bring about

[44] The German term which has been translated as 'validity' is *Geltung*. The primary use of this term is in a legal context and hence the validity in question is not empirical or logical validity, but legal. A legal rule is 'valid' in so far as it is judged binding upon those who recognize the legitimacy of the legal order.—ED.

[45] On the concepts of usage and custom, the relevant parts of vol. ii of Ihering's *Zweck im Recht* are still worth reading. Compare also, K. Oertmann, *Rechtesregelung und Verkehrssitte* (1914); and more recently, E. Weigelin, *Sitte, Recht und Moral,* 1919, which agrees with the author's position as opposed to that of Stammler.

results which are very similar to those which an authoritarian agency, very often in vain, has attempted to obtain by coercion—has aroused a lively interest, especially in economic affairs. Observation of this has, in fact, been one of the important sources of economics as a science. But it is true in all other spheres of action as well. This type, with its clarity of self-consciousness and freedom from subjective scruples, is the polar antithesis of every sort of unthinking acquiescence in customary ways, as well as, on the other hand, of devotion to norms consciously accepted as absolute values. One of the most important aspects of the process of 'rationalization' of action is the substitution for the unthinking acceptance of ancient custom, of deliberate adaptation to situations in terms of self-interest. To be sure, this process by no means exhausts the concept of rationalization of action. For in addition this can proceed in a variety of other directions; positively in that of a conscious rationalization of ultimate values; or negatively, at the expense not only of custom, but of emotional values; and, finally, in favour of a morally sceptical type of rationality, at the expense of any belief in absolute values. The many possible meanings of the concept of rationalization will often enter into the discussion.[46] Further remarks on the analytical problem will be found below.[47]

4. The stability of merely customary action rests essentially on the fact that the person who does not adapt himself to it is subjected to both petty and major inconveniences and annoyances as long as the majority of the people he comes in contact with continue to uphold the custom and conform with it.

Similarly, the stability of action in terms of self-interest rests on the fact that the person who does not orient his action to the interests of others, does not 'take account' of them, arouses their antagonism or may end up in a situation different from that which he had foreseen or wished to bring about. He thus runs the risk of damaging his own interests.

[46] It is, in a sense, the empirical reference of this statement which constitutes the central theme of Weber's series of studies in the Sociology of Religion. In so far as he finds it possible to attribute importance to 'ideas' in the determination of action, the most important differences between systems of ideas are not so much those in the degree of rationalization as in the direction which the process of rationalization in each case has taken. This series of studies was left uncompleted at his death, but all the material which was in a condition fit for publication has been assembled in the three volumes of the *Gesammelte Aufsätze zur Religionssoziologie.*—ED.

[47] It has not been possible to identify this reference of Weber's. It refers most probably to a projected conclusion of the whole work which was never written.—ED.

5: THE CONCEPT OF LEGITIMATE ORDER

Action, especially social action which involves social relationships, may be oriented by the actors to a *belief* (*Vorstellung*) in the existence of a 'legitimate order.' The probability that action will actually empirically be so oriented will be called the 'validity' (*Geltung*) of the order in question.[48]

1. Thus, orientation to the validity of an *order* (*Ordnung*) means more than the mere existence of a uniformity of social action determined by custom or self-interest. If furniture movers regularly advertise at times of the large-scale expiration of leases, this uniformity is determined by self-interest in the exploitation of opportunities. If a salesman visits certain customers on particular days of the month or the week, it is either a case of customary behaviour or a product of some kind of self-interested orientation. But when, on the other hand, a civil servant appears in his office daily at a fixed time, it may involve these elements, but is not determined by custom or self-interest alone, for with these he is at liberty to conform or not as he pleases. As a rule such action in addition is determined by his subjection to an order, the rules governing the department which impose obligations on him, which he is usually careful to fulfil, partly because disobedience would carry disadvantageous consequences to him, but usually also in part because it would be abhorrent to the sense of duty, which, to a greater or lesser extent, is an absolute value to him.

2. The subjective meaning of a social relationship will be called an 'order' only if action is approximately or on the average oriented to certain determinate 'maxims' or rules. Furthermore, such an order will only be called 'valid' if the orientation to such maxims includes, no matter to what actual extent, the recognition that they are binding on the actor or the corresponding action constitutes a desirable model for him to imitate. Naturally, in concrete cases, the orientation of action to an order involves a wide variety of motives. But the circumstance that along with the other sources of conformity the order is also held by at least part of the actors to define a model or to be binding, naturally increases the probability that action will in fact conform to it, often to a very considerable degree.

[48] The term *Gelten* has already been dealt with. From the very use of the term in this context it is clear that by 'order' (*Ordnung*) Weber here means a *normative* system. The pattern for the concept of 'order' is not, as in the law of gravitation, the 'order of nature,' but the order involved in a system of law.

An order which is adhered to from motives of pure expediency is generally much less stable than one upheld on a purely customary basis through the fact that the corresponding behaviour has become habitual. The latter is much the most common type of subjective attitude. But even this type of order is in turn much less stable than an order which enjoys the prestige of being considered binding, or, as it may be expressed, of 'legitimacy.' The transitions between orientation to an order from motives of tradition or of expediency on the one hand to the case where on the other a belief in its legitimacy is involved, are naturally empirically gradual.

3. It is possible for action to be oriented to an order in other ways than through conformity with its prescriptions, as they are generally understood by the actors. Even in the cases of evasion of or deliberate disobedience to these prescriptions, the probability of its being recognized as a valid norm may have an effect on action. This may, in the first place, be true from the point of view of sheer expediency. A thief orients his action to the validity of the criminal law in that he acts surreptitiously. The fact that the order is recognized as valid in his society is made evident by the fact that he cannot violate it openly without punishment. But apart from this limiting case, it is very common for violation of an order to be confined to more or less numerous partial deviations from it, or for the attempt to be made, with varying degrees of good faith, to justify the deviation as legitimate. Furthermore, there may exist at the same time different interpretations of the meaning of the order. In such cases, for sociological purposes, each can be said to be valid in so far as it actually determines the course of action. The fact that, in the same social group, a plurality of contradictory systems of order may all be recognized as valid, is not a source of difficulty for the sociological approach. Indeed, it is even possible for the same individual to orient his action to contradictory systems of order. This can take place not only at different times, as is an everyday occurrence, but even in the case of the same concrete act. A person who fights a duel orients his action to the code of honour; but at the same time, in so far as he either keeps it secret or conversely gives himself up to the police, he takes account of the criminal law.[49] To be sure, when evasion or contravention of the generally understood meaning of an order has become the rule, the order

[49] When this was written (probably about 1913), duelling was still a relatively common practice in Germany and, in certain circles, was regarded as a definite obligation of honour in the face of some kinds of provocation. It was, however, at the same time an explicitly punishable offence under the criminal law.—Ed.

can be said to be 'valid' only in a limited degree and, in the extreme case, not at all. Thus for sociological purposes there does not exist, as there does for the law, a rigid alternative between the validity and lack of validity of a given order. On the contrary, there is a gradual transition between the two extremes; and also it is possible, as it has been pointed out, for contradictory systems of order to exist at the same time. In that case each is 'valid' precisely to the extent that there is a probability that action will in fact be oriented to it.[50]

6: The Types of Legitimate Order

The legitimacy of an order may be guaranteed or upheld in two principal ways:[51] (1) from purely disinterested motives, which may in

[50] Those familiar with the literature of this subject will recall the part played by the concept of 'order' in the brilliant book of Rudolf Stammler, which was cited in the prefatory note, a book which, though like all his works it is very able, is nevertheless fundamentally misleading and confuses the issues in a catastrophic fashion. The reader may compare the author's critical discussion of it, which was also cited in the same place, a discussion which, because of the author's annoyance at Stammler's confusion, was unfortunately written in somewhat too acrimonious a tone.

Stammler fails to distinguish the normative meaning of 'validity' from the empirical. He further fails to recognize that social action is oriented to other things beside systems of order. Above all, however, in a way which is wholly indefensible from a logical point of view, he treats order as a 'form' of social action and then attempts to bring it into a type of relation to 'content,' which is analogous to that of form and content in the theory of knowledge. Other errors in his argument will be left aside. But actually, action which is, for instance, primarily economic, is oriented to knowledge of the relative scarcity of certain available means to want satisfaction, in relation to the actor's state of needs and to the present and probable action of others, in so far as the latter affects the same resources. But at the same time, of course, the actor in his choice of economic procedures naturally orients himself *in addition* to the conventional and legal rules which he recognizes as valid, or of which he knows that a violation on his part would call forth a given reaction of other persons. Stammler succeeds in introducing a state of hopeless confusion into this very simple empirical situation, particularly in that he maintains that a causal relationship between an order and actual empirical action involves a contradiction in terms. It is true, of course, that there is no causal relationship between the *normative* validity of an order in the legal sense and any empirical process. In that context there is only the question of whether the order as correctly interpreted in the legal sense 'applies' to the empirical situation. The question is whether in a *normative* sense it *should* be treated as valid and, if so, what the content of its normative prescriptions for this situation should be. But for sociological purposes, as distinguished from legal, it is only the probability of orientation to the subjective *belief* in the validity of an order which constitutes the valid order itself. It is undeniable that, in the ordinary sense of the word 'causal,' there is a causal relationship between this probability and the relevant course of economic action.

[51] The reader may readily become confused as to the basis of the following classification, as compared with that presented in sec. 7. The first classification is one of motives for

turn be (a) purely affectual, consisting in an emotionally determined loyalty; or (b) may derive from a rational belief in the absolute validity of the order as an expression of ultimate values,[52, 53] whether they be moral, esthetic or of any other type; or (c) may originate in religious attitudes, through the belief in the dependence of some condition of religious salvation on conformity with the order; (2) also or entirely by self-interest, that is, through expectations of specific ulterior consequences, but consequences which are, to be sure, of a particular kind.

A system of order will be called *convention* so far as its validity is externally guaranteed by the probability that deviation from it within a given social group will result in a relatively general and practically significant reaction of disapproval. Such an order will be called *law* when conformity with it is upheld by the probability that deviant action will be met by physical or psychic sanctions aimed to compel conformity or to punish disobedience, and applied by a group of men especially empowered to carry out this function.[54]

1. The term convention will be employed to designate that part of the custom followed within a given social group which is recognized as 'binding' and protected against violation by sanctions of disapproval. As distinguished from 'law' in the sense of the present discussion, it is not enforced by a functionally specialized agency. Stammler distinguishes convention from law in terms of the entirely voluntary character of conformity. This is not, however, in accord with everyday usage and does not even fit the examples he gives. Conformity with convention in such matters as the usual forms of greeting, the mode of dress recognized as appropriate or respectable, and various of the rules governing the restrictions on social intercourse, both in form and in content, is very

maintaining a legitimate order in force, whereas the second is one of motives for attributing legitimacy to the order. This explains the inclusion of self-interested motives in the first classification, but not in the second. It is quite possible, for instance, for irreligious persons to support the doctrine of the divine right of kings, because they feel that the breakdown of an order which depends on this would have undesirable consequences. This is not, however, a possible motive on which to base a direct sense of personal moral obligation to conform with the order.—ED.

[52] The antithesis *innerlich-äusserlich* as applied to elements of motivation does not have any direct English counterpart. The aspect of *innerlich,* however, which is most important in the present context seems to be adequately expressed by the term 'disinterested.' The essential point is that the object of such motivation is valued for its own sake or as a direct expression of ultimate values rather than as a means to some 'ulterior' end.—ED.

[53] *Wertrational.*

[54] On the concept of convention, see beside Ihering, op. cit., and Weigelin, op. cit., F. Tönnies, *Die Sitte.*

definitely expected of the individual and regarded as binding on him. It is not, as in the case of certain ways of preparing food, a mere usage, which he is free to conform to or not as he sees fit. A violation of conventional rules—such as standards of 'respectability'—often leads to the extremely severe and effective sanction of an informal boycott on the part of members of one's group. This may actually be a more severe punishment than any legal penalty. The only thing lacking is the group of men with the specialized function of maintaining enforcement of the order, such as judges, prosecuting attorneys, and administrative officials. The transition, however, is gradual. The case of conventional guarantee of an order which most closely approaches the legal, is the application of a formally threatened and organized boycott. For terminological purposes, this is best considered a form of legal compulsion. Conventional rules may, in addition to mere disapproval, also be upheld by other means; thus domestic authority may be employed to deal with behaviour in defiance of convention. This fact is not, however, important in the present context. The decisive point is that the individual, by virtue of the existence of conventional disapproval, applies these sanctions, however drastic, on his own authority, not as a member of an organized group endowed with a specific authority for this purpose.

2. For the purposes of this discussion the concept 'law' will be made to turn on the presence of a group of men engaged in enforcement, however useful it might be to define it differently for other purposes. The character of this agency naturally need not be at all similar to what is at present familiar. In particular it is not necessary that there should be any specifically 'judicial' authority. The clan, as an agency of blood revenge and of the prosecution of feuds, is such an enforcing agency if there exist any sort of rules which governs its behaviour in such situations. But this is on the extreme borderline of what can be called legal enforcement. As is well known it has often been denied that international law could be called law, precisely because there is no legal authority above the state capable of enforcing it. In terms of the present terminology this would be correct, for a system of order the sanctions of which consisted wholly in expectations of disapproval and of the reprisals of injured parties, which is thus guaranteed entirely by convention and self-interest without the help of a specialized enforcement agency, is not a case of legal order. But for purposes of legal terminology exactly the opposite usage might well be acceptable.

In any case the means of coercion are irrelevant. Even a 'friendly admonition,' such as has been used in various religious sects as a form of gentle pressure on sinners, is to be included if it is carried out according to rules by a specially designated group. Another case is the use of the censure as a means of enforcing norms of moral conduct. Psychic coercion has indeed become the specific disciplinary technique of the church. It is thus naturally just as much a case of 'law' whether an order is upheld by ecclesiastical or by a political organization, whether in conformity with the rules of an association or by the authority of the head of a household. Even the rules contained in a commentary may be regarded, for this terminology, as law. Article 888, sec. 2, of the German Code of Civil Procedure,[55] dealing with unenforceable rights, is a case in point. The *leges imperfectae,* and the category of 'natural obligations,' are forms of legal terminology which express indirectly limits or conditions of the application of compulsion. In the same sense a trade practice which is compulsorily enforced is also law.[56]

3. It is not necessary for a valid order to be of a general and abstract character. The distinction between a legal precept and the decision in a concrete case, for instance, has not always and everywhere been as clearly made as we have to-day come to expect. An 'order' may thus occur simply as the order governing a single concrete situation. The details of this subject belong in the sociology of law.[57] But for present purposes, unless otherwise specified, the modern distinction between a precept and a specific decision will be taken for granted.

4. A system of order which is guaranteed by external sanctions may at the same time be guaranteed by disinterested subjective attitudes. The relations of law, convention, and 'ethics' do not constitute a problem for sociology. From a sociological point of view an 'ethical' standard is one to which men attribute a certain type of value and which, by virtue of this belief, they treat as a valid norm governing their action. In this sense it can be spoken of as defining what is ethically good in the same way that action which is called beautiful is measured by aesthetic standards. It is possible for ethically normative beliefs of this kind to have a pro-

---

[55] *Reichs-Zivil-Prozess-Ordnung.*

[56] See secs. 157 and 242 of the German Civil Code. *Bürgerliches Gesetz-Buch* on the concept of 'common law obligations,' that is, obligations arising out of community standards of acceptable behaviour which come to be sanctioned by law. See the paper of Max Rümelin in *Schwäbische Heimatsgabe für Theodor Häring.*

[57] An extended discussion of this subject is included in the German edition of *Wirtschaft und Gesellschaft,* part ii, chap. vii, pp. 386-512. It is not, however, included in the present translation.—Ed.

found influence on action in the absence of any sort of external guarantee. This is often the case when the interests of others would be little affected by their violation.

Such ethical beliefs are also often guaranteed by religious motives, but they may at the same time in the present terminology be upheld to an important extent by disapproval of violations and the consequent boycott, or even legally with the corresponding sanctions of the criminal law, police measures, or civil penalties. Every system of ethics which has in a sociological sense become validly established is likely to be upheld to a large extent by the probability that disapproval will result from its violation, that is, by convention. On the other hand, it is by no means necessary that all conventionally or legally guaranteed forms of order should claim the authority of ethical norms. Legal rules, much more often than conventional, may have been established entirely on grounds of expediency. Whether a belief in the validity of an order as such, which is current in a social group, is to be regarded as belonging to the realm of 'ethics' or is a mere convention or a mere legal norm, cannot, for sociological purposes, be decided in general terms. It must be treated as relative to the conception of what values are treated as 'ethical' in the social group in question. What these are is, in the relevant respect, not subject to generalization.

7: THE BASES OF LEGITIMACY OF AN ORDER

Legitimacy may be ascribed to an order by those acting subject to it in the following ways:—

(a) By tradition; a belief in the legitimacy of what has always existed; (b) by virtue of affectual attitudes, especially emotional, legitimizing the validity of what is newly revealed or a model to imitate; (c) by virtue of a rational belief in its absolute value,[58] thus lending it the validity of an absolute and final commitment; (d) because it has been established in a manner which is recognized to be *legal*. This legality may be treated as legitimate in either of two ways: on the one hand, it may derive from a voluntary agreement of the interested parties on the relevant terms. On the other hand, it may be imposed on the basis of what is held to be a legitimate authority over the relevant persons and a corresponding claim to their obedience.

[58] *Wertrational.*

All further details, except for a few other concepts to be defined below, belong in the sociology of law and the sociology of authority.[59] For the present, only a few remarks are necessary.

1. The derivation of the legitimacy of an order from a belief in the sanctity of tradition is the most universal and most primitive case. The fear of magical penalties confirms the general psychological inhibitions against any sort of change in customary modes of action. At the same time the multifarious vested interests which tend to become attached to upholding conformity with an order, once it has become established, have worked in the same direction.[60]

2. Conscious departures from tradition in the establishment of a new order have originally been due almost entirely to prophetic oracles or at least to pronouncements which have been sanctioned as prophetic. This was true as late as the statutes of the Greek Aisymnetes. Conformity has then depended on belief in the legitimacy of the prophet. In times of strict traditionalism a new order, that is one which was *regarded* as new, could, without being revealed in this way, only become legitimized by the claim that it had actually always been valid though not yet rightly known, or that it had been obscured for a time and was now being restored to its rightful place.

3. The type case of legitimacy by virtue of rational belief in an absolute value is that of 'Natural Law.' However limited its actual effect, as compared with its ideal claims, it cannot be denied that its logically developed reasoning has had an influence on actual action which is far from negligible. This mode of influence should be clearly distinguished from that of a revealed law, of one imposed by authority, or of one which is merely traditional.

4. To-day the most usual basis of legitimacy is the belief in legality, the readiness to conform with rules which are formally correct and have been imposed by accepted procedure. The distinction between an order derived from voluntary agreement and one which has been imposed is only rela-

[59] The term 'authority' is used to translate *Herrschaft*. It is not adequate for all purposes, but a discussion of the difficulties will be deferred to the point at which the concept becomes of primary importance. See below, sec. 16, p. 152. Weber dealt with this range of problems systematically in two different places, one of which is chapter iii of the present volume. The material of that chapter, however, is expanded and copiously illustrated in part iii of the German edition of *Wirtschaft und Gesellschaft* which is not included in the present translation. This part, like many other parts of the work, was left uncompleted at Weber's death.—ED.

[60] See chap. iii.

tive. For so far as the agreement underlying the order is not unanimous, as in the past has often been held necessary for complete legitimacy, its functioning within a social group will be dependent on the willingness of individuals with deviant wishes to give way to the majority. This is very frequently the case and actually means that the order is imposed on the minority. At the same time, it is very common for minorities, by force or by the use of more ruthless and far-sighted methods, to impose an order which in the course of time comes to be regarded as legitimate by those who originally resisted it. In so far as the ballot is used as a legal means of altering an order, it is very common for the will of a minority to attain a formal majority and for the majority to submit. In this case majority rule is a mere illusion. The belief in the legality of an order as established by voluntary agreement is relatively ancient and is occasionally found among so-called primitive peoples; but in these cases it is almost always supplemented by the authority of oracles.

5. So far as it is not derived merely from fear or from motives of expediency, a willingness to submit to an order imposed by one man or a small group, always in some sense implies a belief in the legitimate *authority* of the source imposing it.[61]

6. Submission to an order is almost always determined by a variety of motives; by a wide variety of interests and by a mixture of adherence to tradition and belief in legality, unless it is a case of entirely new regulations. In a very large proportion of cases, the actors subject to the order are of course not even aware how far it is a matter of custom, of convention, or of law. In such cases the sociologist must attempt to formulate the typical basis of validity.

8: The Concept of Conflict

A social relationship will be referred to as 'conflict'[62] in so far as action within it is oriented intentionally to carrying out the actor's own will against the resistance of the other party or parties. The term 'peaceful' conflict will be applied to cases in which actual physical violence is not employed. A peaceful conflict is 'competition' in so far as it consists in a formally peaceful attempt to attain control over opportunities and

---

[61] This subject will be dealt with separately below. See secs. 13 and 16 and chap. iii.
[62] *Kampf.*

advantages [63] which are also desired by others. A competitive process is 'regulated' competition to the extent that its ends and means are oriented to an order. The struggle, often latent, which takes place between human individuals or types of social status, for advantages and for survival, but without a meaningful mutual orientation in terms of conflict, will be called 'selection.' In so far as it is a matter of the relative opportunities of individuals during their own lifetime, it is 'social selection'; in so far as it concerns differential chances for the survival of inherited characteristics, 'biological selection.'

1. There are all manner of continuous transitions ranging from the bloody type of conflict which, setting aside all rules, aims at the destruction of the adversary, to the case of the battles of medieval chivalry, bound as they were to the strictest conventions, and to the strict regulations imposed on sport by the rules of the game. A classic example of conventional regulation even in war is the herald's call before the battle of Fontenoy: 'Messieurs les Anglais, tirez les premiers.' There are transitions such as that from unregulated competition of, let us say, suitors for the favour of a woman to the competition for economic advantages in exchange relationships, bound as that is by the order governing the market, or to strictly regulated competitions for artistic awards or, finally, to the struggle for victory in election campaigns. The treatment of conflict involving the use of physical violence as a separate type is justified by the special characteristics of the employment of this means and the corresponding peculiarities of the sociological consequences of its use.[64]

2. All typical struggles and modes of competition which take place on a large scale will lead, in the long run, despite the decisive importance in many individual cases of accidental factors and luck, to a selection of those who have in the higher degree, on the average, possessed the personal qualities important to success. What qualities are important depends on the conditions in which the conflict or competition takes place. It may be a matter of physical strength or of unscrupulous cunning, of the level of mental ability or mere lung power and skill in the technique of demagoguery, of loyalty to superiors or of ability to flatter the masses, of creative originality, or of adaptability, of qualities which are unusual, or of those which are possessed by the mediocre majority. *Among* the deci-

---

[63] *Chancen*. This usage of the term is to be distinguished from that translated as probability or likelihood.—ED.

[64] See chaps. ii and iii.

sive conditions, it must not be forgotten, belong the systems of order to which the behaviour of the parties is oriented, whether traditionally, as a matter of rationally disinterested loyalty, or of expediency. Each type of order influences opportunities in the process of social selection differently.

Not every process of social selection is, in the present sense, a case of conflict. Social selection, on the contrary, means only in the first instance that certain types of behaviour, and hence of the corresponding personal qualities, are more favourable than others in procuring differential advantages in attaining to certain social relationships, as in the role of 'lover,' 'husband,' 'member of parliament,' 'official,' 'contractor,' 'managing director,' 'successful business man,' and so on. But the concept does not specify whether this differential advantage in selection for social success is brought to bear through conflict or not, neither does it specify whether the biological chances of survival of the type are affected one way or the other. It is only where there is a genuine competitive process that the term conflict will be used.

It is only in the sense of 'selection' that it seems, according to our experience, that conflict is empirically inevitable, and it is furthermore only in the sense of *biological* selection that it is inevitable in principle. Selection is inevitable because apparently no way can be worked out of eliminating it completely. It is possible even for the most strictly pacific order to eliminate means of conflict and the objects of and impulses to conflict only in that it deals with each type individually. But this means that other modes of conflict would come to the fore, possibly in processes of open competition. But even on the utopian assumption that all competition were completely eliminated, conditions would still lead to a latent process of selection, biological or social, which would favour the types best adapted to the conditions, whether their relevant qualities were mainly determined by heredity or by environment. On an empirical level the elimination of conflict cannot go beyond a point which leaves room for some social selection, and in principle a process of biological selection necessarily remains.

3. From the struggle of individuals for personal advantages and survival, it is naturally necessary to distinguish the 'conflict' and the 'selection' of social relationships. It is only in a metaphorical sense that these concepts can be applied to the latter. For relationships exist only as systems of human action with particular subjective meanings. Thus a process of

selection or a conflict between them means only that one type of action has in the course of time been displaced by another, whether it is action by the same persons or by others. This may occur in various ways. Human action may in the first place be consciously aimed to alter certain social relationships—that is, to alter the corresponding action—or it may be directed to the prevention of their development or continuance. Thus a 'state' may be destroyed by war or revolution, or a conspiracy may be broken up by savage suppression; prostitution may be suppressed by police action; 'shady' business practices, by denial of legal protection or by penalties. Furthermore, social relationships may be influenced by the creation of differential advantages which favour one type over another. It is possible either for individuals or for organized groups to pursue such ends. Secondly, it may, in various ways, be an unanticipated consequence of a course of social action and its relevant conditions that certain types of social relationships (meaning, of course, the corresponding actions) will be adversely affected in their opportunities to maintain themselves or to arise. All changes of natural and social conditions have some sort of effect on the differential probabilities of survival of social relationships. Anyone is at liberty to speak in such cases of a process of 'selection' of social relationships. For instance, he may say that among several states the 'strongest,' in the sense of the best 'adapted,' is victorious. It must, however, be kept in mind that this so-called 'selection' has nothing to do with the selection of types of human individuals in either the social or the biological sense. In every case it is necessary to inquire into the reasons which have led to a change in the chances of survival of one or another form of social action or social relationship, which has broken up a social relationship or which has permitted it to continue at the expense of other competing forms. The explanation of these processes involves so many factors that it does not seem expedient to employ a single term for them. When this is done, there is always a danger of introducing uncritical value-judgments into empirical investigation. There is, above all, a danger of being primarily concerned with justifying the success of an individual case. Since individual cases are often dependent on highly exceptional circumstances, they may be in a certain sense 'fortuitous.' In recent years there has been more than enough of this kind of argument. The fact that a given specific social relationship has been eliminated for reasons peculiar to a particular situation, proves nothing whatever about its 'fitness to survive' in general terms.

9: Types of Solidary Social Relationships

A social relationship will be called 'communal' [65] if and so far as the orientation of social action—whether in the individual case, on the average, or in the pure type—is based on a subjective feeling of the parties, whether affectual or traditional, that they belong together. A social relationship will, on the other hand, be called 'associative' if and in so far as the orientation of social action within it rests on a rationally motivated adjustment of interests or a similarly motivated agreement, whether the basis of rational judgment be absolute values or reasons of expediency. It is especially common, though by no means inevitable, for the associative type of relationship to rest on a rational agreement by mutual consent. In that case the corresponding action is, at the pole of rationality, oriented either to a rational belief in the binding validity of the obligation to adhere to it, or to a rational expectation that the other party will live up to it.[66]

1. The purest cases of associative relationships are: (a) rational free market exchange, which constitutes a compromise of opposed but complementary interests; (b) the pure voluntary association based on self-interest,[67] a case of agreement as to a long-run course of action oriented purely to the promotion of specific ulterior interests, economic or other, of its members; (c) the voluntary association of individuals motivated by an adherence to a set of common absolute values,[68] for example, the rational sect, in so far as it does not cultivate emotional and affective interests, but seeks only to serve a 'cause.' This last case, to be sure, seldom occurs in anything approaching the pure type.

[65] The two types of relationship which Weber distinguishes in this section he himself calls *Vergemeinschaftung* and *Vergesellschaftung*. His own usage here is an adaptation of the well-known terms of Tönnies, *Gemeinschaft* and *Gesellschaft*, and has been directly influenced by Tönnies' work. Though there has been much discussion of them in English, it is safe to say that no satisfactory equivalent of Tönnies' terms have been found. In particular, 'community' and either 'society' or 'association' are unsatisfactory, since these terms have quite different connotations in English. In the context, however, in which Weber uses his slightly altered terms, that of action within a social relationship, the adjective forms 'communal' and 'associative' do not seem to be objectionable. Their exact meanings should become clear from Weber's definitions and comments.—Ed.

[66] This terminology is similar to the distinction made by Ferdinand Tönnies in his pioneering work, *Gemeinschaft und Gesellschaft;* but for his purposes, Tönnies has given this distinction a rather more specific meaning than would be convenient for purposes of the present discussion.

[67] *Zweckverein.*

[68] *Gesinnungsverein.*

2. Communal relationships may rest on various types of affectual, emotional, or traditional bases. Examples are a religious brotherhood, an erotic relationship, a relation of personal loyalty, a national community, the *esprit de corps* of a military unit. The type case is most conveniently illustrated by the family. But the great majority of social relationships has this characteristic to some degree, while it is at the same time to some degree determined by associative factors. No matter how calculating and hard-headed the ruling considerations in such a social relationship—as that of a merchant to his customers—may be, it is quite possible for it to involve emotional values which transcend its utilitarian significance. Every social relationship which goes beyond the pursuit of immediate common ends, which hence lasts for long periods, involves relatively permanent social relationships between the same persons, and these cannot be exclusively confined to the technically necessary activities. Hence in such cases as association in the same military unit, in the same school class, in the same workshop or office, there is always some tendency in this direction, although the degree, to be sure, varies enormously.[69] Conversely, a social relationship which is normally considered primarily communal may involve action on the part of some or even all of the participants, which is to an important degree oriented to considerations of expediency. There is, for instance, a wide variation in the extent to which the members of a family group feel a genuine community of interests or, on the other hand, exploit the relationship for their own ends. The concept of communal relationship has been intentionally defined in very general terms and hence includes a very heterogeneous group of phenomena.

3. The communal type of relationship is, according to the usual interpretation of its subjective meaning, the most radical antithesis of conflict. This should not, however, be allowed to obscure the fact that coercion of all sorts is a very common thing in even the most intimate of such communal relationships if one party is weaker in character than the other. Furthermore, a process of the selection of types leading to differences in opportunity and survival, goes on within these relationships just the same as anywhere else. Associative relationships, on the other hand,

[69] Weber's emphasis on the importance of these communal elements even within functionally specific formal organizations like industrial plants has been strongly confirmed by the findings of research since this was written. One important study which shows the importance of informal social organization on this level among the workers of an industrial plant is reported in Roethlisberger and Dickson, *Management and the Worker.*—Ed.

very often consist only in compromises between rival interests, where only a part of the occasion or means of conflict has been eliminated, or even an attempt has been made to do so. Hence, outside the area of compromise, the conflict of interests, with its attendant competition for supremacy, remains unchanged. Conflict and communal relationships are relative concepts. Conflict varies enormously according to the means employed, especially whether they are violent or peaceful, and to the ruthlessness with which they are used. It has already been pointed out that any type of order governing social action in some way leaves room for a process of selection among various rival human types.

4. It is by no means true that the existence of common qualities, a common situation, or common modes of behaviour imply the existence of a communal social relationship. Thus, for instance, the possession of a common biological inheritance by virtue of which persons are classified as belonging to the same 'race,' naturally implies no sort of communal social relationship between them. By restrictions on social intercourse and on marriage persons may find themselves in a similar situation, a situation of isolation from the environment which imposes these distinctions. But even if they all react to this situation in the same way, this does not constitute a communal relationship. The latter does not even exist if they have a common 'feeling' about this situation and its consequences. It is only when this feeling leads to a mutual orientation of their behaviour to each other that a social relationship arises between them, a social relationship to each other and not only to persons in the environment. Furthermore, it is only so far as this relationship involves feelings of belonging together that it is a 'communal' relationship. In the case of the Jews, for instance, except for Zionist circles and the action of certain associations promoting specifically Jewish interests, there thus exist communal relationships only to a relatively small extent; indeed, Jews often repudiate the existence of a Jewish 'community.'

Community of language, which arises from a similarity of tradition through the family and the surrounding social environment, facilitates mutual understanding, and thus the formation of all types of social relationships, in the highest degree. But taken by itself it is not sufficient to constitute a communal relationship, but only for the facilitation of intercourse within the groups concerned, thus for the development of associative relationships. In the first place, this takes place between *individuals,* not because they speak the same language, but because they have other types of interests. Orientation to the rules of a common language is thus primarily important as a means of communication, not as the content of a social relationship. It is only with the emergence of a consciousness of difference from third persons who speak a different language that the fact that two persons speak the same language, and in that respect share a common situation, can lead them to a feeling of community and to modes of social organization consciously based on the sharing of the common language.

Participation in a 'market' [70] is of still another kind. It encourages association between the individual parties to specific acts of exchange and a social relationship, above all that of competition, between the individual participants who must mutually orient their action to each other. But no further modes of association develop except in cases where certain participants enter into agreements in order to better their competitive situations, or where they all agree on rules for the purpose of regulating transactions and of securing favourable general conditions for all. It may further be remarked that the market and the competitive economy resting on it form the most important type of the reciprocal determination of action in terms of pure self-interest, a type which is characteristic of modern economic life.

10: OPEN AND CLOSED RELATIONSHIPS

A social relationship, regardless of whether it is communal or associative in character, will be spoken of as 'open' to outsiders if and in so far as participation in the mutually oriented social action relevant to its subjective meaning is, according to its system of order, not denied to anyone who wishes to participate and who is actually in a position to do so. A relationship will, on the other hand, be called 'closed' against outsiders so far as, according to its subjective meaning and the binding rules of its order, participation of certain persons is excluded, limited, or subjected to conditions. Whether a relationship is open or closed may be determined traditionally, affectually, or rationally in terms of values or of expediency. It is especially likely to be closed, for rational reasons, in the following type of situation: a social relationship may provide the parties to it with opportunities for the satisfaction of various interests, whether the satisfactions be spiritual or material, whether the interest be in the end of the relationship as such or in some ulterior consequence of par-

---

[70] For definition. See chap. ii, p. 181 ff.

ticipation, or whether it is achieved through co-operative action or by a compromise of interests. If the participants expect that the admission of others will lead to an improvement of their situation, an improvement in degree, in kind, in the security or the value of the satisfaction, their interest will be in keeping the relationship open. If, on the other hand, their expectations are of improving their position by monopolistic tactics, their interest is in a closed relationship.

There are various ways in which it is possible for a closed social relationship to guarantee its monopolized advantages to the parties. Such advantages may be left free to competitive struggle within the group; they may be regulated or rationed in amount and kind, or they may be appropriated by individuals or sub-groups on a permanent basis and become more or less inalienable. The last is a case of closure within, as well as against, outsiders. Appropriated advantages will be called 'rights.' As determined by the relevant order, appropriation may be for the benefit of the members of particular communal or associative groups (for instance, household groups), or for the benefit of individuals. In the latter case, the individual may enjoy his rights on a purely personal basis or in such a way that in case of his death one or more other persons related to the holder of the right by birth (kinship), or by some other social relationship, may inherit the rights in question. Or the rights may pass to one or more individuals specifically designated by the holder. Finally, it may be that the holder is more or less fully empowered to alienate his rights by voluntary agreement, either to other specific persons or to anyone he chooses. This is 'alienable' appropriation. A party to a closed social relationship will be called a 'member'; [71] in case his participation is regulated in such a way as to guarantee him appropriated advantages, a 'privileged' member. Appropriated rights which are enjoyed by individuals through inheritance or by hereditary groups, whether communal or associative, will be called the 'property' of the individual or of groups in question; and, in so far as they are alienable, 'free' property.

The apparently gratuitous tediousness involved in the elaborate definition of the above concepts is an example of the fact that we often neglect to think out clearly what seems to be 'obvious,' because it is intuitively familiar.

1. (a) Examples of communal relationships, which tend to be closed

[71] *Rechtsgenosse.*

on a traditional basis, are those membership in which is determined by family relationship.

(b) Personal emotional relationships are usually affectually closed. Examples are erotic relationships and, very commonly, relations of personal loyalty.

(c) Closure on the basis of rational commitment to values is usual in groups sharing a common system of explicit religious belief.

(d) Typical cases of rational closure on grounds of expediency are economic associations of a monopolistic or a plutocratic character.

A few examples may be taken at random. Whether a group of people engaged in conversation is open or closed depends on its content. General conversation is apt to be open, as contrasted with intimate conversation or the imparting of official information. Market relationships are in most, or at least in many, cases essentially open. In the case of many relationships, both communal and associative, there is a tendency to shift from a phase of expansion to one of exclusiveness. Examples are the guilds and the democratic city-states of Antiquity and the Middle Ages. At times these groups sought to increase their membership in the interest of improving the security of their position of power by adequate numbers. At other times they restricted their membership to protect the value of their monopolistic position. The same phenomenon is not uncommon in monastic orders and religious sects which have passed from a stage of religious proselytizing to one of restriction in the interest of the maintenance of an ethical standard or for the protection of material interests. There is a similar close relationship between the extension of market relationships in the interest of increased turnover on the one hand, their monopolistic restriction on the other. The promotion of linguistic uniformity is to-day a natural result of the interests of publishers and writers, as opposed to the earlier, not uncommon, tendency for class groups to maintain linguistic peculiarities or even for secret languages to be built up.

2. Both the extent and the methods of regulation and exclusion in relation to outsiders may vary widely, so that the transition from a state of openness to one of regulation and closure is gradual. Various conditions of participation may be laid down; qualifying tests, a period of probation, requirement of possession of a share which can be purchased under certain conditions, election of new members by ballot, membership or eligibility by birth or by virtue of achievements open to anyone. Finally, in case of closure and the appropriation of rights within the group, status may be dependent on the acquisition of an appropriated right. There is

a wide variety of different degrees of closure and of conditions of participation. Thus regulation and closure are relative concepts. There are all manner of gradual shadings as between an exclusive club, a theatrical audience the members of which have purchased tickets, and a party rally to which the largest possible number has been urged to come; similarly, from a church service open to the general public through the rituals of a limited sect to the mysteries of a secret cult.

3. Similarly, closure within the group as between the members themselves and in their relations with each other may also assume the most varied forms. Thus a caste, a guild, or a group of stock exchange brokers, which is closed to outsiders, may allow to its members a perfectly free competition for all the advantages which the group as a whole monopolizes for itself. Or it may assign every member strictly to the enjoyment of certain advantages, such as claims over customers or particular business opportunities, for life or even on a hereditary basis. This is particularly characteristic of India. Similarly a closed group of settlers may allow its members free use of the resources of its area or may restrict them rigidly to a plot assigned to each individual household. A closed group of colonists may allow free use of the land or sanction and guarantee permanent appropriation of separate holdings. In such cases all conceivable transitional and intermediate forms can be found. Historically, the closure of eligibility to fiefs, benefices, and offices within the group, and the appropriation on the part of those enjoying them, have occurred in the most varied forms. Similarly, the establishment of rights to and possession of particular jobs on the part of workers may develop all the way from the 'closed shop' to a right to a particular job. The first step in this development may be to prohibit the dismissal of a worker without the consent of the workers' representatives. The development of the 'works councils' in Germany after 1918 might be a first step in this direction, though it need not be.[72]

All the details must be reserved to particular studies. The most extreme form of permanent appropriation is found in cases where particular rights are guaranteed to an individual or to certain groups of them, such as households, clans, families, in such a way that it is specified in the order either that, in case of death, the rights descend to specific heirs, or that

---

[72] This is a reference to the *Betriebsräte* which were formed in German industrial plants during the Revolution of 1918-19 and were recognized in the Weimar Constitution as entitled to representation in the Federal Economic Council. The standard work in English is W. C. Guillebaud: *The German Works Councils.*—ED.

the possessor is free to transfer them to any other person at will. Such a person thereby becomes a party to the social relationship so that, when appropriation has reached this extreme within the group, it becomes to that extent an open group in relation to outsiders. This is true so long as acquisition of membership is not subject to the ratification of the other, prior members.

4. The principal motives for closure of a relationship are: (a) The maintenance of quality, which is often combined with the interest in prestige and the consequent opportunities to enjoy honour, and even profit. Examples are communities of ascetics, monastic orders, especially, for instance, the Indian mendicant orders, religious sects like the Puritans, organized groups of warriors, of retainers [73] and other functionaries, organized citizen bodies as in the Greek states, craft guilds; (b) orientation to the scarcity of advantages in their bearing on consumption needs (*Nahrungsspielraum*).[74] Examples are monopolies of consumption, the most developed form of which is a self-subsistent village community; (c) orientation to the scarcity of opportunities for acquisition (*Erwerbsspielraum*). This is found in trade monopolies such as the guilds, the ancient monopolies of fishing rights, and so on. Usually motive (a) is combined with (b) or (c).

11: REPRESENTATION AND RESPONSIBILITY

The order which governs a social relationship by tradition or by virtue of its legal establishment, may determine that certain types of action of some of the parties to the relationship will have consequences which affect the others. It may be that all are held responsible for the action of *any* one. In that case they will be spoken of as 'solidary' members. Or, on the other hand, the action of certain members, the 'representatives,' may be binding upon the others. That is, the resulting advantages will go to them, they will enjoy the benefits, or conversely bear the resulting losses.

[73] *Ministerialen.*
[74] Weber here refers to *Nahrungsspielraum*. The concept refers to the scope of economic resources and opportunities on which the standard of living of an individual or a group is dependent. By contrast with this, *Erwerbsspielraum* is a similar scope of resources and economic opportunities seen from the point of view of their possible role as sources of profit. The basic distinction implied in this contrast is of central importance to Weber's analysis later on (see chapter ii, sec. 10 ff.).—ED.

Representative authority [75] may be conferred in accordance with the binding order in such a way (a) that it is completely appropriated in all its forms—the case of 'independent' authority; or (b) it may be conferred in accordance with particular criteria, permanently or for a limited term; or (c) it may be conferred by specific acts of the members or of outside persons, again permanently or for a limited term—the case of appointment. There are many different conditions which determine the ways in which social relationships, communal or associative, develop relations of solidarity, or of representation. In general terms, it is possible only to say that one of the most decisive is the extent to which the action of the group is oriented to violent conflict or to peaceful exchange as its end. Besides these, many special circumstances, which can only be discussed in a detailed analysis, may be of crucial importance. It is not surprising that this development is least conspicuous in groups which pursue purely ideal ends by peaceful means. Often the degree of closure against outsiders is closely related to the development of solidarity or of representation. But this is by no means always the case.

1. This 'imputation' of responsibility may in practice involve both active and passive solidarity. All the participants may be held responsible for the action of any one just as he himself is, and similarly may be entitled to enjoy any benefits resulting from his action. This responsibility may be owed to spirits or gods, that is, involve a religious orientation. Or, on the other hand, it may be responsibility to other human beings, as regulated by convention or by law. Examples of regulation by convention are blood revenge carried out against or with the help of members of the kin-group, reprisals against the inhabitants of the town or the country of the offender; of the legal type, formal punishment of relatives, members of the household or fellow-members of a communal group, instead of, or in addition to, the actual offender, and personal liability of members of a household or of a commercial partnership for each other's debts. Solidarity in relation to gods has also had very significant historical results. For instance, in the covenant of Israel with Jahveh, in early Christianity, and in the early Puritan community.

On the other hand, the imputation of solidarity may mean no more than that the participants in a closed social relationship, by virtue of the traditional or legal order, are held legally entitled to enjoy some kind of access to advantages and benefits, especially economic, which a representative has procured. Examples are the control over the powers exer-

[75] *Vertretungsgewalt.*

cised by the 'executive committee' of a club or association, or by the responsible agent of a political or economic association over resources which, as specified in the order, are meant to serve the corporate purpose of the group.

2. Solidarity is typically found in the following cases: (a) In traditional, communal groups based on birth or the sharing of a common life; for example, the household and the kinship unit; (b) in closed relationships which maintain a monopolized position, and control over the corresponding benefits by their own power. The typical case is corporate political groups, especially in the past. But the same situation exists to-day to a high degree, most strikingly in time of war; (c) in profit-making organizations where the participants personally conduct the business. The type case is the business partnership; (d) in some cases, in labour organizations. An example is the Artel. Representation is most frequently found in associations devoted to specific purposes and in legally organized groups, especially when funds have been collected and must be administered in the interests of the group. This will be further discussed in the Sociology of Law.

3. Representative authority is conferred according to 'criteria' (see above) in such cases as when it goes by seniority or some other such rule.

4. It is not possible to carry the analysis of this subject further in general terms. Its elaboration must be reserved to detailed investigation of particular fields. The most ancient and most universal phenomenon in this field is that of reprisal, meant either as revenge or as a means of gaining control of hostages, or some other kind of security against future injury.

12: THE CONCEPT OF 'CORPORATE GROUP' AND ITS TYPES

A social relationship which is either closed or limits the admission of outsiders by rules, will be called a 'corporate group' (*Verband*) [76] so far as its order is enforced by the action of specific individuals whose regu-

[76] The term *Verband*, which is one of the most important in Weber's scheme, has, in the technical sense defined in this paragraph, been translated as 'corporate group.' 'Association' has not been used because it does not imply the formal differentiation between a head or chief and ordinary members. A 'corporation' is, from this point of view, one specific kind of corporate group. The term *Leiter* is not readily translatable. 'Chief' has most frequently been used because it seems to have less objectionable connotations than any alternative. Thus we speak of the 'chief' of the medical staff of a hospital and use the term in other similar connexions.

lar function this is, of a chief or 'head' (*Leiter*) and usually also an administrative staff. These functionaries will normally also have representative authority. The incumbency of a directing position or participation in the functions of the administrative staff constitute 'governing authority' (*Regierungsgewalt*). This may be appropriated, or it may be assigned in accordance with the binding rules of the association according to specific criteria or procedures. It may be assigned permanently, for a term, or for dealing with a specific situation. 'Corporate action' is either the action of the administrative staff, which by virtue of its governing or representative authority is oriented to carrying out the terms of its order, or it is the action of the members as directed by the administrative staff.

1. It is indifferent, so far as the concept is concerned, whether the relationship is of a communal or associative character. It is sufficient for there to be a person or persons in authority—the head of a family, the executive committee of an association, a managing director, a prince, a president, the head of a church—whose action is concerned with carrying into effect the order governing the corporate group. This criterion is decisive because it is not merely a matter of action which is *oriented* to an order, but which is specifically directed to its *enforcement*. Sociologically this adds to the concept of a closed social relationship, a further element, which is of far-reaching empirical importance. For by no means every closed communal or associative relationship is a corporate group. For instance, this is not true of an erotic relationship or of a kinship group without a formalized system of authority.

2. Whether or not a corporate group exists is entirely a matter of the presence of a person in authority, with or without an administrative staff. More precisely, it exists so far as there is a probability that certain persons will act in such a way as to tend to carry out the order governing the group; that is, that persons are present who can be counted on to act in this way whenever the occasion arises. For purposes of definition, it is indifferent what is the basis of the relevant expectation, whether it is a case of traditional or affectual devotion to duty, or a case of devotion by virtue of rational values, any of which may be involved in feudal fealty, loyalty to an office or to a service. It may, on the other hand, be a matter of expediency, as, for instance, a pecuniary interes in the attached salary. Thus for purposes of the terminology of this discussion, the corporate group does not 'exist' apart from the probability that a course of

action oriented in this way will take place. If there is no probability of this type of action on the part of a particular group of persons or of a given individual, there is in these terms only a social relationship, but no corporate group. On the other hand, so long as there is a probability of such action, the corporate group, as a sociological phenomenon, continues to exist, in spite of the fact that the specific individuals whose action is oriented to the order in question, may have been completely changed. The concept has been defined intentionally to include precisely this phenomenon.

3. It is possible (a) that, in addition to the action of the administrative staff itself or that which takes place under its direction, there may be other cases where action of the members is intended to uphold the authority of the order; for instance, contributions or 'liturgies'[77] and certain types of personal services, such as jury service or military service. It is also possible (b) for the binding order to include norms to which it is expected that the action of the members of a corporate group will be oriented in respects other than those pertaining to the affairs of the corporate group as a unit. For instance, the law of the state includes rules governing private economic relations which are not concerned with the enforcement of the state's legal order as such, but with action in the service of private interests. This is true of most of the 'civil' law. In the first case (a) one may speak of action 'oriented to corporate affairs' (*Verbandsbezogenes Handeln*); in the second (b) of action 'subject to corporate regulation' (*Verbandsgeregeltes Handeln*). It is only in the cases of the action of the administrative staff itself and of that deliberately directed by it that the term 'corporate action' (*Verbandshandeln*) will be used. Examples of corporate action would be participation in any capacity in a war fought by a state, or a contribution paid in accordance with a levy authorized by the executive committee of an association, or a contract entered into by the person in authority, the validity of which is recognized by the members and its consequences carried out by them. Further, all administration of justice and administrative procedure belongs in this category.[78]

[77] Weber here uses the term 'liturgies' not in the current religious sense but in that of the institution characteristic of the classical Greek city state. This consisted in the provision of entertainments or services for the public ostensibly as a voluntary gift of an individual, but which were in fact obligatory on persons occupying a given status or office. Weber later uses this term in a technical sense which is defined in chapter ii, sec. 12.—ED.

[78] See also, sec. 14 below.

A corporate group may be either autonomous or heteronomous, either autocephalous or heterocephalous. Autonomy means that the order governing the group has been established by its own members on their own authority, regardless of how this has taken place in other respects. In the case of heteronomy, it has been imposed by an outside agency. Autocephaly means that the chief and his staff act by the authority of the autonomous order of the corporate group itself, not, as in the case of heterocephaly, that they are under the authority of outsiders. Again, this is regardless of any other aspects of the relationship.

A case of heterocephaly is the appointment of the governors of the Canadian provinces by the central government of the Dominion. It is possible for a heterocephalous group to be autonomous and an autocephalous group to be heteromous. It is also possible in both respects for a corporate group to have both characters at the same time in different spheres. The member-states of the German Empire, a federal state, were autocephalous. But in spite of this, within the sphere of authority of the Reich, they were heteronomous; whereas, within their own sphere, in such matters as religion and education, they were autonomous. Alsace-Lorraine was, under German jurisdiction, in a limited degree autonomous, but at the same time heterocephalous in that the governor was appointed by the Kaiser. All these elements may be present in the same situation to some degree. A corporate group, which is at the same time completely heteronomous and completely heterocephalous, is usually best treated as a 'part' of the more extensive group, as would ordinarily be done with a 'regiment' as part of an army. But whether this is the case depends on the actual extent of independence in the orientation of action in the particular case. For terminological purposes, it is entirely a question of convenience.

13: TYPES OF ORDER IN CORPORATE GROUPS

The legally-established order of an associative relationship may originate in one of two ways: by voluntary agreement, or by being imposed (*oktroyiert*) and acquiesced in. The governing authority of a corporate group may claim a legitimate right to impose new rules. The 'constitution' (*Verfassung*) of a corporate group is the empirically existing probability, varying in extent, kind, and conditions, that rules imposed by the governing authority will be acceded to. The system of order may, among these conditions, in particular specify that certain groups or sections of the members must consent, or at least have been heard. Besides this, there may be any number of other conditions.

The system of order of a corporate group may be imposed, not only on its members, but also on non-members who conform to certain criteria. This is especially likely to be true in so far as people are related to a given territorial area, by virtue of residence, birth, or the performance of certain actions within the area. An order which controls by virtue of these criteria possesses 'territorial validity' (*Gebietsgeltung*). A corporate group, the governing order of which is in principle concerned with territorial validity, will be called a 'territorial corporate group' (*Gebietsverband*). This usage will be employed regardless of how far the claim to the authority of its order over its own members is confined to matters pertaining to the area. Such limitation is possible [79] and certainly occurs to some extent.

1. For purposes of this investigation, an order is always 'imposed' to the extent that it does not originate from a voluntary personal agreement of all the individuals concerned. The concept of imposition hence includes 'majority rule,' in that the minority must submit. For that reason there have been long periods when the legitimacy of majority rule has either not been recognized at all, or been held doubtful. This was true in the case of the estates of the Middle Ages, and in very recent times, in the Russian *Obschtschina*. This will be further discussed in the Sociology of Law and of Authority.

2. Even in cases where there is formally 'voluntary' agreement, it is very common, as is generally known, for there to be a large measure of imposition. This is true of the *Obschtschina*. In that case, it is the actual state of affairs which is decisive for sociological purposes.

3. The concept of constitution made use of here is that also used by Lassalle. It is not the same as what is meant by a 'written' constitution, or indeed by 'constitution' in any sort of legal meaning. The only relevant

[79] The concept 'objective possibility' (*objektive Möglichkeit*) plays an important technical role in Weber's methodological studies. According to his usage, a thing is 'objectively possible' if it 'makes sense' to conceive it as an empirically existing entity. It is a question of conforming with the formal, logical conditions. The question whether a phenomenon which is in this sense 'objectively possible' will actually be found with any significant degree of probability or approximation, is a logically distinct question.—ED.

question for sociological purposes is when, for what purposes, and *within what limits,* or possibly under what special conditions (such as the approval of gods or priests or the consent of electors), the members of the corporate group will submit to the governing authority. Furthermore, under what circumstances in these respects the administrative staff and the corporate action of the group will be at the disposal of the supreme authority when it issues orders, or, in particular, imposes new rules.

4. The best cases of the imposition of an order within a territory are the precepts of criminal law and various other legal rules. In such cases political corporate groups use the criteria of whether the actor was resident, born, performed or completed the action, within the area controlled by the corporate group, to decide on the applicability of the rules.[80]

14: TYPES OF ORDER GOVERNING ACTION IN CORPORATE GROUPS

A system of order which governs corporate action as such, will be called an 'administrative' order (*Verwaltungsordnung*). A system of order which governs other kinds of social action and thereby protects the actors in enjoyment of the benefits derived from their relation to the order, will be called a 'regulative' order (*Regulierungsordnung*). So far as a corporate group is solely oriented to the first type of order, it will be called an 'administrative' group (*Verwaltungsverband*). So far as it is oriented to the second type, a 'regulative' group.

1. It goes without saying that the majority of actual corporate groups partake of both characteristics. The type of state, which was the ideal of the theory of absolute laissez faire, would be an example of a purely regulative corporate group. This would, however, assume that the control of the monetary system was left entirely to private enterprise.

2. On the concept of 'corporate action,' see above, sec. 12, para. 3. Under the concept of administrative order would be included all the rules which govern, not only the action of the administrative staff, but also that of the members in their direct relations to the corporate group. This latter type consists in action in the service of ends, the attainment of which is made mandatory in the system of order governing the group, and for which a positive course of action has deliberately been laid down in advance with directions for its execution by the administrative staff and by the members. In a completely communistic economic system, a

---

[80] Compare the concept of *Gebietskörperschaft* as used by Gierke and Preuss.

situation would be approximated where all social action was of this character. In a laissez-faire state, on the other hand, it would include only the functions of judges, police authorities, jurors, soldiers, legislators, and of the general public in the capacity of voters. The distinction between administrative and regulative order coincides in its broad lines, though not always in detail, with the distinction of political theory between public and private law. All further details are treated in the Sociology of Law.

15: TYPES OF ORGANIZATION AND OF CORPORATE GROUPS

An 'organization' (*Betrieb*) is a system of continuous purposive activity of a specified kind. A 'corporate organization' (*Betriebsverband*) is an associative social relationship characterized by an administrative staff devoted to such continuous purposive activity.

A 'voluntary association' (*Verein*) is a corporate group originating in a voluntary agreement and in which the established order claims authority over the members only by virtue of a personal act of adherence.

A 'compulsory association' (*Anstalt*) is a corporate group the established order of which has, within a given specific sphere of activity, been successfully imposed on every individual who conforms with certain specific criteria.[81]

1. The administration of political and ecclesiastical affairs and of the business of associations is included in the concept of 'organization' so far as it conforms to the criterion of continuity.

2. Voluntary and compulsory associations are both types of corporate groups where action is subject to a rationally established order. Or, more accurately, so far as a corporate group has a rationally established order, it will be called a voluntary or compulsory association. The type case of a compulsory association is the state, along with all its subsidiary heterocephalous groups. But, so far as its order is rationally established, the

---

[81] *Betrieb* is a word which in German has a number of different meanings in different contexts. It is only in the present technical use that it will be translated by 'organization.' It should, however, be recognized that the term 'organization' is here also used in a technical sense which conforms with Weber's explicit definition. The distinction of *Verein* and *Anstalt* is one of far-reaching sociological importance, which has not become established in English usage. The terms 'voluntary' and 'compulsory' association seem to be as adequate as any available terms. They should, however, not be interpreted on a common-sense basis but referred to Weber's explicit definitions.—ED.

church [82] is also included. The order governing a compulsory association claims to be binding on all persons to whom the particular relevant criteria apply—such as birth, residence, or the use of certain facilities. It makes no difference whether the individual has, as in the case of a voluntary association, personally assumed the obligation; nor does it matter whether he has taken any part in establishing the order. It is thus a case of imposed order in the most definite sense. One of the most important fields of the compulsory association is the control of territorial areas.

3. The distinction between voluntary and compulsory associations is relative in its empirical application. The rules of a voluntary association may affect the interests of non-members, and recognition of the validity of these rules may be imposed upon them by usurpation or by the exercise of the naked power of the association, as well as by processes of legal promulgation, as in the case of the law governing corporate securities.

4. It is hardly necessary to emphasize that the concepts of voluntary and compulsory associations are by no means exhaustive of all conceivable types of corporate groups. Furthermore, they are to be thought of only as 'polar' antitheses. In the religious sphere, the corresponding types are 'sect' and 'church.'

16: POWER, AUTHORITY, AND IMPERATIVE CONTROL

'Power' (*Macht*) is the probability that one actor within a social relationship will be in a position to carry out his own will despite resistance, regardless of the basis on which this probability rests.

'Imperative control' (*Herrschaft*) [83] is the probability that a command with a given specific content will be obeyed by a given group of persons. 'Discipline' is the probability that by virtue of habituation a command will receive prompt and automatic obedience in stereotyped forms, on the part of a given group of persons.

---

[82] 'Church' (*Kirche*) also is here used in a technical sense. We speak of the 'Baptist Church,' but in Weber's technical terms this is not a church but a sect. The Roman Catholic Church, on the other hand, since it claims jurisdiction over all children of Catholic parents, *is* a church in the technical sense.—ED.

[83] As has already been noted, the term *Herrschaft* has no satisfactory English equivalent. The term 'imperative control,' however, as used by N. S. Timasheff in his *Introduction to the Sociology of Law* is close to Weber's meaning and has been borrowed for the most general purposes. In a majority of instances, however, Weber is concerned with *legitimate Herrschaft*, and in these cases 'authority' is both an accurate and a far less awkward translation. *Macht*, as Weber uses it, seems to be quite adequately rendered by 'power.'—ED.

1. The concept of power is highly comprehensive from the point of view of sociology. All conceivable qualities of a person and all conceivable combinations of circumstances may put him in a position to impose his will in a given situation. The sociological concept of imperative control must hence be more precise and can only mean the probability that a *command* will be obeyed.

2. The concept of 'discipline' includes the 'habituation' characteristic of uncritical and unresisting mass obedience.

The existence of imperative control turns only on the actual presence of one person successfully issuing orders to others; it does not necessarily imply either the existence of an administrative staff, or, for that matter, of a corporate group. It is, however, uncommon to find it not associated with at least one of these. A corporate group, the members of which are by virtue of their membership subjected to the legitimate exercise of imperative control, that is to 'authority,' will be called an 'imperatively co-ordinated' group [84] (*Herrschaftsverband*).

1. The head of a household exercises authority without an administrative staff. A Beduin chief, who levies contributions from the caravans, persons, and shipments of goods which pass his stronghold, exercises imperative control over the total group of changing and indeterminate individuals who, though they are not members of any corporate group as such, have gotten themselves into a particular common situation. But to do this, he needs a following which, on the appropriate occasions, serves as his administrative staff in exercising the necessary compulsion. This type of imperative control is, however, conceivable as carried out by a single individual without the help of any administrative staff.

2. If it possesses an administrative staff, a corporate group is always, by virtue of this fact, to some degree imperatively co-ordinated. But the concept is relative. The usual imperatively co-ordinated group is at the same time an administrative organization. The character of the corporate group is determined by a variety of factors: the mode in which the administration is carried out, the character of the personnel, the objects over which it exercises control, and the extent of effective jurisdiction of its authority. The first two factors in particular are dependent in the highest degree on the way in which the authority is legitimized.[85]

[84] In this case imperative control is confined to the legitimate type, but it is not possible in English to speak here of an 'authoritarian' group. The citizens of any state, no matter how 'democratic,' are 'imperatively controlled' because they are subject to law.—ED.

[85] On the bases of legitimacy. See below, chap. iii.

17: POLITICAL AND RELIGIOUS CORPORATE GROUPS

An imperatively co-ordinated corporate group will be called 'political' if and in so far as the enforcement of its order is carried out continually within a given *territorial* area by the application and threat of physical force on the part of the administrative staff. A compulsory political association with continuous organization (*politischer Anstaltsbetrieb*) will be called a 'state' if and in so far as its administrative staff successfully upholds a claim to the *monopoly* of the *legitimate* use of physical force in the enforcement of its order. A system of social action, especially that of a corporate group, will be spoken of as 'politically oriented' if and in so far as it aims at exerting influence on the directing authorities of a corporate political group; especially at the appropriation, expropriation, redistribution or allocation of the powers of government.

An imperatively co-ordinated corporate group will be called a 'hierocratic' group (*hierokratischer Verband*) if and in so far as for the enforcement of its order it employs 'psychic' coercion through the distribution or denial of religious benefits ('hierocratic coercion'). A compulsory hierocratic association with continuous organization will be called a 'church' if and in so far as its administrative staff claims a monopoly of the legitimate use of hierocratic coercion.

1. It goes without saying that the use of physical force is neither the sole, nor even the most usual, method of administration of political corporate groups. On the contrary, their heads have employed all conceivable means to bring about their ends. But, at the same time, the threat of force, and in case of need its actual use, is the method which is specific to political associations and is always the last resort when others have failed. Conversely, physical force is by no means limited to political groups even as a legitimate method of enforcement. It has been freely used by kinship groups, household groups, the medieval guilds under certain circumstances, and everywhere by all those entitled to bear arms. In addition to the fact that it uses, among other means, physical force to enforce its system of order, the political group is further characterized by the fact that the authority of its administrative staff is claimed as binding within a territorial area and this claim is upheld by force. Whenever corporate groups which make use of force are also characterized by the claim to territorial jurisdiction, such as village communities or even

some household groups, federations of guilds or of trade unions, they are by definition to that extent political groups.

2. It is not possible to define a political corporate group, including the state, in terms of the end to which its corporate action is devoted. All the way from provision for subsistence to the patronage of art, there is no conceivable end which *some* political corporation has not at some time pursued. And from the protection of personal security to the administration of justice, there is none which *all* have recognized. Thus it is possible to define the 'political' character of a corporate group only in terms of the *means* peculiar to it, the use of force. This means is, however, in the above sense specific, and is indispensable to its character. It is even, under certain circumstances, elevated into an end in itself.

This usage does not exactly conform to everyday speech. But the latter is too inconsistent to be used for technical purposes. We speak of the 'open market' policy [86] of a central bank, of the 'financial' policy of an association, of the 'educational' policy of a local authority, and mean the systematic treatment and control of a particular problem. It comes considerably closer to the present meaning when we distinguish the 'political' aspect or implication of a question. Thus there is the 'political' official, the 'political' newspaper, the 'political' revolution, the 'political' club, the 'political' party, and the 'political' consequences of an action, as distinguished from others such as the economic, cultural, or religious aspect of the persons, affairs or processes in question. In this usage we generally mean by 'political,' things that have to do with relations of authority within what is, in the present terminology, a political organization, the state. The reference is to things which are likely to uphold, to change or overthrow, to hinder or promote, the interests of the state, as distinguished from persons, things, and processes which have nothing to do with it. This usage thus seeks to bring out the common features of the various *means* of exercising authority which are used within the state in enforcing its order, abstracting them from the ends they serve. Hence it is legitimate to claim that the definition put forward here is only a more precise formulation of what is meant in everyday usage in that it gives sharp emphasis to what is the most characteristic of these means, the actual or threatened use of force. It is, of course, true that everyday

[86] The German is *Devisenpolitik*. Translation in this context is made more difficult by the fact that the German language does not distinguish between 'politics' and 'policy,' *Politik* having both meanings. The remarks which Weber makes about various kinds of policy would have been unnecessary, had he written originally in English.—ED.

usage applies the term 'political,' not only to groups which are the direct agents of the legitimate use of force itself, but also to other, often wholly peaceful groups, which attempt to influence politically corporate action. It seems best for present purposes to distinguish this type of social action, 'politically oriented' action, from political action as such, the actual *corporate* action of political groups.

3. Since the concept of the state has only in modern times reached its full development, it is best to define it in terms appropriate to the modern type of state, but at the same time, in terms which abstract from the values of the present day, since these are particularly subject to change. The primary formal characteristics of the modern state are as follows: It possesses an administrative and legal order subject to change by legislation, to which the organized corporate activity of the administrative staff, which is also regulated by legislation, is oriented. This system of order claims binding authority, not only over the members of the state, the citizens, most of whom have obtained membership by birth, but also to a very large extent, over all action taking place in the area of its jurisdiction. It is thus a compulsory association with a territorial basis. Furthermore, to-day, the use of force is regarded as legitimate only so far as it is either permitted by the state or prescribed by it. Thus the right of a father to discipline his children is recognized—a survival of the former independent authority of the head of a household, which in the right to use force has sometimes extended to a power of life and death over children and slaves. The claim of the modern state to monopolize the use of force is as essential to it as its character of compulsory jurisdiction and of continuous organization.

4. In formulating the concept of a hierocratic corporate group, it is not possible to use the character of the religious sanctions it commands, whether worldly or other-worldly, material or spiritual, as the decisive criterion. What is important is rather the fact that its control over these sanctions can form the basis of a system of spiritual imperative control over human beings. What is most characteristic of the church, even in the common usage of the term, is the fact that it is a rational, compulsory association with continuous organization and that it claims a monopolistic authority. It is normal for a church to strive for complete imperative control on a territorial basis and to attempt to set up the corresponding territorial or parochial organization. So far as this takes place, the means by which this claim to monopoly is upheld, will vary from case to case. But historically, its control over territorial areas has not been

nearly so essential to the church as to political corporations; and this is particularly true to-day. It is its character as a compulsory association, particularly the fact that one becomes a member of the church by birth, which distinguishes a church from a 'sect.' It is characteristic of the latter that it is a voluntary association and admits only persons with specific religious qualifications. This subject will be further discussed in the Sociology of Religion.[87]

[87] This reference is presumably to the section entitled *Religionssoziologie* which is published as part ii, chap. iv of *Wirtschaft und Gesellschaft,* but is not included in the present translation. In it Weber attempted a systematic typological analysis of the social aspects of religious phenomena. This chapter should not be confused with the three volumes of the *Gesammelte Aufsätze zur Religionssoziologie* which consist of a series of comparative empirical studies of particular religious systems in terms of their bearing on the development of modern capitalism. In the section of *Wirtschaft und Gesellschaft* which he refers to Weber has attempted a more connected and complete typological analysis than is to be found in the comparative study.—ED.

II. Sociological Categories of Economic Action

PREFATORY NOTE

WHAT follows is not intended in any sense to be 'economic theory.' Rather, it consists only in an attempt to define certain concepts which are frequently used and to analyze certain of the simplest sociological relationships in the economic sphere. As in the first chapter, the procedure here has been determined entirely by considerations of convenience. It has proved possible entirely to avoid the controversial concept of 'value.'[1] The usage here, in the relevant sections on the division of labour, has deviated from the terminology of Karl Bücher only so far as seemed necessary for the purposes of the present undertaking. For the present all questions of dynamic process will be left out of account.

1: THE CONCEPT OF ECONOMIC ACTION

Action will be said to be 'economically oriented' so far as, according to its subjective meaning, it is concerned with the satisfaction of a desire for 'utilities' (*Nutzleistungen*). 'Economic action' (*Wirtschaften*) is a peaceful use of the actor's control over resources, which is primarily economically oriented. Economically rational action is action which is rationally oriented, by deliberate planning, to economic ends. An 'economic system' (*Wirtschaft*) is an autocephalous system of economic action. An 'economic organization' (*Wirtschaftsbetrieb*) is a continuously organized system of economic action.

1. It was pointed out above, sec. 1, (b), para. 2, pp. 112-13, that economic action as such need not be social action.

2. The definition of economic action must be as general as possible and must bring out the fact that all 'economic' processes and objects are characterized as such entirely by the meaning they have for human action

[1] In the economic sense.—ED.

in such roles as ends, means, obstacles, and by-products. It is not, however, permissible to express this by saying, as is sometimes done, that economic action is a 'psychic' phenomenon. The production of goods, prices, or even the 'subjective valuation' of goods, if they are empirical processes, are far from being merely psychic phenomena. But underlying this misleading phrase is a correct insight. It is a fact that these phenomena have a peculiar type of subjective meaning. This alone defines the unity of the corresponding processes, and this alone makes them accessible to subjective interpretation.

It is further necessary to formulate the concept of economic action in such a way as to include the modern market economy; so it is not possible to take consumers' wants, and their 'satisfaction,' as a point of departure. The concept must take account, on the one hand, of the fact that utilities are actually sought after—including among them orientation to pecuniary acquisition for its own sake. But, on the other hand, it must also include the fact, which is true even of the most primitive self-sufficient economy, that attempts, however primitive and traditionally limited, are made to assure the satisfaction of such desires by some kind of activity.

3.[2] As distinguished from economic action as such, the term 'economically oriented action' will be applied to two types: (a) every action which, though primarily oriented to other ends, takes account, in the pursuit of them, of economic considerations; that is, of the consciously recognized necessity for economic prudence. Or (b) that which, though primarily oriented to economic ends, makes use of physical force as a means. It thus includes all primarily non-economic action and all non-peaceful action which is influenced by economic considerations. Economic action involves a conscious, primary orientation to economic considerations. It must be conscious, for what matters is not the objective necessity of making economic provision, but the belief that it is necessary.[3]

4. Every type of action, including the use of violence, may be economically oriented. This is true of war-like action in such cases as marauding

---

[2] At this point in the German text there is an error in the numbering of the paragraphs, the number 2 being repeated. It has seemed best to correct this, and the following comments are numbered 3 to 8 incl. instead of 2 to 7. This will, of course, have to be taken account of in any comparison with the original.—ED.

[3] Robert Liefmann has rightly laid emphasis on the subjective character of the concept; that is, the fact that it is the subjectively understandable orientation of action which makes it economic action. He is not, however, correct in attributing the contrary view to all other authorities.

expeditions and trade wars. Franz Oppenheimer, in particular, has rightly distinguished 'economic means' from 'political means.' It is essential to distinguish the latter from economic action. The use of force is unquestionably very strongly opposed to the spirit of economic acquisition in the usual sense. Hence the term 'economic action' will not be applied to the direct appropriation of goods by force and the direct coercion of the other party by threats of force. It goes without saying that exchange is not the *only* economic means, though it is one of the most important. Furthermore, the formally peaceful provision for the means and the success of a projected exercise of force, as in the case of armaments and economic organization for war, is just as much economic action, as any other.

Every course of rational political action is economically oriented with respect to provision for the necessary means, and it is always possible for political action to serve the interest of economic ends. Similarly, though it is not necessarily true of every economic system, certainly the modern economic order under modern conditions could not continue if its control of resources were not upheld by the legal compulsion of the state; that is, if its formally 'legal' rights were not upheld by the threat of force. But the fact that an economic system is thus dependent on protection by force, does not mean that it is itself an example of the use of force.

It is entirely untenable to maintain that economic action, however defined, is only a *means* by contrast, for instance, with the state, as an end in itself. This becomes evident from the fact that it has been possible to define the state itself only in terms of the means which it attempts to monopolize, the use of force. If anything, the most essential aspect of economic action for practical purposes is the prudent choice between alternative ends. This choice is, however, oriented to the scarcity of the means which are available or could be procured for these various ends.

5. Not every type of action which is rational in its choice of means will be called rational economic action, or even economic action in any sense; in particular, the term 'economy' will be distinguished from that of 'technology.' [4] The term 'technology' applied to an action refers to the totality of means employed as opposed to the meaning or end to which the action is, in the last analysis, oriented. Rational technique is a choice

---

[4] The German word *Technik* which Weber uses here covers both the meanings of the English word 'technique' and of 'technology.' Since the distinction is not explicitly made in Weber's terminology, it will have to be introduced according to the context in the translation.

of means which is consciously and systematically oriented to the experience and reflection of the actor, which consists, at the highest level of rationality, in scientific knowledge. What is concretely to be treated as a 'technology' is thus variable. The ultimate significance of a concrete act may, seen in the context of the total system of action, be of a 'technical' order; that is, it may be significant only as a means in this broader context. Then concretely the meaning of the particular act lies in its technical result; and, conversely, the means which are applied in order to accomplish this are its 'techniques.' In this sense there are techniques of every conceivable type of action, techniques of prayer, of asceticism, of thought and research, of memorizing, of education, of exercising political or religious control, of administration, of making love, of making war, of musical performances, of sculpture and painting, of arriving at legal decisions. All these are capable of the widest variation in degree of rationality. The presence of a 'technical question' always means that there is some doubt over the choice of the most efficient means to an end. Among others, the standard of efficiency for a technique may be the famous principle of 'least action,' the achievement of the *optimum* result with the least expenditure of resources, not the achievement of a result regardless of its quality, with the absolute minimum of expenditure.

There is, of course, an analogous principle governing economic action, as is true of every sort of rational action. But in this case it has a different meaning. As long as only questions of technology in the present sense are involved, the only considerations relevant are those bearing on the achievement of this particular end, the pursuit of which is accepted as desirable without question. Given this end, it is a matter of the choice of the most 'economical' means, account being taken of the quality, the certainty, and the permanence of the result. Means, that is, are compared only in terms of the immediate differences of expenditure involved in alternative ways of achieving the end. As long as it is purely a technical question, other wants are ignored. Thus, in a question of whether to make a technically necessary part of a machine out of iron or platinum, a decision on technical grounds alone would, so long as the requisite quantities of both metals for this particular purpose were available, consider only which of the two would in this case bring about the best result and would minimize the other comparable expenditures of resources, such as labour. But once consideration is extended to take account of the relative scarcity of iron and platinum in relation to their potential uses, as every technologist is accustomed to do even in the chemical laboratory, the action is no longer in the present sense purely technical, but *also* economic. From the economic point of view 'technical' questions always involve the consideration of 'costs.' This is a question of crucial importance for economic purposes and in this context always takes the form of asking what would be the effect on the satisfaction of other wants if this particular means were not used for satisfaction of one given want. The 'other wants' may be simultaneous with the one under consideration, but of a different kind, or they may be cases of allocation to the 'same' want at various different times.[5]

The question of what, in comparative terms, is the cost of the use of the various possible technical means for a single technical end depends in the last analysis on their potential usefulness as means to other ends. This is particularly true of labour. A technical problem in the present sense is, for instance, that of what equipment is necessary in order to move loads of a particular kind, or in order to raise mineral products from a given depth in a mine; further, among the alternatives it is a question of knowing which is the most efficient, that is, among other things, which achieves a given degree of success with the least expenditure of effort. It is, on the other hand, an economic problem how, on the assumption of an exchange economy, this equipment can be paid for in money through the sale of goods; or, on the assumption of a planned economy, how the necessary labour and other means of production can be provided without damage to the satisfaction of other wants held to be more urgent. In both cases, it is a problem of the comparison of ends. Economic action is primarily oriented to the problem of choosing the end to which a thing shall be applied; technology, to the problem, given the end, of choosing the appropriate means. For purposes of the theoretical definition of technical rationality it is wholly indifferent whether the product of a technical process is in any sense useful. In practice this is not, however, the case since economic elements are also involved in concrete cases. In the present terminology there could well be a rational technique even of achieving ends which no one desires. It would, for instance, be possible, as a kind of technical amusement, to apply all the most modern methods to the production of atmospheric air. And no one

---

[5] A similar position is taken by Von Gottl in vol. ii of the *Grundriss der Sozialökonomik*. An able and extended statement is to be found in the discussion of Robert Liefmann in his *Grundzüge der Allgemeinen Volkswirtschaftslehre*, pp. 336 ff. He does not, however, in content contribute anything which goes beyond Von Gottl's position. The attempt to reduce all means in the last analysis to the 'irksomeness of labour' will not stand criticism.

could take the slightest exception to the purely technical rationality of the action. Economically, on the other hand, the procedure would under normal circumstances be clearly irrational because there was no demand for the product.[6]

The fact that what is called the technological development of modern times has been so largely oriented economically to profit making is one of the fundamental facts of the history of technology. But however fundamental it has been, this economic orientation has by no means stood alone in shaping the development of technology. In addition, a part has been played by the imagination and cognitation of impractical dreamers, a part by other-worldly interests and all sorts of fantasies, a part by preoccupation with artistic problems, and by various other non-economic factors. None the less, the main emphasis at all times, including the present, has lain in the economic determination of technological development. Had not rational calculation formed the basis of economic activity, had there not been certain very particular conditions in its economic background, rational technology could never have come into existence.

The fact that the aspects of economic orientation, which distinguish it from technology, were not explicitly brought out in the initial definition, is a consequence of the sociological starting point. From a sociological point of view, the weighing of alternative ends in relation to each other and to costs is a consequence of 'continuity.' This is true at least so far as costs mean something other than altogether giving up one end in favour of more urgent ones. An economic theory, on the other hand, would do well to emphasize this criterion from the start.

6. It is essential to include the criterion of power of control and disposal (*Verfügungsgewalt*) [7] in the sociological concept of economic action if for no other reason than that an exchange economy involves a complete network of contractual relationships, each of which originates in a deliberately planned process of acquisition of powers of control and disposal. This, in such an economy, is the principal source of the relation of economic action to the law. But any other type of organization of economic activities would involve some kind of distribution of powers of control and disposal, however different its underlying principles might

[6] On all this, compare Von Gottl, op. cit.

[7] The term *Verfügungsgewalt*, of which Weber makes a great deal of use, is of legal origin, implying legally sanctioned powers of control and disposal. This, of course, has no place in a purely economic conceptual scheme but is essential to a sociological treatment of economic systems. It is another way of saying that concretely economic action depends on a system of property relations.—Ed.

be from those of modern private enterprise with its legal protection of autonomous and autocephalous economic units. Either the central authority, as in the case of socialism, or the subsidiary parts, as in anarchism, must be able to count on having some kind of control over the necessary services of labour and of the means of production. It is possible to obscure this fact by verbal devices, but it cannot be interpreted out of existence. For purposes of definition it is a matter of indifference in what way this control is guaranteed; whether by convention or by law, or whether, even, it does not enjoy the protection of any external sanctions at all, but its security rests only on actual expectations in terms of custom or self-interest. These possibilities must be taken into account, however essential legal compulsion may be for the modern economic order. The indispensability of powers of control for the concept of social action in its economic aspects thus does not imply that *legal* order is part of that concept by definition, however important it may be held to be on empirical grounds.

7. The concept of powers of control and disposal will here be taken to include the possibility of control over the actor's own labour power, whether this is in some way enforced or merely exists in fact. That this is not to be taken for granted is shown by its absence in the case of slaves.

8. It is necessary for the purposes of a sociological theory of economic organization to introduce the concept of 'goods' at an early stage, as is done in sec. 2. For this analysis is concerned with a type of action in which the primary significance is attributed to the *results* of the activity and of the calculations of the actors, even though the role of these can only analytically be distinguished from that of other elements. It is possible that economic theory could proceed differently, though its theoretical results form the basis of a sociology of economic action, however much the latter may find it necessary to theorize on its own account.

2: The Concept of Utility

By 'utilities' (*Nutzleistungen*) will always be meant the specific and concrete, real or imagined, advantages (*Chancen*) or means for present or future use as they are estimated and made an object of specific provision by one or more economically acting individuals. The action of these individuals is oriented to the estimated importance of such utilities as means for the ends of their economic action.

Utilities may be the services of non-human or inanimate objects or of human beings. Non-human objects which are the potential sources of utilities of whatever sort will be called 'goods.' Utilities derived from a human source, so far as this source consists in active conduct, will be called 'services.' Social relationships which are valued as a potential source of present or future disposal over utilities are, however, also objects of economic provision. The opportunities of economic advantage, which are made available by custom, by the constellation of interests, or by a conventional or legal order for the purposes of an economic unit, will be called 'economic advantages.'[8]

1. Goods and services do not exhaust the category of those aspects of his relation to the situation which may be important to an individual for economic purposes and which may hence be an object of economic concern. Such things as good will or the tolerance of economic measures on the part of individuals in a position to interfere with them, and numerous other forms of behaviour, may have the same kind of economic importance and may be the object of economic provision and even, for instance, of contracts. It would, however, result in a confusion of concepts to try to bring such things under either of these two categories. This choice of concepts is thus entirely determined by consideration of convenience.

2. As Böhm-Bawerk has correctly pointed out, it would also be a source of confusion if all the objects significant to life in everyday speech were designated without distinction as 'goods,' and then the concept of a good were identified with any non-human source of utility. In the strict sense of a source of utility it is not a 'horse' or a 'bar of iron' which is an economic 'good,' but the specific ways in which they can be put to desirable and practical uses; for instance, to haul loads, to carry weights, or something of the sort. Above all, the concrete objects dealt with in economic transactions such as purchase and sale, such things as a clientèle, a mortgage, and property, are not 'goods' for purposes of the present terminology. For purposes of simplification, the services of such physical objects when they are made available by a traditional or legal order, or the probable availability of disposal thus guaranteed within an economic system over the utilities of goods and services, will be called 'economic advantages' or 'advantages' without qualification, unless this is likely to be misunderstood.

[8] Compare Böhm-Bawerk, *Rechte und Verhältnisse vom Standpunkt der volkswirtschaftlichen Güterlehre.*

3. The fact that only active conduct, and not merely acquiescence, permission, or omission, are treated as 'services' is a matter of convenience. But it must be remembered that it follows from this that goods and services do not constitute an exhaustive classification of all economically significant utilities.

On the concept of 'labour,' see below, sec. 15.

3: Modes of the Economic Orientation of Action

Economic orientation may be a matter of tradition or of expediency. Even in cases where there is a high degree of rationalization of action, the element of traditional orientation remains considerable. For the most part, rational orientation is primarily significant for the action of the directing agencies, no matter under what form of organization. The development of rational economic action from its origins in the instinctively reactive search for food or in traditional acceptance of inherited techniques and customary social relationships has been to a large extent determined by non-economic events and actions, including those outside everyday routine [9] and also by the pressure of necessity in cases of increasing absolute or relative limitations on subsistence.

1. Naturally there cannot in principle be any scientific standard for any such concept as that of an 'original economic state.' It would be possible to agree arbitrarily to take the economic state on a given technological level, that characterized by the lowest development of tools and equipment, and to treat it and analyse it as the most primitive. But there is no scientific justification for concluding from observations of living primitive peoples on a low technological level that the economic organization of all peoples of the past with similar technological standing has been the same; for instance, as that of the Vedda or of certain tribes of the Amazon region. For, from an economic point of view, this level of technology is compatible with either a large-scale organization of labour or, conversely, its extreme dispersal in small groups.[10] It is impossible to infer which of these would be more nearly approached from the economic aspects of the natural environment alone. Various non-

[9] This is one of the many differences between China and the Western World which Weber related to the difference of orientation to economic activities, growing out of the religious differences of the two civilizations. See his study *Konfuzianismus und Taoismus, Gesammelte Aufsätze zur Religionssoziologie*, Vol. I.—ED.

[10] See below, sec. 16.

economic factors, for instance, military, could make a substantial difference.

2. To be sure, war and migration are not in themselves economic processes, though particularly in early times they have been largely oriented to economic considerations. At all times, however, indeed up to the present, they have often been responsible for radical changes in the economic system. In cases where, through such factors as climatic changes, inroads of sand, or deforestation, there has been an absolute decrease in the means of subsistence, human groups have adapted themselves in widely differing ways according to the structure of interest and to the ways in which non-economic factors have been involved. The typical modes have, however, been a fall in the standard of living and an absolute decrease in population. Similarly, in cases of relative impoverishment in means of subsistence, as determined by a given standard of living and of the distribution of economic advantages, there have also been wide variations. But on the whole, this type of situation has, more frequently than the other, been met by the increasing rationalization of economic activities. It is not, however, possible to discuss this in general terms. So far as the 'statistical' information can be relied upon, there was a tremendous increase of population in China after the beginning of the eighteenth century, but it had exactly the opposite effect from the similar phenomenon of about the same time in Europe. It is, however, possible to say at least something about the reasons for this.[11] The chronic scarcity of the means of subsistence in the Arabian desert has only at certain times resulted in a change in the economic and political structure. And these changes have been most prominent when non-economic religious developments have played a part.

3. A high degree of traditionalism in habits of life, such as characterized the labouring classes in early modern times, has not sufficed to prevent a great increase in the rationalization of economic enterprise under capitalistic direction. The same was, for instance, true of the socialistic rationalization of the taxation system in Egypt. Nevertheless, this traditionalistic attitude had to be at least partly overcome in the Western World before the further development to the specifically modern type of rational capitalistic economy could take place.

[11] See below, sec. 11.

4: TYPICAL MEASURES OF RATIONAL ECONOMIC ACTION

The following are typical measures of rational economic action:

(1) The systematic distribution, as between present and future, of utilities, on the control of which the actor for whatever reason feels able to count. (These are the essential features of saving.)

(2) The systematic distribution of available utilities as between their various potential uses in the order of their estimated relative urgency, according to the principle of marginal utility.

These two cases, the most definitely 'static,' have been most highly developed in times of peace. To-day, for the most part, they take the form of the allocation of money incomes.

(3) The systematic production of utilities through 'manufacture' (*Herstellung*) or transportation, for which all the necessary means of production are controlled by the actor himself. Where action is rational, this type of action will take place so far as, according to the actor's estimate, the urgency of his demand for the expected result of the action exceeds the necessary expenditure, which may consist in (a) the irksomeness of the requisite labour services, and (b) the other potential uses to which the requisite goods could be put; including, that is, the utility of the potential alternative products and their uses. This is 'production' in the broader sense which includes transportation.

(4) The systematic acquisition, by agreement with the present possessors or producers, of assured powers of control and disposal over utilities. The powers of control may or may not be shared with others. The occasion may lie in the fact that utilities themselves are in the control of others, that their means of production are in such control, or that third persons desire to acquire them in such a way as to endanger the actor's own supply.

The relevant associative relationships with the present possessor of a power of control or disposal may consist in (a) the establishment of a corporate group with an order to which the production and use of the utilities is to be oriented, or (b) in exchange. In the first case the purpose of the corporate group may be to ration the production, use, or consumption, in order to limit competition of producers. Then it is a regulative corporate group. Or, secondly, its purpose may be to set up a unified authority for the systematic administration of the utilities which had hitherto been subject to a dispersed control. In this case there is an administrative organization.

'Exchange' is a compromise of interests on the part of the parties in the course of which goods or other advantages are passed as mutual compensation reciprocally from the control of each to that of the others. The exchange may be traditional or conventional;[12] then, especially in the latter case, it is not economically rational. Or, secondly, it may be economically rational both in intention and in result. Every case of a rationally oriented exchange is the resolution of a previously open or latent conflict of interests by means of a compromise. The opposition of interests which is resolved in the compromise involves the actor potentially in two different conflicts. On the one hand, there is the conflict over the price to be agreed upon with the partner in exchange; the typical method is bargaining. On the other hand, there may also be competition against actual or potential rivals, either in the present or in the future, who are competitors for the same market. Here, the typical method is competitive bidding.

1. Utilities and the goods or labour, which are their sources, are at the disposal of an economically acting individual if he is in a position to be able in fact to make use of them at his convenience without interference from other persons, regardless of whether this ability rests on the legal order, on convention, on custom or on a complex of interests. It is by no means true that only the legal assurance of powers of disposal is decisive, either for the concept or in fact. It is, however, to-day empirically an indispensable basis for control of the material means of production.

2. The fact that goods are not as yet consumable may be a result of the fact that while they are, as such, finished, they are yet not in a suitable place for consumption; hence the transportation of goods, which is naturally to be distinguished from trade, a change in the control over the goods, may here be treated as part of the process of production.

3. When there is a lack of control over desired utilities, it is in principle indifferent whether the individual is typically prevented from attempting to use force to interfere with the control of others through a legal order, through convention, through custom, his own self-interest, or his consciously-held moral standards.

[12] It is a striking fact that, particularly in primitive society, a very large proportion of economically significant exchange is formally treated as an exchange of gifts. A return gift of suitable value is definitely obligatory but the specific characteristic of purely economically rational exchange, namely bargaining, is not only absent but is specifically prohibited.—ED.

4. Competition for the means of production may exist under the most various conditions. It is particularly important when supplies depend on territorial control, as in hunting, fishing, lumbering, pasturage, and clearing new land. It is also by no means uncommon for it to exist within a corporate group which is closed to outsiders. The order which seeks to restrain such competition then always consists in the rationing of supplies, usually combined with the appropriation of the advantages thus guaranteed for the benefit of a limited number of individuals or, more often, of households. All agricultural and fishing communities, the regulation of rights of clearing forests, of pasturage and wood gathering, in the common fields and waste, the manuring of Alpine meadows, and so on, have this character. Various types of hereditary property in land have been developed from this type of regulation.

5. Anything which may in any way be transferred from the control of one person to that of another and for which another is willing to give compensation, may be an object of exchange. It is not restricted to goods and services, but includes all kinds of economic advantages; for instance, good will, which exists only by custom or self-interest, and is not subject to any enforcement; in particular, however, it includes all manner of advantages, claims to which are enforceable under some kind of order. Thus, objects of exchange are not necessarily actual utilities.

For present purposes, by 'exchange' in the broadest sense will be meant every case of a formally voluntary agreement involving the offer of any sort of present, continuing, or future utility in exchange for utilities of any sort offered in return. Thus it includes turning over goods for money or placing their services at the disposal of the other party in exchange for a future return of the same kind of goods. It also includes any sort of permission for, or tolerance of, the use of an object in return for 'rent' or 'hire,' or the hiring of any kind of services for wages or salary. The fact that the last example involves, from a sociological point of view, the subjection of the worker to a system of authority and discipline will, for preliminary purposes, be neglected, as will the distinction between loan and purchase.[13]

6. The conditions of exchange may be traditional, partly traditional though enforced by convention, or rational. Examples of conventional exchanges are exchanges of gifts between friends, heroes, chiefs, princes;

[13] See below, sec. 15.

as, for instance, the exchange of armour between Diomedes and Glaucos. It is not uncommon for these to be rationally oriented and controlled to a high degree.[14] Rational exchange is only possible when both parties expect to profit from it, or when one is under compulsion because of his own need or the other's economic power. Exchange may serve either purposes of consumption or of acquisition.[15] It may thus be oriented to provision for the personal use of the actor or to opportunities for profit. In the first case, its conditions are to a large extent differentiated from case to case, and it is in this sense irrational. Thus, for instance, household surpluses will be valued according to the individual marginal utilities of the particular household economy and may on occasion be sold very cheaply. Under certain circumstances the fortuitous desires of the moment determine to a very high degree the marginal utility of goods which are sought in exchange. Thus the thresholds of exchangeability, as determined by marginal utility, are extremely variable. Rational competition develops only in the case of marketable goods and, to the highest degree, when goods are used and sold in a profit system.[16]

7. The modes of intervention of the regulatory system mentioned above,[17] are not the only possible ones, but merely those which are relevant here because they may immediately threaten sources of supply. The regulation of marketing processes will be discussed below.

5: Types of Economic Corporate Groups

According to its relation to the economic system, an economically oriented corporate group may be: (a) a group 'engaged in economic action' (*wirtschaftender Verband*) if the primarily non-economic corporate action oriented to its order includes economic action; (b) an 'economic organization' (*Wirtschaftsverband*) if its corporate action, as governed by the order, is *primarily* autocephalous economic action of a given kind; (c) an organization 'regulating economic activity' (*wirtschaftsregulierender Verband*) if and in so far as the autocephalous economic activity of the members is oriented to the order governing the group because the latter imposes regulations specifying its content; that is, it is heteronomous in that respect; (d) an organization 'enforcing a formal order'

---

[14] Compare the Tell-el-amarna documents.   [16] On these concepts, see secs. 8 and 11.
[15] See below, sec. 11.   [17] See page 168.

(*Ordnungsverband*) [18] if its order guarantees the autocephalous and autonomous activity of its members and the corresponding economic advantages by means of rules which are only formal.

Material control of economic activity cannot in practice be extended
beyond the point where the continuation of a certain type of economic
behaviour is still compatible with the essential requirements of the enterprise being controlled.

1. The state, except for the socialistic or communist type, and all other
corporate groups like churches and voluntary associations are groups
engaged in economic action if they manage their own financial affairs.
This is also true of educational institutions and all other organizations
which are not primarily economic.

2. In the category of economic organizations in the present sense are
included not only business corporations, co-operative associations, cartels,
partnerships, and so on, but all economic organizations which involve
the activities of a plurality of persons all the way from the workshop
relationship of artisans, to a conceivable communistic organization of the
whole world.

3. Organizations regulating economic activity are the following: village
communities, guilds, trade unions, employers' associations, cartels, and
all other groups, the directing authorities of which carry on an 'economic
policy' which seeks to regulate both the ends and the procedures of
economic activity. It thus includes the villages and towns of the Middle
Ages, just as much as a modern state which follows such a policy.

4. An example of a group confined to the enforcement of formal order
is the pure laissez-faire state, which would leave the economic activity of
individual households and enterprises entirely free and confine its regulation to the formal function of settling disputes connected with the fulfilment of free contractual obligations.

5. The existence of corporate groups regulating economic activity or
merely enforcing a formal order presupposes in principle a certain
amount of autonomy in the field of economic activity. Thus there is in
principle a sphere of free disposal over economic resources, though it may
be limited in varying degrees by means of rules to which the actors are

[18] The type case Weber has in mind is the relation of the state to the modern system
of property and contract. Whether or not private citizens will engage in any given activity
is not determined by the law. The latter is restricted to the enforcement of certain formal
rules governing whoever does engage in such activities.—ED.

oriented. This implies, further, at least a relative amount of appropriation of economic advantages over which the actors have, then, an autonomous control. The purest type of this regulation is thus present when all human action is autonomous in content and oriented only to formal conditions of regulation and when all non-human sources of utility are completely appropriated so that individuals can have free disposal of them, especially through exchange. This is the fundamental principle of the modern property system. Any other kind of limitation on appropriation and autonomy implies the regulation of economic activity because it determines the orientation of human activities.

6. The empirical line between the regulation of economic activity and its mere subjection to a formal order is indefinite. For, naturally, the type of formal order not only may, but must, in some way exert a material influence on action; in some cases, a fundamental influence. Numerous modern legal ordinances, which claim to do no more than set up formal rules, are so drawn up that they actually exert a material influence.[19] Indeed, a really strict limitation to purely formal rules is possible only in theory. Many of the recognized principles of the law, of a kind which cannot be dispensed with, imply to an appreciable degree important limitations on the content of economic activity. Especially 'enabling provisions' can under certain circumstances, as in corporation law, involve quite appreciable limitations on economic autonomy.

7. The limits of the material regulation of economic activity may be reached when it results in (a) the abandonment of certain kinds of economic activity, as when a tax on turnover leads to the cultivation of land only for consumption; or (b) in evasion, in such cases as smuggling, bootlegging, etc.

6: MEDIA OF EXCHANGE, MEANS OF PAYMENT, MONEY

An object offered in exchange will be called a 'medium of exchange' so far as it is typically accepted, primarily by virtue of the fact that the recipients estimate that they will, within the relevant space of time, be able to offer it in another exchange to procure other goods which satisfy their wants, regardless of whether it is exchangeable for *all* other goods or only for certain specific goods. The probability that the medium of exchange will be accepted at a given rate for specific other goods will

19 On this, see the Sociology of Law.

be called its 'purchasing power' [20] in relation to these. The use itself will be called the 'formal value.' [21]

An object will be called a 'means of payment' so far as its typical acceptance in payment of specific agreed or imposed obligations is guaranteed by convention or by law. This is the 'formal value' of the means of payment, which may also coincide with its formal value as a means of exchange. Means of exchange or of payment will be called 'chartal' (*Chartal*) [22] when they are artifacts which, by virtue of their specific form, enjoy a significant degree of conventional or legal, agreed or imposed, formal value within the membership of a group of persons or within a territorial area; and when (b) they are divisible in such a way that they represent a particular unit of value or a multiple or a fraction of it, so that it is possible to use them in arithmetical calculations.

Money is a chartal means of payment which is also a means of exchange.

One of the functions of a corporate group may be within the sphere of authority of its order, to maintain by convention of law the formal value of money or of some other means of exchange or of payment. These will be termed internal money, means of exchange or of payment. Means of exchange used in transactions with non-members will be called external means of exchange.

Means of exchange or of payment which are not chartal are 'natural' means. They may be differentiated (a) in technical terms according to their physical characteristics, consisting in such things as ornaments, clothing, useful objects of various sorts; or according to whether their value is a function of weight or not. They may also (b) be distinguished

[20] This distinction Weber expresses in German as that between *materiale Geltung* and *formale Geltung*. Though *Geltung* has been translated in the more general context of obligatoriness of an order as 'validity,' it seems best in the present context to follow the terminology used in current economic discussions in English. The term 'formal value' is, however, used in preference to 'legal,' as it is possible for it to rest on a conventional rather than on a legal basis.—Ed.

[21] At the beginning of this chapter Weber stated that he had found it possible to formulate its concepts without recourse to the controversial concept of 'value' (*Wert*) in the technical economic sense. The term he employs here is not *Wert* but *Geltung*. While in a legal context it is best translated as 'validity,' to do so here would be pedantic as value is far more in accord with ordinary economic usage. The apparent inconsistency with Weber's previous statement is thus not Weber's but one for which the translator must be held responsible.—Ed.

[22] This is a term which is not in general use in German economics, but which Weber took over, as he notes below, from G. F. Knapp. There seems to be no suitable English term and its use has hence been retained.—Ed.

economically according to whether they are used primarily as means of exchange or for purposes of social prestige, the prestige of possession. They may also be distinguished according to whether they are used as means of exchange and payment in internal transactions or in external.

Money means of exchange or of payment are 'tokens' so far as they do not or no longer possess a value independent of their use as means of exchange and of payment. They are, on the other hand, 'material' means so far as their value as such is influenced by their possible use for other purposes, or may be so influenced.

Money may consist either of coins or of notes. Notes are usually adapted to a system of coinage or have a name which is historically derived from it.

(1) Coined money will be called 'free' money or 'market' money so far as the monetary metal will be coined by the mint on the initiative of any possessor of it without limit of amount. This means that in effect the amount issued is determined by the demand of parties to market transactions.

(2) It will be called 'limited' money or 'administrative' money if the issue of coinage is formally subject to the decisions of the governing authority of a corporate group and is in effect primarily oriented to their fiscal needs.

(3) It will be called 'regulated' money if, though its issue is limited, the kind and amount of coinage is effectively subject to rules.

The term 'circulating medium' will be applied to paper money which functions as 'note' money, if it is accepted in normal transactions as 'provisional' money with the expectation that it can, at any time, be converted into 'definitive' money; that is, coins, or a given weight of monetary metal. It is a 'certificate' if this acceptance is conditioned by regulations which require full coverage in coin or bullion.

Within a jurisdiction the relative values of the different natural media of exchange and of payment may be arranged in a scale laid down by law or convention.

The money which, according to the rules of a corporate group, is acceptable in unlimited amounts as a means of payment will be called 'legal tender.' Monetary material is the material from which money is made. The standard money is the same, but limited to the case of market money. The monetary value-scale (*Geldtarifierung*) is the relative valuation of different types of natural or administrative money, which is made the basis for the division and denomination of coins. The monetary ratio is the same as between types of market money differing in material.

'International' means of payment are those means of payment which serve to balance accounts between different monetary systems; that is, so far as payments are not postponed by funding operations.

Every new set of monetary regulations on the part of a corporate group must necessarily take account of the fact that certain means of payment have previously been used for the liquidation of debts. It must either legalize their use as means of payment, or impose new ones. In the latter case a ratio must be established between the old units, whether natural, by weight, or chartal, and the new. This is the principle of the so-called 'historical' definition of money as a means of payment. It is impossible here to discuss how far this affects the value of money as a means of exchange.

It should be strongly emphasized that the present discussion is not an essay in monetary theory, but only an attempt to work out the simplest possible formulations of a set of concepts which will have to be frequently employed later on. In addition, this discussion is concerned primarily with certain very elementary sociological consequences of the use of money. The formulation of monetary theory, which has been most acceptable to the author, is that of Von Mises.[23] The *Staatliche Theorie des Geldes* of G. F. Knapp is the most imposing work in the field and in its way solves the formal problem brilliantly. It is, however, as will be seen below, incomplete for substantive monetary problems. Its able and valuable attempt to systematize terminology and concepts will be left out of account.

1. Means of exchange and means of payment very often, though by no means always, coincide empirically. They are, however, particularly likely not to in primitive conditions. The means of payment for dowries, tribute, obligatory gifts, fines, wergild, etc., are often specified in convention or by law without regard to any relation to the means of exchange actually in circulation. It is only when the economic affairs of the corporate group are administered in money terms that Mises' contention [24] that even the state seeks means of payment only as a means of exchange becomes tenable. This has not been true of cases where the possession of certain means of payment has been primarily significant as a mark of

[23] *Theorie des Geldes und der Umlaufsmittel,* 1912.
[24] Op. cit.

social status.[25] With the introduction of regulation of money by the state, means of payment becomes the legal concept; medium of exchange, the economic concept.

2. There seems at first sight to be an indistinct line between a 'good' which is purchased solely with a view to its future resale and a medium of exchange. In fact, however, even under conditions which are otherwise primitive there is a strong tendency for particular objects to monopolize the function of medium of exchange so completely that there is no doubt about their status. Wheat futures are traded in terms which imply that there will be a final buyer. Therefore they cannot be treated as means of payment or medium of exchange, let alone money.

3. So long as there is no officially sanctioned money, what is used as means of exchange is determined by custom, the play of interests, and all kinds of convention. The agreements of the parties to transactions are then oriented to these. The reasons why specific things have become accepted as means of exchange cannot be gone into here. They have, however, been exceedingly various and tend to be determined by the type of exchange which has been of the greatest importance. By no means every medium of exchange, even within the social group where it has been employed, has been universally acceptable for every type of exchange. For instance, cowry shells, though used for other things, have not in some cases been acceptable in payment for wives or cattle.

4. Sometimes means of payment which were not the usual means of exchange, have played an important part in the development of money to its special status. As G. F. Knapp has pointed out, the fact that various types of debt have existed, such as tributes, dowries, payments for bride purchase, conventional gifts to kings or by kings to each other, wergild, etc., and the fact that these have often been payable in certain specific media, has created for these media, by convention or by law, a special position. Very often they have been specific types of artifact.

5. In the present terminology it is necessary to include as money the one-fifth shekel pieces, which, according to the Babylonian records, circulated bearing the stamp of merchant firms, on the assumption, that is, that they were actually used as means of exchange. On the other hand, bars of bullion, which were not coined, but only weighed, will not be treated as money, but only as means of payment and exchange. The fact, however, that they could be weighed has been enormously important because they could be made the basis of arithmetical calculations. There

---

[25] See K. Schurtz, *Grundriss einer Entstehungsgeschichte des Geldes.*

are naturally many transitional forms, such as the acceptance of coins by weight rather than by denomination.

6. 'Chartal' is a term introduced by Knapp in his *Staatliche Theorie des Geldes*. All types of money which have been stamped or coined, endowed with validity by law or by agreement, belong in this category, whether they were metal or not. It does not, however, seem reasonable to confine the concept to regulations by the state and not to include cases where acceptance is made compulsory by convention or by some agreement. There seems, furthermore, to be no reason why actual minting by the state or under the control of the political authorities should be a decisive criterion. For long periods this did not exist in China at all and was very much limited in the European Middle Ages. As Knapp would agree, it is only the existence of norms regulating the monetary form which is decisive. As will be noted below, value as a means of payment and formal acceptability as means of exchange in private transactions may be made compulsory by law within the jurisdiction of the political authority.

7. Natural means of exchange and of payment may sometimes be used more for internal transactions, sometimes more for external. The details need not be considered here. The question of the purchasing power of money will be taken up later.

8. This is, furthermore, not the place to take up the substantive theory of money in its relation to prices so far as this subject belongs in the field of economic sociology at all. For present purposes it will suffice to state the fact that money, in its most important forms, is used, and then to proceed to develop some of the most general sociological consequences of this fact, which is merely a formal matter when seen from an economic point of view. It must, however, be emphasized that money can *never* be merely a harmless unit of accounting or of calculation so long as it *is* money. Its valuation is always in very complex ways, dependent also on its scarcity or, in case of inflation, on its over-abundance. This has been particularly evident in recent times, but is equally true for all times.

A socialistic regime might issue certificates based on a given quantity of 'labour' which was recognized as useful, which were made valid for the purchase of certain types of goods. These might be saved or used in exchange, but their behaviour would follow the rules of barter exchange, not of money, though the exchange might be indirect.

9. Perhaps the most instructive case of the far-reaching economic consequences of the relations between the monetary and non-monetary uses of a monetary metal, is that of Chinese monetary history. This is because copper had high costs of production and a wide variation in output.

7: THE PRIMARY CONSEQUENCES OF THE USE OF MONEY. CREDIT

The primary consequences of the widespread use of money are:

(1) The so-called indirect type of exchange as a means of satisfying consumers' wants. This makes it possible to obtain goods which are separated from those offered in exchange for them in space, in time, in respect to the persons involved, and, what is very important, in respect to the quantity on each side of the transaction. This results in a tremendous extension of the area of possible exchange relationships.

(2) Closely related to this is the valuation of services, especially reciprocal services to be acquired in exchange—that is, debts—in terms of money.

(3) So-called 'hoarding'; that is, the storing up of money in specie or in the form of claims to payment payable at any time, as a means of insuring future control over economic advantages in exchange.

(4) The increasing transformation of all economic advantages into the ability to control sums of money.

(5) The qualitative individuation of consumption needs and, indirectly, the extension of their area on the part of those who have control of money, of claims to money payment, or of opportunities to acquire money. This means the ability to offer money as a means of obtaining goods and services of all kinds.

(6) The orientation of the production of utilities, as it has become widespread to-day, to their bearing on the marginal utility of the sums of money which the directing authorities of an economic enterprise expect to be able to control in the relevant future.

(7) With this goes the orientation of acquisitive activities to all the opportunities which are made available by the extension of the area of possible exchanges, in time, in place, and with respect to personal agents, as noted above.

(8) All of these consequences are dependent on what is, in principle, the most important fact of all, the possibility of money calculation; that is, the possibility of assigning money values to all goods and services which in any way might enter into transactions of purchase and sale.

In substantive as distinguished from formal terms, monetary valuation means that goods are not valued in terms of their immediate importance as utilities at the time and place and for the person only. On the contrary, these utilities are more or less systematically compared in determining their use, whether for consumption or for production, with all the potential future opportunities of gaining a return. Under some circumstances, this involves their possible use for the purposes of an indefinite number of other persons who can be brought into the situation because they are potential buyers of the powers of control and disposal of the present owner. Where money calculations are highly developed, this will be called the 'market situation.'[26]

The term 'credit' in the most general sense will be used to designate any exchange of goods initially possessed for the promise of a future transfer of disposal over utilities, no matter what they may be. The granting of credit means in the first instance that action is oriented to the probability that this future transfer of disposal will actually take place. In this sense the primary significance of credit lies in the fact that it makes it possible for an economic unit to exchange its expectations of a surplus of future control over goods or money which are not available at the time, for the present control of other goods, which would not otherwise be available for its use. Where the action is rational both parties expect an improvement in their positions, regardless of what it consists in, over what they could procure by any distribution of their present resources.

1. It is by no means necessary for the advantages in question to be economic. Credit may be granted and accepted for all conceivable purposes; for instance, charitable and military.

2. Credit may be granted and accepted in the 'natural' form or in money, and in both cases the promises may be of concrete goods or services or of money payments. Carrying out credit transactions in terms of money, however, means that they become the subject of monetary calculations with all the attendant consequences.[27]

3. This definition (of credit) for the most part corresponds to the usual

[26] The above statement formulates only the simplest and best-known elements of every analysis of money and does not need to be further commented upon. The sociology of the 'market' will not be developed here. On the formal concepts, see secs. 8 and 10.

A very fragmentary beginning of such a study, which Weber unquestionably intended to carry much farther, is included in the German edition of *Wirtschaft und Gesellschaft*, part ii, chap. 5, but not in the present translation.—ED.

[27] These will be discussed below.

one. It is clear that credit relationships may exist between organized groups of all sorts, especially socialistic or communistic groups. In the case of a plurality of such groups with close mutual relationships which are not economically independent, they are unavoidable. When the use of money is completely absent, there is a difficult problem of finding a rational basis of calculation. For the mere fact of the possibility of transactions involving future returns, even long-term credit, does not determine the degree of rationality with which the parties agree on the conditions. Such parties would be in somewhat the same situation as the household economic units of ancient times which exchanged their surpluses for things they had need of. But there is this difference, that in the present situation the interests of huge masses on a long-term basis would be at stake; and for the great masses of the low-income groups, the marginal utility of present consumption is particularly high. Thus there would be a probability that goods urgently needed could only be obtained on unfavorable terms.

4. Credit may be obtained and used for the purpose of satisfying present needs, which are otherwise inadequately provided for. Even in that case it will, so far as the action is economically rational, only be granted in exchange for advantages. This is not, however, historically usual for the earliest type of consumption credit, especially as granted to people in need. That has more frequently consisted in an appeal to ethical obligations.[28]

5. What is the most common basis of credit, in money or in kind, when it is granted for profit, is very obvious. It is the fact that, because the lender is usually in a better economic situation, the marginal utility of future expectations, as compared with present ones, is higher than it is for the debtor. It should, however, be noted that what constitutes a 'better' situation is highly relative.

8: THE MARKET

By the 'market situation' (*Marktage*) for any object of exchange is meant all the opportunities of exchanging it for money which are known

---

[28] This will be discussed in chap. vi on Local Communities.

What Weber meant by this reference cannot be identified with certainty. It seems probable that after completing chap. iv, which was left incomplete, he intended to add at least one, possibly more, other chapters to part i. The most systematic treatment of the material, which is, however, very fragmentary, is to be found in part ii, chap. ii, of *Wirtschaft und Gesellschaft*. This chapter is not included in the translation.—ED.

by the participants in the market situation to be available to them and relevant in orienting their attitudes to prices and to competition.

'Marketability' (*Marktgängigkeit*) is the degree of regularity with which an object tends to be an object of exchange on the market.

'Market freedom' is the degree of autonomy enjoyed by the parties to market relationships in price determination and in competition.

'Regulation of the market,' on the contrary, is the state of affairs where there is a substantive restriction, effectively enforced by the provisions of an order, on the marketability of certain potential objects of exchange or on the market freedom of certain participants. Regulation of the market may be determined (1) traditionally, by the actors' becoming accustomed to traditionally accepted limitations on exchange or to traditional conditions. (2) By convention, through social disapproval of treating certain utilities as marketable or of subjecting certain objects of exchange to free competition and free price determination, in general or when undertaken by certain groups of persons. (3) By law, through legal restrictions on exchange or on the freedom of competition, in general or for particular groups of persons or for particular objects of exchange. Legal regulation may take the form of influencing the market situation of objects of exchange by price regulation or of limiting the possession, acquisition, or exchange of rights of control and disposal over certain goods to certain specific groups of persons. In the latter case it is a legally-guaranteed monopoly or a legal limitation of economic freedom. (4) By voluntary action arising from the play of interests. In this case there is substantive regulation of the market, though the market remains formally free. This type of regulation tends to develop when certain participants in the market are, by virtue of their totally or approximately exclusive control of the possession of or opportunities to acquire certain utilities—that is, of their monopolistic powers—in a position to influence the market situation in such a way as actually to abolish the market freedom of others. In particular, they may make agreements with each other and with typical exchange partners for regulating market conditions. Typical examples are market quota agreements and price cartels.

1. It is convenient, though not necessary, to confine the term 'market situation' to cases of exchange for money because it is only then that uniform numerical statements of relationships become possible. Opportunities for exchange *in kind* are best described simply as exchange opportunities. Different kinds of goods are and have been marketable in widely different and variable degrees, even where a money economy

was well developed. The details cannot be gone into here. In general, articles produced in standardized form in large quantities and widely consumed have been the most marketable; unusual goods, only occasionally in demand, the least. Durable consumption goods which can be made use of over long periods and means of production with a long or indefinite life, above all, agricultural and forest land, have been marketable to a much less degree than finished goods of everyday use or means of production which are quickly used up, which can be used only once, or which give quick returns.

2. The regulation of markets, as an economically rational policy, has been historically associated with the growth of formal market freedom and the extension of marketability of goods. The original modes of market regulation have been various, partly traditional and magical, partly dictated by kinship relations, by class privileges, by military needs, by welfare policies, and not least by the interests and requirements of the governing authorities of corporate groups. But in each of these cases the dominant interests have not been primarily concerned with maximizing the opportunities of acquisition and economic provision of the participants in the market themselves; have, indeed, often been in conflict with them. (1) Sometimes the effect has been to exclude certain objects from market dealings, either permanently or for a time. This has happened in the magical case, by taboo; in that of kinship, by the hereditary appropriation of property; on the basis of social status, with fiefs. In times of famine the sale of grain has been temporarily prohibited. In other cases permission to sell has been made conditional on a prior offer to certain persons, such as kinsmen, co-members of class groups, and of guilds, or fellow-citizens of a town; or the sale has been limited by maximum prices, as is common in war time, or by minimum prices. Thus in the interests of the dignity of magicians, lawyers, physicians, they have not been allowed to accept fees below a certain minimum. (2) Sometimes certain categories of persons, such as members of the nobility, peasants, or sometimes even artisans, have been excluded from market trade in general or with respect to certain commodities. (3) Sometimes the market freedom of consumers has been restricted by regulations, as in regulations specifying consumption for different classes, rationing in case of war or of famine. (4) Another type is the restriction of the market freedom of potential competitors in the interest of the market position of certain groups, such as the professions or the guilds. Finally, (5) certain economic privileges, such as royal monopolies, have been reserved

to the political authorities or to those holding a charter from such authorities. This was typical for the early capitalistic monopolies.

Of all these, the fifth type of market regulation has been the most highly rational in terms of the interests of market participants; the first type, the least. By 'rational' in this sense is meant promoting the interests of the various groups whose action is oriented to the market situations as a means to the advantageous purchase and sale of goods, with consideration for the interests of other groups not thus oriented proportionally minimized. The groups which, relative to these forms of regulation have been most interested in the freedom of the market, have been those whose interests lay in the greatest possible extension of the marketability of goods, whether from the point of view of availability for consumption, or of ready opportunities for sale. Voluntary market regulation has not appeared extensively and permanently except where there have been highly developed profit-making interests. With a view to the securing of monopolistic advantages, this could take several forms: (1) the pure regulation of opportunities for purchase and sale, which is typical of the widespread phenomena of trading monopolies; (2) the monopolization of transportation facilities, as in shipping and railways; (3) the monopolization of the production of goods; and (4) that of the extension of credit and of financing. The last two types generally are accompanied by an increase in the regulation of economic activity by corporate groups other than the immediate participants in the market relationships. But unlike the primitive, irrational forms of regulation, this is apt to be deliberately oriented to the market situation. The starting point of voluntary market regulation has naturally in general been the fact that certain groups with a far-reaching degree of actual control over economic resources have been in a position to take advantage of the formal freedom of the market to establish monopolies. Voluntary associations of consumers, such as consumers' co-operative societies, have, on the other hand, tended to originate among those who were in an economically weak position. They have hence often been able to accomplish savings for their members, but only occasionally and in particular localities have they been able to establish an effective system of market regulation.

9: THE FORMAL AND SUBSTANTIVE RATIONALITY OF ECONOMIC ACTION

The term 'formal rationality of economic action' will be used to designate the extent of quantitative calculation or accounting which is technically possible and which is actually applied. The 'substantive rationality,' on the other hand, is the degree in which a given group of persons, no matter how it is delimited, is or could be adequately provided with goods by means of an economically oriented course of social action. This course of action will be interpreted in terms of a given set of ultimate values no matter what they may be. There is a variety of different possibilities.

1. The terminology suggested above is thought of merely as a means of securing greater consistency in the use of the word 'rational' in this field. It is actually only a more precise form of the meanings which are continually recurring in the discussion of 'socialization' and of evaluation in money and in kind.

2. A system of economic activity will be called 'formally' rational according to the degree in which the provision for needs, which is essential to every rational economy, is capable of being expressed in numerical, calculable terms, and is so expressed. In the first instance, it is quite independent of the technical form these calculations take, particularly whether estimates are expressed in money or in kind. The concept is thus unambiguous, at least in the sense that expression in money terms yields the highest degree of formal calculability. Naturally, even this is true only relatively, so long as other things are equal.

3. On the other hand, the concept of substantive rationality is full of difficulties. It conveys only one element common to all the possible empirical situations; namely, that it is not sufficient to consider only the purely formal fact that calculations are being made on grounds of expediency by the methods which are, among those available, technically the most nearly adequate. In addition, it is necessary to take account of the fact that economic activity is oriented to ultimate ends (*Forderungen*) of some kind, whether they be ethical, political, utilitarian, hedonistic, the attainment of social distinction, of social equality, or of anything else. Substantive rationality cannot be measured in terms of formal calculation alone, but also involves a relation to the absolute values or to the content of the particular given ends to which it is oriented. In principle, there is an indefinite number of possible standards of value which are 'rational' in this sense. Socialistic and communistic standards which, though by no means unambiguous in themselves, always involve elements of social justice and equality, form only one group among the indefinite plurality of possible points of view. Others are action in the interest of a hierarchy of class distinctions or in furtherance of the power

of a political unit, particularly by war. All these and many others are of potential 'substantive' significance. These points of view are, however, significant only as bases from which to judge the *outcome* of economic action. In addition, it is possible to criticize the attitude toward the economic activity itself or toward the means used, from ethical, ascetic or aesthetic points of view. Of all of these, the merely formal calculation in money terms may seem either of quite secondary importance or even as fundamentally evil in itself, quite apart from the consequences of the modern methods of calculation. There is no question in this discussion of attempting value judgments in this field, but only of determining and delimiting what is to be called 'formal.' In this context the concept 'substantive' is itself in a certain sense 'formal'; that is, it is an abstract, generic concept.

10: The Rationality of Monetary Accounting. Management and Budgeting

From a purely technical point of view, money is the most 'efficient' means of economic accounting. That is, it is formally the most rational means of orienting economic activity. Accounting in terms of money, and not its actual use, is thus the specific means of rational, economic provision. So far as it is completely rational, money accounting has the following primary consequences:

(1) The valuation of all the means of achieving a productive purpose in terms of the present or expected market situation. This includes everything which is needed at present or it is expected may be needed in the future; everything actually in the actor's control, which he may come to control or may acquire by exchange from the control of others; everything lost, or in danger of damage or destruction; all types of utilities of means of production or any other sort of economic advantages.

(2) The numerical statement of (a) the prospects of every projected course of economic action and (b) assessment of the results of every completed action in the form of an account comparing costs and returns in money and comparing the estimated net profit to be gained from alternative lines of action by means of these calculations.

(3) A periodical comparison of all the goods and other assets controlled by an economic unit at a given time with those controlled at the beginning of a period, both in terms of money.

THE RATIONALITY OF MONETARY ACCOUNTING

(4) A previous estimate and subseq??ent verification of receipts and expenditures, either those in money itself, or those which can be valued in money, which the economic unit is likely to have available for its use during a period, if it maintains the money value of the means at its disposal intact.

(5) The orientation of provision for consumption to these data by the use of money available during the accounting period for the acquisition of the requisite utilities in accordance with the principle of marginal utility.

The continual use and provision by an economic unit, whether through production or exchange, of goods either for its own consumption or to procure other goods to be consumed, will be called 'budgetary management' (*Haushalt*).[29] Where rationality is maximized, its basis for an individual or for a group economically oriented in this way is the 'budget' (*Haushaltsplan*), which states systematically in what way the means which are expected to be used within the unit for an accounting period—needs for utilities or for means of production—can be covered by the anticipated income.

The 'income' of a 'budgetary unit' is the total of goods valued in money, which, as estimated according to the principle stated above in number 4, has been available during a previous period or, on the availability of which the unit is likely to be able to count by rational calculations for the present or for a future period. The total estimated value of the goods at the disposal of a budgetary unit, which are normally used immediately or as a source of income, will be called its 'resources' (*Vermögen*).[30] The possibility of complete money budgeting for the budgetary unit is dependent on the possibility that its income and resources consist either in money or in goods which are at any time subject to exchange for money; that is, which are in the highest degree marketable.

A rational type of management and budgeting of a budgetary unit is

[29] The concept *Haushalt*, as distinguished from *Erwerb*, is central to Weber's analysis in this context. He means by it essentially what Aristotle meant by the 'management of a household' (Jowett's translation). It is a question of rational allocation of resources in providing for a given set of needs. The concept of budget and budgetary management seems to be the closest English equivalent in common use.—ED.

[30] Corresponding to the distinction of *Haushalt* and *Erwerb*, Weber distinguishes *Vermögen* and *Kapital*. They are, of course, classes of property distinguished, however, in terms of their function in the management of an economic unit. There is no English equivalent of *Vermögen* in this sense, and it has seemed necessary to employ the more general term 'resources.' Where there is danger of confusion, it will be amplified as 'budgetary resources.'—ED.

possible where calculation is carried out in kind, as will be further discussed below. It is true that in that case there is no such thing as a single sum of 'resources' capable of being estimated in money nor is there a single income. Calculations must be worked out in terms of 'possession' of concrete goods and, where acquisition is limited to peaceful means, of concrete 'receipts' from the direct outlay of available goods and services. These receipts will then be administered with a view to attaining the optimum provision for the satisfaction of wants. If the wants are strictly given, this involves a comparatively simple problem from the technical point of view so long as the situation does not require a very precise estimate of the comparative utility to be gained from the allocation of the available resources to each of a large number of very heterogeneous modes of use. If the situation is markedly different, even the simple self-sufficient household is faced with problems which are only to a very limited degree subject to a formally exact solution by calculation. The actual solution is usually found partly by the application of purely traditional standards, partly by making very rough estimates, which, however, may be quite adequate where both the wants concerned and the conditions of provision for them are well known and readily comparable. When possessions consist in heterogeneous goods, as must be the case in the absence of exchange, a formally exact calculable comparison of the state of possession at the beginning and the end of a period, or of the comparison of different possible ways of securing receipts, is possible only with categories of goods which are qualitatively similar. The typical result is that all the available goods are treated as forming a totality of possessions in kind and certain goods are treated as available for consumption so long as it appears that this will not in the long run diminish the available resources. But every change in the conditions of production—as, for instance, through a bad harvest—or any change in wants necessitates a new allocation since it alters the scale of relative marginal utilities. Under conditions which are simple and adequately understood, this adaptation may be carried out without much difficulty. Otherwise, it is technically more difficult than if money terms could be used. For then any change in the price situation in principle influences the satisfaction only of the wants which are marginal on the scale of relative urgency, which are thus met with the final (variable) increments of income.

As far as accounting in kind becomes more and more rational, and is thus emancipated from tradition, the estimation of marginal utilities in terms of the relative urgency of wants encounters grave complications; whereas, if it were carried out in terms of money resources and income, it would be relatively simple. In the latter case the question is merely whether to apply more labour or whether to satisfy or sacrifice, as the case may be, one or more wants, rather than others. For when the problems of budgetary management are expressed in money terms, this is the form that 'costs' take. But where calculations are in kind, it is necessary, in addition to having a scale of urgency of wants, to estimate (1) the various possible modes of use of the means of production, including their value in terms of previous labour applied to them; that is, it is necessary to evaluate a variant and changeable relationship between want satisfaction and expenditure of resources. This involves further (2) estimating the amount of labour which it would be necessary to expend in order to secure various forms of new receipts; and (3) the ways in which the various resources could be used in carrying out each of a series of potential productive processes. It is one of the most important tasks of economic theory to analyse the various possible ways in which these evaluations can be rationally carried out. It is, on the other hand, a task for economic history to follow out the ways in which the budgetary management of resources in kind has actually worked out in the course of various historical epochs. In general, the following may be said: (1) that the degree of formal rationality has, generally speaking, fallen short of the level which was even empirically possible, to say nothing of the theoretical maximum. As a matter of necessity, the accounting of non-monetary budgetary management units has in the great majority of cases remained strongly bound to tradition. (2) In the larger units of this type, precisely because an expansion and refinement of everyday wants has not taken place, there has been a tendency to employ surpluses for uses outside the everyday standard of living, above all, for artistic purposes. This is an important basis of the tendency of societies with an economy on a low level of the use of money to develop cultures with a strong emphasis on style and an artistic type of orientation.

1. The category of 'resources' includes more than physical goods. It also includes all the economic advantages over which the budgetary unit has an assured control, whether that control is due to custom, to the play of interests, to convention, or to law. The clientèle of a profit-making organization, whether it be a medical or legal practice, or a retail shop, belongs to the resources of the owner if it is for whatever reason relatively stable. In case such resources are legally appropriated, they may,

according to the definition in Chapter 1, sec. 10, constitute part of its property.

2. Money accounting is found without the actual use of money or with its use limited to the settlement of balances which cannot be paid in kind in the goods being exchanged on both sides. Evidence of this is common in the Egyptian and Babylonian records. The use of money accounting as a measure of payments in kind is found in the code of Hammurabi and in the late Roman and early Medieval law, in the permission for a debtor to pay an amount due in whatever form he is able. The establishment of equivalents may in such cases have been carried out on the basis of traditional prices or of prices laid down by decree.

3. Apart from this, the above discussion contains only commonplaces, which are introduced to facilitate the formulation of a precise concept of the rational budgetary unit as distinguished from that of a rational profit-making enterprise—the latter will be discussed presently. It is important to state explicitly that both can take rational forms. The satisfaction of needs is not something more 'primitive' than profit-seeking; 'resources' is not necessarily a more primitive category than capital; income, than profit. It is, however, true that historically the budgetary unit has been prior and has been the dominant form in most periods of the past.

4. It is indifferent what unit is the bearer of a budgetary management economy. Both the budget of a state and the family budget of a worker fall under the same category.

5. Empirically the administration of budgetary units and profit-making are not mutually exclusive alternatives. The business of a consumers' co-operative, for instance, is normally oriented to the economical provision for wants; but in the form of its activity, it tends to be a profit-making business without being oriented to profit as a substantive end. In the action of an individual, the two elements may be so intimately intertwined, and in the past have typically been so, that only the conclusion of the course of action, whether its product was sold or consumed, can serve as a basis for interpreting the meaning of the action. This has been particularly true of small peasants. Exchange may well be a part of the process of budgetary management where it is a matter of acquiring consumption goods by exchange and of disposing of surpluses. On the other hand, the budgetary economy of a prince or a landowner may, at least in part in the sense of the following discussion, be a profit-making enterprise. This has been true on a large scale in earlier

times. Whole industries have developed out of the heterocephalous and heteronomous enterprises which landowners, monasteries, princes, etc., have established to exploit the products of their lands. All sorts of profit-making enterprises to-day are part of the economy of such units as local authorities or even states. In these cases it is legitimate to include in the 'income' of the units, if they are rationally administered, only the net profits of these enterprises. Conversely, it is possible for profit-making enterprises to establish various types of heteronomous budgetary units under their direction for such purposes as providing subsistence for slaves or wage workers—among them are 'welfare' organizations, housing and eating facilities. Net profits are money surpluses after the deduction of all money costs. See above, para. 2 of this section.

6. It has been possible here to give only the most elementary starting points for analysing the significance of economic calculations in kind for general social development.

11: The Concept and Types of Profit Making. The Role of Capital

'Profit-making' (*Erwerben*) [31] is activity which is oriented to opportunities for seeking new powers of control over goods on a single occasion, repeatedly, or continuously. 'Profit-making activity' is activity which is partly oriented to profit-making. Profit-making is economic if it is oriented to acquisition by peaceful methods. It may be oriented to the exploitation of market situations. 'Means of profit' (*Erwerbsmittel*) are those goods and other economic advantages which are used in the interests of economic profit-making. Exchange for profit is that which is oriented to market situations in order to increase control over goods, rather than to secure means for consumption. Credit may be extended as a means of increasing control over the necessary requisites of profit-making activity.

There is a form of monetary accounting which is peculiar to rational economic profit-making; namely, 'capital accounting.' Capital accounting is the valuation and verification of opportunities for profit and of the success of profit-making activity. It involves the valuation of the total assets of the enterprise, whether these consist in goods in kind or

[31] In common usage the term *Erwerben* would perhaps best be translated as 'acquisition.' This has not, however, been used as Weber is here using the term in a technical sense as the antithesis of *Haushalten*. 'Profit-Making' brings out this specific meaning much more clearly.—Ed.

in money, at the beginning of a period of activity; and the comparison of this with a similar valuation of the assets still present or newly acquired, at the end of the process. In the case of a profit-making organization operating continuously, it is a matter of accounting periods. But in any case, a balance is drawn between the initial and final states of the enterprise. 'Capital' is the sum of money in terms of which the means of profit-making which are available to the enterprise are valued. 'Profit,' and correspondingly 'loss,' is the difference between the valuations as revealed by the initial balance and that drawn at the conclusion of the period. 'Capital risk' is the estimated probability of loss as expressed in terms of a balance. A profit-making 'enterprise' (*Unternehmen*) is a system of action capable of autonomous orientation to capital accounting. This orientation takes place by means of calculation. On the one hand, there is a calculation, prior to actual action, of the probable risks and chances of profit; on the other hand, at the conclusion of a measure, verification of the actual profit or loss resulting. 'Profitability' (*Rentabilität*) means, in the rational case, one of two things: (1) the amount of profit estimated as possible by previous calculations, the attainment of which is made an objective of the entrepreneur's activity; or (2) that which an audit shows actually to have been earned in a given period and which is available for the consumption uses of the entrepreneur, without prejudice to his future chances of profit making. In both cases it is usually expressed in ratios—to-day, percentages—in relation to the capital of the initial balance.

Enterprises based on capital accounting may be oriented to the exploitation of opportunities of acquisition afforded by the market or they may be oriented toward other channels of acquisition, such as exploitation of the ability to use force, as in the case of tax farming or the sale of offices.

Each individual operation undertaken by a rational profit-making enterprise is oriented to estimated profitability by means of calculation. In the case of profit-making activities on the market, capital accounting requires: (1) that there exist, subject to estimate beforehand, adequately extensive and assured opportunities for sale of the goods which the enterprise produces; that is, normally a high degree of marketability. (2) That, similarly, the means of carrying on the enterprise such as instruments of production and the services of labour are available in the market at costs which can be estimated with an adequate degree of certainty. Finally, (3) that the technical and legal conditions to which the process is subjected, from the acquisition of the means of production to final sale, including transport, manufacturing operations, storage, etc., can be taken account of as calculable money costs.

The extraordinary importance of the highest possible degree of calculability as the basis for efficient capital accounting will be evidenced again and again throughout the discussion of the sociological conditions of economic activity. It is far from the case that only economic factors are important to it. On the contrary, it will be shown that the most various sorts of external and subjective barriers have existed to account for the fact that capital accounting has arisen as a basic form of economic calculation only in the Western World.

As distinguished from the calculation appropriate to a budgetary unit, the capital accounting and calculation of the market entrepreneur, are oriented not to marginal utility, but to profitability. To be sure, the probabilities of profit are in the last analysis dependent on the income of consumption units and, through this, on the marginal utility of the available income of the final consumers of consumption goods. As it is usually put, it depends on their 'purchasing power' for the relevant commodities. But from a technical point of view, the accounting calculations of a profit-making enterprise and of a consumption unit differ as fundamentally as do the ends of want satisfaction and of profit-making which they serve. For purposes of economic theory, it is the marginal consumer who determines the direction of production. In actual fact, given the actual distribution of power this is only true in a limited sense for the modern situation. To a large degree, even if the consumer is in a position to buy, his wants are 'awakened' and 'directed' by the entrepreneur.

In a market economy every form of rational calculation, hence, especially, of capital accounting, is oriented to expectations of prices and their changes as they are determined by the conflicts of interests in bargaining and competition and the resolution of these conflicts. In the estimation of profitability this is made particularly clear by the form of bookkeeping, the double entry type, which is the most highly developed from a technical point of view. For here, in the system of accounting, there is introduced the fiction of exchange transactions between the different parts of a single enterprise; or, between different accounts in order to develop a technique of estimating the bearing of each particular measure on the profitability of the enterprise. Thus the highest degree of rational capital accounting presupposes the existence of competition on a large scale. And this in turn involves a further very specific condition. It is not possible in *any* economic system for subjective wants to correspond directly to effective demand; that is, to that which enters into calculations for provision by the acquisition of goods. For whether or not a subjective want can be satisfied depends, on the one hand, on its place in the scale of relative urgency; on the other hand, on the goods̄ which are actually or potentially estimated to be available for its satisfaction. Satisfaction does not take place if the utilities needed for it are applied to other more urgent uses, or if they either cannot be procured at all, or only by such sacrifices of labour and goods that future wants, which are still, from a present point of view, adjudged more urgent, could not be satisfied. This is true of consumption in every kind of economic system including a communistic one.

In an economy which makes use of capital accounting and which is thus characterized by the appropriation of the means of production by individual units, that is by property, profitability depends on the prices which the 'consumers,' according to the marginal utility of money in relation to their income, can and will pay. It is only possible to produce profitably for those consumers who, in these terms, have sufficient income. A need may fail to be satisfied, not only when an individual's own demand for other goods takes precedence, but also when the greater purchasing power of others, in relation to any kind of demand, withdraws the relevant good from the market. Thus the fact that competition on the market is an essential condition of the existence of rational money accounting further implies that the outcome of the economic process is decisively influenced by the ability of persons who are plentifully supplied with money to outbid the others, and of those more favourably situated for production to underbid their rivals on the selling side. The latter are particularly those well supplied with goods essential to production or with money. In particular, rational money accounting presupposes the existence of effective prices and not merely of fictitious prices conventionally employed for technical accounting purposes. These, in turn, presuppose money which functions as an effective circulating medium of exchange and in demand as such, and not merely as a technical accounting unit.[82] Thus the orientation of action to money prices and to profit

[82] Since Weber wrote, there has been an extensive discussion of the problem of whether rational allocation of resources was possible in a completely socialistic economy in which there were no independent, competitively determined prices. The principal weight of technical opinion seems at present to take the opposite position from that which Weber defends here. A recent discussion of the problem will be found in the book on the *Economic Theory of Socialism,* edited by B. E. Lippincott. This book includes a bibliography on the subject.—Ed.

has the following consequences: (1) that the distribution of the amount of money or of marketable goods at the disposal of the different parties in the market is decisive in determining the direction taken by the production of goods, so far as it is carried on by profit-making enterprises. For it is only demand which is made effective through purchasing power which is and can be satisfied. Further, (2) the question, what type of demand is to be satisfied by the production of goods, becomes in turn dependent on the profitability of production itself. Production is, to be sure, in formal terms a rational process of want satisfaction. But it does not respond to actual wants unless their possessors are in a position to make them effective by sufficient purchasing power on the market.

'Capital goods,' as distinguished from ordinary possessions or the resources of a budgetary unit, are all such goods as are administered and so long as they are administered on the basis of capital accounting. 'Interest on capital,' as distinct from various other possible kinds of interest on loans, is: (1) what is estimated to be the minimum normal profitability of the use of material means to profit making; (2) the rate of interest at which profit-making enterprises can obtain money or capital goods.[33]

1. The concept of capital has been defined strictly with reference to the individual enterprise and in accordance with accounting practice, which was, indeed, the most convenient method for present purposes. This usage is much less in conflict with everyday speech than with the usual scientific use of the term, which, furthermore, has by no means been consistent. In order to test the usefulness of the present accounting term, which is being increasingly employed in scientific writings again, it is necessary only to ask the following simple questions: (1) What does it mean when we say that a company has an original capital of a million pounds? When (2) that capital is 'written down'? When (3) laws dealing with financing make rules which lay down what may and may not be included in original capital? The first question means that when profit is being divided, it is only when the excess of credits over debits as stated in the balance sheet exceeds a million pounds, that it can be treated as profit and divided among the share-holders to do what they like with. In the case of a one man enterprise, it means that only this surplus may be used for his private expenditures. The second question

[33] This exposition only repeats generally known things in a somewhat more precise form. For the technical aspects of capital accounting, compare the standard textbooks of accountancy, which are, in part, excellent. E.g. those of Leitner, Schär, etc.

concerns the situation where there have been heavy losses. It means that the division of profit need not be postponed until a surplus of over a million pounds has been accumulated but that the division of 'profits' may begin at a lower figure. In order to do this, it is necessary to 'write down' the capital and this is the purpose of the operation. Finally, the purpose of rules as to how capital liability can be 'covered' by acquisition of assets and when and how it can be written down or up is to give creditors and shareholders a guarantee that the division of profits will be carried out correctly according to the rules of the enterprise; in such a way, that is, (a) that profitability is maintained, and (b) that the security of the creditors is not impaired. The rules as to what may be entered in the balance sheet are concerned essentially with how objects may be reckoned as capital. (4) What does it mean when we say that as a result of unprofitability 'capital turns to other channels of investment'? The statement may refer to the resources of a budgetary unit, for 'investment' may be a category of the administration of budgetary resources, as well as of profit-making enterprise. But it may mean that capital goods partly have ceased to be such by being sold, for instance as scrap or junk, partly are transferred to other uses as capital. (5) What is meant when we speak of the 'power of capital'? We mean that the possessors of control over the means of production and of economic advantages which can be used as capital goods in a profit-making enterprise enjoy, by virtue of this control and of the orientation of economic action to the principles of capitalistic acquisition, a specific position of power in relation to others.

In the earliest beginnings of rational profit-making activity capital appears, though not under this name, as a sum of money used in accounting. Thus in the 'commenda' relationship various types of goods were entrusted to a travelling merchant to sell in a foreign market, and possibly he was also commissioned to purchase other goods wanted for sale at home. The profit or loss was then divided in a particular proportion between the travelling merchant and the entrepreneur who advanced the capital. But for this to take place it was necessary to value the goods in money; that is, to strike balances at the beginning and the conclusion of an enterprise. The 'capital' of the commenda relationship or the *societas maris* was simply this money valuation, which served only the purpose of settling accounts between the parties and no other.

What is meant when the term 'capital market' is used? It means that goods, especially money, are in demand in order to be used as capital goods. Furthermore, it means that there are profit-making enterprises, especially various kinds of 'banks,' which make profits by the provision of goods, especially money, for this purpose as a regular business. In the case of so-called 'loan capital,' which consists in handing over money in lieu of a promise to return the same amount at a later time with or without the addition of 'interest,' the term capital will only be used if lending is the object of a profit-making enterprise. Otherwise, the term 'money loans' will be used. Everyday speech tends to use the term capital in so far as 'interest' is paid because the latter is usually reckoned as a proportion of the nominal value of the loan. It is only because of this basis of calculation that we speak of the amount of a loan or a deposit as capital. It is true that this is the origin of the term. *Capitale* was the principal sum of a loan which is said, though it cannot be proved, to derive from the heads counted in a loan of cattle. But this is irrelevant. Even in very early times a loan of goods in kind was reckoned in money terms; and it was on this basis that interest was calculated, so that even in such cases capital goods and capital accounting are typically related, as has been true in later times. In the case of an ordinary loan, which is made simply as a phase in the administration of a budgetary unit and so far as it is employed for the needs of the budgetary unit, the term 'loan capital' will not be used. The same, of course, applies to the lender.

The concept of a profit-making enterprise is in accord with ordinary usage, except for the fact that the orientation to capital accounting, which is usually taken for granted, is made explicit. This is done in order to emphasize that not every case of search for profit as such constitutes an 'enterprise,' but only when it is capable of orientation to capital accounting, regardless of whether it is on a large or a small scale. At the same time it is indifferent whether this capital accounting is in fact rationally carried out according to rational principles. Similarly the terms 'profit' and 'loss' will be used only as applying to enterprises oriented to capital accounting. The earnings or other modes of acquisition without relation to capital, of such persons as authors, physicians, lawyers, civil servants, professors, clerks, technicians, or workers, is naturally 'acquisition,' [34] but it is not 'profit.' Even everyday usage would not call it profit. 'Profitability' is a concept which is applicable to every sort of act which is oriented in terms of business accounting technique to profit and loss, such as the employment of a particular worker, the purchase of a new machine, the determination of rest periods in the working day, etc.

[34] *Erwerb.*

It is not expedient in defining the concept of interest on capital to start with interest on any type of loan. If somebody helps out a peasant by giving him seed and demands an increment on its return, or if the same is done in the case of money loaned to a household to be returned with interest, it is not expedient to call this a 'capitalistic' process. It is possible, where action is rational, for the lender to secure an additional amount because his creditor is in a position to expect benefits from the use of the loan greater than the amount of the interest he pays; when, that is, the situation is seen in terms of what it would be if he had had to do without the loan. Similarly, the lender, being aware of the situation, is in a position to exploit it, in that for him the marginal utility of his present control over the goods he lends is exceeded by the marginal utility at the relevant future time of the repayment with the addition of the interest. This is essentially a matter of the administration of budgetary units and their resources, not of capital accounting. Even a person who secures a loan for his urgent personal needs from a 'usurer' is not for purposes of the present discussion said to be paying interest on capital, nor does the lender receive such interest. It is rather a case of return for the loan. But the person who makes a business of lending calculates interest, in case he acts rationally, in terms of its relation to his business capital, and must consider that he has suffered a 'loss' if the returns from loans do not come up to the requisite rate of profitability. This is a case of interest on capital; the former is simply interest. Thus for the present terminological purposes, interest on capital is always that which is calculated on the basis of capital, not that which is a return for capital. It is always oriented to money valuations, and thus to the sociological fact that disposal over means to making profit, whether through the market or not, is in private hands; that is, appropriated. Without this, capital accounting, and thus calculation of interest, would be unthinkable.

In a rational profit-making enterprise, the interest, which is charged on the books to a capital sum, is the minimum of profitability. It is in terms of whether or not this minimum is reached that a judgment of the advisability of this particular mode of use of capital goods is arrived at. Advisability in this context is naturally conceived from the point of view of maximizing profit. The rate for this minimum profitability is, it is well known, only approximately that at which it is possible to secure credit on the capital market at the time. But nevertheless, the existence of the capital market is the reason why calculations are made on this basis, just as the existence of market exchange is the basis for making entries against the different accounts. It is one of the fundamental phenomena of a capitalistic economy that entrepreneurs are permanently willing to pay interest for loans. This phenomenon can only be explained by understanding how it is that the average entrepreneur may hope in the long run to earn a profit, or that entrepreneurs on the average in fact do earn it, over and above what they have to pay as interest on loans.

Economic theory approaches this problem in terms of the relative marginal utilities of goods under present and under future control. No objection is to be made to this procedure. But the sociologist wishes to know in addition how this supposed relation of marginal utilities affects human action so that actors are in a position and willing to make differences in time preference a basis of the payment of interest. For it is by no means obvious that this would happen at all times and places. In fact, it is a phenomenon specific to profit-making economies. The primary basis of it is the economic market structure which mediates between the profit-making enterprises, on the one hand, and the budgetary units on the other, which not only consume the goods offered on the market but also provide certain essential means of production, notably labour. It is only where there is such a market that profit-making enterprises are founded and administered permanently with a capitalistic orientation. Such enterprises are further dependent on an expectation of earning the minimum rate of interest on capital. In terms of economic theory, which is subject to numerous variations, it might well be said that this type of exploitation of the situation was a consequence of positions of power deriving from private property in the means of production and in the products. It is only this type of economically-acting individuals who are in a position to orient their economic activity to interest payments.

2. The budgetary administration of resources and profit-making enterprises may be outwardly so similar as to appear identical. They are in fact in the analysis only distinguishable in terms of the difference in meaningful orientation of the corresponding economic activities. In the one case, it is oriented to maintaining and improving profitability and the market position of the enterprise; in the other, to the security and increase of resources and income. It is, however, by no means necessary that this fundamental orientation should always, in a concrete case, be decisively turned in either direction; and sometimes it is impossible to decide it. In cases where the private resources of the entrepreneur are identical with his business control over its business resources and his

private income is identical with the profit of the business, the two things seem to go entirely hand in hand. All manner of personal considerations may in such a case cause the entrepreneur to enter upon business policies which, in terms of the rational maximization of profit, are irrational. But very generally, private resources and those of the business are not identical. Furthermore, such factors as personal indebtedness of the proprietor, his personal demand for a higher present income, and the like, often exert what is, in terms of business considerations, a highly irrational influence on the business. Such situations often lead to measures intended to eliminate these influences altogether, as in the incorporation of family businesses.

The tendency to separate the sphere of private affairs from the business is thus not fortuitous. It is a consequence of the fact that, from the point of view of business interest, the interest in maintaining the private resources of the owner is often irrational, as is his interest in income receipts at any given time from the point of view of the profitability of the enterprise. Considerations relevant to the profitability of a business are also not identical with those governing the private interests of persons who are related to it as workers or as consumers. Conversely, the interests growing out of the private fortunes and income of persons or corporate groups having powers of control over an enterprise, do not necessarily lie in the same direction as the long-run considerations of maximizing its profitability and its market position. This is definitely, even especially, true when a profit-making enterprise is controlled by a producers' co-operative association. The objective interests of rational management of a business enterprise and the personal interest of the individuals who control it, are by no means identical and are often opposed. This fact implies the distinction in principle of the budgetary unit and the enterprise, even where both, with respect to powers of control and objects controlled, are identical.

It is essential for purposes of a clear and convenient terminology to maintain a sharp distinction between the budgetary unit and the profit-making enterprise. The purchase of securities on the part of a private investor who wishes to consume the proceeds, is not an investment of capital but of personal resources. A money loan made by a private individual for obtaining the interest is, when regarded from the standpoint of the lender, entirely different from one made by a bank to the same borrower. On the other hand, a loan made to a consumer and one to an entrepreneur for business purposes are quite different from the point of

THE CONCEPT AND TYPES OF PROFIT MAKING

view of the borrower. The bank is investing capital and the entrepreneur is borrowing capital; but in the first case, it may be for the borrower a matter simply of borrowing for purposes of budgetary management; in the second it may be, for the lender, a case of investment of his private resources. This distinction between private resources and capital, between the budgetary unit and the profit-making enterprise, is of far-reaching importance. In particular, without it, it is impossible to understand the economic development of the ancient world and the limitations on the development of capitalism in those times.[35]

3. By no means all profit-making enterprises with capital accounting are doubly oriented to the market in that they both purchase means of production on the market and sell their product there. Tax farming and all sorts of financial operations have been carried on with capital accounting but without selling any products. The very important consequences of this will be discussed later. It is a case of capitalistic profit-making which is not oriented to the market.

4. For reasons of convenience, acquisitive activity and profit-making enterprise have been distinguished. Anyone is engaged in acquisitive activity so far as he seeks, among other things, in given ways to acquire goods—money or others—which he does not yet possess. Thus it includes the official and the worker, no less than the entrepreneur. But the term 'profit-making enterprise' will be confined to those types of acquisitive activity which are continually oriented to market advantages by virtue of the fact that goods are used as means to secure profit, either (a) through the production and sale of goods in demand, or (b) through the offer of services in demand in exchange for money, which may occur through free exchange or through the exploitation of appropriated advantages, as has been pointed out above. The person who is a mere investor is, in the present terminology, not engaged in profit-making, no matter how rationally he administers his resources.

5. It goes without saying that in terms of economic theory the direction in which goods can be profitably produced by profit-making enterprises is determined by their marginal utilities for final consumers in conjunction with the latter's incomes. But from a sociological point of view, it should not be forgotten that, to a large extent, in a capitalistic economy (a) new wants are created and others allowed to disappear and (b) capitalistic enterprises, through their aggressive advertising policies, exer-

[35] The well-known articles of Rodbertus are in spite of their errors and incompleteness still important. They should be compared with the excellent discussion of Karl Bücher.

cise an important influence on the demand functions of consumers. Indeed, these are essential traits of a capitalistic economy. It is true that this does not apply primarily to wants of the highest degree of necessity, but even types of food provision and housing are importantly determined by the producers in a capitalistic economy.

12: Calculations in Kind

Calculations in kind can occur in the most varied form. We speak of a 'money economy,' meaning an economy where the use of money is typical and where action is typically oriented to market situations in terms of money prices. The term 'natural economy,'[36] on the other hand, means an economy where money is not used. The different economic systems known to history can be classified according to the degree to which they approximate the one or the other.

The concept 'natural economy' is not, however, very definite, since it can cover systems with widely varying structures. It may mean an economy where no exchange at all takes place or one where exchange is only by barter, and thus money is not used as a medium of exchange. The first type may be an individual economic unit organized on a completely communistic basis, or with some determinate distribution of rights of participation. In both cases, there would be a complete lack of autonomy or autocephaly of the component parts. This may be called a 'closed household economy.' Or, secondly, it may be a combination of otherwise autonomous and autocephalous individual units, all of which, however, are obligated to make contributions in kind to a central organization which exists for the exercise of authority or as a communal institution. This is an economy based on payments in kind, such as the Greek *oikos* or a 'liturgically'[37] organized political group. In both cases, so far as the pure type is conformed to, there is only calculation in kind.

In the second place, where exchange is involved there may be natural economies where exchange is only by barter without either the use of money or calculation in money terms. Or there may be economies where there is exchange in kind, but where calculation is occasionally or even typically carried out in money terms. This was typical of the Orient in ancient times and has been common everywhere.

For the purposes of analysing calculation in kind, it is only the cases

[36] *Naturalwirtschaft.*
[37] In Weber's technical sense.

of the first type which are of interest, where the unit is either completely self-sufficient, or the liturgies are produced in rationally organized units. This would be inevitable in attempting to employ modern technology in a completely socialized economy.

Calculation in kind is in its essence oriented to consumption, the satisfaction of wants. It is, of course, quite possible to have something analogous to profit-making on this basis. This may occur (a) in that, without resort to exchange, available objective means of production and labour are systematically applied to the production and transportation of goods on the basis of calculations, according to which the state of want satisfaction thus attained is compared with the state which would exist without these measures or if the resources were used in another way, and thus a judgment as to the most advantageous procedure arrived at. Or (b) in an exchange economy, goods may be disposed of and acquired by exchange even in systematically repeated ways, though strictly by barter. Such action would be systematically oriented to securing a supply of goods which, as compared with the state which would exist without them, is judged to be a more adequate provision for the needs of the unit. It is, in such cases, only when quantities of goods which are qualitatively similar are compared that it is possible to use numerical terms unambiguously and without a wholly subjective valuation. It is naturally possible to set up typical combinations of consumable goods, such as salaries paid in kind and benefices, consisting of income in kind, which have been particularly common in the Orient. These may even become the objects of exchange transactions in a way somewhat similar to our government securities. In certain cases involving goods of highly uniform quality, such as the grain of Egypt, it has been possible to store them and to trade on the basis of certificates of ownership, just as if they were silver bars or bank credit. Similarly, what is more important, it has been possible to express the technical efficiency of a process of production in numerical terms and thereby compare it with other types of technical process. This may be done, if the final product is the same, by comparing the relative requirements of different processes in both the quantity and the type of means of production. Or, where the means of production are the same, the different products which result from different procedures may be compared. It is often, though by no means always, possible in this way to secure numerical comparisons for the purposes of particular problems. But the more difficult problems of calculation begin when it becomes a question of comparing different kinds of means of production, their different possible modes of use, and qualitatively different final products.

Every capitalistic enterprise is, to be sure, continually concerned with calculations in kind. For instance, given a certain type of loom and a certain quality of yarn, it is a question of ascertaining, in relation to the other relevant data, such as the efficiency of machines, the humidity of the air, the rate of consumption of coal, lubricating oil, etc., what will be the product per hour per worker and thus the amount of the product which is attributable to any individual worker for each unit of time. For industries with typical waste products or by-products, this can be determined without any use of money accounting and is in fact so determined. Similarly, under given conditions, it is possible to work out, in technical terms without the use of money, the normally expected annual consumption of raw materials by the enterprise according to its technical production capacity, the depreciation period for buildings and machinery, the typical loss by spoiling or other forms of waste. But the comparison of different kinds of processes of production with the use of different kinds of raw materials and different ways of treating them, is carried out to-day by making a calculation of comparative profitability in terms of money costs. For accounting in kind, on the other hand, there are formidable problems involved here which are incapable of objective solution. Though it does not at first sight seem to be necessary, a modern enterprise tends to employ money terms in its capital calculations without regard to these difficulties. But even this is not entirely fortuitous. In the case of the distribution of items to the different accounts, for example, money accounting is used because this is the method of forecasting the conditions of future productivity of the business which combines the greatest degree of certainty with the greatest flexibility in relation to changing circumstances. Without such a means of checking the bearing on future profitability, any provision of stocks of materials or any other mode of provision in kind would be irrational and it would be very difficult to know where to stop. It is difficult to see, without money accounting, how 'reserves' could be built up without being specified in detail. Further, an enterprise is always faced with the question as to whether any of its parts is operating irrationally: that is, unprofitably, and if so, why. It is a question of what parts of the expenditure of resources in kind, that is, of 'costs,' could be saved and, above all, could be more rationally used elsewhere. This can be determined with relative ease and accuracy in terms of money accounting by means of striking a balance between proceeds and costs on the books, which must include the interest payment assigned to that account. But it is exceedingly difficult to do this entirely in terms of material goods, and indeed it can be accomplished at all only in very simple cases. This is not a matter of circumstances which could be overcome by technical improvements in the methods of calculation, but of fundamental limitations, which make really exact accounting in terms of calculations in kind impossible in principle.

It is true this might be disputed, though naturally not with arguments drawn from the Taylor system, nor from the possibility of achieving improvements in efficiency by making use of a system of premiums or points without the use of money. The essential question is that of how it is possible to discover at what point in the organization it would be profitable to employ such measures because there existed at that point certain elements of irrationality. It is in finding out these points that accounting in kind encounters difficulties which cannot be solved by a subsequent assessment in money terms. The fundamental limitations of accounting in kind as the *basis* of calculation in enterprises—of a type which would include the heterocephalous and heteronomous units of a planned organization of production—are to be found in the problem of imputation. This involves much more than a simple matter of the arbitrary assignment of values in bookkeeping. It is rather a matter of the type of highly complex considerations analyzed by the theory of marginal utility. A system of accounting in kind would have to set up indices of the value of the various significant resources which would play the role of the accounting prices of modern business. But it is not clear how these indices could be established and regulated; for instance, whether they would vary from one unit to another, according to special conditions, or whether they would be uniform for the whole economy, to take account of social utility, that is, the present and future conditions of consumers' demand.

Nothing is gained by assuming that, if only the problem of a non-monetary economy were seriously enough attacked, a suitable accounting method would be discovered or invented. The problem is fundamental to any kind of complete socialization. We cannot speak of any kind of a 'rational planned economy' so long as at this decisive point we have no way of working out a rational plan.

The difficulties of accounting in kind become more marked when the question is considered of whether, from the point of view of efficiently satisfying the wants of a given group of persons, it is rational to locate a certain enterprise with a given productive function at one or an alternative site. The same difficulties arise if we want to determine whether a given economic unit, from the point of view of the most rational use of the labour and raw materials available to it, would do better to obtain certain products by exchange with other units or by producing them itself. It is true that the basis of the location of industries lies in the natural environment and its simplest data are capable of formulation in non-monetary terms.[38] Nevertheless, the concrete determination of whether, according to the relevant circumstances of its particular location, a given unit is better assigned one or a somewhat different role in the system of production, is, in terms of calculation in kind, capable of solution only in terms of very crude estimates apart from the few cases where the solution is given by some natural peculiarity, such as a unique source of a raw material. But in spite of the numerous unknowns which may be present, the problem in money terms is always capable of a determinate solution in principle.

Finally, there is the independent problem of the comparative importance of the satisfaction of different wants, provision for which is, under the given conditions, equally feasible. In the last analysis, this problem is, in at least some of its implications, involved in every particular case of the calculations of a productive unit. Under conditions of money accounting, it has a decisive influence on profitability and thereby on the direction of production of profit-making enterprises. But where calculation is only in kind, it is in principle soluble only in one of two ways: by adherence to tradition or by an arbitrary dictatorial regulation which, on whatever basis, lays down the pattern of consumption and requires obedience. Even when that is resorted to, it still remains a fact that the problem of imputation of the part contributed to the total product of an economic unit by the different factors of production and different executive decisions is not capable of the kind of solution which is at present attained by calculations of profitability in terms of money. It is precisely the process of provision for mass demand by mass production so typical of the present day which would encounter the greatest difficulties.

[38] On this, see the contribution of Alfred Weber to the present series, English edition translated by Carl Joachim Friedrich, *Theory of the Location of Industries*, Chicago, Ill., University of Chicago Press, 1929.—ED.

1. The problems of accounting in kind have been raised in a particularly penetrating form by Dr. Otto Neurath in his numerous works apropos of the tendencies to 'socialization' in recent years. The problem is a central one in any discussion of complete socialization; that is, that which would lead to the disappearance of effective prices. It may, however, be explicitly noted that the fact that it is incapable of rational solution serves only to point out some of the consequences, including economic ones, which would have to be faced as a result of such a socialist experiment. This does not, however, touch the question of the justification of such a programme so far as it does not rest on technical considerations, but like most such movements, on ethical postulates or other forms of absolute value. A 'refutation' of these is beyond the scope of any science. From a purely technical point of view, however, the possibility must be considered that the maintenance of a certain density of population within a given area is possible only on the basis of accurate calculation. In so far as this is true, a limit to the possible degree of socialization would be set by the necessity of maintaining a system of effective prices. That cannot, however, be considered here. It may be noted, though, that the distinction between 'socialism' and 'social reform,' if there is any such, should be made in these terms.

2. It is naturally entirely correct that mere money accounts, whether they refer to single enterprises, to any number of them, or to all enterprises—indeed, even the most complete statistical information about the movement of goods in money terms—tell us nothing whatever about the nature of the real provision of a given group with what it needs; namely, real articles of consumption. Furthermore, estimates of national income in money are only to be taken seriously so far as they serve fiscal ends; that is, they determine taxable income and property. But this no longer holds true in anything like the same degree for income statistics in money terms so far as the prices of goods in money are known. But even then there is no possibility of checking real welfare in terms of substantive rationality. It is further true, as has been convincingly shown for the case of extensive farming in the Roman *campagna* by Sismondi and Sombart, that satisfactory profitability, which, in the *campagna* existed for all the participants, in numerous cases has nothing to do with an optimum use of the available productive resources for the provision of consumers' goods for population. The mode of appropriation, especially,

though not solely that of land,[39] leads to a system of claims to rent and services of various kinds which may well obstruct the development of even a technical optimum in the exploitation of productive resources. This is, however, very far from being a peculiarity of capitalistic economies. In particular, the much-discussed limitation of production in the interest of profitability was very highly developed in the economy of the Middle Ages and the modern labour movement is acquiring a position of power which may lead to similar consequences. But there is no doubt that this phenomenon exists in the modern capitalistic economy.

The existence of statistics of changes in money prices or of money estimates has not, as some writers have tended to give the impression, hindered the development of statistics of physical quantities. This is true, however much fault we may find with the available statistics when measured by ideal standards. Probably more than nine-tenths of economic statistics are not in terms of money, but of physical quantity.

The work of a whole generation of economists has been concentrated almost entirely on a critique of the orientation of economic action to profitability so far as it has been related to the provision of the population with real income. All the work of the so-called *Kathedersozialisten* was, in the last analysis, quite consciously concerned with this. They have, however, employed as a standard of judgment a mode of social reform which was oriented to social welfare.[40] This, as contrasted with complete socialization, has presupposed the continuance of effective prices and these have, indeed, been considered inevitable in an economy which either at that time or any other provided for mass production. It is naturally quite possible to treat this as a half measure, but it is not in itself a nonsensical policy. It is true that the problems of a non-monetary economy, and especially of the possibility of rational action in terms of calculations in kind, have not received much attention. Indeed most of the attention they have received has been historical and not concerned with present problems. But the World War, like every war in history, has brought these problems emphatically to the fore in the form of the problems of war economy and the post-war adjustment. It is, indeed, one of the merits of Dr. Neurath to have produced an analysis of just these problems, which, however much it is open to criticism both in principle and in detail was one of the first and was very penetrating. That

---

[39] This much must be conceded to Franz Oppenheimer.
[40] *Sozialpolitik*.

economic science has taken little notice of his work is not surprising because until now we have had only stimulating suggestions, which are, however, so very broad that it is difficult to use them as a basis of intensive analysis. The problem only begins at the point where the public discussion has left off.

3. It is only with the greatest caution that the results and methods of war economy can be used as a basis for criticizing the substantive rationality of forms of economic organization. In war time the whole economy is oriented to what is in principle a single clear goal, and the authorities are in a position to make use of powers which would generally not be tolerated in peace except in cases where the subjects are 'slaves' of an authoritarian state. Furthermore, it is a type of economy which inherently tends toward bankruptcy. The overwhelming urgency of the immediate end overshadows almost any concern for welfare in the coming era of peace. Precision of calculation exists only on the technical level. Economically, however, except for materials of which a grave shortage threatens, and above all, for labour services, calculations are very rough. Hence calculation has predominantly, though not exclusively, a technical character. So far as it has a genuinely economic character—that is, so far as it takes account of alternative ends and not only of means for a given end—it is restricted to what is, from the standpoint of careful monetary calculation, a relatively primitive level of calculation according to the principle of marginal utility. In type this belongs to the class of budgetary calculations and it is not meant to establish a permanent basis for the allocation of labour and the means of production. Hence, however illuminating the experience of war-time and post-war adjustments is for the analysis of the possible range of variation of economic forms, it is unwise to draw conclusions from the type of accounting in kind found under war conditions for their suitability in a permanent peacetime economy.

It may be freely conceded: (1) That it is necessary in money accounting to make arbitrary assumptions in connexion with means of production which have no market price. This is particularly common in the case of agricultural accounting; (2) that to a less extent something similar is true of the allocation of overhead costs among the different branches of a complicated enterprise; (3) that the formation of cartel agreements, no matter how rational their basis in relation to the market situation may be, immediately diminishes the stimulus to accurate calculation on the basis of capital accounting, because calculation does not take place, at all or with a high degree of accuracy, in the absence of an objective need for it. But if calculation were in kind, the situation described under (1) would be universal. Furthermore, any type of accurate allocation of overhead costs, which, however roughly, is now somehow achieved in money terms, would become impossible; and, finally, every stimulus to exact calculation would be eliminated and would have to be created anew by artificial means, the effectiveness of which would be questionable.

It has been suggested that the clerical staff of a business concern, which is actually to a large extent concerned with calculations, should be turned into a universal statistical bureau which would have the function of replacing the monetary calculations of the present system with a statistical accounting in kind. This idea not only fails to take account of the fundamentally different motives underlying 'statistics' and 'calculation,' it also fails to distinguish their fundamentally different functions. They differ essentially as the bureaucrat differs from the entrepreneur.

4. Both calculation in kind and in money are rational techniques. They do not, however, by any means exhaust the totality of economic action. There also exist aspects of action which, though actually oriented to economic considerations, are unrelated to calculation. Economic action may be traditionally oriented or may be affectually determined. All the more primitive aspects of the search for food on the part of human beings is closely related to that of animals, dominated as the latter is by instinct. But apart from this, when economically oriented action is dominated by a religious faith, by war-like passions, or by attitudes of personal loyalty and similar modes of orientation, the level of rational calculation is likely to be very low, even though the motives are fully self-conscious. Bargaining is excluded 'between brothers,' whether they be brothers in the kinship sense, in a guild, or in a religious group. It is not usual to be calculating within a family, a group of comrades, or of disciples. At most, in cases of necessity, a rough sort of rationing is resorted to, which is a very modest beginning of calculation.[41] Everywhere it has been money which has been the means in terms of which calculation has been developed. This explains the fact that calculation

[41] In chap. v, the process by which calculation gradually penetrates into the earlier form of family communism will be taken up. (*Editor's note*—What Weber here refers to is not included in the present translation. As the work was finally edited after his death, there is no chap. v, but the reference is probably in part to the material in part ii, chap. ii, pp. 194 ff. of the German text. The full treatment he intended was probably never written.)

in kind has remained on an even lower technical level than the actual nature of its problems might have necessitated.[42]

13: THE FORMAL AND SUBSTANTIVE RATIONALITY OF A MONEY ECONOMY

It is thus clear that the formal rationality of money calculation is dependent on certain quite specific substantive conditions. Those which are of a particular sociological importance for present purposes are the following: (1) Market competition of economic units which are at least relatively autonomous. Money prices are the product of conflicts of interest and compromises; they thus result from systems of power relationships. Money is not a mere token or sign for unspecified utilities, which could be altered at will without any fundamental effect on the character of the price system, for the latter results from the competitive process. Money is rather, primarily, an instrument in the competitive struggle, and prices are competitive in their significance. Money, even as a unit of account, is essentially significant as a means of quantitative expression of estimated opportunities and risks met in the pursuit of competitive advantages; (2) money accounting attains the highest degree of rationality as a means of orientation of economic action by calculation when it takes the form of capital accounting. This implies the substantive condition of far-reaching market freedom in the sense both of the absence of monopolistic limitations which are imposed or are economically irrational, and of those which are voluntary and economically rational through orientation to the securing of market advantages. The competition to dispose of products, which results under these circumstances, gives rise to a number of expenses, especially for a marketing organization and for advertisement in the broadest sense. In the absence of competition, these expenses would, as in a planned economy or with complete monopoly, be unnecessary. Capital accounting is further dependent on the social conditions of a disciplined organization and the appropriation of the means of production. This implies the existence of a system of imperatively co-ordinated relationships; [43] (3) it is not wants as such, but effective [44] demand for utilities, which regulates the production of goods by

[42] In this respect Otto Neurath appears to be right. While the above was in press, the essay of Ludwig von Mises, dealing with these problems, appeared. Unfortunately it was impossible to comment upon it. See the *Archiv für Sozialwissenschaft,* vol. xlvii.

[43] See chap. i, sec. 16, p. 152.

[44] 'Effective' in the sense of being backed by the requisite purchasing power. Weber says *kaufkräftiger Begehr.*—ED.

profit-making enterprises oriented to capital accounting. What is to be produced is thus determined by the structure of marginal utilities in the income group which has both the inclination and the resources to purchase a given utility. This will depend on the distribution of wealth in the particular society. Where complete market freedom is given, the highest degree of formal rationality in capital accounting is absolutely indifferent to all the substantive considerations involved. But it is precisely the existence of these substantive factors underlying monetary calculations which determine a fundamental limitation on its rationality. This rationality is of a purely formal character. No matter what the standards of value by which they are measured, the requirements of formal and of substantive rationality are always in principle in conflict, no matter how numerous the individual cases in which they may coincide empirically. It is true that they may be made to coincide theoretically in all cases, but only under assumptions which are wholly unrealistic. The formal rationality of money accounting has as such no implications for the actual distribution of goods. This must always be considered separately. If the standard used is that of the provision of a certain minimum of subsistence for the maximum size of population, the experience of the last few decades would seem to show that formal and substantive rationality coincide to a relatively high degree. The reasons lie in the nature of the incentives which underlie the type of economic orientation of social action which is alone adequate to the large-scale use of money calculations. Under all circumstances, it holds true that formal rationality can explain anything about the type of real want satisfaction only when it is combined with knowledge of the distribution of income.[45]

14: MARKET ECONOMIES AND PLANNED ECONOMIES

Want satisfaction will be said to take place through a 'market economy' so far as it results from action oriented to advantages in exchange on the

---

[45] Weber seems to have said in this passage in a somewhat involved way what has come to be generally accepted among the more critical economic theorists. A simpler way of stating the same point is provided by the doctrine of maximum satisfaction. This states the conditions under which, to use Weber's phrase, formal and substantive rationality would coincide. It is generally conceded that among these conditions is the absence of certain types of inequality of wealth. One of the best statements of the problem is that of Frank H. Knight in his essay *The Ethics of Competition*, which is reprinted in the book of that title. The problem of the relations of formal and substantive rationality has for Weber, however, wider ramifications.—ED.

basis of self-interest and where co-operation takes place only through the exchange process. It results, on the other hand, from a 'planned economy' so far as action is oriented systematically to the established order, whether agreed or imposed, which is valid within a corporate group.

Want satisfaction through a market economy normally and in proportion to the degree of rationality presupposes money calculation. Where capital accounting is used it presupposes the economic separation of the budgetary unit and the enterprise. Want satisfaction by means of a planned economy is dependent, in ways which vary in kind and degree according to its extensiveness, on calculation in kind as the ultimate basis of the substantive orientation of economic action. Formally, however, the action of the producing individual is oriented to the instructions of an administrative staff, the existence of which is indispensable. In a market economy the individual units are autocephalous and their action is autonomously oriented. In the administration of budgetary units, the basis of orientation is the marginal utility of money holdings and of anticipated money income in relation to the market situation for the purposes of particular purchases. In profit-making enterprises, capital accounting is the basis of orientation. In a planned economy, all economic action, so far as it is carried through, is oriented heteronomously in terms of the administration of the budgetary unit, to rules which enjoin certain modes of action and forbid others, and which establish a system of rewards and punishments. When, in a planned economy, the prospect of individual income is used as a means of stimulating self-interest, the type and direction of the action thus rewarded is heteronomously determined. It is possible for the same thing to be true of a market economy, though in a formally voluntary way. This is particularly true where the unequal distribution of wealth, and particularly of capital goods, forces the low-income group to comply with the authority of others in order to obtain any return at all for the utilities they can offer on the market. It may be they are subjected to the authority of a wealthy householder or to that of the owners of capital interested in maximizing the profit from it, or of their agents. In a purely capitalistic organization of production, this is the fate of the entire working class.

The following are decisive as elements of the motivation of economic activity under the conditions of a market economy: (1) For those without substantial property; (a) the fact that they run the risk, both for themselves and their personal dependents, such as children, wives, sometimes parents, of going without any provision; (b) that, in varying degrees subjectively they value economically productive work as a mode of life. (2) For those who enjoy a privileged position by virtue of wealth or the education which is usually in turn dependent on wealth; (a) opportunities for large income from profitable undertakings; (b) ambition; (c) the valuation as a 'calling'[46] of types of work enjoying high prestige, such as intellectual work, artistic performance, and work involving high technical competence. (3) For those involved in the fortunes of profit-making enterprises; (a) the risk to the individual's own capital and conversely his own opportunities for profit, combined with (b) the valuation of rational acquisitive activity as a 'calling.' The latter may be significant as a proof of the individual's own achievement or as a symbol and a means of autonomous control over the individuals subject to his authority, or of control over economic advantages which are culturally or materially important to an indefinite plurality of persons—in a word, power.

A planned economy oriented to want satisfaction must, in proportion as it is radically carried through, weaken the incentive to labour so far as the risk of lack of support is involved. For it would, at least so far as there is a rational system of provision for wants, be impossible to allow a worker's dependents to suffer the full consequences of his lack of efficiency in production. Furthermore, autonomy in the direction of organized productive units would have to be greatly reduced or, in the extreme case, eliminated. Hence it would be impossible to retain capital risk and proof of merit by a formally autonomous achievement. The same would be true of autonomous power over other individuals and important features of their economic situation. Along with opportunities for special material rewards, a planned economy may have command over certain ideal motives of what is in the broadest sense an altruistic type, which can be used to stimulate a level of achievement in economic production comparable to that which autonomous orientation to opportunities for profit, by producing for the satisfaction of effective demand, has been able to achieve in a market economy. Where a planned economy is radically carried out, it must further accept the inevitable reduc-

---

[46] In the most general sense as employed below (see sec. 24) *Beruf* may be translated as occupation. In the present context, however, Weber has a more specific meaning in mind, that of an occupational role which embodies an especially strong element of ethical valuation. It is this type of attitude toward an occupational role which Weber found exemplified in the Protestant ethic, especially in the use of the term 'calling,' in Puritan literature. It has hence seemed to be the most appropriate translation in this passage.—ED.

tion in formal rationality of calculation which would result from the elimination of money and capital accounting. This is merely an example of the fact that substantive and formal rationality are inevitably largely opposed. This fundamental and, in the last analysis, unavoidable element of irrationality in economic systems is one of the important sources of all the problems of social policy, above all, the problems of socialism.[47]

1. The above exposition obviously formulates only things which are generally known, in a somewhat more precise form. The market economy is by far the most important case of typical widespread social action predominantly oriented to 'self-interest.' The process by which this type of action results in the satisfaction of wants is the subject matter of economic theory. Knowledge of it in general terms is here presupposed. The use of the term 'planned economy' (*Planwirtschaft*) naturally does not imply acceptance of the well-known proposals of the former minister of economic affairs. The term has been chosen because, while it does not do violence to general usage, it has, since it was used officially, been widely accepted. This fact makes it preferable to the term used by Neurath, *Verwaltungswirtschaft,* which would otherwise be suitable.

2. So far as it is oriented to profit-making, the economic activity of corporate groups, or that regulated by corporate groups, is not included in the concept of planned economy, whether the group be a guild, a cartel, or a trust. Planned economy includes the economic activity of corporate groups only so far as it is oriented to the provision for needs. Any system of economic activity oriented to profit-making, no matter how strictly it is regulated or how stringently controlled by an administrative staff, presupposes effective prices, and thus capital accounting as a basis of action. In the limiting case of a total system of cartels, prices would be determined by negotiation between the cartel groups and by negotiated wage agreements with labour organizations. In spite of the identity of their objectives, complete socialization in the sense of a planned economy administered purely as a budgetary unit, and partial socialization of various branches of production with the retention of capital accounting, are technically examples of quite different types. A preliminary step in the direction of the budgetary planned economy is to be found wherever consumption is rationed or wherever measures are taken to control the spontaneous distribution of goods. A centrally planned organization of production, whether it is undertaken by voluntary agreement, by authoritatively imposed cartels, or by agencies of the

47 The following remarks apply to both secs. 13 and 14.

government, is primarily concerned with a rational organization of the use of means of production and labour resources and cannot, on its own terms, do without prices. It is thus by no means fortuitous that the type of socialism which attempts to ration goods tends to become intimately connected with 'Guild Socialism,'[49] oriented as the latter is to the interests of workers in their jobs. This has happened against the will of the leaders of the latter movement who have been interested in a completely rational scheme.

3. It will not be possible to enter at this point on a detailed discussion of the formation of such economic corporate groups as cartels, corporations or guilds. Their general tendency is orientation to the regulation or monopolistic exploitation of opportunities for profit. They may arise by voluntary agreement, but are more generally imposed even where formally voluntary.[50]

The conflict between two rival forms of socialism has not died down since it was started in Marx's *Misère de la Philosophie*. On the one hand, there is the type, which includes especially the Marxists, which is evolutionary and oriented to the problem of production; on the other, the type which takes the problem of distribution as its starting point and advocates a rational planned economy. The latter is again to-day coming to be called 'communism.' The conflict within the Russian socialistic movement, especially as exemplified in the vigorous disputes between Plechanov and Lenin, was in the last analysis essentially concerned with the issue. While the internal divisions of present-day socialism are very largely concerned with competition for leadership and for 'benefices,' along with these issues and underlying them goes the same set of problems. In particular, the economic experience of war time has given impetus to the idea of a rationally planned economy, but at the same time, to the development of interests in appropriation.

The question of whether a planned economy, in whatever meaning or extent, *should* be introduced, is naturally not in this form a scientific problem. On scientific grounds it is possible only to inquire what would probably be the results of any given specific proposal, and thus what un-

---

[49] The expression which has been translated as 'guild socialism' is *'Betriebsrats'—Sozialismus*. This was the movement in Germany which looked upon the Works Councils as the entering wedge for a completely socialistic organization of the national economy. This is sufficiently similar to the movement known in England as 'Guild Socialism' to justify this translation.—ED.

[50] Compare in the most general terms, chap. i, sec. 10, and also the discussion of the appropriation of economic advantages, sec. 19 ff. of the present chapter.

foreseen or undesired consequences would have to be accepted if the attempt were made. Honesty requires that all parties should admit that, while some of the factors are known, many of those which would be important are only very partially understood. In the present discussion, it is not possible to enter into the details of the problem in such a way as to arrive at concretely conclusive results. The points which will be taken up can be dealt with only in a fragmentary way in connexion with forms of corporate groups, particularly the state. It was possible above only to introduce an unavoidably brief discussion of the most elementary aspects of the technical problem. The phenomenon of a regulated market economy has, for the reasons noted above, not yet been taken up.

4. The organization of economic activity on the basis of a market economy presupposes the appropriation of the non-human sources of utilities on the one hand, and market freedom on the other. The extent of market freedom is a function of the degree to which these sources of utility, particularly the means of transport and production, are appropriated. For, the higher the degree of marketability, the more will economic action be oriented to market situations. But market freedom is further a function of the degree to which appropriation is limited to *non-human* sources of utility. Every case of the appropriation of human beings through slavery or serfdom, or of economic advantages through control of persons, as in market monopolies, restricts the range of human action which can be so oriented. Fichte in his *Geschlossener Handelsstaat* was right in treating this limitation of the concept of 'property' to non-human goods, along with the extension of autonomy of control over the things included, as characteristic of the modern property system with its intimate relations to the market economy. All the parties to market relations have had an interest in the development of this form of property right because it increased the area within which they could orient their action to the opportunities of profit offered by the market situation. The development of this type of property system is hence primarily attributable to their influence.

5. For reasons of convenience, the common term 'collective economy' (*Gemeinwirtschaft*) has been avoided. It suggests a 'collective interest' or 'a community of sentiment' as the normal thing, but for purposes of definition it is not necessary to include them. The economic organization of the estate of a feudal lord or of a monarch like the Pharaohs of the New Kingdom, belongs to the same category in the present termi-

nology as does that of a family household. Both are equally to be distinguished from a market economy.

6. For the purposes of the definition of a market economy, it is indifferent whether or to what extent economic action is 'capitalistic,' that is, is oriented to capital accounting. The budgetary satisfaction of wants in money terms may involve a market economy; indeed, that is the more common case. It would be a mistake to assume that the development of capitalistic enterprises occurred in direct proportion to that of the satisfaction of wants through a money economy. It would be particularly untenable to maintain that this was true of capitalistic forms of the particular type which have developed in the Western World. In fact, the contrary is true. The extension of money economy might well go hand in hand with the increasing monopolization of the larger sources of profit by the household economy of a prince. The Egypt of the Ptolemies is an outstanding example. According to the evidence of the accounts which have survived, it was a highly developed money economy, but its accounting remained budgetary accounting and did not develop into capital accounting. It is also possible that with the extension of a money economy could go a process of 'feudalization' (*Verpfründung*) of fiscal advantages resulting in a traditionalistic stabilization of the economic system. This happened in China, as will be shown later.[51] Finally, the capitalistic investment of money resources could take place in relation to sources of potential profit which were not oriented to opportunities of exchange in a free commodity market and were thus not oriented to the production of goods. For reasons which will be discussed below, this has been almost universally true outside the area of the modern Western economic order.

15: Types of Economic 'Division of Labour'

Every type of social action in a group which is oriented to economic considerations and every associative relationship of economic significance involves to some degree a particular mode of division and organization of human services in the interest of production. A mere glance at the

[51] What this refers to is not entirely clear. It is certainly not any part of the present translation. Weber's most extensive treatment of China is in the first volume of the *Religionssoziologie*. There are also various scattered references in the untranslated portions of *Wirtschaft und Gesellschaft*, the most extensive of which is pp. 707 ff. Very likely he intended a more extensive treatment which remained unwritten.—Ed.

facts of economic action reveals that different persons perform different types of work and that these are combined in the service of common ends, with each other and with the non-human means of production, in the most varied ways. The complexity of these phenomena is extreme, but yet it is possible to distinguish a few types.

Human services for economic purposes may be distinguished as (a) 'managerial,' or (b) oriented to the instructions of a managerial agency. The latter type will be called 'labour' for purposes of the following discussion.

It goes without saying that managerial activity constitutes 'labour' in the most definite sense if labour is taken to mean the expenditure of time and effort as such. The use of the term labour in contradistinction to managerial activity has, however, come to be generally accepted for social reasons and this usage will be followed in the present discussion. For more general purposes, the terms 'services' or 'work' will be used.

Within a social group the ways in which labour or other work may be carried on typically may be classified in the following way: (1) technically, according to the way in which the services of a plurality of co-operating individuals are divided up and combined, with each other and with the non-human means of production, to carry out the technical procedures of production; (2) socially. In the first place, forms of labour may vary according to whether particular services do or do not fall within the jurisdiction of autocephalous and autonomous economic units, and according to the economic character of these units. Closely connected with this is variation according to the modes and extent to which the various services, the non-human means of production, and opportunities for economic profit, used as sources of profit or as means of acquisition, are or are not appropriated. These factors determine the mode of occupational differentiation, a social phenomenon, and the organization of the market, an economic phenomenon; (3) finally, in every case of combination of services with each other and with non-human means of production, it is important, in determining their division among economic units and the modes of appropriation, to know whether they are used in a context of budgetary administration or of profit-making enterprise.[52]

---

[52] For this and the following section, see especially the authoritative discussion of Karl Bücher in his article 'Gewerbe' in the *Handwörterbuch der Staatswissenschaften* and in his book, *Die Entstehung der Volkswirtschaft*. These are fundamentally important works. Both the terminology and the classification here presented have departed from Bücher's only

1. It should be emphatically stated that the present discussion is concerned only with a brief summary of the sociological aspects of these phenomena, so far as they are relevant to its context. The economic aspect is included only in so far as it is expressed in what are formally sociological categories. In a substantive sense, the discussion would be economic only if the conditions of price determination and market relationships, which have heretofore been dealt with only on a theoretical level, were introduced into it. It would, however, be possible to treat such substantive aspects of the problem in such a general introduction to the field only in terms which would involve a very unfortunate kind of one-sidedness. Furthermore, attempts to explain these things in *purely* economic terms are both misleading and open to question. To take an example: The Dark Ages in the tenth to the twelfth centuries have been held to be the decisive period for the development of that type of Medieval labour which, though subject to corporate regulations, was in a sense free labour. In particular, it is held that the lords were in a situation of having to compete for the fees and income arising from the control over land, personal status, and jurisdiction; and that this situation permitted peasants, miners, and artisans to profit from the competition of the lords. It is further held that the decisive period for the development of capitalism was that of the great long-drawn-out price revolution of the sixteenth century. This led both to an absolute and a relative increase in the prices of almost all products of the land in the Western World. It is only necessary to apply well-known principles of agricultural economics to see that this both made possible and stimulated the development of enterprises which sold products on the market. This in turn led to the development of large-scale production, in part, as in England, of the capitalistic type; in part, as between the Elbe and Russia, more on the basis of patriarchal estates. Furthermore, it meant, in most cases, an absolute rise of prices, but, relatively in the normal case, a fall in the price of important industrial products. Then, so far as the necessary forms of organization and other conditions, both external and subjective, were given, there would be a stimulus to the development of market enterprises related in a competitive system. These were, to be sure, not present in Germany, but this fact is held to account for the economic decline which started there about that time. The consequence of all this is the development of capitalistic

where it seemed necessary for reasons of convenience. There is little reason to cite other references for the following exposition does not pretend to achieve new results, but only to provide a scheme of analysis useful for the purposes of this work.

enterprises in the industrial field. Its necessary prerequisite was the development of extensive markets. An indication that this was actually happening is seen in certain changes of English commercial policy, to say nothing of other phenomena.

In order to verify theoretical reasoning about the substantive economic conditions of the development of economic structures, it would be necessary to employ theses, such as these and similar ones. This cannot, however, be attempted in the present discussion. These and numerous other equally controversial theories, even so far as they could be proved not to be wholly erroneous, cannot be incorporated into the present scheme which is intentionally limited to sociological *concepts*. In that the present discussion renounces any attempt to take account of this type of data, however, the following exposition in this chapter explicitly repudiates any claim to concrete 'explanation' and restricts itself to working out a sociological typology. The same is true of the previous discussion in that it consciously omitted to develop a theory of money and price determination. This must be strongly emphasized. For the facts of the economic situation provide the flesh and blood for a genuine explanation of the process by which even a sociologically relevant development takes place. What can be done here is only to provide a scaffolding which is adequate to enable the analysis to work with relatively clear and definite concepts.

It is obvious, not only that no attempt is here made to do justice to the empirical historical aspect of economic development, but even the typology of the genetic order of possible forms is neglected. The present aim is only to develop a systematic scheme of classification.

2. A common and correct objection to the usual terminology of economics, is that it fails to make a distinction between the 'organization' and the 'enterprise.' [53] In the field of economically oriented action, 'organization' is a technical category which designates the ways in which various types of services are continuously combined with each other and with non-human means of production. Its antithesis is one of two things: either intermittent activity or that which is discontinuous from the technical point of view, as is true empirically of every household. The antithesis of enterprise, denoting as it does a type of economic orientation,

[53] *Betrieb* and *Unternehmung*. In a good deal of his discussion, Weber uses the term *Betrieb* in a context where this distinction is not important. Thus he speaks of an *Erwerbsbetrieb;* hence *Betrieb* has often been translated as 'enterprise.' But where the distinction is important in the context, 'organization' is used.—ED.

namely, profit-making, is the budgetary unit which is oriented to provision for needs. Classification of types of economic orientation in terms of profit-making enterprise and budgetary units is not, however, exhaustive. There are actions oriented to acquisition which are not covered by the concept of enterprise. All cases of seeking earnings from work, like the work of the author, the artist, the official, are neither one nor the other. The receipt and use of incomes from investment is a clear case of budgetary administration.

Despite the mixture of categories, a profit-making organization (*Erwerbsbetrieb*) [54] is spoken of wherever there is continuous permanent co-ordinated action on the part of an entrepreneur. Such action is in fact unthinkable without an 'organization,' though, in the limiting case, it may be merely the organization of his own activity, without any help from others. Here it is a matter primarily of distinguishing the budgetary unit from the enterprise and its attendant organization. The term 'profit-making organization,' instead of a continuous profit-making enterprise is, it may now be noted, to be accepted, because there it is unambiguous, only for the simplest case where the unit of technical organization coincides with the unit of enterprise. But in a market economy, it is possible for a number of technically separate organizations or 'plants' to be combined in a single enterprise. The latter receives its unity by no means alone through the personal relationship of the various units to the same entrepreneur, but by virtue of the fact that they are all controlled in terms of some kind of consistent plan in their exploitation for purposes of profit. It is hence possible that there should be transitional forms. Where the term 'organization' or 'plant' is used by itself, it will always refer to the technically distinct unit consisting in buildings, equipment, labour forces, and technical management. The latter is possibly heterocephalous and heteronomous. This state of affairs would still exist, as even ordinary usage recognizes, in a communistic economy. The term 'profit-making organization' will be used from now on only in cases where the technical and the economic unit, the enterprise, coincide.[55]

The relation between organization and enterprise raises particularly difficult terminological questions in the case of such categories as 'factory'

[54] See above note. In most cases it has seemed best to translate *Erwerbsbetrieb* with 'enterprise,' as to speak of a profit-making organization as distinguished from an enterprise would unduly complicate the terminology without bringing out sufficiently important empirical distinctions.—ED.

[55] As has already been noted, it does not seem necessary to introduce this terminological complication into the translation.—ED.

and 'putting-out industry.'[56] The latter is clearly a category of enterprise. From the point of view of organization, there are two types of units: The commercial organization and those which are parts of the workers' households without any centralized workshop except in certain cases where a master craftsman organizes one on his own initiative. The organizations in the worker's household perform certain specified functions for the commercial organization, and vice versa. The process is thus not understandable in terms of technical organization alone. It is necessary in addition to employ the categories of market, profit-making enterprise, household (of the individual worker), and exploitation of contracted services for profit.

The concept of 'factory' could, as has often been proposed, be defined in entirely non-economic terms as a mode of technical organization, leaving aside consideration of the status of the workers, whether free or unfree, the mode of division of labour, involving the extent of internal technical specialization, and the type of means of production, whether machines or tools. This would make it equivalent to an organized workshop. But besides this, it is necessary to include in the definition the mode of appropriation in the hands of an owner of the premises and the means of production. Otherwise, the concept becomes confused with that of an 'ergasterion.'[57] If this distinction is made, it seems more appropriate to define both factory and 'putting-out system' as strictly economic categories of capitalistic enterprise. Then, in a strictly socialistic economy, there would neither be factories nor 'putting-out' enterprises, but only workshops, buildings, machines, tools, and various types of labour in the shop or at home.

3. The question of stages of economic development will be considered only in so far as it is absolutely necessary, and then only incidentally. The following points will suffice for the present.

It has fortunately become more common lately to distinguish types of economic system from types of economic policy. The stages which Schönberg first suggested, and, which in a somewhat altered form, have become identified with Schmoller's name, 'domestic economy,' 'vil-

---

[56] *Hausindustrie.* This is often translated as 'domestic industry.' As Weber points out, however, this term designates the unit of technical organization, namely the household, and not of business enterprise. For this reason such authorities as Professor E. F. Gay prefer the term 'putting out industry.'—ED.

[57] Weber himself takes over the Greek word, and since the closest English equivalent, 'workshop,' is too indefinite, it seems best to retain his own term.—ED.

lage economy,' the economy of landed estates and royal households, 'town economy,' 'territorial economy,' and 'national economy,'[58] have been formulated according to the type of corporate group regulating economic activity. But there is no implication of any specific mode of variation even in the type of regulation to which economic activity has been subjected by the different corporate groups thus classified in terms of the extent of their jurisdiction. Thus the territorial economic policies of the German states consisted to a large extent simply in taking over the measures developed in the town economy. Furthermore, their innovations were not greatly different from the 'mercantilistic' policies, which were typical of those of the patrimonial states which had already achieved a relatively high level of rationality. They were thus similar to 'national economic policies,' to use the common term, which is, however, not very appropriate. This classification, further, clearly does not imply that the inner structure of the economic system, the modes in which work roles were assigned, differentiated and combined, the ways in which these different functions were divided between independent economic units, and the modes of appropriation of control over labour, means of production, and opportunities for profit, in any way ran parallel to the extent of jurisdiction of the corporate group, which might be responsible for economic policy. Above all, it does not imply that this structure was a simple function of the extent of corporate jurisdiction. To demonstrate the untenability of this view, it is only necessary to compare the Western World with Asia and the situation in modern Europe with that of Antiquity. At the same time, in considering economic structure, it is by no means legitimate to ignore the existence or absence of corporate groups with substantive powers of regulation of economic activity, nor to ignore the essential purposes of their regulation. The modes of profit-making activity are strongly influenced by such regulation, but it is by no means only political corporations which are important in this respect.

4. In this connexion, as well as others, the purpose of the discussion has been to determine the optimum conditions for the formal rationality of economic activity and its relation to the various types of substantive demands which may be made on the economic system.

[58] The corresponding German terms are: *Hauswirtschaft, Dorfwirtschaft, Stadtwirtschaft, Territorialwirtschaft,* and *Volkswirtschaft.*—ED.

16: Types of the Technical Division of Labour

From a technical point of view the division of labour may take the following forms: In the first place, it may vary according to modes of differentiation and combination of work services as such: (1) They may vary according to the type of functions undertaken by the same person. He may combine managerial functions with those of carrying out specifications; or his work may be specialized in terms of one or the other.

The distinction is naturally relative. It is common for an individual who normally supervises to take a hand in the work from time to time, as in the case of the peasants with larger holdings. The type cases of combination of the two functions are: The small peasant, the independent artisan, or the small boatman.

A given individual may perform functions which are technically different and contribute to different results, or he may perform only technically specialized functions. In the first case, the lack of specialization may be due to the technical level of work which does not permit further dividing up, to seasonal variation, or to the exploitation of labour services as a side line at times when they are not taken up by their primary occupation. In the second case, the function may be specialized in terms of the product in such a way that the same worker carries out all the processes necessary for this product, though they differ technically from each other. In a sense, this involves a combination of different functions and will be called the 'specification of function.' On the other hand, the functions may be differentiated according to the type of work, so that the product is brought to completion only by combining, simultaneously or successively, the work of a number of persons. This is the 'specialization of function.' The distinction is to a large extent relative, but it exists in principle and is historically important.

The case where there is little division of labour because of the low technical level is typical of primitive household economies. There, with the exception of the differentiation of sex roles, every individual performs every function as the occasion arises. Seasonal variation has been common in the alternation of agricultural work in the summer with the crafts in the winter. An example of side lines is the tendency for urban workers to take up agricultural work at certain times, such as the harvest, and also the various cases of secondary functions undertaken in otherwise free time, which is common even in modern offices.

The case of specification of function is typical of the occupational structure of the Middle Ages. Then, there was a large number of crafts, each of which specialized in the production of a particular article, but with no reference to the technical heterogeneity of the functions involved. There was thus a combination of functions. The specialization of functions, on the other hand, is crucial to the modern development of the organization of labour. There are, however, important physiological and psychological reasons why it has virtually never been pushed to the absolute extreme of isolation, even on the highest levels of specialization. There is almost always an element of specification of function involved. It is not, however, as in the Middle Ages, oriented to the final product.

(2) The differentiation and combination of different functions may further vary according to the modes in which the services of a plurality of persons are combined to achieve a co-ordinated result. There are two main possibilities: First, the 'accumulation' of functions; that is the employment of a number of persons all performing the same function to achieve a result. This may be organized in such a way that the functions are co-ordinated but technically independent of each other, are thus parallel; or they may be organized on a technical basis in relation to a single common purpose.

Examples of the first case are the functions performed by carpenters or plasterers, several of whom work at the same time on the same job. The second type is exemplified on a grand scale in ancient Egypt in such cases as the transportation of huge stones by thousands of workers, large numbers of them performing the same acts, such as pulling on ropes, at the same time.

The second type is the 'combination' of functions—that is, of functions which are qualitatively different, and thus specialized—in order to achieve a result. These functions may be technically independent and either simultaneous or successive; or they may involve technically organized co-operation in the simultaneous performance of technically complementary functions.

1. A particularly simple example of simultaneous, technically independent functions is furnished by the parallel spinning of the warp and the woof for a given cloth. In the same class are to be placed a very large number of processes which are, from a technical point of view, undertaken independently, but are all designed as part of the production of the same final product.

2. An example of the successive type of technically independent processes is furnished by the relation of spinning, weaving, fulling, dyeing, and finishing. Similar examples are to be found in every industry.

3. The combination of specialized functions is found all the way from the case of an assistant holding a piece of iron while a blacksmith forges it, a case which is repeated in every modern foundry, to the complicated situations, which, though not specific to modern factories, are an important characteristic of them. One of the most highly developed types outside the factory is the organization of a symphony orchestra or of the cast of a theatrical production.

17: TYPES OF THE TECHNICAL DIVISION OF LABOUR—(*Continued*)

The division of labour varies also, from a technical point of view, in terms of the extent and nature of combinations with the non-human means of production.

1. Forms may vary according to whether they consist purely in personal services, as in the case of wash-women, barbers, the performance of actors, or whether they produce or adapt goods by 'working up' or transporting raw materials. The latter may consist in construction work, as that of plasterers, decorators, and stucco workers, in production of commodities and in transport of commodities. There are many transitional forms between them.

2. They may be further distinguished according to the stage at which they stand in the process from original raw material to consumption; thus from the original products of agriculture and mining, to goods which are not only ready to consume, but available at the desired place for consumption.

3. The forms may further vary according to the ways in which they use: (a) Fixed plant and facilities.[59] These may consist in sources of power; that is, means of harnessing energy, either that of natural forces, such as the power of water, wind, or heat from fire, or that which is produced mechanically, especially steam and electrical power, or in special premises for work, or they may use (b) implements of work,[60] which include tools, apparatus, and machines. In some cases only one or another of these means of production may be used, or none. 'Tools' are those aids to labour, the design of which is adapted to the physiological and

[59] *Anlagen.*
[60] *Arbeitsmittel.*

psychological conditions of manual labour. 'Apparatus' is something which is 'tended' by the worker. 'Machines' are mechanized apparatus. These rather vague distinctions have a certain significance for characterizing epochs in the development of industrial technology.

The use of mechanized sources of power and of machinery is characteristic of modern industry. From a technical point of view, the latter presupposes specialization of functions and the saving of human labour, and also a peculiar uniformity and calculability of performance, both in quality and quantity. It is thus rational only where there exists a sufficiently wide demand for particular types of products. In the case of a market economy, it presupposes adequate purchasing power for the relevant goods; and this in turn depends on a certain type of income distribution.

It is quite out of the question here to undertake to develop even the most modest outline of a theory of the evolution of the technology and economics of tools and machinery. The concept of 'apparatus' refers to such things as the type of loom which was operated by a foot-pedal and to numerous other similar devices. These already involve a certain relative independence on the part of the mechanical process, as distinguished from the functioning of the human or, in some cases, the animal organism. Without such apparatus—which included in particular various devices for moving materials in mines—machines, with their importance in modern technology, would never have come into existence. Leonardo's famous inventions were types of apparatus.

18: Social Aspects of the Division of Labour

From the social point of view, types of the division of labour may be classified in the following way: In the first place, there is the question of the ways in which qualitatively different, especially complementary functions, are divided between more or less autocephalous and autonomous economic units, which may further be distinguished economically according to whether they are budgetary units or profit-making enterprises. There are two polar possibilities:

(1) A 'unitary' economy (*Einheitswirtschaft*) where the specialization of functions is wholly internal, completely heterocephalous and heteronomous and carried out on a purely technical basis. The same would be true of the co-ordination of function. A unitary economy may, from an

economic point of view, be either a budgetary unit or a profit-making enterprise.

On the largest possible scale a communistic organization of a national economy would be a unitary budgetary economy. On the smallest scale an example is the primitive family unit, which included all or the great majority of productive functions—a closed household economy. The type case of a profit-making enterprise with a high degree of internal specialization and co-ordination of functions is naturally the great vertical combination [61] which treats with outsiders only as an integrated unit. These two distinctions will suffice for the moment as a treatment of the development of autonomous economic units; (2) the differentiation of functions may, on the other hand, exist as between autocephalous economic units. (a) It may consist in the specialization or specification of functions between units which are heteronomous, but are autocephalous, which are thus oriented to an order established by agreement or imposed. The order, in turn, may be substantively oriented in a variety of ways. Its main concern may be to provide for the needs of a superior economic unit, which may be the budgetary unit of a lord, an *oikos,* or a profit-making enterprise controlled by a political body. The order may, on the other hand, be concerned with providing for the needs of the members of some organized group. From an economic point of view, this may be accomplished by the organization of subsidiary budgetary units, or of profit-making enterprises. The corporate group in question may exercise any one of a large number of functions. It may be confined to the regulation of economic activity or may, at the same time, be engaged in economic action on its own account. (b) The other main type is the specialization of autocephalous and autonomous units in a market economy, which are oriented on the one hand substantively only to their own self-interest, formally only to the order of a corporate group, such as the laissez-faire state, which enforces only formal, rather than substantive rules.[62]

1. A typical example of the corporate group which, limiting its function to the regulation of economic activity, takes the form of a budgetary unit administered by an association of the members, is the organization

[61] What Weber apparently has in mind is the type of 'trust' which controls all stages of the process of production from raw material to the finished product. Thus many of our steel enterprises have not only blast furnaces and rolling mills, but coal mines, coke ovens, railways and ships, and iron ore mines. The most notable example in Germany in Weber's time was the Stinnes combine.—Ed.

[62] See above, chap. i, sec. 15.

of village handicrafts in India. Corporate groups, which are themselves engaged in economic activity, like the household of a great noble, are illustrated by the organizations which provide for the wants of great landlords or slaveowners by means of contributions from the individual holdings of subjects, dependents, serfs, slaves, cottars, or sometimes village craftsmen. These phenomena have been found spontaneously developed in every part of the world. Cases of production of compulsory payments in kind to a landlord or to a town corporation, have, in so far as they have not served substantive, but as has often been the case, only fiscal ends, constituted only the regulation of economic activity. This type of control has served profit-making ends in cases where the services of household industries have been exploited for the benefit of the controlling unit.

The types where there is specialization and specification of function, as between heteronomous units, are all cases of the imposition of specialized functions. They have been common in many very old small-scale industries. The Solingen metal trade was originally organized in terms of a voluntary association determining the division of labour by agreement. It was only later that it became organized in terms of imperative co-ordination—that is, became a 'putting-out industry.' The type where the autocephalous economic units are subject only to regulation by a corporate group is illustrated by innumerable cases of the rules established by village communities and town corporations for the regulation of trade, so far at least as these have a substantive influence on the processes of production.

The case of specialization as between units in a market economy is best illustrated by the modern economic order.

2. A few further details may be added. The rules of those corporate groups which attempt to provide for the wants of their members on a budgetary basis, are related to the component budgetary units in a particular way—that is, they are oriented to the prospective needs of the individual members, not of the organized group, such as a village, itself. Specified services of this kind will be called demiurgic liturgies; [63] and this type of provision for needs, correspondingly, demiurgic. It is always a question of corporate regulation governing the division of labour and, in some cases, the ways in which specialized functions are co-ordinated.

This term will not, on the other hand, be applied to a corporate group,

[63] The term 'demiurgic' is taken over directly from Weber, who introduced it in this technical sense. It is not, apparently, current in the German literature.—ED.

whether it is imperatively co-ordinated or based on voluntary co-operation, if it carries on economic activity on its own account, contributions to which are assigned on a specialized basis. The type cases of this category are the specialized and specified contributions in kind of feudal manors, landed estates, and other types of large household units. But assigned obligations are also common in various types of corporate groups which are not primarily oriented to economic ends, such as the households of princes, political groups and the budgetary administration of local communities. These contributions are generally for the benefit of the budgetary needs of the governing authority or for corporate purposes. This way of providing for the needs of a budgetary unit by means of qualitatively specified liturgies and payments in kind on the part of peasants, craftsmen, and merchants, will, when they are owed to a personal superior, be called the *'oikos'* [64] type of organization. Where they are received by the corporate budgetary unit as such, they will be called 'corporate liturgies in kind.' The principle governing this mode of provision for the budgetary needs of a corporate group engaged in economic action, is 'liturgical' provision. This mode of organization has played an exceedingly important historical role and will have to be discussed frequently. In many political corporations, it has taken the place of modern taxation and, in economic groups, it has made possible a decentralization of the central organization by providing for its needs through agencies which were not included in the single common unit. On the contrary, each unit has managed its own affairs, but has assumed the obligation to fulfil certain functions for the central unit and to that extent has been dependent on it. Examples are peasants and serfs, subject to various kinds of labour services and payments in kind; craftsmen attached to an estate; and a large number of other types. Rodbertus was the first to apply the term *'oikos'* to the large-scale household economies of Antiquity. He used as the principal criterion the tendency to self-sufficiency in provision for needs by using the services of members of the household unit itself or of others dependent on it. In all these cases, the non-human means of production were made available without relation to the market. It is a fact that the landed estates, and still more the royal households of antiquity, especially in the New Kingdom in Egypt, were cases where the greater part of the needs of the unit were provided by services and payments in

[64] The term *oikos* is, of course, taken over from the Greek. As Weber notes below, however, it was introduced into economic discussion by Rodbertus and has been used in the German literature ever since.—ED.

kind, which were obligations of dependent household units. At the same time, the degree of approach to the pure type varies widely. The same phenomena are to be found at times in China and India, and to a less extent in our own Middle Ages, beginning with the *capitulare de villis*. It is true that exchange with the outside world has generally not been entirely lacking, but has tended to have the character of budgetary exchange. Obligations to money payment have also not been uncommon, but have generally played a subsidiary part in the main provision for needs and have tended to be traditionally fixed. It has also not been uncommon for the economic units subject to liturgical obligations to be involved in exchange relations. The decisive point, however, is that the main emphasis lay on the fact that the subsistence of the members was regarded as a return for the services of the land and equipment the members were privileged to use. There are, of course, many transitional forms. But in each case there is some kind of regulation of functions by a corporate group which is concerned with the mode of division of labour and of its co-ordination.

3. The cases where a corporate group regulating economic activity is oriented to considerations of economic profit, are well illustrated by the economic regulations of the communes of Medieval Europe and by the guilds and castes of China and India. The regulations governed the number of master craftsmen and their functions and also the technique of the craft, thus the way in which labour was oriented in the handicrafts. They belonged to this type so far as the rules were intended not primarily to secure provision for a given standard of living of the craftsmen, but, as was often though not always the case, to secure their market position by maintaining the quality of performance and by dividing up the market. Like every other type of economic regulation, that of the guilds, of course, involved limitations on market freedom and hence on fully autonomous orientation of craftsmen to the maximization of their profits. It was unquestionably intended to maintain the income standards of the existing craft shops and to that extent, in spite of its formal resemblance to profit-making enterprise, still involved a budgetary mode of orientation.

4. The cases where the corporate group carrying on economic activity has been concerned with profit making, are illustrated, apart from the cases of putting-out industry already discussed, by the agricultural estates of north-eastern Germany. These have been carried out by semi-independent tenants bound by a common system of rules. In the north-west it has

taken the form of the part-time labour by individuals with small independent holdings (*Heuerlingswirtschaft*). These estates, like the putting-
out industries, have been profit-making enterprises of the landlord as
were those of the 'putter-out.' The economic activities of the tenants and
of the domestic workers are oriented primarily to the obligations which
have been imposed upon them both in the division of functions and in
their co-ordination. These obligations determine the organization of
labour on the estate as they determine the mode of dependency of the
domestic worker. Apart from this, they are budgetary units. Their contribution to the profit-making activity is not autonomous, but is a heteronomous function on behalf of the enterprise of the landlord or the
putter-out. According to the degree in which this orientation is substantively standardized, the technical aspects of the division of labour within
a single organization may approach the kind which is typical of the
factory.

19: SOCIAL ASPECTS OF THE DIVISION OF LABOUR—(*Continued*)

From a social point of view, the modes of the division of labour may
be further classified according to the mode in which the economic advantages, which are regarded as returns for the different functions, are
appropriated. The objects of appropriation [65] may be opportunities for
realizing returns on work, non-human means of production, or opportunities for profit from the exercise of managerial functions.

When the returns from labour services are appropriated, the service
may be owed to a particular recipient, such as a lord, or a particular corporate group; or it may be disposed of on the market. In either case,
there may be any one of four radically different possibilities: (a) Monopolistic appropriation of opportunities for return by the individual
worker—the case of 'free guild labour.' This may be hereditary but
alienable, as for the Indian village craftsman; or personal and inalienable, as for the Medieval craftsman, who in addition disposed of his
services on the market. Rights of elegibility for office are personal and
inalienable, but not marketable. Or finally, they may be hereditary, but
inalienable, as was the case with certain of the rights attached to the
Medieval handicrafts, but above all, the Indian handicrafts and various
types of Medieval offices. In all these cases the appropriation may be unconditional or subject to various substantive conditions; (b) The second

---

[65] On the sociological concept of appropriation, see above, chap. i, sec. 10.

possibility is that the return for labour services should be appropriated by an 'owner' of the worker—the case of 'unfree labour.' There may be free appropriation which is both hereditary and alienable—the case of slavery proper. Or, though it is hereditary, it may not be freely alienable, but may, for instance, be bound to the non-human means of production, particularly the land. This includes serfdom and hereditary dependency.[66]

The appropriation of the use of labour by a lord may be limited by substantive conditions, as in serfdom. The worker cannot leave his status of his own free will, but neither can it arbitrarily be taken from him.

The appropriation of returns of labour may be used by the owner for purposes of budgetary administration, as a source of income in kind or in money, or as a source of labour service in the unit, as in the case of domestic slaves or serfs. Or it may be used as a means of profit. In that case the dependent may be obligated to contribute goods or to work on raw materials provided by the owner. The owner will then sell the product. This is unfree domestic industry. He may, finally, be used as a labourer in an organized shop—a slave or serf workshop.

The person herein designated as the 'owner' is very generally involved in the work process himself in a managerial capacity or even in part as a worker, but this need not be true. It may be that his position as owner, *ipso facto,* makes him the managing agent. But this is by no means necessary and is very generally not the case.

The use of slaves and serfs, the latter including various types of dependents, as part of a process of budgetary administration and not as workers in a profit-making enterprise, was typical of Antiquity and of the early Middle Ages. There are, for instance, inscriptions which mentioned slaves 'of a Persian prince who were bound out as apprentices on the understanding that they might be used for labour services in the household, but might also be allowed, in return for a payment to the owner,[67] to work independently for customers.' Though by no means without exception, this tended to be the rule for Greek slaves; and in Rome this type of independent economic activity became a legal institution which involved providing the slave with a *peculium* or *merx peculiaris*. He was naturally obligated to make payments to his owner. In the Middle Ages, body serfdom frequently involved merely a right to claim payments. This was usual in western and southern Germany. In Russia, also, an actual limitation to the receipt of these payments (*obrok*) from

[66] *Erbuntertänigkeit.*

[67] In Greek, 'ἀποφορά'; Russian, '*obrok*'; German, '*Hals*' or '*Leibzips*.'

an otherwise free serf was, though not universal, very common. Its legal status was, however, precarious.

The use of unfree labour for profit-making purposes has taken the following principal forms, particularly in the domestic industries on the estates of landlords, including various royal estates, among them probably those of the Pharaohs: (1) Unfree obligation to payments in kind—the delivery of goods in kind, the raw material for which was produced by the workers themselves as well as worked on by them. Flax is an example; (2) unfree domestic industry—work on material provided by the lord. The product could be sold at least in part for money by the lord. But in many cases, as in Antiquity, the tendency was to confine market sale to occasional instances. In early modern times, however, particularly in the border regions between the Germans and the Slavs, this was not the case, particularly, though not alone, where domestic industries have developed on the estates of landlords. The use of unfree labour in a continuous organization could take the form of unfree domestic labour or of labour in a workshop. Both forms are common. The latter was one of the various forms of the *Ergasterion* of Antiquity. It also was found on the estates of the Pharaohs, in temple workshops, and from the testimony of the frescoes on tombs, on the estates of private owners or lords. It also existed in the Orient, in Greece (Demosthenes' shop in Athens) in the Roman estate workshops, in Byzantium, in the Caroligian 'genitium,' and in modern times, for example, in Russian factories operated with serf labour; [68] (c) the third possibility is the absence of every sort of appropriation—in this sense, formally free labour. The services of labour are treated as the subject of a contractual relationship which is formally free on both sides. The contract may, however, be substantively regulated in various ways through a conventional or legal order governing the conditions of labour.

Freely contracted labour may be used in various ways. In the first place, in a budgetary unit, as occasional labour,[69] either in the household of the employer [70] or in that of the worker himself. Or it may be permanent, again performed in the household of the employer, as in the case of domestic service, or in that of the worker, as typical of the colonate. It may, on the other hand, be used for profit, again on an occasional or a permanent basis; and in both cases either in the worker's own home or

[68] See Von Tugan-Baranowski's book on the Russian factory.
[69] What Bücher calls *Lohnwerk*.
[70] *Stör.*

on premises provided by the employer. The latter is true of workers on an estate or in a workshop, but especially of the factory.

Where the worker is employed in a budgetary unit, he is directly in the service of a consumer who supervises his labour. Otherwise, he is in the service of a profit-making entrepreneur. Though the form is often legally identical, economically the difference is fundamental. Coloni may be in either status; but it is more typical for them to be workers in an *oikos;* (d) the fourth possibility is that opportunities for return for labour services may be appropriated by an association of workers, either without any appropriation by the individual worker or with important limitations on such appropriation. This may involve absolute or relative closure against outsiders and also prohibition of the dismissal of workers from employment by management without consent of the workers, or at least some kind of limitations on power of dismissal.

Examples of the type of appropriation involving closure of the group are castes of workers, the type of miners' association found in the Medieval mining industry, the organized groups or retainers sometimes found at courts, or the threshers on a landed estate. This type of appropriation is found throughout the social history of all parts of the world in an endless variety of forms. The second type involving limitations on powers of dismissal, which is also very widespread, plays an important part in the modern situation in the 'closed shop' of trade unions and especially in the 'works councils.'

Every form of appropriation of jobs by workers in profit-making enterprises, like the converse case of appropriation of the services of workers by owners, involves limitations on the free recruitment of the labour force. This means that workers cannot be selected solely on grounds of their technical efficiency, and to this extent there is a limitation on the formal rationalization of economic activity. These circumstances further impose substantive limitations on technical rationality in so far as: (1) The exploitation of the products of labour is appropriated by an owner. This may occur through the tendency to arbitrary restriction of the production of labour by tradition, by convention, or by contract. Or it may occur by the reduction or complete disappearance of the worker's own interest in maximizing the production. The latter occurs when, as in slavery, the worker is freely appropriated by an owner; (2) limitations on technical rationalization may also result from appropriation on the part of the worker. There may be a conflict of the self-interest of the worker, which lies in the maintenance of his traditional mode of life, with the attempts of his employer to get him to produce at the optimum technical level or to use other modes of production in place of his labour. For employers, there is always the possibility of transforming their exploitation of labour into a mere source of income. The tendency for the exploitation of the products to be appropriated by the workers thus under favourable circumstances generally leads to a more or less complete exclusion of the owner from management. But it also regularly tends to place workers in a state of dependence on people with whom they deal who enjoy a more favourable market position. These, such as putting-out entrepreneurs, then tend to assume a managerial position.

1. The tendency of appropriation of jobs by workers and that of workers by owners are formally antithetical. But in practice they have very similar results. This should not be surprising. In the first place, the two tendencies are very generally formally related. This is true when appropriation of the workers by an owner coincides with appropriation of opportunities for jobs by a closed corporate group of workers, as has happened in feudal courts. In such cases it is natural that exploitation of services should, to a large extent, be stereotyped; hence that production should be restricted and the worker have little interest in maximizing it. The result is generally a successful resistance of workers against any sort of technical innovation. But even where this does not occur, the fact that workers are appropriated by an owner means in practice that he is obliged to make use of this particular labour force. He is not in a position like that of the modern factory manager to select according to technical needs, but must utilize those he has without selection. This is particularly true of slave labour. Any attempt to exact performance from appropriated workers beyond that which has become traditionally established, encounters traditionalistic obstacles. These could only be overcome by the most ruthless methods, which are not without their danger from the point of view of the employer's own self-interest, since they might undermine the traditionalistic bases of his authority. Hence almost universally the production of appropriated workers has shown a tendency to restriction. Even where, as was particularly true of eastern Europe in early modern times, this has been broken up by the power of the propertied classes, the development of much higher technical levels of production has still been impeded by the absence of the selective process and by the absence of any element of self-interest or independent risk on the part of the appropriated workers. When jobs have been formally

appropriated by workers, the same result has come about even more rapidly.

2. Appropriation by workers was particularly common in the development of the early Middle Ages, from the tenth to the thirteenth centuries. The Carolingian 'beunden' and all the other beginnings of large-scale agricultural enterprise declined and disappeared. The income of feudal lords and landed proprietors became stereotyped at a very low level; and an increasing proportion of the products in kind, in agriculture and mining, and of the money proceeds from the handicrafts, went to the workers. In just this form this development was peculiar to the Western World. The principal circumstances which favoured it were as follows: (a) The fact that the propertied classes were heavily involved in political and military activity; (b) the absence of a suitable administrative staff. These two circumstances made it impossible to treat these workers in any other way than as a source of stereotyped income; (c) the fact that the freedom of movement of workers as between the potential employers competing for their services could not easily be restricted; (d) the numerous opportunities of opening up new land, new mines, and new local markets; (e) the primitive level of the technical tradition. The more the appropriation of opportunities for profit by the workers took the place of the appropriation of workers by owners, the more the owners became merely recipients of income. Classical examples are the mining industry and the English guilds. But this, even at an early period, tended to go further to the point of repudiation of payments to a lord altogether, as exemplified in the saying, 'A townsman is a freeman.' Almost immediately all this led to a broadening of opportunities of making profit by market transactions, arising either from within the group of workers themselves or from without through the development of trade.

20: Social Aspects of the Division of Labour—(*Continued*)

The Appropriation of the Non-Human Means of Production

The non-human means of production may be appropriated by workers as individuals or as corporate groups, by owners, or by regulating groups consisting of third parties.

When appropriated by workers, it may be by the individual worker who then becomes the 'owner' of the non-human means of production;

or the appropriation may be carried out by a more or less completely closed group of workers so that, though the individual worker is not the owner, the corporate group is. Such a corporate group may carry out its functions as a unitary economy as on a 'communistic' basis, or with appropriation of shares.[71] In all these cases, appropriation may be used for the purposes of budgetary administration or for profit making.

Appropriation by individual workers may exist in a system of completely free market relations, as between small peasants, artisans, boatmen, or taxi-drivers, each owning his own means of production. Where it is not the individual but a corporate group which is the agent of appropriation, there is a wide variety of possibilities, varying particularly with the extent to which the system is of a budgetary or a profit-making character. The household economy, which is in principle neither necessarily primitive nor in fact communistic, may be oriented wholly to provision for its own needs. Or it may, perhaps only occasionally, dispose of surpluses of certain types of raw material accumulated by virtue of a favourable location, or of products derived from some particular technical skill, as a means to better provision. This occasional sale may then develop into a regular system of profit-making exchange. In such cases it is common for 'tribal' crafts to develop with an interethnic specialization of function and exchange. Generally speaking, marketability depends on maintaining a monopoly, which in turn is usually secured by inherited secrets. These may develop into wandering craft groups or possibly pariah [72] crafts. It is also possible, as in India, where these groups are united in a political structure and where there are ritual barriers between the ethnic elements, for them to develop into castes.

The case where members of the group possess appropriated shares is that of 'producers' co-operation.' [73] Household economies may, with the development of money accounting, approach this type. Otherwise, it is only occasionally found, as an organization of workmen. There is, how-

---

[71] *Genossenschaftlich.*

[72] The term *Paria* is used by Weber in a technical sense to designate a group occupying the same territorial area as others, but separated from them by ritual barriers which severely limit social intercourse between the groups. It has been common for such groups to have specialized occupations, particularly occupations which are despised in the larger society.—Ed.

[73] What is ordinarily called a 'producers' co-operative association' would be included in this type, but Weber conceives the type itself more broadly. In certain respects, for instance, the medieval manor and other types of village community could be considered as examples.—Ed.

ever, one important case closely approaching this type—the mining industry of the early Middle Ages.

Since appropriation by organized groups of workers has already been discussed, appropriation by 'owners' or organized groups of them can mean only the expropriation of the workers from the means of production, not merely as individuals, but as a whole. An owner may in this connexion appropriate one or more of the following items: land, including water; subterranean wealth; sources of power; work premises; labour equipment, such as tools, apparatus and machinery; and raw materials. In any given case all these may be concentrated in a single ownership or they may be appropriated by different owners. The owners may employ the means of production they appropriate in a context of budgetary administration, as means to provide for their own needs, or as sources of income by loans. In the latter case, the loans may in turn be used for budgetary purposes or as means for earning a profit, in which case they may be used in a profit-making enterprise without capital accounting, as capital goods in another's enterprise or as capital goods in the owner's own enterprise.

The appropriating agency may be a corporate group engaged in economic activity. In this case, all the alternatives just outlined are open to it. It is, however, also possible that the means of production should be appropriated by a corporate group which only *regulates* economic activity. In this case, they are neither used as capital goods nor as a source of income, but are placed at the disposal of the members.

1. When land is appropriated by isolated economic units, it is usually for the period of actual cultivation until the harvest or, so far as, by virtue of clearing or irrigation, land is itself an artifact, for the period of continuous cultivation.

It is only when scarcity of land has become noticeable that it is common for rights of cultivation, pasturage and use of timber to be reserved to the members of a settlement group, and for the extent of their use to be limited: (1) When that happens, appropriation may be carried out by a corporate group. This may be of differing sizes, according to the mode of use to which the land is put—for gardens, meadows, arable land, pastures, or woodland. These have been appropriated by progressively larger groups from the individual household to the whole tribe. Typical cases are the appropriation of arable land, meadows, and pastures by a kinship group or a local community, usually a village. It has been usual for woodland to be appropriated by broader territorial groups,

SOCIAL ASPECTS OF THE DIVISION OF LABOUR   241

differing greatly in character and extent. The individual household has typically appropriated garden land and the area around the house and has had shares in arable fields and meadows. The assignment of these shares may take various forms. Where a wandering agricultural people takes over new areas, it may involve rigid equality. In a sedentary agricultural regime, there may be a rationally systematic redistribution. This usually occurs only as a consequence of fiscal claims when villagers are collectively responsible for taxes, or of claims of the members to political equality. The unit of technical organization has normally been the household group; (2) the subject of appropriation may be a landlord. This status may, as will be discussed later, be based primarily on the individual's position of authority in a kinship group or as political chieftain with claims to exact labour services, or on fiscal or military authority, or on some form of organization for the systematic exploitation of new land or an irrigation project.

Proprietorship over land may be made a source of utilities by the employment of the unfree labour of slaves or serfs. This, in turn, may be administered as part of a budgetary unit, through deliveries in kind or labour services, or as a means of profit, as a 'plantation.' On the other hand, it may be exploited with free labour. Here again it may be treated in budgetary terms, drawing income from the land in the form of payments in kind or from share-cropping by tenants or of money rents from tenants. In both cases the equipment used may be provided by the tenant himself or may be loaned to him by the landlord. A landlord may also exploit his holdings as a source of profit in the form of a large-scale rational enterprise.

Where the land is used as part of a budgetary economy with unfree labour, the landlord is apt to be bound traditionally in his exploitation of it, both with respect to his labour personnel, which is not subject to selection, and to their functions. The use of unfree labour in a profit-making organization, the 'plantation,' has only occurred in a few cases, notably in Antiquity in Carthage and in Rome, and in modern times in the plantations of colonial areas and in the Southern States of North America. Its use in large-scale profit-making enterprises with free labour has occurred only in the modern Western World. It is the mode of development of land proprietorship, in particular the way in which it was broken up, which has been most decisive in determining the modern forms of land appropriation. To-day, only the following pure types are found: the owner of land, the capitalistic tenant, and the propertyless agricultural labourer. The latter type is exceptional, found principally in England.

Sources of wealth adapted to exploitation by mining may be appropriated in the following ways: (a) By the owner of the land, who in the past has usually been a *landlord*; (b) by a political overlord or authority; (c) by any person discovering deposits worthy of mining; (d) by a corporate group of workers; and (e) by a profit-making enterprise.

Landlords and political authorities may administer their holdings themselves, as they did occasionally in the early Middle Ages; or they may use them as a source of income, by leasing them to an organized group of workers or to any discoverer whatever or anyone who was a member of a given group. This was the case with the 'free mines' of the Middle Ages and was the origin of the institution of 'mining freedom.' [74]

In the Middle Ages, the groups of organized mine workers were typically sharing co-operatives where each member was under obligation either to the owner or to the other solidary members to work in the mine. This obligation was balanced by a right to a share in the products. There was also the type of association of owners which distributed shares of the proceeds and each of whom had to make contributions. The tendency was for the owners to be progressively expropriated in favour of the workers; but these, in turn, as their need for equipment increased, became more and more dependent on groups with command over capital goods. Thus in the end, the appropriation took the form of a capitalistic enterprise, a limited liability company.

2. Means of production which are bound to a fixed position, such as sources of power, particularly water power, 'mills' for various different purposes, and workshops, sometimes including the apparatus in them, have in the past, particularly in the Middle Ages, generally been appropriated in one of the following ways: (a) by princes or landlords; (b) by towns; (c) by associations of workers, such as guilds, without the development, in any of them, of a unified productive organization.

In the first two cases, they are usually exploited as a source of income, a charge being made for their use. This has often been combined with monopoly position and the compulsory use of the facilities. Each productive unit would make use of the facilities in turn, according to need or, under certain circumstances, it was made the monopoly of a closed, regulative group. Baking ovens, various kinds of grinding mills for grain

[74] *Bergbaufreiheit.*

or oil, fulling mills, polishing equipment, slaughter-houses, dye works, bleaching equipment, forges—which were usually, to be sure, leased—breweries, distilleries, other equipment including particularly shipyards in the possession of the Hanseatic towns, and all kinds of market booths have been appropriated in this way. Under pre-capitalistic conditions, these have all tended to be exploited by allowing workers to use them in return for a payment; thus as part of the budgetary resources of the owner, rather than as capital, whether the owner were an individual or a corporate group, including town corporations. This type of production and budgetary exploitation as a source of investment income for the owning individual or group, or possibly production by a producers' co-operative group, has preceded their transformation into the 'fixed capital' of individual business units. Those using such equipment have tended to treat them in part as means of meeting their own needs, especially in the case of baking ovens, but also of equipment for brewing and distilling. In part they have used them in profit-making operations.

3. For maritime commerce the typical arrangement in past times has been the appropriation of the ship by a plurality of owners who have tended to become more and more sharply differentiated from the workers on ships. The organization of maritime enterprise has tended then to develop into a system of sharing risks with shippers in which ship owners, officers, and even the crew, were associated. This did not, however, produce any fundamentally new forms of appropriation, but affected only the forms of calculation and hence the distribution of profit and loss.

4. To-day, it is usual for all kinds of equipment and tools to be appropriated under one controlling agency, as is essential to the modern factory; but in earlier times, this has been exceptional. In particular, the economic character of the Greek and Byzantine 'ergasterion' and the corresponding Roman 'ergastulum' has been highly equivocal, a fact which historians have persistently ignored. It was a 'workshop' which might, on the one hand, be a part of a household unit in which slaves might carry out production for the owner's own needs, as on a landed estate. Or it might be a place where slaves carried out some subsidiary process of production of goods for sale. But, on the other hand, the workshop might be used as a source of profit in the ownership of a private individual or of a corporate group, which latter might be a town, as was true of the workshops of the Piraeus. A property would then be leased to individuals or to organized groups of workers in return for

payment. Thus when it is stated that people worked in an ergasterion, especially in a town, it is always necessary to inquire further to whom it belonged and who was the owner of the other means of production necessary for the work process. Did it employ free labour? Did they work for their own profit? Or did it employ slaves, in which case it is necessary to know who their owners were and whether they were working on their own account, though making a ἀποφορά payment to their master, or directly for their master. According to the ways in which these questions are answered, the structure would be radically different from an economic point of view. In the great majority of cases, even as late as the Byzantine and Mohammedan types, the ergasterion seems to have been primarily a source of budgetary income and was hence fundamentally different from the modern factory and should not be treated as an early stage of its development. From an economic point of view, this category is, in lack of definiteness, most closely comparable to the various types of mills, found in the Middle Ages.

5. Even in cases where the workshop and the means of production are appropriated by an individual owner who hires labour, the situation is not, from an economic point of view, necessarily what would usually be called a factory to-day. It is necessary in addition to have the use of mechanical power, of machinery, and of an elaborate internal differentiation and combination of functions. The factory to-day is a category of the capitalistic economy. Hence in the present discussion, the concept will be confined to a type of organization which is at least potentially under the control of a profit-making enterprise with fixed capital. It thus takes the form of an organized workshop with internal differentiation of function, with the appropriation of all the non-human means of production and with a high degree of mechanization of the work process by the use of mechanical power and machinery. The great workshop of Jack of Newbury, which was famous among its sixteenth-century contemporaries, did not have any of these features. It is alleged to have contained hundreds of hand looms which were his property, and the entrepreneur bought the raw material for the workers, and maintained all manner of welfare arrangements for them. But each worker worked independently as if he were at home. It was possible for an internal differentiation and combination of functions to exist in an ergasterion in which a master employed unfree labourers in Egypt, Greece, Byzantium, and in the Mohammedan world. There is no doubt that such cases have existed. But the Greek texts show clearly that even in such cases it was

common for the master to be content with the payment of an ἀποφορά from each worker though perhaps a higher one from persons in a supervisory position. This alone is sufficient to warn us not to consider such a structure economically equivalent to a factory or even to a workshop like that of Jack of Newbury. The closest approximation to the factory in the usual sense is found in royal manufactures, like the imperial Chinese porcelain manufactures and the European manufactures of court luxuries which were modelled on it. The best case of all is the manufacture of military equipment. No one can be prevented from calling these 'factories.' The Russian workshops operating with serf labour seem at first sight to stand even closer to the modern factory. Here the appropriation of the workers themselves is added to that of the means of production. But for present purposes the concept 'factory' will, for the reasons stated, be limited to organized workshops where the non-human means of production are fully appropriated by an owner, but the workers are not; where there is internal specialization of functions, and where mechanical power and machines which must be 'tended' are used. All other types of organized workshops will be designated as such with the appropriate additional description.

21: SOCIAL ASPECTS OF THE DIVISION OF LABOUR—(*Concluded*)

The Appropriation of Managerial Functions

In all cases of the management of traditional budgetary units, it is typical for the appropriation of managerial functions to take place either by the titular head himself, such as the head of the family or the kinship group, or by members of an administrative staff appointed for the management of the unit, such as household servants or officials.

In the case of profit-making enterprises, it occurs in the following situations: (a) When management and ordinary labour are entirely or very nearly identical. In this case there is usually also appropriation of the non-human means of production by the worker. This type of appropriation may be unlimited, that is, hereditary and alienable on the part of the individual, with or without a guaranteed market. It may, on the other hand, be appropriated by an organized group, with appropriation of the function by the individual restricted to personal tenure [75] or subject to substantive regulation, thus limited and dependent on various

[75] That is without rights of inheritance or alienation. See above chap. i, sec. 10.

conditions. Again, a market may or may not be guaranteed; (b) where management and ordinary work are differentiated, there may be a monopolistic appropriation of entrepreneurial functions in various possible forms, notably by co-operative groups, such as guilds, or monopolies granted by the political authority.

In cases where managerial functions are, from a formal point of view, wholly unappropriated, the appropriation of the means of production or of the credit necessary for securing control over them is, in practice, in a capitalistic form of organization, identical with appropriation of control of management by the owners of the means of production. Owners can, in such cases, exercise their control by personally managing the business or by appointment of the actual managers. Where there is a plurality of owners, they will co-operate in the selection.[76]

Wherever there is appropriation of technically complementary means of production, it generally means, in practice, at least some degree of effective voice in the selection of management and, to a relative extent at least, the expropriation of the workers from management. The expropriation of individual workers does not necessarily imply the expropriation of workers in general. Though they are formally expropriated, it is possible for an association of workers to be in fact in a position to play an effective part in management or in the selection of managing personnel.

22: THE EXPROPRIATION OF WORKERS FROM THE MEANS OF PRODUCTION

The expropriation of the individual worker from ownership of the means of production is in part determined by the following purely technical factors: (a) The fact that sometimes the means of production require the services of many workers, at the same time or successively; (b) the fact that sometimes sources of power can only be rationally exploited by using them simultaneously for many similar types of work under a unified control; (c) the fact that often a technically rational organization of the work process is possible only by combining many complementary processes under continuous common supervision; (d) the fact that sometimes special technical training is needed for the management of co-ordinated processes of labour which, in turn, can only be exploited rationally on a large scale; (e) the fact that, if the means of production and raw materials are under unified control, there is the possibility of subjecting labour to a stringent discipline and thereby con-

[76] These points are so obvious that there is no need of comment.

trolling both the speed of work and standardization and quality of products.

These factors, however, do not exclude the possibility of appropriation by an organized group of workers, a producers' co-operative. They necessitate only the separation of the *individual* worker from the means of production.

The expropriation of workers in general, including clerical personnel and technically trained persons, from possession of the means of production depends on the following principal economic factors: (a) The fact that, other things being equal, it is generally possible to achieve a higher level of technical efficiency if the management has extensive control over the selection and the modes of use of workers, as compared with the situation created by the appropriation of jobs or the existence of rights to participate in management. These latter conditions produce technically, as well as economically, irrational obstacles to efficiency. In particular, considerations appropriate to small-scale budgetary administration and the immediate interests of consumers are often in conflict with the efficiency of the organization; (b) in a market economy a management which is not hampered by any established rights of the workers, and which enjoys unrestricted control over the goods and equipment which underlie its borrowings, is in a superior credit position. This is particularly true if the management consists in individuals experienced in business affairs and with a good reputation for 'safety' derived from their continuous conduct of business; (c) from a historical point of view, the expropriation of labour has developed since the sixteenth century in an economy characterized by a progressive development of the market system, both extensively and intensively, by the sheer technical superiority and actual indispensability of a type of autocratic management oriented to the particular market situations, and by the structure of power relationships in the society.

In addition to these general conditions, the effect of the fact that enterprise has been oriented to the exploitation of market advantages has been to favour such expropriation: (a) As compared with every type of economic attitude which, from the point of view of calculation is less rational, it has favoured the maximum of technical rationality in capital accounting. This, however, has been a function of the complete appropriation of economic resources by owners; (b) it has favoured commercial abilities in management as opposed to the technical. It has also favoured the maintenance of technical and commercial secrets; (c) it has favoured a speculative business policy which again has required expropriation; (d) apart from any considerations of technical rationality, expropriation has been favoured by the bargaining superiority which management, by virtue of its possession of property, has enjoyed, both on the labour market in relation to the worker, and in the commodity market, by virtue of its capital accounting, and its command over capital goods and credit. In these ways it is superior to any type of competitor operating on a lower level of rationality in methods of calculation or less well situated with respect to capital and credit resources. The upshot of all these considerations is that the maximum of formal rationality in capital accounting is possible only where the workers are subjected to the authority of business management. This is a further specific element of substantive irrationality [77] in the modern economic order; (e) finally, free labour and the complete appropriation of the means of production create the most favourable conditions for discipline.

23: The Expropriation of Workers from the Means of Production—(*Continued*)

The expropriation of *all* the workers from the means of production may have the following effects in practice: (1) That management is in the hands of the administrative staff of a corporate group. This would be true very particularly of any rationally organized socialistic economy. The expropriation of all the workers would be retained and merely brought to completion by the expropriation of private owners; (2) that the managerial functions are, by virtue of their appropriation of the means of production, exercised by the owners or by persons they appoint. The appropriation of control over the persons exercising managerial authority by the interests of ownership may have the following consequences: (a) Management by one or more entrepreneurs who are at the same time owners—the immediate appropriation of managerial functions. This situation, however, does not exclude the possibility that a wide degree of control over the policies of management may rest in hands outside the organization, by virtue of their powers over credit or financing; for instance, the bankers who finance the enterprise; (b) the

---

[77] Attention should be called again to Weber's peculiar use of the term 'irrational.' He means that the maximum of formal rationality in his specific sense can be attained only in a structure which is in conflict with certain important values or ideas of welfare.—Ed.

THE EXPROPRIATION OF WORKERS FROM THE MEANS OF PRODUCTION 249

separation of managerial functions from appropriated ownership, especially through limitations of the functions of owners to the appointment
of management and to the free appropriation of shares of the profits,
these powers exercised by the owners of capital shares. From this situation to the purely personal type of appropriation there are all manner
of gradual transitions. The separation of ownership and management is
formally rational in the sense that, as contrasted with the case of permanent and hereditary appropriation of managerial functions, it permits the
selection for managerial posts of the persons best qualified from the
standpoint of profitability. But this can have various different practical
consequences. By virtue of their ownership, control over managerial positions may rest in the hands of property interests outside the organization as such. They may be shareholders who are, above all, concerned
with maximizing their investment returns. Or control over managerial
positions may lie, by virtue of a temporary market situation, in the hands
of speculative interests outside the organization, such as shareholders
who are interested in profits from the sale of their shares. Or, finally,
control over managerial positions may be in the hands of other business
interests, such as banks or others, which by virtue of their power over
markets or over credit are in a position to exercise control. These may
pursue their own interests, which are often foreign to those of the organization as such.

Interests are spoken of as 'outside the firm' so far as they are not
primarily oriented to the long-run profitability of the enterprise. This
may be true of all sorts of property interests. It is particularly true, however, of interests having control of the plant and capital goods of the
enterprise or of a share in it, which is not exercised as a permanent investment, but as a means of making a speculative profit. The types of outside interest which are most readily reconciled with those of the enterprise are those of pure investment; they are, that is, interests in long-run
profitability.

The ways in which these outside interests play into the modes of control over managerial position constitutes another specific element of substantive irrationality in the modern economic order. This is the more
true the higher the degree of rationality exercised in selection. It is possible for entirely private property interests to exercise control, or others
which are oriented to ends having no connexion with the organization,
or finally, those concerned only with gambling. By gaining control of
shares, these can control the appointment of the managing personnel

and, more important, the business policies they pursue. The influence exercised on the market situation, especially that for capital goods, and in turn on the orientation of production of goods for profit, by speculative interests outside the producing organizations themselves, is *one* of the sources of the phenomena known as the 'crises' of the modern market economy. This cannot, however, be further discussed here.

24: The Concept of Occupation and Types of Occupational Structure

The term 'occupation' (*Beruf*) will be applied to the mode of specialization, specification, and combination of the functions of an individual so far as it constitutes for him the basis of a continual opportunity for income or for profit. Occupations may be distributed in the following ways: (1) By a heteronomous assignment of functions and provision of maintenance within a corporate group regulating economic activity—the unfree differentiation of occupations—or through autonomous orientation to the state of the market for occupational services—free differentiation of occupations; (2) its distribution may rest on the specification of functions or the specialization of functions; (3) it may involve economic exploitation of the services by their bearers on either an autocephalous or a heterocephalous basis.

The structure of occupational differentiation and that of opportunities for income and profit are closely related. This will be discussed in relation to the problems of social stratification.[78]

1. The unfree organization of occupations exists in cases where there is compulsory assignment of functions within the organization of a royal estate, a state, a feudal manor, or a commune on the basis of liturgies or of the *oikos* type of structure. The free type of distribution arises from the successful offer of occupational services on the labour market or successful application for free 'positions.'

2. As was pointed out above in sec. 16, the specification of functions was typical of the organization of the handicrafts in the Middle Ages; specialization is characteristic of the modern form of rational organization. Occupational distribution in a market economy consists to a large

[78] See chap. iv, with particular reference to occupation as a basis of social prestige and class status.

All of this chapter, which is to be found in the German edition, is included in the present translation. It is, however, a mere fragment which Weber intended to develop on a scale comparable with the others. Hence most of the material to which this note refers was probably never written down.—Ed.

extent of technically irrational specification of functions, rather than of rational specialization of functions, because it is oriented to the market situation and hence to the interests of purchasers and consumers. These interests determine what services will be offered to and selected by a given productive unit, often independently of the technical aspects of the specialization of functions. And this often necessitates modes of combinations of functions which are technically irrational.

3. Cases of autocephalous occupational specialization are the independent 'business' of an artisan, a physician, a lawyer, or an artist. The factory worker and the government official, on the other hand, occupy heterocephalous occupational positions.

The occupational structure of a given social group may vary in the following ways: (a) According to the degree in which well-marked and stable occupations have developed at all. The following circumstances are particularly important in this connexion; the development of consumption standards, the development of techniques of production, and the development of large-scale budgetary units in the case of unfree occupational organization, or of market systems in that of free organization; (b) according to the mode and degree of occupational specification or specialization of individual economic units. This will be decisively influenced by the market situation for the services or products of specialized units, which is in turn dependent on adequate purchasing power. It will also be influenced by the modes of distribution of control over capital goods; (c) according to the extent and kind of continuity or change in occupational status. This in turn depends above all on two factors: on the one hand, on the amount of training required for the specialized functions, and on the other hand the degree of stability or instability of opportunities for earnings from them. The latter is in turn dependent on the type and stability of distribution of income and on the state of technology.

Finally, it is always important in studying occupational structure to know the system of social stratification, including the distribution of opportunity in the different classes and the types of education which are available for the various types of occupations requiring specialized training, notably the learned professions.

It is only functions which require a certain minimum of training and for which opportunity of continuous remuneration is available which become the objects of independent and stable occupations. The choice of occupation may rest on tradition, in which case it is usually hereditary, on considerations of expediency, especially the maximization of money returns, on charismatic devotion to the task, on affectual grounds, and finally, in particular, on grounds of prestige with particular reference to class status. Originally, the more individualistic occupations seem to have been dependent primarily on charismatic, particularly magical, elements; while all the rest of the occupational structure, so far as in a differentiated form it existed at all, was traditionally fixed. The requisite qualities, so far as they were not charismatic and thus specifically personal, tended to become the object of a traditional training in closed groups, or of a hereditary tradition. Specialized occupations which were not of a strictly charismatic character first appeared on a liturgical basis in the large-scale households of princes and landed proprietors, and then oriented to a market economy in the towns. Alongside of this, however, related to magical ritual or clerical training there have developed literary forms of education which have tended to enjoy high class prestige.

From what has been said it will be seen that occupational specialization does not necessarily imply continuous employment either on a liturgical basis for an organized unit, as, for instance, in a royal household [80] or in relation to a completely free market. Other forms are not only possible, but common: (1) Propertyless occupationally specialized workers may be employed on an occasional basis as needed in the service of a relatively stable group of customers in household units or of employers in profit-making enterprises. In the first case, if the worker has no property of his own, the employer provides the raw material and is hence the owner of the product. This type of work may be carried on on a purely itinerant basis or sedentarily in the service of a local group of household units.[81] It is also possible for the work to be carried on in the worker's own fixed shop, which may at the same time also be his household, but on behalf of the household unit.[82]

In all such cases the employing household provides the raw materials but it is usual for the worker to own his own tools—the mower, his scythe; the seamstress, her sewing equipment, etc. In the first type, the

[80] Following this, in the German text, occur the words *oder eine Fabrik*. Since the inclusion of the factory as a form with liturgical organization of occupations is directly contradictory to Weber's explicit definition above, this must be either an error on Weber's part, or a misprint. That it is a correct expression of his meaning seems so improbable that the phrase has been omitted in translation.—ED.

[81] This is usually called *Stör* in German.—ED.

[82] *Lohnwerk*.

relationship to the employer involves temporary membership in the latter's household.[83]

Occupationally specialized workers may be employed on an occasional basis by profit-making enterprises when at least the raw material, and thus also control over the product, belongs to the employer. In this case there may be migratory labour for a variety of different employers in different units, or occasional or seasonal work for an employer, the work being done in the worker's own household. Migratory harvest labour is an example of the first type. The second type is illustrated by the common cases of homework which supplements that of the workshop; (2) the same type of thing may occur where the means of production are appropriated by the economic units in question: (i) Where there is capital accounting and partial appropriation of the means of production by owners, particularly appropriation restricted to spatially fixed equipment and premises. Examples are workshop organizations employing wage labour, and, above all, the 'factories'[84] of the putting-out industries. The first of these forms has long existed, while the latter has recently become common; (ii) when the means of production are completely appropriated by the workers: (a) In a small-scale unit without capital accounting, producing for households, who are the ultimate consumers, or for profit-making enterprises. The latter is a case of domestic industry without expropriation of the means of production. The worker is formally a free craftsman, but is actually bound to a monopolistic group of merchants who are buyers for his product; (b) on a large scale with capital accounting and production for a fixed group of purchasers. This is usually, though not always, the result of market regulation by cartels.

Finally, it must be pointed out that every case of earning is by no means necessarily part of profit-making as an occupation; nor is it necessary that involvement in acquisitive action, however frequent, should imply a continuous specialization with a constant meaningful orientation.

Occasional acquisition is found as a result of the disposal of surpluses produced in a budgetary unit. Corresponding to these are both purchases and sales of goods by large-scale budgetary units, especially landed estates, as the occasion offers. From this starting point, it is possible to trace a continuous series of occasional acquisitive acts, such as the occa-

[83] Karl Bücher has used the term *Preiswerk* for the case where *all* the means of production are owned by the worker.

[84] This usage is apparently inconsistent with Weber's explicit definition of the factory.—ED.

sional speculation of a person living on income from investment, occasional publication of an article or a poem by a person who is not a professional author, and similar modern phenomena, to the case where such things constitute a 'subsidiary' occupation.[85]

It should furthermore be remembered that there are ways of making a living which are continually shifting and in essence fundamentally unstable. A person may shift continually from one type of profitable activity to another; or even between normal legitimate earning and begging, stealing, or highway robbery.

The following must be treated in special terms: (a) Support from purely charitable sources; (b) maintenance in an institution on other than a charitable basis, notably a penal institution; (c) regulated acquisition by force; and (d) criminal acquisition; that is, acquisition by force or fraud in violation of the rules of an order. The cases of (b) and (d) are of relatively little interest; (a) has often been of tremendous importance for the economy of religious groups, such as mendicant orders; while (c) has been crucial for many political groups in the form of the booty gained from war. It is characteristic of both these cases that they lie outside the realm of economic activity as such. Hence this is not the place to enter into a more detailed classification. The forms will be treated elsewhere.[86] For reasons which are in part, though only in part, the same, the earnings of bureaucratic officials, including military officers, have been mentioned below (sec. 39) only in order to give them a place as a sub-type of the earnings of labour, but without going into the details. To do this, it would be necessary to discuss the structure of relations of authority and imperative co-ordination in the context of which these types of earnings are to be placed.

24A: THE PRINCIPAL FORMS OF APPROPRIATION AND OF MARKET RELATIONSHIP

According to the theoretical schema which has been developed, starting with sec. 15, the classification of the modes of appropriation in their

---

[85] *Nebenberuf.*

[86] The part of the present translation most relevant to this subject is the discussion of 'the financing and economic support of administrative staffs in systems of authority.' It runs through various parts of chap. iii. More detailed discussion of certain aspects of the subject is to be found in part iii of *Wirtschaft und Gesellschaft,* which is not included in the present translation. In this, as in other respects, however, this part of the work is seriously incomplete.—ED.

technical aspects and in relation to the market is exceedingly complex. But actually, only a few of the many theoretical possibilities play a really important role.

(1) With respect to agricultural land: (a) There is the migratory household economy, which changes its location whenever the land has been worked out. The land is usually appropriated by the tribe while its use is temporarily or permanently appropriated by neighbourhood groups. It is only appropriation of the use of land for a period which is enjoyed by the individual household.

The extent of the household group may vary from the individual conjugal family, through various types of extended family groups, to organized kin groups or a widely extended household community. Agriculture is migratory as a rule only in relation to arable land, much less commonly and at longer intervals for farm buildings.

(b) Sedentary agriculture. This is usually regulated by territorial or village communities with a smaller household group enjoying rights of use of arable fields, meadows, pastures, woodland, and water. Gardens and the land immediately surrounding the buildings are normally appropriated by the immediate family; arable fields, usually meadows, and pastures, by the village community; woodland, by more extensive territorial groups. Redistribution of land is usually possible according to the law, but has generally not been systematically carried through and is hence usually obsolete. Economic activities have generally been regulated by a system of rules applying to the whole village. This is a 'primary village economy.'

It is only in exceptional cases, such as China, that the extended kinship group has constituted an economic unit. Where this is the case, it has generally taken the form of a rationalized corporate group, such as a clan association.

(c) Landed proprietorship and serfdom. The estate is controlled by a landlord, and dependent peasant farms are obligated to deliveries in kind and labour services. Land ownership and the workers are appropriated by the lord, the use of the land and rights to work by the peasants. This is a simple case of an organization of reciprocal relations between a landlord and his sources of income in kind.

(d) The monopoly of control over the land by a landlord or a fiscal unit with communal responsibility of the peasant community for meeting fiscal obligations. This leads to communal cultivation and a regular systematic redistribution of the land. The land is, as a correlate of the fiscal burden, permanently appropriated by the organized peasant community, not the individual household; the latter enjoys only rights of use and these are subject to redistribution. Economic activity is regulated by the rules imposed by the landlord or the political authority.

(e) Free landed proprietorship with exploitation of the dependent peasants as a source of budgetary income. The land is thus appropriated by a landlord; but colonies, sharecroppers,[87] or tenants paying money rent carry out the actual economic activities.

(f) The plantation. The land is freely appropriated and worked by slaves. The owner uses both as means of profit making in a capitalistic enterprise with unfree labour.

(g) A 'landed estate.'[88] The land is appropriated by owners who receive rent by leasing it to large-scale farmers or who farm it themselves as a source of profit. In both cases free labour is used. Various sorts of equipment may be either owned by the tenant or provided by the lord. In both cases, again, all agricultural products may be produced on the estate or, in the limiting case, all consumption needs met through the market.

(h) The absence of landed proprietorship. This is a peasant economy with appropriation of the land by the peasant who farms it. In practice, this form of appropriation may mean that the land farmed is predominantly inherited land, or, on the other hand, that the land is freely bought and sold. The former is typical of settlements with scattered farms and large-scale peasant proprietors; the latter, where settlement is in villages and the scale is small.[89]

Where tenants pay a money rent and where peasant proprietors buy and sell land, it is necessary to presuppose an adequate local market for the products of peasant agriculture.

(2) In the field of industry and transport, including mining, and of trade:

(a) Household industry carried on primarily as a means of occasional exchange of surpluses, only secondarily as a means of profit. This

---

[87] *Teilpachtbauer.* Apparently this institution is similar to the French *metoyer* system.

[88] *Gutswirtschaft.*

[89] It seems curious that in this classification Weber failed to mention the type of agricultural organization which has become predominant in the staple agricultural production of much of the United States and Canada. Of the European types this comes closest to large-scale peasant proprietorship, but is much more definitely oriented to the market for a single staple, such as wheat. Indeed, in many respects this type of farm is closely comparable to some kinds of small-scale industrial enterprise.—ED.

may involve an inter-ethnic division of labour, out of which in turn caste occupations have developed. In both cases it is usual for sources of raw materials to be appropriated by craft groups, and hence, the production of raw materials to be carried on by them. The purchase of raw materials and work for wages are secondary phenomena. In the case of inter-ethnic specialization, formal appropriation is often absent. There is, however, generally, and in the case of caste, always, appropriation of opportunities for earning from a specified function by kinship or household group.

(b) A restricted craft working for specific customers. The specification of function for an organized group of consumers. This may be a group exercising authority, such as an *oikos* or a landed estate, or it may be a communal group.

There is no market sale. In the first case, there is an organization of functions on a budgetary basis, or of labour in a workshop, as part of the ergasterion of the lord. In the second case, there is hereditary appropriation of the status of the workers which may, however, become alienable. Work is carried out for an appropriated group of customers who are consumers. There are the following very limited possibilities of development: (i) The workers, who are formally unfree but with specified functions, may be appropriated by a lord as a source of income, but in spite of their formal unfreedom, may remain for the most part in fact free to work for customers as they will. They may also be appropriated as unfree workers in the lord's own household for his profit. They may, finally, be employed in an ergasterion for profit; (ii) this may also develop into a liturgical specification of functions for fiscal purposes, similar to the type of caste occupations.

In the field of mining, there are similar forms, notably the use of unfree labour, slaves or serfs, in productive units controlled by princes or landed proprietors.

In inland transportation, it is common for transportation equipment to be appropriated as a source of income. Services are then compulsorily imposed on specified small peasant holdings. Another possibility is small-scale caravan trade co-operatively regulated. The traders would then appropriate the goods themselves.

In the field of maritime transportation: (i) The ownership of ships by an *oikos* or a landlord or a patrician who manages it himself; (ii) co-operative construction and ownership of the ship. The captain and the crew also participate on their own account. Small travelling merchants would also participate as shippers. All the parties were associated in the bearing of risks. Actual voyages were made by strictly regulated 'caravans.' In all these cases 'trade' was still identical with inter-local trade; that is, with transport.

(c) Free industry.[90] Free production for consumers in return for a wage, either on the customer's premises or the worker's own. Usually the raw materials were appropriated by the customer, the tools by the worker, and premises and stationary equipment, if they were involved at all, by a lord as a source of income or by organized groups with rights of use in rotation. Another possibility is that both raw materials and tools should be appropriated by the worker who thus managed his own work, whereas premises and stationary equipment belonged to an organized group of workers, such as a guild. In all these cases, it is usual for the regulation of profit-making activity to be carried on by guilds.

In mining, deposits have usually been appropriated by political authorities or by landlords as sources of income, while the rights of exploitation have been appropriated by organized groups of workers. Mining operations have been regulated on a guild basis, oriented to the obligation toward the owner to secure his interest in royalties and to the working group who were responsible to him as a group and had an interest in the proceeds.

In the field of inland transport are found guilds of boatmen and land carriers with fixed itineraries and regulations of their opportunities for profit.

In the field of maritime shipping have existed the ownership of shares, 'caravans' of ships, and travelling merchants acting as agents on a commission basis.

There are the following stages in the development toward capitalism: (a) Effectual monopolization of money capital by entrepreneurs who have used it as a means to make advances to labour. Connected with this is the assumption of powers of management of the process of production by virtue of the extension of credit and of control of the product, in spite of the fact that appropriation of the means of production has continued formally in the hands of the workers, as in the handicrafts and in mining; (b) appropriation of the right of marketing products

---

[90] The German term *Gewerbe* may sometimes be translated as 'handicraft,' but as generally used is somewhat broader. Industry here should be taken in the broadest sense to include any process of non-agricultural production.—ED.

on the basis of previous monopolization of knowledge of the market and hence of market opportunities and monopolization of money capital. This was made possible by the imposition of a monopolistic system of guild regulation or by privileges granted by the political authority. Such privileges were granted in return for periodical payments or for loans; (c) the subjective disciplining of workers who stood in a dependent relationship in the putting-out system, and the supply of raw materials and apparatus by the entrepreneur. A special case is that of the rational monopolistic organization of domestic industries on the basis of privileges granted in the interests of national finances or of the employment of the population. The conditions of work were thereby regulated by imposition from above as part of the concession which made profit-making activity possible; (d) the development of workshops without a rational specialization of labour in the process of production, by means of the appropriation by the entrepreneur of all the non-human means of production. In mining this included the appropriation by individual owners of mineral deposits, galleries, and equipment. In transportation, shipping enterprises fell into the hands of large owners. The universal result is the expropriation of the workers from the means of production; (e) the final step in the transition to capitalistic organization of production is the mechanization of the productive process and of transportation and its orientation to capital accounting. All the non-human means of production become fixed or working capital; all the workers become 'hands.' As a result of the transformation of enterprises into associations of security owners, even the management itself becomes expropriated and assumes the formal status of an official. Even the owner becomes effectively an agent for, or unofficial representative of, the suppliers of credit, the banks.

Of all these various types, the following instances may be noted:

1. In agriculture, type (a), migratory agriculture, is universal. But the sub-type where the effective unit has been the large-scale household community or kinship group, is found only occasionally in Europe, but has been very common in eastern Asia, particularly China. Type (b), sedentary agriculture with village communities, has been indigenous to Europe and India. Type (c), unfree landed proprietorship, has been found everywhere and is still common in some parts of the Orient. Type (d), proprietorship by a landlord or a fiscal unit, with a systematic redistribution of peasant holdings, has been, in the context of landed

proprietorship, primarily found in Russia, and in a somewhat different form, involving the redistribution of land rents, in India. The predominantly fiscal form has been found in Eastern Asia, the Near East, and Egypt. Type (e), free ownership of land, drawing rent from small tenants, is typical of Ireland, but also occurs in Italy, southern France, China, and the eastern parts of the Hellenistic world in Antiquity. Type (f), the plantation with unfree labour, was characteristic of Carthage and Rome in Antiquity, of modern colonial areas, and of the Southern States of the United States. Type (g), the landed estate, in the form which involves separation of ownership and exploitation, has been typical of England; in the form of owner management, of eastern Germany, parts of Austria, Poland, and western Russia. Finally, type (h), peasant proprietorship, has been found in France, southern and western Germany, parts of Italy, Scandinavia, with certain limitations in south-western Russia, and with modifications, particularly in modern China and India.

These wide variations in the forms which the organization of agriculture has finally assumed are only partially explicable in economic terms, involving such factors as the difference between the cultivation of forest clearings and of the areas subjected to irrigation. In addition, it is necessary to take account of a variety of special historical circumstances, especially the forms taken by political and fiscal obligations and military organization.

2. In the field of industry, the following outline of the distribution of types may be given. Our knowledge of the situation in transportation and mining is not sufficiently complete to give such an outline for those fields.

(a) The first type, the tribal craft, has been found universally; (b) organization on the basis of occupational castes has become the predominant form only in India. Elsewhere it has existed only for occupations considered discreditable and sometimes ritually impure; (c) the organization of industry on the basis of the *oikos* is found in all royal households in early times, but has been most highly developed in Egypt. It has also existed on landed estates all over the world. Production by a co-operative group for a fixed market [91] occurs occasionally everywhere, including the Western World, but has become the predominant form only in India. The special case of the use of control over unfree persons simply as a source of income was common in Mediterranean Antiquity.

[91] *Demiurgische Gewerbe.*

The liturgical specification of functions is characteristic of Egypt, of the Hellenistic world, of the later Roman Empire, and has been found at times in China and India; (d) the free handicraft organization with guild regulation is classically illustrated in the European Middle Ages and became the predominant form only there. It has, however, been found all over the world; and guilds, in particular, have developed very widely, especially in China and the Near East. It is notable, however, that this type was entirely absent from the economic organization of classical Antiquity. In India, the caste took the place of the guild. Of the stages in the development toward capitalism, only the second was reached on a large scale outside the Western World. This difference cannot be explained entirely in purely economic terms.[92]

25: Conditions Underlying the Calculability of the Productivity of Labour

1. In the three typical communistic forms of organization, non-economic motives play a predominant part.[93] But apart from these cases, there are three primary conditions affecting the maximization of calculable performance by labour in carrying out specifications: (a) The optimum of aptitude for the function; (b) the optimum of skill acquired through practice; (c) the optimum of incentive for the work.

Aptitude, regardless of whether it is the product of hereditary or environmental and educational influences, can only be determined by testing. To-day, in large-scale business firms this usually takes the form of special aptitude tests. The Taylor system involves an attempt to work out rational methods of accomplishing this.

Practice, and the resulting skill, can only be perfected by rational and continuous specialization. To-day, it is worked out on a basis which is largely empirical, guided by considerations of minimizing costs in the interest of profitability, and limited by these interests. Rational specialization with reference to physiological conditions is only in its beginnings. Here again the Taylor system is a pioneer.

Incentives to work may be oriented to any one of the ways which are

[92] The above proposition is one of the most important conclusions of Weber's comparative study in the Sociology of Religion. An attempt to throw light on the problems raised by the materialistic interpretation of history was one of the principal reasons for his embarking on these studies.—Ed.

[93] See below, sec. 26.—Ed.

open to any other mode of action.[94] But in the specific sense of carrying
out the intentions of the actor himself or of persons supervising his
work, it must be determined either by a strong interest in the outcome
on his own part, or by direct or indirect compulsion. The latter is
particularly important in relation to work which carries out the aims
of others. This compulsion may consist in the immediate threat of
physical force or of other undesirable consequences, or in the probability
that unsatisfactory performance will have an adverse effect on earnings.

The second type, which is essential to a market economy, appeals immensely more strongly to the worker's self-interest. It also necessitates
freedom of selection according to performance, both qualitatively and
quantitatively, though naturally from the point of view of its bearing on
profit. In this sense it has a higher degree of formal rationality, from
the point of view of technical considerations, than any kind of direct
compulsion to work. It presupposes the expropriation of the workers
from the means of production and their dependence on competition for
paid employment. This in turn presupposes that the appropriation of
the means of production by owners is protected by force. As compared
with direct compulsion to work, the system of free labour involves responsibility for reproduction, in the family, and part of the responsibility
for selection according to aptitude is turned over to the workers themselves. Further, both the need for capital and the risks to which it is
subjected are, as compared with the use of unfree labour, lessened and
made more calculable. Finally, through the payment of money wages
on a large scale, the market for goods which are objects of mass consumption is broadened.

Other things being equal, positive motives for work are not, in the
absence of direct compulsion, to the same extent obstructed as they are
for unfree labour. It is, however, true that whenever technical specialization has reached very high levels, the extreme monotony of operations
tends to limit incentives to purely material wage considerations. It is
only when wages are paid in proportion to performance on a piece-rate
basis that there is an incentive to increasing productivity. In the capitalistic system, the most immediate bases of willingness to work are opportunities for high piece-rate earnings and the danger of dismissal.[95]

The following observations may be made of the situation of free labour

---

[94] See above, chap. i, sec. 2.

[95] Investigations carried out since this was written have tended to show that the situation is not as simple as Weber seemed to think. There is, in most cases, not so direct a

separated from the means of production: (a) Other things being equal, the likelihood that people will be willing to work on affectual grounds is greater in the case of specification of functions than in that of specialization of functions. This is true because the product of the individual's own work is more clearly evident. In the nature of the case, this is particularly true where quality of performance is important; (b) traditional incentives to work are particularly common in agriculture and in domestic industries, where in both cases the general attitude toward life is traditional. It is characteristic of this that the level of performance is oriented either to products which are stereotyped in quantity and quality or to a traditional level of earnings, or both. Where such an attitude exists, it is difficult to manage labour on a rational basis and production cannot be increased by such incentives as piece rates. Experience shows, on the other hand, that a traditional patriarchal relationship to a lord or owner is capable of maintaining a high level of affectual incentive to work; (c) incentives based on absolute values are usually the result of religious orientations or of the high social esteem in which the particular form of work as such is held. Observation seems to show that all other sources of incentive are transitional forms between this and other types.

It goes without saying that the 'altruistic' concern of the worker for his own family is a typical element of duty contributing to willingness to work generally.

2. The appropriation of the means of production and personal control, however formal, over the process of work constitute among the strongest incentives to unlimited willingness to work. This is the fundamental basis of the extraordinary importance of small units in agriculture, whether in the form of small-scale proprietorship or small tenants who hope to rise to the status of owner. The classical locus of this type of organization is China. The corresponding phenomenon in the functionally specified skilled trades is most marked in India. But it is very important in all parts of Asia and also in Europe in the Middle Ages. In the latter case, the most crucial conflicts have been fought out over the issue of formal autonomy of the individual worker. The existence of the small peasant in a sense depends directly on the absence of capital accounting and on retaining the unity of household and enterprise. His is a speci-

relation between the level of effort and effective earnings as he maintained. It also appears that other factors, notably the informal social relationships of the working group, play an important role. See especially Roethlisberger and Dickson, *Management and the Worker*.

fied and not a specialized function, and he tends both to devote more intensive labour to it and to restrict his standard of living in the interest of maintaining his formal independence. In addition, this system of agriculture makes possible the use of all manner of by-products and even 'waste' in the household in a way which would not be possible to a large organization. All the information we have available [96] goes to show that capitalistic organization in agriculture is, where management is in the hands of the owner, far more sensitive to cyclical movements than small-scale peasant farming.

In industry, the corresponding small-scale type has retained its importance right up to the period of mechanization and of the most minute specialization and combination of functions. Even as late as the sixteenth century, as actually happened in England, it was possible simply to forbid the maintenance of workshops, like that of Jack of Newbury, without catastrophic results for the economic situation of the workers. This was true because the combination in a single shop of looms, appropriated by an owner and operated by workers, could not, under the market conditions of the time, without any far-reaching increase in the specialization and co-ordination of labour functions, lead to an improvement in the prospects of profit for the entrepreneur large enough to compensate with certainty for the increase in risk and for the costs of operating the shop. It is above all true that in industry an enterprise with large investments in fixed capital is not only, as in agriculture, sensitive to cyclical fluctuations, but also in the highest degree to every form of irrationality—that is, lack of calculability—in public administration and the administration of justice. This factor has everywhere been of crucial importance, except in the modern Western World. It has hence been possible, as in competition with the Russian factory and everywhere else, for decentralized domestic work to dominate the field. This was true up to the point, which was reached before the introduction of mechanical power and machine tools, where, with the broadening of market opportunities, the need for exact cost accounting and standardization of product became marked. In combination with technically rational apparatus, using water power and horses, this led to the development of forms of organization with internal specialization. Mechanical motors and machines could then be introduced. Though they did occasionally appear, it would, until this point was reached, have been possible for all the large-scale industrial establishments in the world to be eliminated without any serious

[96] See the author's figures in the *Verhandlungen des deutschen Juristentags,* vol. xxiv.

prejudice to the economic situation of all those involved in them and without any serious danger to the interest of consumers. This situation has been changed only with the appearance of the factory. But willingness to work on the part of factory labour has been primarily determined by a combination of the transfer of responsibility for maintenance to the workers personally and the corresponding powerful indirect compulsion to work as symbolized in the English workhouse system. It is furthermore permanently bound to the compulsory guarantee of the property system. This is demonstrated by the marked decline in willingness to work at the present time, which has resulted from the breakdown of this compulsory power in the revolution.[97]

26: Types of Communal Organization of Labour

Communistic systems for the communal or associational organization of work are unfavourable to calculation and to the consideration of means for obtaining optimum production; they tend, rather, to be based on the direct feeling of mutual solidarity. They have thus tended historically, up to the present, to develop on the basis of common value attitudes of a primarily non-economic character. There are three main types: (1) The household communism of the family, resting on a traditional and affectual basis; (2) the military communism of comrades in an army; (3) the communism based on love and charity in a religious community.

Cases (2) and (3) rest primarily on a specific emotional or charismatic basis. They always, however, (a) stand in direct conflict with the specialized rational or traditional economic organization of their environment. The communistic group then either works itself or is supported purely by contributions from without, or both. Or (b) it may constitute a budgetary organization of privileged persons who exercise control over other budgetary units which are not members and are supported by the contributions or liturgies of the latter. Or (c) finally, it is a purely consuming unit, distinct from any profit-making enterprises, but drawing income from them, and hence in an associative relationship with them.

The first of these modes of support (a) is typical of communities based on religious belief or some other community of sentiment—such as

97 Weber means the Revolution of 1918 in Germany.—ED.

monastic communities which renounce the world altogether or carry on communal labour, sectarian groups and utopian socialists.

The second mode (b) is typical of military groups which rest on a wholly or partially communistic basis. Examples are the 'men's house' in many primitive societies, the Spartan 'mess,' the Ligurian pirate groups, the entourage of the Calif Omar, the communism, in consumption and partly in requisitioning, of armies in the field in every age. A similar state of affairs is found in authoritarian religious groups— as in the Jesuit state in Paraguay and communities of mendicant monks in India and elsewhere.

The third mode (c) is typical of family households in a market economy.

Willingness to work and consumption without calculation are, within these communities, a result of the non-economic attitudes characteristic of them. In the military and religious cases, they are to an appreciable extent based on a feeling of separateness from the ordinary everyday world and even of conflict with it. Modern communistic movements are, so far as they aim for a communistic organization of the masses, dependent on devotion to absolute values for their following. In their propaganda, however, they also make use of arguments from expediency, touching the efficiency of production. But in both cases, they rest their position on specifically rational considerations which are, as contrasted with military and religious communities, concerned with the everyday profane world.[98] Their prospects of success under ordinary conditions rest on entirely different subjective conditions from those governing groups which are oriented to exceptional activities, to other-worldly values, or to other primarily non-economic considerations.

[98] Weber uses the term *Alltag* in a technical sense, which is contrasted with *Charisma*. The antithesis will play a leading role in chap. iii. In his use of the terms, however, an ambiguity appears of which he was probably not aware. In some contexts, *Alltag* means routine, as contrasted with things which are exceptional or extraordinary and hence temporary. Thus, the charismatic movement led by a prophet is, in the nature of the case, temporary, and if it is to survive at all must find a routine basis of organization. In other contexts, *Alltag* means the profane, as contrasted with the sacred. The theoretical significance of this ambiguity has been analysed in the *Structure of Social Action*, chap. xvii. Weber's fullest discussions of the concepts of *Charisma* and *Alltag* and their relation are, apart from chap. iii of the present translation, to be found in the section on *Religionssoziologie* in *Wirtschaft und Gesellschaft*, part ii, chap. iv, and in part iii, especially chaps. ix and x. —ED.

27: CAPITAL GOODS AND CAPITAL ACCOUNTING

Capital goods are usually first found in their earlier stages in the form of commodities which are objects of exchange between different areas or tribes. This implies that 'trade' or 'commerce'[99] occurs which is clearly distinct from the mere production of goods by budgetary units. For trade, when carried on by the budgetary unit itself, cannot be oriented to a system of capital accounting. The products of household, clan or tribal crafts, which are sold to other groups, are commodities; and the means of production, so long as they are used to produce directly for consumption, are tools and raw materials, not capital goods. The same is true of the salable products and means of production of peasants and feudal estates, so long as production is not carried on in terms of even a primitive form of capital accounting of the type which Cato, for example, mentions.

It is obvious that the internal movement of goods within the domain of a feudal lord or of an *oikos,* including occasional exchange and the common forms of internal exchange of products, is the antithesis of trade based on capital accounting. Even the trade engaged in by an *oikos,* like that of the Pharaohs, when it is not concerned solely with provision for need, and is thus not a budgetary unit but one oriented to profit, is not for present purposes necessarily capitalistic. This would only be the case if it were oriented to capital accounting, particularly to an estimate, beforehand, in money, of the chances of profit from a transaction. This did occur in the case of professional travelling merchants, whether they were engaged in selling their own goods, in selling as agents for others, or in disposing of goods co-operatively marketed by an organized group. It is here, in the form of occasional profit-making enterprise, that the source of capital accounting and of the use of goods as capital is to be found.

Human beings, such as slaves and serfs, and all sorts of fixed premises and equipment which are used by owners and landlords as sources of consumption income, are in the nature of the case only income-producing property and not capital goods. The same is true to-day of securities which yield interest or dividends to the private investor, even though he may be ready to take advantage of any opportunity for speculative

[99] *Handel.*

gain. Investment in this sense should be clearly distinguished from even a temporary use of resources as capital of an enterprise. Goods which a landlord or a personal overlord receives from his dependents in payment of the obligations due him by virtue of his status of authority, and then puts up for sale, are not capital goods for the present terminological purposes, but only commodities. In such cases capital accounting—and above all, estimates of cost—are lacking in principle, not merely in practice. On the other hand, where slaves are used in an enterprise as a means of profit, particularly where there is an organized slave market, and widespread purchase and sale of slaves, they do constitute capital goods. Where productive organization works with unfree labour which is not, however, freely alienable, but consists in hereditary dependents, even when they are oriented to profit-making, it will not be called a capitalistic enterprise, but only a profit-making enterprise with unfree labour. It is the fact that the lord is bound to the worker which is decisive. Whether it is a case of agricultural production or unfree domestic industry is indifferent.

In industry, production for sale by free workers with their own raw materials and tools [100] is a case of small-scale capitalistic enterprise. The putting-out industry is capitalistic, but decentralized; whereas every case of an organized workshop under capitalistic control is centralized capitalistic organization. All types of wage employment of occasional workers, whether in the employer's or in the worker's home, are mere forms of relation of workers and employer. They are sometimes exploited in the interest of the budgetary economy, sometimes in the interest of the employer's profit.

The decisive point is thus not so much the empirical fact of the use of capital accounting, as the question of whether, in principle, it is possible.

28: THE CONCEPT OF COMMERCE AND ITS PRINCIPAL FORMS

In addition to the various types of specialized and specified functions, which have already been discussed, every market economy, even normally those subject to substantive regulation, is characterized by another; namely, mediation in the process of disposing of a producer's own control over goods or acquiring such control from others. This function can

[100] *Preiswerk.*

be carried out in any one of the following forms: (1) By the members of the administrative staff of an organized economic group, in return for payments in kind or in money which are fixed or vary with the services performed; (2) by an organized group created especially to provide for the selling and purchasing needs of its members; (3) by the members of a specialized occupational group working for their own profit and remunerated by fees or commissions without themselves acquiring control of the goods they handle; they act, that is, as agents, but in terms of a wide variety of legal forms; (4) by a specialized occupational group engaged in trade as a capitalistic profit-making enterprise. Such persons purchase goods with the expectation of being able to resell them at a profit, or sell for future delivery with the expectation of being able to cover their obligations in the meantime at a profitable figure. This may be done by buying and selling entirely freely in the market or subject to substantive regulation; (5) by a continuous regulated process of expropriation of goods with compensation on the part of an organized political group, and their exchange for compensation on a free market or under compulsion of the buyers—compulsory trade; (6) by the loan of money or provision of credit on the part of a specialized occupational group in order to make payments necessary in the course of business or for the acquisition of means of production through the granting of credit. Such loans may be granted to profit-making enterprises or to other organized groups, particularly to political bodies. Economically, the credit may be designed as a source of payment or for the acquisition of capital goods.

Cases (4) and (5), and only these, will be called 'commerce.' Case (4) is 'free commerce,' case (5) 'compulsory monopolistic commerce.'

Type (1) is illustrated, for budgetary units, by the *negotiatores* and *actores* who have acted on behalf of princes, landlords, monasteries, etc., for profit-making enterprises, by various types of agents; type (2) is illustrated by various kinds of co-operative buying and selling agencies, including consumers' co-operative societies; type (3) includes brokers, commission merchants, forwarding agents, insurance agents, and various other kinds of agents; type (4) is illustrated, for the case of free merchants, by modern commerce, for the regulated case by various types of heteronomously imposed or autonomously agreed divisions of the market for transactions with customers, or for the purchase and sale of different types of commodities, or the substantive regulation of the terms of exchange by the order of a political body, or some other type of co-operative group; type (5) is illustrated by the state monopoly of the grain trade.[101]

29: THE CONCEPT OF COMMERCE AND ITS PRINCIPAL FORMS —(*Continued*)

Free commerce, which alone will be dealt with for the present, is always a matter of profit-making enterprise, never of budgetary administration. It is hence under all normal conditions, if not always, a matter of earning money profits by contracts of purchase and sale. It may, however, be carried on by an organization subsidiary to a budgetary economy, or it may be an inseparable part of a total function through which goods are brought to a state of direct consumability by a unit.

The first type is illustrated by cases where members of a budgetary unit are designated to dispose of surpluses on their own account. If it is a matter simply of occasional sale by different members at different times, it is not even a subsidiary enterprise, but where the members in question devote themselves entirely and on their own financial responsibility to sale or purchase, it is an example of the fourth type, though somewhat modified. If, on the other hand, they act on behalf of the unit as a whole, it is a case of the first type.

The second form is illustrated by pedlers and other small traders who travel carrying their own goods with them, who thus primarily perform the function of transporting goods to the place of sale. They have hence been mentioned above in connexion with the function of transportation. Travelling *commenda* traders may be a transitional form between types (3) and (4). It is generally quite indefinite as to whether the transportation service is primary and the trading profit secondary, or *vice versa*. In any case all the persons included in these categories are 'traders' or 'merchants.'

Commerce on the individual's own account (type 4) is always carried on on the basis of appropriation of the means of production, even though his control is only made possible by borrowing. It is always the trader who bears the capital risk on his own account; and, correspondingly, it is he who, by virtue of his appropriation of the means of production, enjoys the opportunity for profit.

---

[101] The primary example is, of course, that carried on for many centuries by the Roman State.—ED.

Specialization and specification of functions in the field of free commercial enterprise may take place in a variety of different ways. From an economic point of view, it is for the present most important to distinguish them according to the types of economic unit between which the merchant mediates: (i) Trade between budgetary units with a surplus and other units which consume the surplus; (ii) trade between profit-making enterprises, themselves producers or merchants, and budgetary units which consume the product. The latter units include, of course, all types of corporate groups, in particular, political bodies; (iii) trade between one profit-making enterprise and another.

The first two cases come close to what is usually called 'retail trade' and involve sale to consumers without reference to the source from which the goods were obtained. The third case corresponds to 'wholesale trade.'

Commerce may be carried out on the market. In that case it may be a consumers' market, normally with the goods actually present. It may on the other hand, be a market for profit-making enterprises, in which case the goods may actually be present, as at fairs and expositions, which are usually, though not necessarily, seasonal, or the goods may not be present, as in trade on exchanges. Usually, though not necessarily, such markets are permanent.

Trade may, on the other hand, be carried on for customers, providing for the needs of a relatively fixed group of purchasers. These may be budgetary units, as in the custom retail trade, or profit-making enterprises. The latter may in turn be producing units or retail enterprises or, finally, other wholesale enterprises. There may be various levels of middlemen in this sense, varying from the one nearest the producers to the one who sells to the retailer.

According to the geographical source of the goods disposed of, trade may be 'interlocal' or 'local.'

The merchant may be in a position in fact to secure purchases on his own terms from the economic units which sell to him. He may, on the other hand, be in a position to dictate the terms of his sales to the economic units which buy from him, the case of sellers' monopoly. The first type is closely related to the putting-out organization of industry and is generally found combined with it. The second is substantively regulated commerce, one variety under type (4).

It goes without saying that every profit-making enterprise involved in market relationships must market its own goods. This is true even if it is primarily a producing enterprise. This type of marketing is not, however, 'mediation' in the sense of the above definition so long as members of the administrative staff are not present whose functions are specialized for this purpose on their own financial responsibility. Only then can they be said to be performing a commercial function of their own. There are, of course, all manner of transitional forms.

The calculations underlying commercial activity will be called 'speculative' to the extent to which they are oriented to possibilities, the realization of which is regarded as fortuitous and is in this sense uncalculable. In this sense the merchant assumes the burden of 'uncertainty.'[102] The transition from rational calculation to what is in this sense speculative calculation is entirely continuous, since no calculation which attempts to forecast future situations can be completely secured against unexpected 'accidental' factors. The distinction thus has reference only to a difference in the degree of rationality.

The forms of technical and economic specialization and specification of function in commerce do not differ substantially from those in other fields. The department store corresponds to the factory in that it permits the most extensive development of internal specialization of function.

29a: The Concept of Commerce and Its Principal Forms
—(*Concluded*)

The term 'banks' will be used to designate those types of profit-making commercial enterprise which make a specialized function of administering or creating money.

Money may be administered for private households by taking private deposit accounts and caring for the property of private individuals. It may also be administered for political bodies, as when a bank carries the account of a state, and for profit-making enterprises, by carrying business deposits and their current accounts.

Money may be created for the needs of budgetary units, as in extending private consumption credit to private individuals, or in extending credit to political bodies. It may be created for profit-making enterprises, for making payments to third persons, as in money changing, or providing checks or drafts for payments. It may also be used to

[102] There are several different factors involved in the inability to predict future events with complete certainty. Perhaps the best known analysis of these factors is that of Professor F. H. Knight in his *Risk, Uncertainty and Profit*.—Ed.

anticipate future payments due from customers, especially in the form of the discount of bills of exchange. It may, finally, be used to give credit for the purchase of capital goods.

The bank may (1) advance this money from its own funds or promise to make it available on demand, as in the provision for over-drafts of a current account, and the loan may or may not be accompanied by a pledge or any other form of security provided by the borrower. (2) Also, the bank may, by some type of guarantee or otherwise, influence others to grant funds. For formal purposes, it is indifferent which of these forms is taken.

In practice, the business policy of banks is normally aimed to make a profit by relending funds which have been lent to them or placed at their disposal.

The funds which a bank lends may be obtained from stocks of bullion or of coin from the existing mints which it holds on credit, or by its own creation of certificates or of circulating bank notes. Or, finally, it may secure them from the deposits of private individuals who have placed their money at its disposal.

In every case in which a bank either borows or creates media of circulation, its business policy must, so far as it is rationally conducted, be concerned with making provision for liquidity through coverage; that is, through having available a sufficiently large reserve of liquid assets ready to be paid out, or to arrange the terms of its own loans in such a way as to be able to meet its normal obligations for payment as they arise.

As a general rule, though not always, the maintenance of a standard of liquidity for banks which create money, i.e. note-issuing banks, is assured by the imposition of regulations on the part of corporate groups, such as guilds of merchants or political bodies. These regulations are generally designed as far as possible at the same time to protect the monetary system of an area, once it has been established, against changes in the substantive value of money. This, in turn, tends to protect the formally rational economic calculations of budgetary units, especially those of political bodies, and of profit-making enterprises, from disturbance by irrational factors. Furthermore, the attempt is usually made to maintain the stablest possible rate of exchange of the money of that area with that of others with which it stands in important credit and trading relationships. Such policy, which attempts to control the factors of irrationality in the monetary field will, following G. F. Knapp, be called 'lytric' policy. In the strictly laissez-faire state, this is the most important function in the realm of economic policy which the state would undertake. In its rational form this type of policy is entirely restricted to the modern state.

The measures of the Chinese government regulating the status of copper coins and paper money, and the Roman coinage policy, will be discussed at the proper point; but they did not constitute a modern type of monetary policy. Only the bank money policy of the Chinese guilds, which formed the model for the Hamburg mark banks, has come up to modern standards of rationality.[103]

The term 'financing'[104] will be applied to all business transactions which are oriented to obtaining control of favourable opportunities for profit-making by business enterprise, regardless of whether they are carried on by banks or by other agencies, including individuals, as an occasional source of profit or as a subsidiary enterprise, or as part of the speculative operations of a 'financier': (a) Financing may take place through the transformation of rights to appropriated opportunities for profit into securities or other negotiable instruments, and by the acquisition of these securities, either directly or through such subsidiary enterprises as are described below under (c); (b) by the systematic tender or refusal of business credit; (c) when it is necessary or desired, by forcing co-operation between hitherto competing enterprises. (i) This may take the form of monopolistic regulation of enterprises at the same stage of production—the cartel; (ii) it may mean a monopolistic unification of previously competing enterprises under a single management in order to suppress the least profitable—'mergers'; (iii) it may be a combination, which may or may not be monopolistic, of enterprises occupying successive stages in the process of production—a 'vertical combination'; (iv) finally, it may mean the attempt to direct a number of enterprises from one source by control of their securities, through such devices as the 'trust,' or holding company, and, in many cases, the deliberate creation of new enterprises for increasing profits or for extending power.

Of course, financing operations are often carried out by banks and, as a general rule, unavoidably involve their participation. But the main control often lies in the hands of stock brokers, like Harriman, or of

[103] This reference is probably to an extended historical discussion of monetary policy which Weber included in his plans for *Wirtschaft und Gesellschaft* but never actually wrote.—ED.

[104] *Finanzierungsgeschäfte.*

individual large-scale entrepreneurs in the productive field, like Carnegie. The formation of cartels is also often the work of large-scale entrepreneurs, like Kirdorf; while that of trusts is more likely to be the work of 'financiers,' like Graed, Rockefeller, Stinnes, and Rathenau. This will be further discussed below.

30: The Conditions of Maximum Formal Rationality of Capital Accounting

The following are the principal conditions necessary for obtaining a maximum of formal rationality of capital accounting in productive enterprises: (1) the complete appropriation of all the non-human means of production by owners and the complete absence of all formal appropriation of opportunities for profit in the market; that is, market freedom; (2) complete autonomy in the selection of management by the owners, thus complete absence of formal appropriation of rights to managerial functions; (3) the complete absence of appropriation of jobs and of opportunities for earning by workers and, conversely, the absence of appropriation of workers by owners. This involves free labour, freedom of the labour market, and freedom in the selection of workers; (4) complete absence of substantive regulation of consumption, production, and prices, or of other forms of regulation which limit freedom of contract or specify conditions of exchange. This may be called substantive freedom of contract; (5) the maximum of calculability of the technical conditions of the productive process; that is, a mechanically rational technology; (6) complete calculability of the functioning of public administration and the legal order and a reliable formal guarantee of all contracts by the political authority. This is formally rational administration and law; (7) the most complete possible separation of the enterprise and its conditions of success and failure, from the household or private budgetary unit and its property interests. It is particularly important that the capital at the disposal of the enterprise should be clearly distinguished from the private wealth of the owners, and should not be subject to division or dispersion through inheritance. For large-scale enterprises, this condition tends to approach an optimum from a formal point of view in the fields of transport, manufacture, and mining, when they are organized in corporate form with freely transferrable shares and limited liability. In the field of agriculture, relatively long-term leases on a large scale constitute formally the most favourable situation; (8) a monetary system with the highest possible degree of formal rationality.

Only a few points are in need of comment, though even these have already been touched on:

(1) With respect to the freedom of labour and of jobs from appropriation, it is true that certain types of unfree labour, particularly full-fledged slavery, have guaranteed what is formally a more complete power of disposal over the worker than is the case with employment for wages. But there are various reasons why this is less favourable to rationality and efficiency than the employment of free labour: (a) The amount of capital which it was necessary to invest in human resources through the purchase and maintenance of slaves has been much greater than that required by the employment of free labour; (b) the capital risk attendant on slave ownership has not only been greater but specifically irrational in that slave labour has been exposed to all manner of non-economic influences, particularly to political influence in a very high degree; (c) the slave market and correspondingly the prices of slaves have been particularly subject to fluctuation, which has made a balancing of profit and loss on a rational basis exceedingly difficult; (d) for similar reasons, particularly involving the political situation, there has been a difficult problem of recruitment of slave labour forces; (e) when slaves have been permitted to enjoy family relationships, this has made the use of slave labour more expensive in that the owner has had to bear the cost of maintaining the women and of rearing children. Very often, he has had no way in which he could make rational economic use of these elements as part of his labour force; (f) hence the most complete exploitation of slave labour has been possible only when they were separated from family relationships and subjected to a ruthless discipline. Where this has happened it has greatly accentuated the difficulties of the problem of recruitment; (g) it has in general been impossible to use slave labour in the operation of tools and apparatus, the efficiency of which required a high level of responsibility and of involvement of the operator's self-interest; (h) perhaps most important of all has been the impossibility of selection, of employment only after trying out in the job, and dismissal in accordance with fluctuations of the business situation or when personal efficiency declined.

Hence the employment of slave labour has only been possible in general under the following conditions: (a) Where it has been possible to maintain slaves very cheaply; (b) where there has been an opportunity for regular recruitment through a well-supplied slave market; (c) in agricultural production on a large scale of the plantation type, or in very simple industrial processes. The most important examples of this type of relatively successful use of slaves are the Carthaginian and Roman plantations, those of colonial areas and of the Southern United States, and the Russian 'factories.' The drying up of the slave market, which resulted from the pacification of the Empire, led to the decay of the plantations of Antiquity.[105] In North America, the same situation led to a continual search for cheap new land, since it was impossible to meet the costs of slaves and pay a land rent at the same time. In Russia, the slave 'factories' were barely able to meet the competition of the Custar type of household industry and were totally unable to compete with free factory labour. Even before the emancipation of the serfs, petitions for permission to dismiss workers were common, but they disappeared with the introduction of shops using free labour.

When workers are employed for wages, the following advantages to industrial profitability and efficiency are conspicuous: (a) Capital risk and the necessary capital investment are smaller; (b) the costs of reproduction and of bringing up children fall entirely on the worker. His wife and children must seek employment on their own account; (c) largely for this reason, the risk of dismissal is an important incentive to the maximization of production; (d) it is possible to select according to ability and willingness to work.

(2) The following comment may be made on the separation of enterprise and household. In England there has developed a sharp separation of capitalistic tenant farming from the entailed system of land ownership. This is by no means fortuitous, but is the outcome of a continuous development extending over centuries. It was made possible largely by the absence of protection of the status of the peasants, which in turn was the result of the insular position. The tendency to combine land ownership with the economic exploitation of the land has a number of consequences. It tends to make the land an economic capital good and thereby increases both the need for capital and the risks involved. It tends to obstruct the separation of household and budgetary interests from those of the enterprise, as, for instance, when legacies have to be

---

[105] In a well-known essay, *Die sozialen Gründe des Untergangs der antiken Kultur*, Weber attributed to this factor an important role in the economic decline and through this the cultural changes of the Roman Empire. This essay is reprinted in *Gesammelte Aufsätze zur Social- und Wirtschaftsgeschichte*, pp. 289-311.—Ed.

paid out of the resources of the enterprise. It reduces the liquidity of the entrepreneur's capital and introduces a number of irrational factors into his capital accounting. Hence the separation of land ownership from the organization of agricultural production is, from a formal point of view, a step which promotes the rationality of capital accounting. It goes without saying, however, that the substantive valuation of the phenomenon is quite another matter and may be decided quite differently according to the values underlying the judgment.

31: The Principal Modes of Capitalistic Orientation of Profit Making

There are a number of qualitatively different modes in which it is possible for the orientation to profit to be determined in a capitalistic manner; that is, in proportion to its rationality in terms of capital accounting.

1. Profit-making activity may be oriented to the exploitation of market advantages in a continuous process of purchase and sale on the market where exchange is free; that is, formally not subject to compulsion and materially, at least relatively, free. Or it may be oriented to the maximization of profit in continuous productive enterprises which make use of capital accounting.

2. It may be oriented to opportunities for profit by trade and speculation in money, taking over debts of all sorts, and creating means of payment. A closely related type is the professional extension of credit, either for consumption or for profit-making purposes.

3. It may be oriented to opportunities for acquiring 'booty' from corporate political groups or persons connected with politics. This includes the financing of wars or revolutions and the financing of party leaders by loans and supplies.

4. It may be oriented to opportunities for continuous profit by virtue of domination by force or of a position of power guaranteed by the political authority. There are two main sub-types: colonial capitalism operated through plantations with compulsory payments or compulsory labour and by monopolistic and compulsory trade. On the other hand there is the fiscal type, profit making by farming of taxes and of offices, whether in the home area or in colonies.

5. The orientation to opportunities for profit opened up by unusual transactions with political bodies.

6. The orientation to opportunities for profit of the following types: (a) To purely speculative transactions in standardized commodities or in the securities of an enterprise; (b) by carrying out the continuous financial operations of political bodies; (c) by the promotional financing of new enterprises in the form of sale of securities to investors; (d) by the speculative financing of capitalistic enterprises and of various other types of economic organization with the purpose of a profitable regulation of market situations or of attaining power.

Types (1) and (6) are to a large extent peculiar to the modern Western World. The other types have been common all over the world for thousands of years where the possibilities of exchange, money economy, and money financing have been present. In the Western World they have not had such a dominant importance as modes of profit-making as they had in Antiquity, except in restricted areas and for relatively brief periods, particularly in times of war. Where large areas have been pacified for a long period, as in the Chinese and later Roman Empires, these have tended to decline, leaving only commerce, money changing and lending, as forms of capitalistic acquisition. The capitalistic financing of political activities has always depended on two conditions: a competition of states with one another for power and the corresponding competition for control of capital which was free as between them. All this has ended only with the establishment of large-scale, unified states.[106]

It is only in the modern Western World that rational capitalistic enterprises with fixed capital, free labour, the rational specialization and combination of functions, and the allocation of productive functions on the basis of capitalistic enterprises, bound together in a market economy, are to be found. This involves the capitalistic type of organization of labour, which in formal times is purely voluntary, as the typical and dominant mode of providing for the wants of the masses of the population, with expropriation of the workers from the means of production and appropriation of the enterprises by security owners. It is also only here that we find public credit in the form of issues of government securities, the legal form of the business corporation, the issue of securities, and financing carried on as the business of rational enterprises, trade in commodities and securities or organized exchanges, money and capital markets,

[106] The point of view here stated has, if the author's memory is accurate, been previously put forward in the clearest form by J. Plenge in his *Von der Diskontpolitik zur Herrschaft über den Geldmarkt.* Before that a similar position seems to have been taken only in the author's article, '*Agrarverhältnisse im Altertum*' (reprinted in *Gesammelte Aufsätze zur Social- und Wirtschaftsgeschichte.*—ED.)

monopolistic associations as a type of economically rational organization of the production of goods by profit-making enterprises as opposed to the mere trade in them.

This difference calls for an explanation and the explanation cannot be given on economic grounds alone. Types (3) to (5) inclusive will be treated here together as 'politically oriented capitalism.' The whole of the later discussion will be devoted particularly, though not alone, to the problem of explaining the difference.[107] In general terms, it is possible only to make the following statement:—

1. It is clear from the very beginning that the types of political events and processes which open up the kind of opportunities for profit which are exploited by political capitalism are, seen in economic terms—that is, from the point of view either of orientation to market advantages or of the consumption needs of budgetary units—irrational.

2. It is further clear that purely speculative opportunities for profit and pure consumption credit are, from the point of view both of want satisfaction and of the production of goods, irrational because they are determined by the fortuitous distribution of ownership and of market advantages. The same may also be true of opportunities for promotion and financing, under certain circumstances; but this is by no means necessarily always the case.

Apart from the rational capitalistic enterprise, the modern economic order is unique in its mode of regulation of the monetary system and in the commercialization of bills of exchange and securities. Both these peculiarities must be discussed—first the monetary system.

32: The Monetary System of the Modern State and the Different Kinds of Money

1. (a) The modern state has universally assumed the monopoly of regulation of the monetary system by legislation; (b) it has, almost without exception, assumed the monopoly of creating money, at least of the issue of coinage.

---

[107] As has been noted in the introduction, this problem, the factors involved in the emergence of the specific forms of capitalistic organization characteristic of the modern Western World, was the dominant empirical interest of Weber's sociological work as a whole. It is probable that he intended to sum up all that he had to say on the subject in this one monumental work. The state of incompleteness in which it was left at his death is, however, such that only a fragmentary impression of his total argument can be gained, even when the parts not included in this translation are taken into account.—Ed.

Originally, purely fiscal considerations were decisive in the creation of this monopoly—minting fees and other profits from coinage. This was the origin of the prohibition of the use of foreign money. But the monopolization of issue of money has not been universal even up to the present. Thus, up until the recent reform of the currency foreign coins were current in Bremen.

With the increasing importance of its taxation and its own economic enterprises, the state has become both the largest receiver of payments and the largest spender in the society, either on its own account, or through the accounts maintained on its behalf. Quite apart from the monopoly of monetary regulation and issue, because of the tremendous importance of the financial transactions of the state, which are always decisive for the monetary situation, it is crucial what attitude the authorities of the state take toward money. Above all, the question arises what types of money they actually have control over and can pay out, and what kind of money is imposed on the general public as legal. There is further the question, what money they will, on the one hand, accept in payment, on the other, will partly or wholly repudiate.

Thus paper money is partly repudiated when the payment of customs must be made only in coin. Full repudiation is illustrated by the cases of the final status of the *assignats* of the French Revolution, the money of the Confederate States of America, and that issued by the Chinese Government during the Tai Ping Rebellion.

Money can be defined as 'legal' only when it constitutes 'legal tender' which everyone, including, in particular, the public authorities, is obligated to accept or to pay, either up to given amounts, or without limit. 'Public money' may be defined as that which public bodies accept or themselves use in payment. 'Compulsory legal money' is that which is imposed on the public. The imposition of a type of money may be carried out on the basis of a long-standing legal authority for reasons of monetary policy; thus talers and five-franc pieces were issued after the cessation of silver coinage. But this did not, as is well known, succeed.

Or money may be imposed because the state is unable to make payment in any other monetary medium. In such a case an existing legal authority to issue money may be made use of for the first time or an *ad hoc* legal authority to impose a new means of payment may be created. This is almost always true of cases of resort to paper money. In this last case, what usually happens is that a means of exchange, which was previously in general use, whether legally possible or not, becomes in fact unredeemable.

Legally, it is possible for a state to make any object whatever a legal means of payment and every chartal object into money in the sense of a means of payment. It can establish any desired set of relations between the values of different objects; in the case of circulating money, it can establish parities. There are, however, certain formal disturbances of the monetary system which the state is either powerless to prevent at all or can prevent only with great difficulty.

(a) In the case of administrative money, the forgery of notes, which is almost always very profitable; and (b) with all forms of metallic money, the non-monetary use of the metal as a raw material, where its products have a high value. This is particularly true when the metal in question is in an undervalued monetary relation to others. It is also exceedingly difficult to prevent the export of metal to other countries where that metal has a higher value. Finally, it is difficult to compel the offer of a legal monetary metal for coinage where it is undervalued in its coinage rate, as compared with its market price.

With paper money the rate of interchange of one unit of the metal with its nominal equivalent of paper always becomes too unfavourable for the metal when redeemability of the notes is suspended, and this is what happens when it is no longer possible to make payments in metallic money.

The exchange ratios between several kinds of commercial money may be determined (a) by fixing the relation for each particular case; (b) by establishing rates periodically; and (c) by legal establishment of permanent rates, as in bimetallism.

Only in cases (a) and (b) is it usual for there to be only one public and effective standard metal, which in the Middle Ages was silver, with the others used as trading coins with varying rates. The complete separation of the specific modes of use of different types of market money is rare in modern monetary systems, but has at times been common, as in China and in the Middle Ages.

2. From a sociological point of view the definition of money as legal tender and as a product of the lytric administration of political bodies, is not exhaustive. As G. F. Knapp says, it starts from the fact of the existence of debts, especially obligations to make payment of taxes and interest to states. For meeting the legal obligation, what is essential is that the nominal amount of money should remain the same, even though the

monetary metal may have changed in the meantime. If, on the other hand, the nominal unit has changed, it is the 'historical' definition which is decisive. But in addition to this, the individual to-day values the nominal monetary unit not as a chartal metallic coin or note, but as a certain proportion of his money income.

It is true that the state is in a position by legislation and by the action of its administrative agencies to dictate formally the valid monetary standard within the area under its control.[108]

The value of money, however, is not merely a matter of dealing with existing debts, but also with exchange in the present and the contraction of new debts to be paid in the future. In this connexion, however, it is necessary to consider primarily the status of money as a means of exchange. This lends primary importance to the probability that it will be at some future time acceptable in exchange for specified or unspecified goods in a price relationship which is capable of approximate estimate.

1. Under certain circumstances the probability that urgent debts can be paid off to the state or private individuals from the proceeds may also be importantly involved. This case may, however, be left out of account here because it only arises in emergency situations.

2. In spite of the fact that it is within its limits correct and brilliantly executed, hence of permanently fundamental importance, it is at this point that the incompleteness of G. F. Knapp's *Staatliche Theorie des Geldes* becomes evident.

Furthermore, the state on its part needs the money which it receives through taxation or from other sources, both as a means of exchange and, often to a very large extent, for the payment of interest on its debt. Its creditors, in turn, will then wish to employ it as a means of exchange; indeed this is the main reason why they desire money. It is almost always true that the state needs money to a large degree, sometimes even entirely, as a means of exchange to cover future purchases of goods and supplies in the market. Hence, however necessary it is to distinguish it analytically, it is not the fact that money is a means of payment which is decisive.

The value of a monetary unit in exchange for other specific goods,

[108] This is true if it employs modern methods of administration. It was not, however, possible at all times, for instance, in China. There in earlier times it has generally not been possible because payments by and to the government were too small in relation to the total field of transactions. Even recently it appears that the Chinese Government has not been able to make silver into a restricted currency with a cash reserve since it was not sufficiently powerful to suppress the counterfeiting which would undoubtedly have ensued.

which rests on its valuation in relation to marketable goods, will be called its 'substantive' value as opposed to its formal, legal value as a means of exchange.

In principle, as an observable fact, a monetary unit has a substantive value only in relation to particular kinds of goods and only for each separate individual as his own valuation on the basis of the marginal utility of money for him, which will vary with his income. This valuation is changed for the individual with any increase in the sums of money at his disposal. Thus the marginal utility of money to the issuing authority falls, not only, but above all, when it creates administrative money and uses it for obtaining goods by exchange or forces it on the public as a means of payment. There is a secondary change in the same direction for those persons who deal with the state and who, because of the higher prices resulting from the lowered marginal utility of money to public bodies, become the possessors of larger money funds. The increased purchasing power resulting from this—that is, the lowering of the marginal utility of money for these possessors—can in turn result in an increase in prices paid to those from whom *they* purchase, etc. If, on the other hand, the state were to withdraw part of the notes it receives from circulation—that is, should not pay them out again, but destroy them—the result would be that in proportion to the decrease in its expenditures the marginal utility of money for its lessened funds would rise and its market demand in money terms correspondingly fall. The results would be the exact opposite of those just outlined. It is hence possible for administrative money, though by no means only this, to have an important effect on the price structure in any given monetary area.[109]

3. It has universally been true that a cheapening and increase in the supply, or vice versa, a rise in cost and curtailment of the supply in the production of monetary metals could have a similar effect in all countries using it for monetary purposes. Monetary and non-monetary uses of metals are closely interdependent, but the only case in which the non-monetary basis of valuation has been decisive for its value as money, has been that of copper in China. In different areas money must always enjoy an equivalent valuation of the nominal standard metal unit less costs of coining as long as it is used as a means of payment between monetary areas and is also the money of market transactions in the monetary area of the leading commercial powers, as is true to-day of gold. In the past

---

[109] The speed at which this will occur and the different ways in which it affects different goods cannot be discussed here.

this was true of silver and would be to-day if silver were in the same situation as gold. A metal which is not used as a means of payment between monetary areas, but constitutes market money in some of them, will naturally be valued nominally in some definite relation to the monetary units of those areas. But these in turn will, according to the costs of adding to the supply and according to the quantities in circulation, and, finally, according to the so-called 'balance of payments,' have a fluctuating exchange relationship. Finally, a precious metal which is universally used for limited coinage into administrative money, but not as market money, is primarily valued on the basis of its non-monetary use. The question is always whether the metal in question can be profitably produced and at what rate. When it is completely demonetized, this depends entirely on its money cost of production reckoned in international means of payment in relation to the non-monetary demand for it. If, on the other hand, it is used universally as market money and as an international means of payment, its production will depend on costs in relation primarily to the monetary demand for it. When, finally, it has a limited use as market or administrative money, its production will depend in the long run on whether and how much the demand for it, as expressed in terms of international means of payment, is able to outweigh the costs of production. If its use as market money is limited, it is unlikely in the long run that its monetary use will be decisive. For the relation of this limited area of use to other monetary areas will in the long run tend to reduce its value. And it is only when domestic prices are completely cut off from this influence that they will not be affected. This has actually happened in China and Japan and is to-day true of the areas which are still actually cut off from each other by the war. Even in the case where a metal was used only as regulative administrative money, this possibility of use as a strictly monetary unit would play a decisive role in determining its value only when coinage rates were unusually high, and even then it will end in the same way as in the case of specialized free coinage and for the same reasons.

Though it was temporarily realized in practice in China, the monopolization of the total production and use of a monetary metal is essentially a theoretical, limiting case. If several competing monetary areas are involved and wage labour is used, it does not alter the situation as much as possibly might be expected. For if all payments by government agencies were made in terms of this metal, every attempt to limit its coinage or to tax it very heavily, which might well yield large profit, would have the same result as it did in the case of the very high Chinese seignorage. First in relation to the crude metal, the money would become very highly valued; and if wage labour were used, mining operations would to a large extent become unprofitable. As the amount in circulation declined, there would result a 'contra-inflation'; and it is possible, as actually happened in China, where this led at times to complete freedom of coinage, that this would go so far as to lead to the use of money substitutes and to a large extension of the area of natural economy. This also happened in China. If a market economy is to continue, it is hardly possible for monetary policy in the long run to act otherwise than as if free coinage were legally in force. The only difference is that minting would no longer be left to the initiative of interested parties. With complete socialism, on the other hand, the problem of money would cease to be significant and the precious metals would hardly be produced at all.

4. The fact that the precious metals have normally become the monetary standard and the material from which money is made is historically an outcome of their function as ornaments and hence, specifically, as gifts. But apart from purely technical factors, this use was also determined by the fact that they were goods which were typically dealt with by weight. Their maintenance in this function is not at first sight understandable since to-day, for all except the smallest payments, everyone normally uses notes, especially bank-notes, and expects to receive them in payment. There are, however, important motives underlying retention of metal standards.

5. In all modern states, not only is the issue of money in the form of notes legally regulated, but it is monopolized by the state. It is either carried out directly by the state itself, or by one or a few issuing agencies enjoying special privileges but subject to the control of the state—the banks of issue.

6. The term 'public legal tender money'[110] will be applied only to money which is actually paid out by public agencies. On the other hand, any other money which, though not paid out under compulsory acceptance, is used in transactions between private individuals by virtue of formal legal provisions, will be called 'accessory standard money.' Money which may legally be used in private transactions only up to a given maximum amount, will be called 'subsidiary money.'[111]

[110] This terminology is based on that of Knapp. This is even more definitely true in what follows.
[111] *Regiminales Kurantgeld.*

'Definitive' currency means public legal tender money; whereas any type of money is to be called 'provisional' currency so far as it is in fact effectively exchangeable for or redeemable in terms of definitive currency.

7. In the long run, public legal tender currency must naturally coincide with the effective currency. It cannot be a separate official money with only a legal validity. Effective currency, however, is necessarily one of three things: (a) free market money; (b) unregulated; or (c) regulated, administrative money. The public treasury does not make its payments simply by deciding to apply the rules of a monetary system which somehow seems to it ideal, but its acts are determined by its own financial interests and those of important economic groups.

With regard to its chartal form, an effective standard money may in the first place be metallic money. Only metallic money can be a free market money, but this is not necessarily the case for all metallic money.

It is free market money when the lytric administration will coin any quantity of the standard metal or will exchange it for chartal coins— free coinage.[112] According, then, to the precious metal which is chosen as the standard, there will be an effective gold, silver, or copper standard. Whether the lytric administration is in fact in a position to maintain an actual system of free coinage, does not depend simply on its own desires, but on whether there are individuals present who are interested in presenting metal for coinage.

It is thus possible for free coinage to exist 'officially' without existing in fact. Whatever the official position may be, it is not effectively present (a) when, given free coinage of a plurality of metals in an official ratio, one or more of these comes to be undervalued in relation to the current market price of bullion. In that case, of course, only the overvalued metal will be offered by private individuals for minting or will be used to make payments. If public agencies withdraw the overvalued coins, they will have to remain in their hands until no other means of payment are available. If the price discrepancy is sufficiently large, the undervalued coins will then be melted down or sold as a commodity by weight in exchange for the overvalued coins.

(b) Free coinage is also not effective if persons making payments, including especially public agencies under stress of necessity, continually and on a large scale make use of their formal right or usurped power to compel acceptance of another form of means of payment, whether in

---

[112] *Hydrolomic*—a term introduced by G. F. Knapp.—ED.

metal or notes. This must not only be a form of provisional money, but must either have been accessory money or, if previously provisional, have ceased to be redeemable because of the inability of the issuing agency to pay.

In case (a) free coinage always ceases for the undervalued metal, and the same thing happens in case (b) when accessory forms of money or forms which are no longer effectively provisional are forced on the public persistently on a large scale.

The outcome in case (a) is to confine free coinage to the overvalued metal which becomes the only free market money, thus resulting in a new metallic standard. In case (b) the accessory metal or notes which are no longer effectively provisional become the standard money. In the first case we get a limited money standard; in the second, a paper standard.

It is also possible for free coinage to be effective without being official in the sense of being legally established.[113]

In view of what has just been said, a monometallic standard, which may be gold, silver, or copper, will be said to have existed when one metal is legally freely coined. A multimetallic standard, on the other hand, exists when more than one (it may be two or three) is freely coined in a fixed ratio to each other. A parallel standard exists when more than one metal is freely coined without a fixed ratio. A standard metal and a metallic standard will only be spoken of where the metal or metals are effectively freely coined; thus, in practice, constitute actual market money.

Bimetallism existed legally in all the countries of the Latin Union until the suspension of the free coinage of silver which followed the German currency reform. Effectively, however, only the metal which was for the time being overvalued was actually as a rule a standard metal. The process of stabilization through the ratio, however, worked so effectively that the change was often scarcely noted and there seemed to be effective bimetallism. But in so far as the standard shifted, the coins of the undervalued money became accessory money.[114] At least where there is competition between several autocephalous and autonomous issuing agencies, bimetallism is an effective monetary standard

[113] An example is the competition of the various coining authorities in the Middle Ages, determined by their fiscal interest in seignorage, to mint as much as possible of the monetary metals. As yet, there was no formal establishment of free coinage, but the actual situation was much as if there had been.

[114] This account of the matter coincides closely with that of Knapp.

only as a transitory phenomenon and is usually only a legal, as opposed to an effective, state of affairs.

The fact that the undervalued money is not brought to the mint is naturally the result, not of administrative action, but of the changed market situation in relation to the persistence of the legal coinage ratio of the metals. It would, of course, be possible for the mint to continue to coin that metal at a loss as administrative money, but since the non-monetary uses of the money are more profitable, it could not be kept in circulation.

33: RESTRICTED MONEY [115]

Any type of metallic money which is legal tender will be called 're-stricted' money if it is not freely coined. Restricted money may circulate as accessory money; that is, having a fixed relationship to some other legal tender money in the same monetary area. This latter may be an-other form of restricted money, paper money, or a market money.

Or restricted money may be oriented to an international standard. This is the case when it is the sole legal tender money in its own area, and provision is made for having international means of payment avail-able for making payments abroad, either in coin or in bullion. This is an international restricted money standard with a reserve fund of for-eign exchange.

(a) Restricted money will be called 'particular' when it is the only legal tender money, but is not oriented to an international standard.

Restricted money may then be valued internationally *ad hoc* each time international means of payment or foreign exchange is bought; or, when this is possible, it may be given a fixed relation to the interna-tional standard. Talers and silver five-franc pieces were restricted money with a fixed relation to the other money of the same country; thus both were accessory. The Dutch silver gulden have been oriented to the inter-national gold standard after having been particular for a short time after the restriction of coinage, and now the rupee is in the same position. This is also true of the Chinese dollar, which according to the coinage regulations of 24 May 1910, is particular as long as free coinage, which is not mentioned in the statute, does not exist. The orientation to the international gold standard, as recommended by the American Com-mission, was rejected.

[115] *Sperrgeld.*

Where money is restricted, free coinage would be very profitable to the private owners of the precious metals. Nevertheless, and precisely for this reason, restriction is maintained because it is feared that the introduction of free coinage of the formerly restricted metals would lead to abandonment as unprofitable of free coinage of the other metal which was fixed in too low a ratio to it. The monetary stock of this metal, which would now become obstructed,[116] would be put to more profitable non-monetary uses. The reason why a rational lytric administration wishes to avoid this is that the other metal, which would be forced out, is an international means of payment; (b) restricted legal tender money will be called 'obstructed' market money when, contrary to the case just cited, free coinage exists legally, but is unprofitable to private business and hence does not take place. This lack of profitability may rest on an unfavourable relation between the market price of the metal and its monetary ratio to the market money, if a metal, or to paper money. Such money must at some time in the past have been market money; but, with multimetallism, there would have to have been changes in the relative market prices of the metals or, with it and monometallism, financial catastrophes, which have made the payment of metallic money by the government impossible and forced it to adopt paper money which had been made irredeemable. The result has been the impossibility of the operation of free coinage by an appeal to private business interests. At least so far as action is rational, this money then ceases to be used in transactions; (c) apart from restricted legal standard money, which has alone been called restricted money here, there may be restricted metallic subsidiary money; that is, money which must be accepted as legal tender only up to a given amount. Usually, though not necessarily, it is then intentionally coined at a rate which undervalues it in relation to standard coin to protect it from being melted down. Usually, then, it has the status of provisional money in that it is redeemable at certain places.[117]

All subsidiary money and many types of restricted metallic money occupy a place in monetary systems similar to that of paper money. They differ from it only in that the monetary metal has a non-monetary use which is of some importance. Restricted metallic money is very closely related to a circulatory medium when it is provisional money; that is, when there is adequate provision for redemption in market money.

[116] See next paragraph.

[117] This case is a phenomenon of everyday experience and has no special importance for present purposes.

34: Paper Money

Paper money naturally is always administrative money. For the purposes of a sociological theory of money, it is always the specific chartal form of document including the specific formal meaning printed on it which constitutes 'money.' It is not the claim to something else which may, though it need not, be involved. Indeed, in the case of unredeemable paper money, this is altogether absent.

From a formal legal point of view, paper money may consist in an officially redeemable certificate of indebtedness, acknowledged by a private individual, as in the case of the English goldsmiths in the seventeenth century, by a privileged bank, as in the case of bank-notes, or by a political body, as in the case of government paper. If it is effectively redeemable and thus functions only as a circulating medium or provisional money, it may be fully covered—thus constituting a certificate— or it may be covered only sufficiently to meet normal demands for redemption, which makes it a circulating medium. Coverage may be in terms of specified weights of bullion or of metal coin.

It is almost always the case that paper money has first been issued as a redeemable form of provisional money. In modern times, it has been typically a medium of circulation, almost always in the form of bank-notes. They have thus been denominated in terms of units of an existing metallic standard.

1. Naturally the first part of the last paragraph is not true of cases where one form of paper money has been replaced by another; for example, where government paper has been replaced by bank-notes, or vice versa. But this is not a case of primary issue of money.

2. It is of course true that means of exchange and of payment may exist which do not take a chartal form, as coins or notes or otherwise. There is no doubt of this. It is not, however, expedient to speak of these as 'money,' but, to use the term 'unit of account' or some other terms, which, according to the particular case, is appropriate. It is characteristic of money that it is associated with particular quantities of chartal objects. This is a property which is very far from being superficial or of secondary importance.

If what has previously been provisional money has its redeemability suspended, it is important to distinguish whether the interested parties regard this as a temporary measure or as definitive for as long as they can predict. In the first case it would be usual, since metallic money or bullion is sought after for international payments, for the paper money to fall to a discount in relation to its nominal metal equivalent. This is not, however, by any means inevitable; and the discount is often moderate. The discount may, however, become large if the need for foreign exchange is very acute. In the second case, after a time a definite paper money standard will develop. Then it is no longer appropriate to speak of the monetary unit as discounted, but rather, as history tends to show, of devaluation.

It is not beyond the range of possibility that the market price of the standard metal of the money which was originally the basis of the note but is now obstructed, may for some reason fall radically relative to international means of payment, while the fall in the value of the paper money is less marked. This must have the result, as it actually did in Austria and Russia, that in the long run what was earlier the formal nominal unit of weight of silver could be purchased with a smaller nominal amount than before in the notes, which had now become independent of it. That is readily understandable. In the initial stages following introduction of pure paper standard, the paper money is without exception valued at a lower figure than the same nominal amount of metal, because this step always results from inability to pay. But, as in the cases of Austria and Russia, the subsequent development depends on various things; on the development of the balance of payments, which determines the foreign demand for domestic means of payment, on the amount of paper money issued, and on the degree of success with which the issuing authority is able to obtain an adequate supply of international means of payment. It is possible for these three factors to be combined in such a way that the paper money is, in its relation to the international means of payment, in this case gold, the more stable, or even rises in value; whereas the earlier standard metal, on account of increased and cheapened production of silver and of its progressive demonetization, has continually fallen in relation to gold. A true independent paper standard exists in the case where there is no longer any prospect of effective resumption of redemption in terms of metal at the former rate.

35: The Formal and Material Value of Money

It is true that by law and administrative action a state can insure the formal value of a form of money as the standard in its own area of jurisdiction if it is itself in a position to make payments in this money.

It is not in a position to do this if it has allowed, in the case of metallic money, what was previously an accessory or provisional type of money to become free market money, or if it permits the development of an autonomous paper money. This is because these types of money must accumulate in the hands of the government until it commands no other kind and is hence forced to use them in its own payments.[118]

But naturally this formal power implies nothing as to the substantive value of money; that is, the rate at which it will be accepted in exchange for commodities. Nor does it yield any knowledge of whether and to what extent the monetary authorities can influence its substantive value. Experience shows that it is possible for the political authority by such measures as the rationing of consumption, the control of production, and the enforcement of maximum or minimum prices, to attain a high degree of control so far as it is a question of goods or services which are present or produced within its own territory. It is equally demonstrable from experience, however, that there are exceedingly important limits to the effectiveness of this kind of control, which will be discussed elsewhere. But in any case, such measures obviously do not belong in the category of monetary administration. The rational type of modern monetary policy has, on the contrary, had quite a different aim. The tendency has been to attempt to regulate the material value of domestic currency in terms of foreign currency; thus to influence the foreign exchange rate with other currencies, usually to maintain stability or in some cases the highest possible ratio. Among the interests determining such policy are those of prestige and political power. But on the economic side, the decisive ones are financial interests, with particular reference to future foreign loans, and other very powerful business interests, notably of importers and of industries which have to use raw materials from abroad. Finally, the interests as consumers of those elements in the population which purchase imported goods are involved. To-day there can be no doubt that 'lytric' policy is in fact primarily concerned with regulation of the foreign exchanges.[119]

It is probable that England accepted the gold standard reluctantly be-

---

[118] Knapp has rightly maintained that this is the normal process in the case of obstructional changes in the standard.

[119] Both this and what follows are closely in agreement with Knapp. Both in its form and content, his book is one of the greatest masterpieces of German literary style and scientific acumen. It is unfortunate that most of the specialist critics have concentrated on the problems which he deliberately ignored, which, though relatively few, are in some cases, however, not unimportant.

cause silver, though considered the more desirable standard, was under-valued by the official ratio. But all the other states in the modern world with a modern form of organization have chosen their monetary stand-ard with a view to the most stable possible exchange relation with sterling. This has led to a pure gold standard, to a gold standard with restricted accessory silver money, or to a restricted silver standard, or, finally, to a regulated paper standard. In both the latter cases, lytric policy has been concerned primarily with the maintenance of gold re-serves for international payments. The adoption of pure paper standards has always been a result of political catastrophe where it has been the only way to meet the problem of inability to pay in what was previously the standard money. This is happening on a large scale to-day.[120]

It seems to be true that for the purpose of stabilizing foreign exchange in relation to gold, the free coinage of gold in one's own monetary sys-tem is not the only possible means. The parity of exchange between dif-ferent types of freely minted gold coins may in fact be seriously disturbed, even though the possibility of obtaining means of making international payments in foreign trade by exporting or recoining gold, may be very greatly facilitated by the internal free coinage of gold; and, further-more, so long as this free coinage exists, only natural obstacles to trade or embargoes on the export of gold can lead to temporary large disturb-ances. On the other hand, experience shows that under normal peace-time conditions, it is also possible for an area with a well-ordered legal system, favourable conditions of production and a lytric policy which is deliberately oriented to procuring adequate foreign exchange for interna-tional payments, to maintain a relatively stable exchange situation. It is true, however, that other things being equal, this involves markedly higher costs to financial operations and to persons in need of gold. Exactly the same would be true, of course, if silver were the principal means of payment in international transactions and were recognized as such in the principal trading nations of the world.

36: Methods and Aims of Monetary Policy

Among the more elementary of the typical methods of lytric policy in relation to foreign exchange are the following:—[121]

[120] It should be borne in mind that this was written in 1919 or 1920. The situation has clearly been radically changed by the developments since that time.—Ed.

[121] Specific measures will not in general be dealt with here.

(a) In countries with free coinage of gold: (1) The backing of the circulating medium, so far as it is not covered by gold, with commercial paper; that is, claims to payments for goods which have been sold and which are guaranteed by safe persons, in other words, proved entrepreneurs. The transactions of the note issuing banks on their own account are as far as possible limited to dealing with such bills, to making loans on the security of stocks of goods, to the receipt of deposits, the clearing of check payments, and, finally, acting as financial agent for the state; (2) the 'discount policy' of the banks of issue. This consists in raising the rate of interest charged on bills discounted when there is a probability that payments abroad will create a demand for gold sufficient to threaten the internal stock of gold, especially that in the hands of the issuing bank. The purpose is to encourage foreigners to take advantage of the higher rate of interest and to discourage internal borrowing.

(b) In areas with a restricted metal standard other than gold or with a paper standard the following are the principal measures: (1) Discount policy similar to that described under (a)(2) in order to check undue expansion of credit; (2) a gold-premium policy. This is a measure which is also common in gold-standard areas with an accessory restricted silver currency; (3) a deliberate policy of gold purchase and sale and deliberate control of foreign exchanges by purchase and sale of foreign bills.

This policy is in the first instance oriented purely to lytric considerations, but under certain circumstances it may come to involve substantive regulation of economic activity. The note-issuing banks occupy a position of great power in the system of commercial banks, since the latter are in many cases dependent on the credit extended by the bank of issue. The latter may influence the other banks to regulate the money market, that is, the conditions on which short-term credit is given, in a uniform way and thereby aim at a deliberate regulation of business credit, thereby influencing the direction of the production of goods. This is, within the framework of a capitalistic economic order, the closest approach to a planned economy. It is formally merely a matter of monetary administration, but actually involves substantive regulation of economic activity within the area controlled by the political authority in question.

These measures were all typical before the war. They were used in the interest of a monetary policy which was primarily oriented to the stabilization of a currency. But in case changes were desired, in countries with restricted or paper money, the authorities usually attempted to bring about a gradual rise in the foreign exchange value of their currency. It was, thus, in the last analysis, oriented to the freely coined monetary systems of the most important trading nations. But strong interests have made themselves felt which desired just the reverse policy. They have favoured a lytric policy of the following type: (1) Measures which would lead to a fall in the foreign exchange position of their own money in order to improve the position of exporting interests; (2) by increasing the issue of money through free coinage of silver in addition to gold (which would have meant *instead of* it), and even in some cases deliberate issue of paper money, to decrease the value of money in relation to domestic goods and thereby, what is the same thing, to raise the money prices of domestic goods. The object has been to improve prospects for profit in the production of such goods since the increase in their prices as reckoned in terms of domestic currency would probably be the first consequence of the increase of the amount of money in circulation and of the attendant fall in its foreign exchange position. This process is termed 'inflation.'

The following points may be noted: (1) though its quantitative importance is still controversial, it is very probable that with any type of free coinage a very great cheapening in the production of the precious metal or other source of increase in its supply, as through very cheap forced seizures, will lead to a noticeable tendency toward a rise in the prices at least of many products in areas where that metal is the monetary standard, and in differing degrees of all products. (2) It is at the same time an undoubted fact that, in areas with an independent paper standard, situations of severe financial pressure, especially war, lead the monetary authorities to orient their policy overwhelmingly to the financial necessities of the moment. It is equally clear that countries with free coinage or with restricted metallic money have, in similar circumstances, not only suspended redemption of their paper currency, but have gone further to establish definitely a pure paper standard. But in the latter case, the metal money, since its premium in relation to notes is ignored, has become accessory and could only be used for non-monetary purposes. It has thus disappeared from circulation. Finally, it is established that in cases of that kind of shift to a pure paper standard, occurring along with unlimited issues of paper money, inflation has in fact ensued with all its consequences on a grand scale.

When all these processes are compared, it will be seen that so long as freely coined market money exists, the possibility of inflation will be narrowly limited. This will be true in the first place for mechanical reasons. Though it is somewhat elastic, the quantity of the precious metal in question available for monetary use is strictly limited. Secondly, there are economic reasons in that under free coinage the production of money normally takes place only on the initiative of private interests so that the demand for coinage is oriented to the needs of the economic system for means of payment. Inflation, then, is only possible if metal money which was previously restricted is thrown open to free coinage, as is the case to-day with silver in gold-standard countries. When, however, the restricted metal can be produced very cheaply and in large quantities, the effect may be very great.

Inflation through increase in the quantity of redeemable currency notes is conceivable over a very long period only as the result of gradual increase in the circulation through credit expansion. The limits are elastic but in the last resort this process is strictly limited by the necessity for maintaining the solvency of the note-issuing bank. There is acute danger of inflation only if there is danger that the bank will become insolvent. Normally this is likely to occur only where there is a paper standard resulting from war needs.[122]

Where an independent paper standard exists, there may not be any greater danger of inflation itself since in time of war almost all countries soon go over to a paper standard. But in general there is a noticeably greater probability of the results of inflation being felt. Various financial difficulties are likely to arise; and once inflationary tendencies are started, the resulting higher prices lead to demands for increases in salaries and wages and to higher costs in other respects. Even though it would be possible to avoid inflation by making large sacrifices—and there is no absolute necessity to resort to it—there is a strong tendency for financial administrations to continue the inflationary process. As the differences between the conduct during the war of the Allied Powers, of Germany, and of Austria and Russia show, the difference is only one of degree, but nevertheless significant.

Lytric policy may thus, especially when there is an accessory restricted monetary metal or paper money, be an inflationary policy. In a country which, like the United States, has had relatively so little interest in the

[122] Cases like the gold inflation of Sweden during the war, resulting from the export of war materials, are the result of such special circumstances that they need not be considered here. (Since this was written a somewhat similar tendency, or at least the possibility of it, has developed in the United States as a result of the forces which have concentrated the great bulk of the world's monetary gold in that country.)—ED.

foreign exchange value of her money, this has been true for a time under quite normal conditions without being based on any motives derived from the field of public finance. In a number of countries which fell into inflationary measures during the War, the pressure of necessity has been such as to lead to its continuance after the War.

This is not the place to discuss the theory of inflation. Inflation always means, in the first place, a particular way of increasing the purchasing power available to certain interests. It must, however, be pointed out that, though it seems to be much easier to develop a planned rational course of monetary policy with administrative money, especially paper money, it is from the point of view of stabilization of the exchanges particularly easy for this to come under the influence of irrational interests.

The formal economic rationality of lytric policy and thus of the monetary system could, in conformity with the meaning of the term 'rationality' consistently held to here, only mean the exclusion of such interests. These interests are either, like the financial interest of the state, not oriented to the market at all, or not to the maintenance of stable exchange relations with other currencies as an optimum basis for rational calculation. What they wish is rather, on the contrary, to augment certain types of purchasing power for certain groups of interests by means of inflation and to maintain it even without financial pressure. Whether this phenomenon is to be regarded as desirable or regrettable, is naturally not a question capable of empirical solution. But there is no doubt of its real existence.

It is furthermore true that a point of view which is oriented to substantive social ideals can find a very important opening for criticism of free market money in this fact. It is true, namely, that the production of money and currency is, in a pure market economy, made an object of the play of interests from the point of view of profitability and is not considered in terms of the right sort of volume or type of money. It can be rightly argued that it is only administrative money which can be rationally controlled, but not market money. Thus the use of administrative money, especially paper money, which can be cheaply produced in any desired form and quantity is, from a substantively rational point of view, the correct way to handle the monetary question. This argument is conclusive in formal logical terms. Its value, however, is naturally limited in view of the fact that in the future as in the past it will be the interests of individuals rather than ideas which determine economic policy.[123] Thus, the possibility of conflict between formal rationality in the present sense and the substantive rationality which would theoretically be open to any lytric authority which was entirely free of any obligation to maintain free coinage of metal, has been demonstrated. That was the sole purpose of this discussion.

It is evident that this whole treatment of money consists only in a kind of discussion with Knapp's excellent book, *Die Staatliche Theorie des Geldes,* a discussion which is, however, confined to points relevant to the present problems and carried out on a highly schematic basis, entirely neglecting the finer points. Quite at variance with its author's intentions, though perhaps not entirely without fault on his part, the work immediately became a battleground for value judgments. It was naturally greeted with especial warmth by the Austrian lytric administration, with its partiality to paper money. Events have by no means disproved Knapp's theory in any point, though they have shown, what was known beforehand, that it is incomplete in its treatment of the substantive value of money. It will now be necessary to justify this statement in more detail.

36a: CRITICAL NOTE ON THE 'STATE THEORY OF MONEY'

Knapp succeeds in demonstrating that in every case the recent monetary policy both of states themselves and of agencies under the direction of the state have, in their efforts to adopt a gold standard or some other standard approximating this as closely as possible, been primarily concerned with the exchange value of their currency in relation to others, particularly the English. The object has been to maintain par of exchange with the English gold standard since this has been the money of the world's largest trading area and has been most universally used as a means of payment in international trade. To accomplish this, Germany first demonetized silver; then France, Switzerland, and the other countries of the Latin Union, Holland, and finally India ceased to treat silver as market money and made it into restricted money. Apart from this, indirectly, they undertook measures providing for foreign payments

---

[123] This is an application of Weber's general theory of the relations of interests and ideas, which is much further developed in his writings on the Sociology of Religion. The most important point is that he refused to accept the common dilemma that a given act is motivated either by interests or by ideas. The influence of ideas is rather to be found in their function of defining the situations in which interests are pursued. Beside in Weber's own works, this point is developed in the editor's article 'The Role of Ideas in Social Action,' *American Sociological Review,* October 1938.—Ed.

in gold. Austria and Russia did the same by using unredeemable, independent paper money and also took measures to maintain its parity with gold and to be in a position to make at least foreign payments in gold at any time. They were thus concerned entirely with maintaining the greatest possible stability of their foreign exchanges. It is this on which Knapp bases the opinion that this is the only respect in which a metallic standard and free coinage are important. He concludes that this end of foreign exchange stability would be just as well served by the use of indirect measures to insure adequate gold reserves, if carried out by authorities using paper money or by the direct measures of the type undertaken by Austria and Russia. This is not, other things being equal, strictly and literally true for areas of free coinage. For, so long as two areas, which maintain the same kind of free coinage, refrain from embargoes on the exportation of monetary metal, whether they are both gold-standard or silver-standard countries, the fact of the existence of free coinage on both sides undoubtedly facilitates the maintenance of exchange parity considerably. Under normal conditions this is to a large extent the fact. But even so far as it is true, it does not prove that in the choice of a monetary standard—above all to-day in the choice between a metallic standard, whether gold or silver, and a paper standard—this would be the only set of considerations which would be important.[124]

This would imply that a paper standard and a metallic standard would in other respects behave in the same way. But even from a formal point of view the difference is significant. Paper money is necessarily a form of administrative money, which may be true of metallic money, but is not necessarily so. It is impossible for paper money to be freely coined. The difference between depreciated paper money, such as the *assignats,* and the type of depreciation of silver which might at some future time result from its universal demonetization, making it exclusively an industrial raw material, is not negligible.[125]

Paper has been and is to-day by no means a free good, just as the precious metals are not. But the difference, both in the objective possibility of increased production and in the costs of production in relation to probable demand, is enormous, since the production of metals is to a relative degree so definitely dependent on the existence of mineral deposits. This difference justifies the proposition that a lytic adminis-

[124] The special circumstances which are involved in bimetallism and restricted money have already been discussed and can reasonably be left aside here.
[125] It is true that Knapp occasionally grants this.

tration was, before the war, in a position to produce paper money, if it so desired, in the unlimited quantities. This is a significant difference even from copper, as used in China, certainly from silver, and very decidedly from gold. The costs would be, relatively speaking, negligible. Furthermore, the nominal value of the notes can be determined arbitrarily and need bear no particular relation to the amount of paper used. In the case of metallic money, this last has been true only of its use as subsidiary money; thus not in any comparable degree or sense. It is not true of standard metal. In the latter case, the available quantity has been somewhat elastic but has been subject to an immensely more rigid limit than is the case of the produceability of paper. This fact has imposed limits on the arbitrariness of monetary policy. It is of course true that, so far as the lytric administration has been oriented exclusively to the maintenance of the greatest possible stability of foreign exchange rates, it would be subject to no technically rigid limits in its production of paper money. This is the objection Knapp would make; and in saying this he would be right but only from a formal point of view.

What has been the actual history of independent paper money? Knapp would cite the cases of Austria and Russia to show that it was the same for them. The only difference was that the mechanical limits imposed by the scarcity of metal were absent. The question is whether this difference is unimportant, a question which Knapp ignores. He would no doubt say that there is no cure known to prevent the 'death' of a monetary standard. If the present [126] very abnormal limits to the production of paper be ignored, there unquestionably have been and still are certain factors tending to unlimited issue of paper money. In the first place, there are the interests of those in political authority who Knapp also assumes will bear ultimate responsibility for monetary policy, and there are also certain private interests. These are not of necessity primarily concerned with the maintenance of stable foreign exchange. It is even true, at least for certain periods, that their interests may lie in the opposite direction. These interests can, either from within the political and monetary administration or by exercising a strong pressure on it, have an important influence on policy which would lead to inflation. Knapp, who strictly avoids the term, could only describe this as a case of issue of paper money that was not oriented to the international rate of exchange. He would have to admit that it could occur.

[126] It should be kept in mind that this was written under the abnormal conditions of Germany in 1920.—ED.

There are, in the first place, financial temptations to resort to inflation. An average depreciation of the German mark by inflation to $\frac{1}{20}$th of its former value in relation to the most important internal commodities and property would—once profits and wages had become adapted to this level of prices—mean, it may here be assumed, that all internal commodities and labour would nominally be valued 20 times as highly as before. This would further mean, for those in this fortunate situation, a reduction of the war debt to $\frac{1}{20}$th of its original level. The state, which would receive a proportionate increase in its income from taxation as nominal money incomes rose, would at least enjoy important relief from this source. This is indeed an attractive prospect. It is clear that someone would have to bear the costs, but it is not clear that it is either the state or one of these two categories of private individuals, entrepreneurs and wage earners. The prospect is even more attractive of being able to pay old foreign debts in a monetary unit which can be manufactured at will and at negligible cost. Apart from the possibility of political intervention, there is of course the objection that the use of this policy toward foreign loans would endanger future credit. But the state is often more concerned with the present than with the more or less remote future. Furthermore, there are entrepreneurs who would be only too glad to see the prices of their products increased twenty-fold through inflation if, as is altogether possible, their workers, because of lack of bargaining power or through lack of understanding of the situation or for any other reason, were allowed to increase their nominal wages only by five- or possibly ten-fold.

It is usual for acute inflation from financial motives of this kind to be sharply disapproved by experts in economic policy. It is a fact that it is not compatible with Knapp's form of foreign exchange policy. On the other hand, a deliberate but very gradual increase of the quantity of money in circulation, of the type which is sometimes undertaken by central banks by facilitating the extension of credit, is often looked upon favourably as a means of stimulating speculative attitudes. By holding out prospect of greater profits, it is held to stimulate the spirit of enterprise and with that an increase in capitalistic production by encouraging the investment of free money in profit-making enterprise, rather than its investment in fixed interest-bearing securities.

The question arises, however, of the way in which this more conservative policy is related to the stability of foreign exchange. Its direct effect—that is, the consequences of the stimulation of the spirit of enterprise—may be to create a more favourable balance of payment, or at least to check the fall in the foreign exchange position of the domestic currency. How often this works out and how strong the influence is, is, of course, another question. Also, no attempt will here be made to discuss whether the effects of a moderate increase in the circulation of money derived from financial sources would be similar. The costs of this enrichment of the supply of standard money, which are relatively harmless to the foreign exchange position, will be gradually paid by the same groups which would be subject to 'confiscation' in a case of acute financial inflation. This includes all those whose nominal income remains the same or who have securities with a constant nominal value, above all, the receivers of fixed investment income, and those who earn salaries which are fixed in that they can be raised only through a severe struggle. It is thus not possible to interpret Knapp as meaning that it is only the stability of foreign exchange which is significant for the management of paper money; indeed, he does not claim this. Nor is it legitimate, however, to believe as he does that there is a very high probability that this will in fact be alone decisive. It cannot, however, be denied that it would be the only consideration which would weigh with a completely rational lytric policy; that is, one which sought as far as possible to prevent disturbances of the price structure resulting from monetary sources. But it cannot be admitted, and Knapp does not claim this either, that the practical significance of the kind of monetary policy formulated is limited to the question of the stability of foreign exchange rates.

Inflation has here been spoken of as a source of price revolutions or at least changes in the price structure, and it has been pointed out that it may be influenced by the desire to bring about price changes. Naturally, an inflation so extensive as to create a price revolution, will inevitably upset the stability of foreign exchange; though this is by no means necessarily true of gradual increases in the circulating medium. Knapp would admit that. He obviously assumes, and rightly, that there is no place in his theory for a currency policy concerned with commodity prices, whether it be revolutionary, evolutionary, or conservative. Why does he do this? Presumably for the following formal reasons:—

The exchange relationship between the standards of two or more countries is expressed daily in a small number of formally specific and uniform foreign exchange rates, which can be used as a guide to a rational lytric policy. It is further possible for a monetary authority, especially one concerned with the volume of currency, to make certain

estimates on the basis of facts which are made available through a periodical demand for them. These, which are only estimates, concern the
probable variation in the quantity of means of payment for purposes of
making payments alone, which a given population involved in market
relationships with one another will, so long as conditions remain approximately the same, have need of for a certain future time. On the other
hand, it is not in the same sense possible to estimate, quantitatively, the
effect of an inflationary or deflationary process of a given magnitude on
prices. To do this, it would, in the case of inflation, to which attention
will be confined, be necessary to know the following additional facts:
(1) The existing distribution of income; (2) connected with this, the
present expectations of the direction of economic action for the different
individuals engaged in economic activity; (3) the channels the inflationary process would follow, that is, who would be the primary and
subsequent recipients of newly-issued money. This would involve knowing the order in which nominal incomes are raised by the inflation and
the extent to which this would take place; (4) the way in which the
newly-created demand for goods would be exercised, for consumption,
for building up property investments, or for new capital. This would be
important quantitatively, but even more so qualitatively; (5) the directions and the extent to which it would be possible that the production of
goods would be further stimulated as a result of the changes in the price
structure, the resultant changes in the distribution of income, and, finally,
in turn, in purchasing power.

All these are data which would depend entirely on the decisions made
by individuals when faced with the new economic situation. And these
decisions would in turn react on the expectations as to prices of other
individuals. These latter expectations would only be verified or the reverse as a result of the prices as actually determined by the future play
of interests. In such a situation there can clearly be no question of forecasting in the form of such prediction as that the issue of an additional
billion of currency units would result in a pig-iron price of 'X' or a grain
price of 'Y.' The prospect is made even more difficult by the fact that it
is possible temporarily to establish effective price regulation of domestic
commodities, even though these can only be maximum and not minimum prices and their effectiveness is definitely limited. But even if this
impossible task of calculating specific prices were accomplished, it would
be of relatively little use. This would only determine the amount of
money required as a means of payment, but in addition to this, and on a

much larger scale, money would be required in the form of credit as a means of obtaining capital goods. Here, possible consequences of a proposed inflationary measure are involved which are inaccessible to any kind of accurate forecasting. It is thus understandable that, all things considered, Knapp should have entirely neglected the possibility of inflationary price policies being used in the modern market economy as a deliberate rational policy comparable to the maintenance of foreign exchange stability.

But historically the existence of such policies is a fact. To be sure, in a crude form and under much more primitive conditions of money economy, inflation and deflation have been repeatedly attempted in terms of the Chinese copper currency, though they have led to serious failures. In America, inflation has been proposed. Knapp, however, since his book operates on the basis only of what he calls demonstrable assumptions, contents himself with giving the advice that the state ought to be careful in the issue of independent paper money. Since he is entirely concerned with the maintenance of stable foreign exchange, this advice *appears* to be relatively unequivocal; he is merely pointing out that inflationary devaluation and depreciation in foreign exchange are usually very closely associated. But they are not identical, and it is far from true that every inflation is primarily caused by the foreign exchange situation. Knapp does not explicitly admit, but neither does he deny, that an inflationary price policy has been urged among others by the American silver producers during the free silver campaign and by the farmers who demanded 'greenbacks.' It is probably comforting to him that it has never been successful over a long period.

But the situation is by no means so simple as this. Whether or not they have been intended simply to raise the price level, inflations have in fact often taken place; and even in the Far East, to say nothing of Europe, such catastrophes as met the *assignats* are by no means unknown. This is a fact which a substantive theory of money must deal with. Knapp surely would not maintain that there is no difference whatever between the depreciation of silver and the depreciation of the *assignats*. Even formally this is not the case. What has been depreciated is not silver coin, but, on the contrary, the raw silver for industrial purposes. Coined silver, on the contrary, being restricted, has often had the opposite fate. On the other hand, it is ridiculous to speak of the paper which is available for industrial purposes being 'depreciated.' The term is applicable only to the chartal *assignats*. It is true, as Knapp would rightly point out, that they would fall to zero or to their values to collectors or as museum pieces only when they had finally been repudiated by the state. Thus even this results from a public action by the state. This may be granted, but their material value may have fallen to a minute proportion of what it formerly was, before their formal repudiation, in spite of the fact that they were still nominally valid for making payments of public obligations.

But quite apart from such catastrophes, history provides a considerable number of examples of inflation, and, on the other hand, in China, of deflationary movements as a result of non-monetary use of monetary metals. It is necessary to note in this connexion that under some circumstances, though by no means always, certain kinds of money which were not accessory before, have become so. They have tended to accumulate in the hands of the state and render obstructional changes in the standard necessary. Furthermore, it is imperative for a substantive theory of money, at least to formulate the problems of the ways in which prices and income, and hence the whole economic system, are influenced in such cases. How far it will be able to achieve a theoretical solution of such problems is, for the reasons which have been given, perhaps questionable. Similarly, a problem is suggested by the fact that, as a result of relative decline in the prices of either silver or gold in terms of the other, France, which has been formally a country of bimetallism, in fact has operated at times on a gold standard alone, and at others on a silver standard while the other metal became accessory. In such a case it is not sufficient merely to call attention to the fact that the resulting price changes originate from a *monetary* source. The same is true in other cases where monetary standards have been changed.

In addition to such considerations, it is necessary to inquire what are the sources of an increase in the supply of a precious metal, whether it has come from the booty of conquest (as in the case of Cortez and Pizarro), through the channels of trade (as in China early in the Christian era and since the sixteenth century), or from an increase of production. So far as the latter is the source, has production merely increased, or has it also become cheaper, and why? What is the part which may have been played by changes in the non-monetary uses of the metal? It may be that for a particular economic area, as, for instance, the Mediterranean area in Antiquity, a definitive export has taken place to an entirely distinct area like China or India, as happened in the early centuries of the Christian era. Or the reasons may lie wholly or partly in a change in the monetary demand arising from changes in customs touching the use of money, such as use in small transactions. It is necessary to consider how these and various other possibilities tend to affect the situation.

Finally, it is necessary to discuss the regulation of the demand for money in a market economy, and to inquire into the meaning of this concept. One thing is clear, that it is the actual demand for means of payment on the part of the parties to market relationships which determines the creation of free market money under free coinage. Furthermore, it is the effective demand for means of payment and, above all, for credit, on the part of market participants, in combination with care for the solvency of the banks of issue and the norms which have been established with this in view, which determines the currency policies of modern banks of issue. All this is in conformity with the general character of the modern economic order.

It is only this which, under the formal legal conditions of our economic system, can correctly be called 'demand for money.' This concept is thus quite indifferent with respect to substantive criteria, as is the related one of effective demand for goods. In a market economy there is an inherent limit to the creation of money only in the case of metallic money. But it is precisely the existence of this limit, as has already been pointed out, which constitutes the significance of the precious metals for monetary systems. The restriction of standard money to a material which is not capable of unlimited production at will, particularly to one of the precious metals, in combination with the coverage of currency by this standard, sets a limit to any sort of production of money. Even though it does not exclude a certain elasticity and does not make an evolutionary type of credit inflation altogether impossible, it still has a significant degree of rigidity. Where money is made out of a material which is, for practical purposes, capable of unlimited production, like paper, there is no such mechanical limit. In this case, there is no doubt that it is really a matter of the free decision of the political authorities freed from such mechanical barriers. That, however, means, as has been indicated, determination by their conception of the financial interests of the authority or even, under certain circumstances, the purely personal interests of the members of the administrative staff, as was true of the use of the printing presses by the Red armies. The significance of metallic standards to-day lies precisely in the elimination of these interests from influence on the monetary situation, or more precisely, since it is always *possible* for the state to abandon them in favour of a pure paper standard, a check on such interests. In spite of the mechanical character of its operation, a metallic standard nevertheless makes possible a higher degree of formal rationality in a market economy because it permits action to be oriented wholly to market advantages. It is of course true that the monetary policy of lytric authorities under a pure paper standard, is not necessarily oriented either to the purely personal interests of the authority or the administrative staff, or the financial interests of the state. This is demonstrated by the cases of Austria and Russia. It is also not necessary that the cheapness of the monetary standard should be a ruling consideration. But there is, none the less, continually present a danger that these considerations will become dominant, which is not present in a comparable sense under free coinage. From the point of view of the formal order of a market economy, the existence of this danger is an 'irrational' factor present in any other form of monetary system than a freely coined metallic standard. This is true in spite of the fact that it may be readily admitted that, on account of its mechanical character, such a monetary system possesses only a relative degree of formal rationality. So much Knapp could and should admit.

However incredibly primitive the older forms of the quantity theory of money were, there is no denying that any inflation with the issue of paper money determined by financial needs is in danger of causing depreciation. Nobody, not even Knapp, would deny this. But his reasons for dismissing it as unimportant are not convincing. The claim that each individual is equally a debtor and a creditor, so that the value of money is indifferent to him, which Knapp in all seriousness puts forward as proof of the absolute indifference of depreciation, is, as we now see, a phantom. What becomes of this assumption, not only in the case of the receiver of fixed interest, but of people living on fixed salaries or income? Their income remains nominally constant or, at best, the financial situation will perhaps permit its doubling, and even that is dependent on the decisions of administrative authority, while his expenditures may very well have nominally increased twenty-fold. What happens to long-term creditors? The effect of this kind of radical alterations in the purchasing power of money is to-day to produce a chronic tendency toward social revolution in spite of the fact that many entrepreneurs are in a position to make unusual profits from the foreign exchange situation and that a few of the workers are powerful enough to secure increases in their nominal wages. It is, of course, open to anyone to welcome this revolutionary tendency and the accompanying tremendous unsettlement of the market economy. Such an opinion cannot be scientifically refuted. Rightly or wrongly, it is possible to hope that this tendency will lead to the transformation of a market economy into socialism. Or some may think that it proves that only a regulated economy with small-scale production is substantively rational, regardless of the sacrifices its establishment would entail. It is impossible for science to decide such questions, but at the same time it is its duty to state the facts about these effects as clearly and objectively as possible. Knapp's assumption that people are both debtors and creditors in the same degree, which in the generalized form he gives the proposition is quite untenable, serves only to obscure the situation. There are particular errors in his work, but the above seems to be the most important element of *incompleteness* in his theory. It is this which has led certain scholars to attempt to attack him on grounds of principle. This seems to be altogether unnecessary.

37: THE NON-MONETARY SIGNIFICANCE OF POLITICAL BODIES FOR THE ECONOMIC ORDER

Apart from their relation to the monetary system, the fact that independent political units exist is important for the economic system primarily in the following respects:—

(1) It is a fact that, other things being nearly equal, they tend to prefer their own subjects as sources of supply for the utilities they need. The significance of this fact is the greater the more the economy of these political bodies has a monopolistic character or that of a system of budgetary economic units.

(2) There is a possibility, through substantive measures, of deliberately encouraging, checking, or regulating trade over its boundaries.

(3) There is a possibility of various types of formal and substantive regulation of economic activity by political bodies, differing in stringency and in type.

(4) There are important consequences of the very great differences in the structure of authority and of political power and in the closely related structure of administration and of social classes, especially of those which enjoy the highest prestige. From these facts are generally derived the principal attitudes toward earning and profit-making.

(5) There may or may not be competition among the directing authorities of these political bodies to increase their own power and to provide

the members under their authority with means of consumption and acquisition and with the corresponding opportunities for earnings and profits.

(6) There are differences in ways in which these bodies provide for their own needs. On this see the following paragraphs.

38: THE FINANCING OF POLITICAL BODIES

The most direct connexion between the economic system and primarily non-economic corporate groups lies in the way in which they secure the means of carrying on their corporate activity as such; that is, the activity of the administrative staff itself and that which is directed by it.[127] This mode of provision may be called 'financing' in the broadest sense, which includes the provision of goods in kind.

Financing—that is, the provision of corporate activity with economically produced means—may, considering only the simplest types, be organized in the following ways:—

(1) Intermittently, which may in turn be based on purely voluntary contributions or services. Such contributions may take one of three forms:

(a) That of large gifts or endowments.[128] This is typical in relation to charitable, scientific, and other ends which are primarily neither economic nor political.

(b) By begging. This is typical of certain kinds of ascetic communities.

In India, however, profane castes of beggars are also found; and elsewhere, particularly in China, organized groups of beggars. Begging may be extensively monopolized and systematized with a distribution of areas. Also, because response is regarded as a duty or as meritorious, begging may lose its intermittent character and even tend to be treated as a regular source of income.

(c) By gifts, which are formally free, to persons or organizations which are recognized as politically or socially superior. This includes gifts to chiefs, princes, patrons, landlords, or body lords. Because of the fact that they have become conventional, these may in fact be closely approximated to compulsory payments. But usually, they are not worked

---

[127] See chap. i, sec. 12.

[128] *Mäzenatisch*. This term is commonly used in German but not in the precise sense which Weber gives it here. There seems to be no equivalent single term in English, so the idea has been conveyed by a phrase.—ED.

out on a basis of rational expediency, but are generally made on certain traditional occasions, such as particular anniversaries or on the occasion of events of family or political significance.

Intermittent financing may, on the other hand, be based on compulsory contributions.

The type case is furnished by such organizations as the *Camorra* in southern Italy and the *Mafia* in Sicily, and similar organized groups elsewhere. In India there have existed ritually separate castes of 'thieves' and 'robbers,' in China, sects and secret societies with a similar method of economic provision. The payments are only, *prima facie,* intermittent because they are formally extra-legal. In practice they often assume the character of a periodic rate and it is common for certain services to be offered in exchange—notably, a guarantee of security. About twenty years ago, a Neapolitan manufacturer replied to the author's questions concerning the unfavourable effect of the *Camorra* on business, 'Signor, the *Camorra* takes ten lire a month from me, but guarantees me security. The state might take ten times ten, but would guarantee me nothing.' The secret societies which are typical of Africa, perhaps as survivals of the former 'men's house,' function in the same way, and thus guarantee security. Political groups may, like the Ligurian 'pirate state,' rest primarily on the profits of booty. But this has never been the exclusive source of support over a long period.

(2) Financing may, on the other hand, be organized on a permanent basis.

A.—This may take place without any independent economic production on the part of the corporate group. Then, it may consist in contributions of goods, which may be based on a money economy. If so, funds are collected by money contributions and provision is made by the money purchase of the necessary utilities. In this case, all compensation of members of the administrative staff takes the form of money salaries. It may, on the other hand, be organized on the basis of a natural economy. Then, members are assessed with specific contributions in kind. Within this category, there are the following sub-types: the administrative staff may be provided for by benefices in kind and the needs of the group met in the same way. On the other hand, the contributions which were collected in kind may be sold wholly or in part for money and provision made in monetary terms.

Whether in money or in kind, the principal elementary types of contribution are the following:—

(a) Taxes; that is, contributions of a proportion of all possessions or, in money terms, property; or of all receipts, or, in money terms, incomes; or finally, from the means of production in the hands of certain kinds of profit-making enterprises, the so-called 'profit tax.'

(b) Fees; that is, payments for using or taking advantage of facilities provided by the corporate group, of its property or of its services.

(c) 'Duties' on such things as various kinds of use or consumption of commodities, specific kinds of transactions, above all, the transportation of goods (tariffs) and the turn-over of goods (excise duties and sales tax).

Contributions may be collected by the corporate group itself or leased out ('farmed') or lent out or pledged. The leasing of collection for a fixed sum of money ('tax farming') may have a rational effect on the fiscal system since it may be the only possible way to budget accounts. Lending and pledging are usually irrational from the fiscal point of view, normally resulting from financial necessity or usurpation on the part of the administrative staff, a result of the absence of a dependable administrative organization.

A permanent appropriation from the receipts from contributions by creditors of the state, by private guarantors of the army or of tax payments, by unpaid mercenary chieftains and soldiers, and, finally, by holders of rights to official positions, will be called the granting of benefices.[129] This may in turn take the form of individual appropriation or collective appropriation with freedom of replacement from the group which has collectively carried out the appropriation.

Financing without any economic production on the part of the corporate group itself may also take place by imposing obligations to personal services; that is, direct personal services with specification of the work to be done.

B.—Permanent financing may further, contrary to the above cases, be based on the existence of a productive organization under the direct control of the corporate group. Such an organization may be a budgetary unit, as an *oikos* or a feudal domain, or it may be a profit-making enterprise, which, in turn, may compete freely with other profit-making enterprises or be a monopoly.

Once more, exploitation may be directly under the administration of the corporate group or it may be farmed out, leased, or pledged.

C.—Finally, it is possible for financing to be organized 'liturgically' by means of burdens which are associated with privileges. These may

[129] *Verpfründung.*

involve positive privileges, as when a group is freed from the burden of making particular contributions, or negative privileges, as when greater burdens are placed on other particular groups. The latter are usually either social classes [130] as such or property or income groups. Finally, the liturgic type may be organized correlatively by associating specific monopolies with liability to the burden of performing certain services or supplying certain goods. This may be organized by social classes, by compulsorily forming the members of the corporate group into hereditarily closed liturgical classes on the basis of property and occupation, each enjoying class privileges. Or it may be carried out capitalistically, by creating closed guilds or cartels, with monopolistic rights and a corresponding obligation to make money contributions.

This very rough classification applies to all kinds of corporate groups. Examples, however, will be given only in terms of political bodies.

The system of provision through money contributions without economic production is typical of the modern state. It is, however, quite out of the question to attempt even a schematic analysis of modern systems of taxation at the present point. The place where it belongs in a sociological analysis will be at a later point [131] in relation to the kind of structure of authority which has typically influenced the development of its type of contribution, such as fees, excises, and taxes.

Contributions in kind, even in cases of fees, customs, excises, and sales taxes, were common throughout the Middle Ages. Their commutation into money payments is a relatively modern phenomenon.

Deliveries of goods in kind are typical in the form of tribute or of assessments of products laid upon dependent economic units. The transportation of goods in kind is only possible for small political units or under exceptionally favourable transportation conditions, as were provided by the Nile and the Chinese Grand Canal. Otherwise it is necessary for the contributions to be converted into money if the final recipient is to benefit from them. This was common in Antiquity. It is also possible for them to be exchanged for objects with different specified prices according to the distance they have to be transported. This is said to have been done in Ancient China.

Examples of obligations to personal service are obligations to military

[130] *Stände.*
[131] This is apparently a plan which Weber did not succeed in fulfilling, as there is no extended discussion of taxation in *Wirtschaft und Gesellschaft.*—Ed.

service, to act in courts [132] and on juries, to maintain roads and bridges, to work on a dyke or in a mine, and all sorts of compulsory service for corporate purposes which are found in various types of corporate groups. The type case is furnished by the compulsory labour state,[133] of which the best example is the New Kingdom of Ancient Egypt. Similar conditions are found at some periods in China, to a lesser extent in India, and to a still less extent in the late Roman Empire and in many groups in the early Middle Ages. Support by the granting of benefices is illustrated by the following cases: (1) In China, the recognition of the collective claims of successful examinees to official position; (2) in India to the private guarantors of military forces and tax payments; (3) to unpaid mercenary leaders and soldiers, as in the late Caliphate and under the regime of the Mamelukes; (4) to creditors of the state, as in the very common sale of offices.

Provisions from the group's own productive organization administered on a budgetary basis, is illustrated by the exploitation of domains under the direct control of the political authority. Also, the obligation of subjects to compulsory services has been used, as in Egypt, to produce goods needed by the court or for political purposes. Modern examples are factories maintained by the state for the manufacture of munitions or of military clothing.

The use of productive organizations for profit in free competition with private enterprise is rare, but has occurred occasionally, for instance, in maritime trade. On the other hand, the monopolistic type is very common in all periods of history but reached its highest development in the Western World from the sixteenth to the eighteenth centuries.

Positive privileges on a liturgical basis are illustrated by the exemption of the literate classes in China from feudal obligations. There are similar exemptions of privileged groups from the more menial tasks all over the world. In many countries educated people have been exempt from military service.

Negative privilege is to be found in the extra liturgical burdens placed upon wealth in the democracies of Antiquity. It is also illustrated by the burden placed on the classes who did not enjoy the exemptions in the cases just mentioned.

To take the correlative case, subjecting particular classes to specifically liturgical obligations is the most important form of systematic provision

---

[132] As the court of a lord in feudalism.—Ed.
[133] *Fronstaat.*

for public needs on a different basis than that of regular taxation. In China, India, and Egypt, the countries with the earliest development of bureaucracy, which was usually based on irrigation, there has been a liturgical organization based on obligations to payments and services in kind. It was also in part taken over from these sources by the Hellenistic states and by the late Roman Empire, though there, to be sure, to an important extent, it took the form of liturgical obligations to pay money taxes rather than deliver goods. This type of provision always involves the organization of the population in terms of occupationally differentiated classes. It is by no means out of the question that it might reappear again in the modern world in this form if public provision by taxation should fall down and the satisfaction of private wants by capitalistic enterprise become subject to extensive regulation by the state. Up until now, the financial difficulties of the modern state have been adequately met by imposing burdens on the propertied classes in exchange for various privileges. A simple example is the compulsory control of the manufacture of explosives in Spain where they are monopolistically protected against competition in return for heavy taxation by the state. It is always tempting to use the socialization of particular branches of industry, starting with coal, in this way. Compulsory cartels or combinations could be imposed with obligations to pay large sums in taxes. Thus they could be made useful for fiscal purposes and production would be allowed to continue to be oriented rationally to the price situation.

39: Repercussions of Financing on Private Economic Activity

The way in which political and hierocratic bodies provide for their corporate needs has a very important influence on the structure of private economic activity. If the finances of the state are based on money taxation, and even then only if taxes are collected under its own authority, the development of capitalistic enterprise rationally oriented to the market is given the most favourable opportunities. It is a further favouring circumstance if personal services are required by the state only for political and legal purposes. A state which collects money taxes by tax farming is a favourable environment for the development of politically oriented capitalism, but it does not encourage the orientation of profit-making activity to the market. The granting of rights to contributions and their distribution as benefices normally tends to check the development of capitalism by creating vested interests in the maintenance of existing sources of fees and contributions. It thus tends to stereotyping and traditionalizing of the economic system.

A political body based on deliveries in kind does not promote the development of capitalism. On the contrary, it hinders it to the extent to which it involves rigidly binding the decisions as to what will be economically produced to compulsory political needs, in a form which, from a point of view of profit-making enterprise, is irrational.

A system of provision by compulsory services in kind hinders the development of market capitalism; above all, in that it maintains control of labour forces and thus prevents the development of a free labour market. It is unfavourable to politically oriented capitalism because it removes the typical prospective advantages which enable it to develop.

Financing by means of monopolistic profit-making enterprises has in common with the use of contributions in kind which are sold for money and with liturgical obligations on property, the fact that they are all unfavourable to the development of a type of capitalism which is autonomously oriented to the market. On the contrary, they tend to repress it in favour of fiscal considerations which, from the point of view of the market, are irrational, such as the establishment of privileges and of opportunities for money making through other channels. They are, on the other hand, under certain conditions, favourable to politically oriented capitalism.

What is important for profit-making enterprises with fixed capital and careful capital accounting is, in formal terms, above all, the calculability of the tax load. Substantively, it is important that there shall not be unduly heavy burdens placed on the capitalistic employment of resources, above all, on market turnover. On the other hand, a speculative commercial type of capitalism is compatible with any form of organization of public finance which does not, through tying it to liturgical obligations, directly inhibit the commercial exploitation of goods as commodities.

Though important, the form of organization of the obligations imposed by public finance is not sufficient to determine completely the direction of development which the orientation of economic activity will take. In spite of the apparent absence of all the more important obstacles of this type, no important development of rational capitalism has occurred in large areas and for long periods. On the other hand, there are cases where, in spite of what appear to be very serious obstacles placed in the way by public finance, such a development has taken place. Various factors seem to have played a part. Substantively, economic policy may be very largely oriented to non-economic ends. The development of the intellectual disciplines, notably science and technology, is important. But above all, there have been obstructions in the types of value-attitude derived from ethical and religious sources which have tended to limit the development of an autonomous capitalistic system of the modern type to certain areas. It must, furthermore, not be forgotten that forms of organization and of enterprise must, like technical products, be 'invented.' From a historical point of view, it is possible only to cite circumstances which exert a negative influence on the relevant thought processes—that is, one which impedes or even obstructs them—or a positive favouring influence. It is not, however, possible to prove a strictly inevitable causal relationship in such cases, any more than it is possible in the case of any other kind of strictly individual events.[134]

Apropos of the last statement, it may be noted that concrete individual events in the field of the natural sciences can be rigorously reduced to their particular causal components only under very special circumstances. There is thus no difference in principle between the field of action and other fields.

At this point it is possible to give only a few provisional indications of the fundamentally important inter-relationships between the form of organization and administration of political bodies and the economic system.

1. Historically, the most important case of obstruction of the development of market capitalism by turning public contributions into privately held benefices is China. The leasing of contributions, which is often identical with this, has existed in the Near East since the time of the Caliphs. Both will be discussed in the proper place. Tax farming is found in India, in the Near East, and in the Western World in Antiquity and the Middle Ages. Particularly, however, in Antiquity, as in the development of the Roman Equestrian Order, it became decisive in determining the mode of orientation of capitalistic acquisition. In India and the Near East, on the other hand, it was more important in determining the development and distribution of wealth, notably of land ownership.

[134] The methodological problems touched here have been further discussed in various of the essays collected in the volume *Gesammelte Aufsätze zur Wissenschaftslehre*. The most essential point is that Weber held that no scientific analysis in the natural or the social field ever exhausts the concrete individuality of the empirical world. Scientific conceptual schemes and the causal explanations attained through their use are always in important respects abstract.—Ed.

2. The most important case in history of the obstruction of capitalistic development by a liturgical organization of public finance is that of later Antiquity. It was also perhaps important in India after the Buddhist era and at certain periods in China. This also will be discussed later.

3. The most important historical case of the monopolistic diversion of capitalism is, following the Hellenistic, especially the Ptolemaic models, the period of royal monopolies and monopolistic concessions in early modern times, which again will be discussed in the proper place. This was first initiated in certain measures introduced by Frederick II in Sicily, perhaps following a Byzantine model. It was finally doomed by the struggle under the Stuarts.

This whole discussion in such an abstract form has been introduced only in order to make an approximately correct formulation of problems possible. But before returning to the stages of development of economic activity and the conditions underlying that development, it is necessary to undertake a strictly sociological analysis of the non-economic components.

40: The Influence of Economic Factors on the Organization of Corporate Groups

Economic considerations have one very general kind of sociological importance for the organization of corporate groups if, as is almost always true, the directing authority and the administrative staff are remunerated. If this is the case, an overwhelmingly strong set of economic interests become bound up with the continuation of the organization, even though its primary ideological basis may in the meantime have ceased to exist.

It is an everyday occurrence that organizations of all kinds which, even in the eyes of the participants have become 'meaningless,' continue to exist because an executive secretary or some other official makes his 'living' out of it and without it would have no means of support.

Every advantage which is appropriated, or even under certain circumstances which has not been formally appropriated, *may* have the effect of stereotyping existing forms of social action. Among the opportunities for economic profit or earnings in the field of the peaceful provision for everyday wants, it is in general *only* the opportunities open to profit-making enterprise which constitute autonomous forces which are revolutionary in a rational sense; but even of them this is not always true.

For example, the interests of bankers in maintaining their commissions long obstructed the recognition of endorsements on checks. Similar cases of the obstruction of formally rational institutions by vested interests, which may well be interests in capitalistic profits, will frequently be met with below. They are, however, appreciably rarer than obstructions resulting from such factors as appropriation of benefices, class status, and various economically irrational forces.

41: MOTIVES OF ECONOMIC ACTIVITY [135]

All economic activity in a market economy is undertaken and carried through by individuals to make provision for their own ideal or material interests. This is naturally just as true when economic activity is oriented to the patterns of order of corporate groups, whether they themselves are partly engaged in economic activity, are primarily economic in character, or merely regulate economic activity. Strangely enough, this fact is often not taken account of.

Even if an economic system were organized on a socialistic basis, there would be no fundamental difference in this respect. It is true that the decisions involved in control and management would lie primarily in the hands of the central authority. The functions of the normal individual engaged in the production of goods would be limited to the performance of 'technical' services; that is, of 'labour' in the sense of the term employed here. This would be true so long as the central authority followed a 'dictatorial' policy, proceeding autocratically without consultation with others. As soon as any rights of being consulted were granted, this would, even on a formal basis, immediately open the door to conflicts of interests. Such conflicts would inevitably influence policies in the organization of production, above all, those concerned with the amount of saving. But this is not the decisive point. What is important is that, even then, the individual will ask first of all how far the real in-

[135] The title of this section is somewhat misleading. It actually does not contain what most people would expect under a treatment of the motivation of economic activity. Indeed, it carries this problem only to the point of establishing the structural basis of an interest in income, without attempting to analyze the underlying motivation any farther. Important contributions to various phases of this problem are to be found in other parts of Weber's work. Beside the references already given, this is one of the central themes of the comparative studies in the Sociology of Religion. A systematic generalized statement was, however, never made in the later stages of Weber's career, and his position must be pieced together from many different sources.—ED.

come allotted to him and the labour service required of him, especially as compared with the situation of others, appear to conform with his interests. This would be the basis of his behaviour. According to the prevailing judgment of such interests, any one of a number of different developments might take place. There might be struggles for power over the alteration or maintenance of established allotments of real income, whether, for instance, there should be special allowances for heavy work; over appropriation of or expropriation from particular jobs, which were sought after because of extra remuneration or particularly favourable conditions of work; over the cessation of work by strikes or lockouts; over restriction of production to force alterations in the conditions of work in particular industries; over boycotts and the forcible dismissal of unpopular supervisors. In short, the moment the function of the worker goes beyond the purely technical sphere, all sorts of processes of appropriation and of conflicts of interests would become the normal thing. The fact that they would for the most part be fought out through organized groups and that advantages would be enjoyed on the one hand by the workers engaged in the most essential services, on the other hand by those who were physically strongest, would simply reflect the existing situation. But however that might be, it would be the interests of the individual, possibly organized in terms of the similar interests of many, especially as opposed to those of others, which would underlie all action. The structure of interests and the relevant situation might change; there would be other means of pursuing interests, but this fundamental factor would remain just as relevant as before. It is of course true that economic action which is oriented on purely ideological grounds to the interests of others does exist. But it is even more certain that the mass of men do not act in this way, and it is an induction from experience that they cannot do so and never will.

In a completely socialized planned economy there would be scope only for the following: (a) the distribution of real income by rationing in conformity with a systematic pattern of consumption; (b) the production of goods and services in kind according to a plan of production. The monetary category of 'income' would necessarily disappear, but rationed 'receipts' would be possible.

In a market economy the interest in the maximization of income is necessarily the ultimate driving force [136] of all economic activity. For

---

[136] *Triebfeder.* Weber certainly cannot mean that the maximization of money income is the ultimate basis of all economic motivation in general. This would be radically in con-

any activity which requires goods and services which are not available to the actors as free goods, presupposes the orientation of action to the acquisition of and control over future income. Furthermore, practically every case of existing control over goods and services presupposes a previous income as its source. All the profits of business enterprise in a market economy become at some stage and in some form parts of the income of economically acting individuals. In a regulated economy the principal aim of the regulatory provisions is generally to influence the distribution of income.[137]

Income and receipts may, from a sociological point of view, take the following principal forms and be derived from the following principal sources:—

A.—Incomes and receipts from personal services derived from specialized or specified functions:

(1) Wages, (a) which may be freely contracted wage income or receipts calculated according to the time worked. (b) Income and receipts paid according to an established scale, as in salaries and the remuneration of officials. (c) Conditional piece rates paid to employees. (d) The proceeds of entirely free labour contracts.

(2) Profits. (a) Profits from free exchange transactions involving the production of goods or services by business enterprises. (b) Regulated profits from exchange transactions by the same kinds of operation. In cases (a) and (b), net returns are arrived at by deducting costs. (c) The proceeds of 'booty.' (d) Profits arising from appropriation of rights such as those of exercising power, of occupying offices, of tax farming; acquisition through bribery, and from similar sources. In cases (c) and (d) costs must be deducted if these methods of acquisition are carried on as a permanent business. Otherwise, this does not always take place.

B.—Income and receipts from property, derived from the exploitation of control over important means of production:

(1) Those which are normally treated as net income after the deduction of costs. (a) Income derived from property in human beings, such

tradiction to his earlier analysis in chap. i, particularly secs. 6 and 7, and to much of what follows in chap. iii. What he means is rather that, in so far as action is *economically* oriented in a market economy, it must strive for the maximization of income. Thus this is not an ultimate 'motive,' but rather a generalized goal which is inherent in certain kinds of social structures, relatively independently of what the deeper motives may be.—ED.

137 In natural economies, according to the terminology adopted here, 'income' does not exist, but only 'receipts' which consists of goods and services in kind, but which cannot be valued and added in terms of the units of a means of exchange.

as slaves, serfs or freedmen. These may be receipts in money or in kind; they may be fixed in amount or consist in shares after the deduction of costs of maintenance. (b) Appropriated income associated with positions of authority, usually after deducting costs of administration. (c) Income from land ownership. This may be based on leases dividing shares of the crop, on leases for fixed periods, or on receipts in the capacity of landlord, rather than merely owner. It may be in money or in kind. It should be reckoned after the deduction of taxes and costs of maintenance. (d) House rents after deduction of costs. (e) Receipts from appropriated monopolies—exclusive privileges, patents, etc., after deduction of fees.

(2) Property income which is normally reckoned without deduction of costs. (a) Income from fixed means of production [138] derived from permission to use such facilities in return for the payment to a budgetary unit or a profit-making enterprise of a 'rent.' [139] (b) Payments for the use of domestic animals.[140] (c) Interests on loans in kind and conditional allowances in kind. (d) Interest on money loans. (e) Money interest on mortgages. (f) Money returns from securities, which may consist in fixed interest or in dividends varying with profitability. (g) Other shares in profits, such as shares in exceptional profits and profits from rational speculative operations and a rationally assigned share in the long-run profits of all sorts of enterprises.

All 'profits' and the income derived from securities are either not arranged in advance at all or only with respect to certain assumptions such as their purchase price or agreed rates of interest. Fixed interest and wages, leases of land, and house rents are stipulated in advance. Income from the exercise of power, from ownership of human beings, from authority over as well as ownership of the land, and from 'booty,' all involve appropriation by force. Income from property may be divorced from any occupation in case the recipient does not administer the property himself, but through agents. Wages, salaries, labour profits, and entrepreneur's profits are, on the other hand, occupational incomes. Other types of property income and profit may be either one or the other. It is not possible here to enter into a detailed classification.

Of all types of income, it is particularly those from business profits and from stipulated or free labour contracts which have a dynamic, revolutionary significance for economic life. Next to these stand incomes de-

[138] An 'administrative staff.' See chap. i, 12.
[139] *Viehrenten.*
[140] *Anlagen.*

rived from free exchange and, in quite different ways, under certain circumstances, from 'booty.'

Those having a static conservative influence on economic activity are above all incomes fixed in accordance with a scale, namely salaries, time wages, profits from the exploitation of official positions, and normally all kinds of fixed interest and rent.[141]

In an exchange economy, the economic source of income lies in the great majority of cases in the exchange situation of the market with respect to goods and labour services. Thus, in the last analysis, it is determined by consumers' demand in connexion with the more or less strong naturally or socially determined monopolistic position of the parties to market relationships.

The economic source of receipts in a natural economy generally lies in the monopolistic appropriation of advantages; that is, in opportunities to exploit property or services for a return.

Underlying all these types of income is the possibility of the use of force in protecting appropriated advantages. 'Booty' and similar means of acquisition are the results of the actual use of force.

This sketch has been so rough that it has been impossible to make any attempt at refined systematization.[142]

---

[141] The distinction here made between those types of economic interest having a dynamic and a static influence on economic activity respectively, is strikingly similar to that made by Pareto between 'speculators' and 'rentiers,' see *The Mind and Society,* especially secs. 22, 34 ff.—ED.

[142] Though it is not acceptable in a good many particular points, the treatment of 'income' in Robert Liefmann's works is one of the most valuable available. Here, the economic problem cannot be explored further. The relations of economic dynamics and the social order will have to be discussed again and again as the analysis proceeds.

III. The Types of Authority and Imperative Co-ordination

I. THE BASIS OF LEGITIMACY [1]

1: THE DEFINITION, CONDITIONS, AND TYPES OF IMPERATIVE CONTROL

'IMPERATIVE co-ordination' was defined above [2] as the probability that certain specific commands (or all commands) from a given source will be obeyed by a given group of persons. It thus does not include every mode of exercising 'power' or 'influence' over other persons. The motives of obedience to commands in this sense can rest on considerations varying over a wide range from case to case; all the way from simple habituation to the most purely rational calculation of advantage. A criterion of every true relation of imperative control, however, is a certain minimum of voluntary submission; thus an interest (based on ulterior motives or genuine acceptance) in obedience.

Not every case of imperative co-ordination makes use of economic means; *still less* does it always have economic objectives. But normally (not always) the imperative co-ordination of the action of a considerable number of men requires control of a staff of persons.[3] It is necessary, that is, that there should be a relatively high probability that the action of a definite, supposedly reliable group of persons will be primarily oriented to the execution of the supreme authority's general policy and specific commands.

The members of the administrative staff may be bound to obedience

[1] In this chapter Weber departs from his previous practice and, in addition to the usual division into numbered sections, has a system of somewhat more comprehensive subdivisions. These will be designated by capital letters.—ED.

[2] Chap. i, p. 152. The translation problem raised by the term *Herrschaft* was commented upon at that point.—ED.

[3] An 'administrative staff.' See chap. i, 12.

to their superior (or superiors) by custom, by affectual ties, by a purely material complex of interests, or by ideal (*wertrational*) motives. *Purely* material interests and calculations of advantage as the basis of solidarity between the chief and his administrative staff result, in this as in other connexions, in a relatively unstable situation. Normally other elements, affectual and ideal, supplement such interests. In certain exceptional, temporary cases the former may be alone decisive. In everyday routine life these relationships, like others, are governed by custom and in addition, material calculation of advantage. But these factors, custom and personal advantage, purely affectual or ideal motives of solidarity, do not, even taken together, form a sufficiently reliable basis for a system of imperative co-ordination. In addition there is normally a further element, the belief in legitimacy.

It is an induction from experience that no system of authority voluntarily limits itself to the appeal to material or affectual or ideal motives as a basis for guaranteeing its continuance. In addition every such system attempts to establish and to cultivate the belief in its 'legitimacy.' But according to the kind of legitimacy which is claimed, the type of obedience, the kind of administrative staff developed to guarantee it, and the mode of exercising authority, will all differ fundamentally. Equally fundamental is the variation in effect. Hence, it is useful to classify the types of authority according to the kind of claim to legitimacy typically made by each. In doing this it is best to start from modern and therefore more familiar examples.

1. The choice of this rather than some other basis of classification can only be justified by its results. The fact that certain other typical criteria of variation are thereby neglected for the time being and can only be introduced at a later stage is not a decisive difficulty. The 'legitimacy' of a system of authority has far more than a merely 'ideal' significance, if only because it has very definite relations to the legitimacy of property.

2. Not every 'claim' which is protected by custom or by law should be spoken of as involving a relation of authority. Otherwise the worker, in his claim for fulfilment of the wage contract, would be exercising 'authority' over his employer because his claim can, on occasion, be enforced by order of a court. Actually his formal status is that of party to a contractual relationship with his employer, in which he has certain 'rights' to receive payments. At the same time the concept of a relation of authority naturally does not exclude the possibility that it has originated in a formally free contract. This is true of the authority of the

employer over the worker as manifested in the former's rules and instructions regarding the work process; and also of the authority of a feudal lord over a vassal who has freely entered into the relation of fealty. That subjection to military discipline is formally 'involuntary' while that to the discipline of the factory is voluntary does not alter the fact that the latter is also a case of subjection to authority. The position of a bureaucratic official is also entered into by contract and can be freely resigned, and even the status of 'subject' can often be freely entered into and (in certain circumstances) freely repudiated. Only in the limiting case of the slave is formal subjection to authority absolutely involuntary.

Another case, in some respects related, is that of economic 'power' based on monopolistic position; that is, in this case, the possibility of 'dictating' the terms of exchange to contractual partners. This will not, taken by itself, be considered to constitute 'authority' any more than any other kind of 'influence' which is derived from some kind of superiority, as by virtue of erotic attractiveness, skill in sport or in discussion. Even if a big bank is in a position to force other banks into a cartel arrangement, this will not alone be sufficient to justify calling it a relation of imperative co-ordination. But if there is an immediate relation of command and obedience such that the management of the first bank can give orders to the others with the claim that they shall, and the probability that they will, be obeyed purely as such regardless of particular content, and if their carrying out is supervised, it is another matter. Naturally, here as everywhere the transitions are gradual; there are all sorts of intermediate steps between mere indebtedness and debt slavery. Even the position of a 'salon' can come very close to the borderline of authoritarian domination and yet not necessarily constitute a system of authority. Sharp differentiation in concrete fact is often impossible, but this makes clarity in the analytical distinctions all the more important.

3. Naturally, the legitimacy of a system of authority may be treated sociologically only as the probability that to a relevant degree the appropriate attitudes will exist, and the corresponding practical conduct ensue. It is by no means true that every case of submissiveness to persons in positions of power is primarily (or even at all) oriented to this belief. Loyalty may be hypocritically simulated by individuals or by whole groups on purely opportunistic grounds, or carried out in practice for reasons of material self-interest. Or people may submit from individual weakness and helplessness because there is no acceptable alternative. But these considerations are not decisive for the classification of types of im-

perative co-ordination. What is important is the fact that in a given case the particular claim to legitimacy is to a significant degree and according to its type treated as 'valid'; that this fact confirms the position of the persons claiming authority and that it helps to determine the choice of means of its exercise.

Furthermore a system of imperative co-ordination may—as often occurs in practice—be so completely assured of dominance, on the one hand by the obvious community of interests between the chief and his administrative staff as opposed to the subjects (bodyguards, Pretorians, 'red' or 'white' guards), on the other hand by the helplessness of the latter, that it can afford to drop even the pretence of a claim to legitimacy. But even then the mode of legitimation of the relation between chief and his staff may vary widely according to the type of basis of the relation of authority between them, and, as will be shown, this variation is highly significant for the structure of imperative co-ordination.

4. 'Obedience' will be taken to mean that the action of the person obeying follows in essentials such a course that the content of the command may be taken to have become the basis of action for its own sake. Furthermore, the fact that it is so taken is referable only to the formal obligation, without regard to the actor's own attitude to the value or lack of value of the content of the command as such.

5. Subjectively, the causal sequence may vary, especially as between 'submission' and 'sympathetic agreement.' This distinction is not, however, significant for the present classification of types of authority.

6. The scope of determination of social relationships and cultural phenomena by authority and imperative co-ordination is considerably broader than appears at first sight. For instance, the authority exercised in the school has much to do with the determination of the forms of speech and of written language which are regarded as orthodox. The official languages of autonomous political units, hence of their ruling groups, have often become in this sense orthodox forms of speech and writing and have even led to the formation of separate 'nations' (for instance, the separation of Holland from Germany). The authority of parents and of the school, however, extends far beyond the determination of such cultural patterns which are perhaps only apparently formal, to the formation of the character of the young, and hence of human beings generally.

7. The fact that the chief and his administrative staff often appear formally as servants or agents of those they rule, naturally does nothing whatever to disprove the authoritarian character of the relationship. There

will be occasion later to speak of the substantive features of so-called 'democracy.' But a certain minimum of assured power to issue commands, thus of 'authority,' must be provided for in nearly every conceivable case.

2: THE THREE PURE TYPES OF LEGITIMATE AUTHORITY

There are three pure types of legitimate authority. The validity of their claims to legitimacy may be based on:

1. Rational grounds—resting on a belief in the 'legality' of patterns of normative rules and the right of those elevated to authority under such rules to issue commands (legal authority).

2. Traditional grounds—resting on an established belief in the sanctity of immemorial traditions and the legitimacy of the status of those exercising authority under them (traditional authority); or finally,

3. Charismatic grounds—resting on devotion to the specific and exceptional sanctity, heroism or exemplary character of an individual person, and of the normative patterns or order revealed or ordained by him (charismatic authority).

In the case of legal authority, obedience is owed to the legally established impersonal order. It extends to the persons exercising the authority of office under it only by virtue of the formal legality of their commands and only within the scope of authority of the office. In the case of traditional authority, obedience is owed to the *person* of the chief who occupies the traditionally sanctioned position of authority and who is (within its sphere) bound by tradition. But here the obligation of obedience is not based on the impersonal order, but is a matter of personal loyalty within the area of accustomed obligations. In the case of charismatic authority, it is the charismatically qualified leader as such who is obeyed by virtue of personal trust in him and his revelation, his heroism or his exemplary qualities so far as they fall within the scope of the individual's belief in his charisma.

1. The usefulness of the above classification can only be judged by its results in promoting systematic analysis. The concept of 'charisma' ('the gift of grace') is taken from the vocabulary of early Christianity. For the Christian religious organization Rudolf Sohm, in his *Kirchenrecht,* was the first to clarify the substance of the concept, even though he did not use the same terminology. Others (for instance, Hollin, *Enthusiasmus und Bussgewalt*) have clarified certain important consequences of it. It is thus nothing new.

2. The fact that none of these three ideal types, the elucidation of which will occupy the following pages, is usually to be found in historical cases in 'pure' form, is naturally not a valid objection to attempting their conceptual formulation in the sharpest possible form. In this respect the present case is no different from many others. Later on (§ 11 ff.) the transformation of pure charisma by the process of routinization will be discussed and thereby the relevance of the concept to the understanding of empirical systems of authority considerably increased. But even so it may be said of every empirically historical phenomenon of authority that it is not likely to be 'as an open book.' Analysis in terms of sociological types has, after all, as compared with purely empirical historical investigation, certain advantages which should not be minimized. That is, it can in the particular case of a concrete form of authority determine what conforms to or approximates such types as 'charisma,' 'hereditary charisma' (§ 10, 11), 'the charisma of office,' 'patriarchy' (§ 7), 'bureaucracy' (§ 4), the authority of status groups,[4] and in doing so it can work with relatively unambiguous concepts. But the idea that the whole of concrete historical reality can be exhausted in the conceptual scheme about to be developed is as far from the author's thoughts as anything could be.

II. LEGAL AUTHORITY WITH A BUREAUCRATIC ADMINISTRATIVE STAFF [5]

3: LEGAL AUTHORITY: THE PURE TYPE WITH EMPLOYMENT OF A BUREAUCRATIC ADMINISTRATIVE STAFF

The effectiveness of legal authority rests on the acceptance of the validity of the following mutually inter-dependent ideas.

1. That any given legal norm may be established by agreement or by imposition, on grounds of expediency or rational values or both, with a claim to obedience at least on the part of the members of the corporate group. This is, however, usually extended to include all persons within the sphere of authority or of power in question—which in the case of territorial bodies is the territorial area—who stand in certain social relationships or carry out forms of social action which in the order governing the corporate group have been declared to be relevant.

[4] *Ständische*. There is no really acceptable English rendering of this term.—ED.
[5] The specifically modern type of administration has intentionally been taken as a point of departure in order to make it possible later to contrast the others with it.

2. That every body of law consists essentially in a consistent system of abstract rules which have normally been intentionally established. Furthermore, administration of law is held to consist in the application of these rules to particular cases; the administrative process in the rational pursuit of the interests which are specified in the order governing the corporate group within the limits laid down by legal precepts and following principles which are capable of generalized formulation and are approved in the order governing the group, or at least not disapproved in it.

3. That thus the typical person in authority occupies an 'office.' In the action associated with his status, including the commands he issues to others, he is subject to an impersonal order to which his actions are oriented. This is true not only for persons exercising legal authority who are in the usual sense 'officials,' but, for instance, for the elected president of a state.

4. That the person who obeys authority does so, as it is usually stated, only in his capacity as a 'member' of the corporate group and what he obeys is only 'the law.' He may in this connexion be the member of an association, of a territorial commune, of a church, or a citizen of a state.

5. In conformity with point 3, it is held that the members of the corporate group, in so far as they obey a person in authority, do not owe this obedience to him as an individual, but to the impersonal order. Hence, it follows that there is an obligation to obedience only within the sphere of the rationally delimited authority which, in terms of the order, has been conferred upon him.

The following may thus be said to be the fundamental categories of rational legal authority:—

(1) A continuous organization of official functions bound by rules.

(2) A specified sphere of competence. This involves (a) a sphere of obligations to perform functions which has been marked off as part of a systematic division of labour. (b) The provision of the incumbent with the necessary authority to carry out these functions. (c) That the necessary means of compulsion are clearly defined and their use is subject to definite conditions. A unit exercising authority which is organized in this way will be called an 'administrative organ.' [6]

There are administrative organs in this sense in large-scale private organizations, in parties and armies, as well as in the state and the church.

[6] *Behörde.*

An elected president, a cabinet of ministers, or a body of elected representatives also in this sense constitute administrative organs. This is not, however, the place to discuss these concepts. Not every administrative organ is provided with compulsory powers. But this distinction is not important for present purposes.

(3) The organization of offices follows the principle of hierarchy; that is, each lower office is under the control and supervision of a higher one. There is a right of appeal and of statement of grievances from the lower to the higher. Hierarchies differ in respect to whether and in what cases complaints can lead to a ruling from an authority at various points higher in the scale, and as to whether changes are imposed from higher up or the responsibility for such changes is left to the lower office, the conduct of which was the subject of complaint.

(4) The rules which regulate the conduct of an office may be technical rules or norms.[7] In both cases, if their application is to be fully rational, specialized training is necessary. It is thus normally true that only a person who has demonstrated an adequate technical training is qualified to be a member of the administrative staff of such an organized group, and hence only such persons are eligible for appointment to official positions. The administrative staff of a rational corporate group thus typically consists of 'officials,' whether the organization be devoted to political, religious, economic—in particular, capitalistic—or other ends.

(5) In the rational type it is a matter of principle that the members of the administrative staff should be completely separated from ownership of the means of production or administration. Officials, employees, and workers attached to the administrative staff do not themselves own the non-human means of production and administration. These are rather provided for their use in kind or in money, and the official is obligated to render an accounting of their use. There exists, furthermore, in principle complete separation of the property belonging to the organization, which is controlled within the sphere of office, and the personal property of the official, which is available for his own private uses. There is a corresponding separation of the place in which official

---

[7] Weber does not explain this distinction. By a 'technical rule' he probably means a prescribed course of action which is dictated primarily on grounds touching efficiency of the performance of the immediate functions, while by 'norms' he probably means rules which limit conduct on grounds other than those of efficiency. Of course, in one sense all rules are norms in that they are prescriptions for conduct, conformity with which is problematical.—Ed.

functions are carried out, the 'office' in the sense of premises, from living quarters.

(6) In the rational type case, there is also a complete absence of appropriation of his official position by the incumbent. Where 'rights' to an office exist, as in the case of judges, and recently of an increasing proportion of officials and even of workers, they do not normally serve the purpose of appropriation by the official, but of securing the purely objective and independent character of the conduct of the office so that it is oriented only to the relevant norms.

(7) Administrative acts, decisions, and rules are formulated and recorded in writing, even in cases where oral discussion is the rule or is even mandatory. This applies at least to preliminary discussions and proposals, to final decisions, and to all sorts of orders and rules. The combination of written documents and a continuous organization of official functions constitutes the 'office' [8] which is the central focus of all types of modern corporate action.

(8) Legal authority can be exercised in a wide variety of different forms which will be distinguished and discussed later. The following analysis will be deliberately confined for the most part to the aspect of imperative co-ordination in the structure of the administrative staff. It will consist in an analysis in terms of ideal types of officialdom or 'bureaucracy.'

In the above outline no mention has been made of the kind of supreme head appropriate to a system of legal authority. This is a consequence of certain considerations which can only be made entirely understandable at a later stage in the analysis. There are very important types of rational imperative co-ordination which, with respect to the ultimate source of authority, belong to other categories. This is true of the hereditary charismatic type, as illustrated by hereditary monarchy and of the pure charismatic type of a president chosen by plebiscite. Other cases involve rational elements at important points, but are made up of a combination

[8] *Bureau.* It has seemed necessary to use the English word 'office' in three different meanings, which are distinguished in Weber's discussion by at least two terms. The first is *Amt,* which means 'office' in the sense of the institutionally defined status of a person. The second is the 'work premises' as in the expression 'he spent the afternoon in his office.' For this Weber uses *Bureau* as also for the third meaning which he has just defined, the 'organized work process of a group.' In this last sense an office is a particular type of 'organization,' or *Betrieb* in Weber's sense. This use is established in English in such expressions as 'the District Attorney's Office has such and such functions.' Which of the three meanings is involved in a given case will generally be clear from the context.—Ed.

of bureaucratic and charismatic components, as is true of the cabinet form of government. Still others are subject to the authority of the chief of other corporate groups, whether their character be charismatic or bureaucratic; thus the formal head of a government department under a parliamentary regime may be a minister who occupies his position because of his authority in a party. The type of rational, legal administrative staff is capable of application in all kinds of situations and contexts. It is the most important mechanism for the administration of everyday profane affairs. For in that sphere, the exercise of authority and, more broadly, imperative co-ordination, consists precisely in administration.

4: Legal Authority: The Pure Type with Employment of a Bureaucratic Administrative Staff—(Continued)

The purest type of exercise of legal authority is that which employs a bureaucratic administrative staff. Only the supreme chief of the organization occupies his position of authority by virtue of appropriation, of election, or of having been designated for the succession. But even *his* authority consists in a sphere of legal 'competence.' The whole administrative staff under the supreme authority then consists, in the purest type, of individual officials who are appointed and function according to the following criteria:[9]

(1) They are personally free and subject to authority only with respect to their impersonal official obligations.

(2) They are organized in a clearly defined hierarchy of offices.

(3) Each office has a clearly defined sphere of competence in the legal sense.

(4) The office is filled by a free contractual relationship. Thus, in principle, there is free selection.

(5) Candidates are selected on the basis of technical qualifications. In the most rational case, this is tested by examination or guaranteed by diplomas certifying technical training, or both. They are *appointed,* not elected.

(6) They are remunerated by fixed salaries in money, for the most part with a right to pensions. Only under certain circumstances does the employing authority, especially in private organizations, have a

---

[9] This characterization applies to the 'monocratic' as opposed to the 'collegial' type, which will be discussed below.

right to terminate the appointment, but the official is always free to resign. The salary scale is primarily graded according to rank in the hierarchy; but in addition to this criterion, the responsibility of the position and the requirements of the incumbent's social status may be taken into account.[10]

(7) The office is treated as the sole, or at least the primary, occupation of the incumbent.

(8) It constitutes a career. There is a system of 'promotion' according to seniority or to achievement, or both. Promotion is dependent on the judgment of superiors.

(9) The official works entirely separated from ownership of the means of administration and without appropriation of his position.

(10) He is subject to strict and systematic discipline and control in the conduct of the office.

This type of organization is in principle applicable with equal facility to a wide variety of different fields. It may be applied in profit-making business or in charitable organizations, or in any number of other types of private enterprises serving ideal or material ends. It is equally applicable to political and to religious organizations. With varying degrees of approximation to a pure type, its historical existence can be demonstrated in all these fields.

1. For example, this type of bureaucracy is found in private clinics, as well as in endowed hospitals or the hospitals maintained by religious orders. Bureaucratic organization has played a major role in the Catholic Church. It is well illustrated by the administrative role of the priesthood [11] in the modern church, which has expropriated almost all of the old church benefices, which were in former days to a large extent subject to private appropriation. It is also illustrated by the conception of the universal Episcopate, which is thought of as formally constituting a universal legal competence in religious matters. Similarly, the doctrine of Papal infallibility is thought of as in fact involving a universal competence, but only one which functions 'ex cathedra' in the sphere of the office, thus implying the typical distinction between the sphere of office and that of the private affairs of the incumbent. The same phenomena are found in the large-scale capitalistic enterprise; and the larger it is, the greater their role. And this is not less true of political parties, which will be discussed separately. Finally, the modern army is essentially a bureau-

---

[10] See below, chap. iv.
[11] *Kaplanokratie.*

cratic organization administered by that peculiar type of military functionary, the 'officer.'

2. Bureaucratic authority is carried out in its purest form where it is most clearly dominated by the principle of appointment. There is no such thing as a hierarchy of elected officials in the same sense as there is a hierarchical organization of appointed officials. In the first place, election makes it impossible to attain a stringency of discipline even approaching that in the appointed type. For it is open to a subordinate official to compete for elective honours on the same terms as his superiors, and his prospects are not dependent on the superior's judgment.[12]

3. Appointment by free contract, which makes free selection possible, is essential to modern bureaucracy. Where there is a hierarchical organization with impersonal spheres of competence, but occupied by unfree officials—like slaves or dependents, who, however, function in a formally bureaucratic manner—the term 'patrimonial bureaucracy' will be used.

4. The role of technical qualifications in bureaucratic organizations is continually increasing. Even an official in a party or a trade-union organization is in need of specialized knowledge, though it is usually of an empirical character, developed by experience, rather than by formal training. In the modern state, the only 'offices' for which no technical qualifications are required are those of ministers and presidents. This only goes to prove that they are 'officials' only in a formal sense, and not substantively, as is true of the managing director or president of a large business corporation. There is no question but that the 'position' of the capitalistic entrepreneur is as definitely appropriated as is that of a monarch. Thus at the top of a bureaucratic organization, there is necessarily an element which is at least not purely bureaucratic. The category of bureaucracy is one applying only to the exercise of control by means of a particular kind of administrative staff.

5. The bureaucratic official normally receives a fixed salary. By contrast, sources of income which are privately appropriated will be called 'benefices.'[13] Bureaucratic salaries are also normally paid in money. Though this is not essential to the concept of bureaucracy, it is the arrangement which best fits the pure type. Payments in kind are apt to have the character of benefices, and the receipt of a benefice normally implies the appropriation of opportunities for earnings and of positions. There are, however, gradual transitions in this field with many intermediate

[12] On elective officials, see below, sec. 14.
[13] *Pfründen*. On this concept, see below, sec. 7.—ED.

types. Appropriation by virtue of leasing or sale of offices or the pledge of income from office are phenomena foreign to the pure type of bureaucracy.

6. 'Offices' which do not constitute the incumbent's principal occupation, in particular 'honorary' offices, belong in other categories, which will be discussed later.[14] The typical 'bureaucratic' official occupies the office as his principal occupation.

7. With respect to the separation of the official from ownership of the means of administration, the situation is essentially the same in the field of public administration and in private bureaucratic organizations, such as the large-scale capitalistic enterprise.

8. Collegial bodies will be discussed separately below.[15] At the present time they are rapidly decreasing in importance in favour of types of organization which are in fact, and for the most part formally as well, subject to the authority of a single head. For instance, the collegial 'governments' in Prussia have long since given way to the monocratic 'district president.'[16] The decisive factor in this development has been the need for rapid, clear decisions, free of the necessity of compromise between different opinions and also free of shifting majorities.

9. The modern army officer is a type of appointed official who is clearly marked off by certain class distinctions. This will be discussed elsewhere.[17] In this respect such officers differ radically from elected military leaders, from charismatic condottieri,[18] from the type of officers who recruit and lead mercenary armies as a capitalistic enterprise, and, finally, from the incumbents of commissions which have been purchased.[19] There may be gradual transitions between these types. The patrimonial 'retainer,' who is separated from the means of carrying out his function, and the proprietor of a mercenary army for capitalistic purposes have, along with the private capitalistic entrepreneur, been pioneers in the organization of the modern type of bureaucracy. This will be discussed in detail below.[20]

[14] See below, sec. 14.

[15] See sec. 15.

[16] *Regierungs präsident.*

[17] See chap. iv. As has already been remarked, chap. iv was left incomplete and the part which is available contains no discussion of this subject.—ED.

[18] See sec. 10.

[19] See sec. 8.

[20] The parts of Weber's work included in this translation contain only fragmentary discussions of military organization. It was a subject in which Weber was greatly interested and to which he attributed great importance for social phenomena generally. This factor

5: THE MONOCRATIC TYPE OF BUREAUCRATIC ADMINISTRATION

Experience tends universally to show that the purely bureaucratic type of administrative organization—that is, the monocratic variety of bureaucracy—is, from a purely technical point of view, capable of attaining the highest degree of efficiency and is in this sense formally the most rational known means of carrying out imperative control over human beings. It is superior to any other form in precision, in stability, in the stringency of its discipline, and in its reliability. It thus makes possible a particularly high degree of calculability of results for the heads of the organization and for those acting in relation to it. It is finally superior both in intensive efficiency and in the scope of its operations, and is formally capable of application to all kinds of administrative tasks.

The development of the modern form of the organization of corporate groups in all fields is nothing less than identical with the development and continual spread of bureaucratic administration. This is true of church and state, of armies, political parties, economic enterprises, organizations to promote all kinds of causes, private associations, clubs, and many others. Its development is, to take the most striking case, the most crucial phenomenon of the modern Western state. However many forms there may be which do not appear to fit this pattern, such as collegial representative bodies, parliamentary committees, soviets, honorary officers, lay judges, and what not, and however much people may complain about the 'evils of bureaucracy,' it would be sheer illusion to think for a moment that continuous administrative work can be carried out in any field except by means of officials working in offices. The whole pattern of everyday life is cut to fit this framework. For bureaucratic administration is, other things being equal, always, from a formal, technical point of view, the most rational type. For the needs of mass administration to-day, it is completely indispensable. The choice is only that between bureaucracy and dilletantism in the field of administration.

The primary source of the superiority of bureaucratic administration lies in the role of technical knowledge which, through the development of modern technology and business methods in the production of goods, has become completely indispensable. In this respect, it makes no differ-

is one on which, for the ancient world, he laid great stress in his important study, *Agrarverhältnisse im Altertum*. Though at various points in the rest of *Wirtschaft und Gesellschaft* the subject comes up, it is probable that he intended to treat it systematically but that this was never done.—ED.

ence whether the economic system is organized on a capitalistic or a socialistic basis. Indeed, if in the latter case a comparable level of technical efficiency were to be achieved, it would mean a tremendous increase in the importance of specialized bureaucracy.

When those subject to bureaucratic control seek to escape the influence of the existing bureaucratic apparatus, this is normally possible only by creating an organization of their own which is equally subject to the process of bureaucratization. Similarly the existing bureaucratic apparatus is driven to continue functioning by the most powerful interests which are material and objective, but also ideal in character. Without it, a society like our own—with a separation of officials, employees, and workers from ownership of the means of administration, dependent on discipline and on technical training—could no longer function. The only exception would be those groups, such as the peasantry, who are still in possession of their own means of subsistence. Even in case of revolution by force or of occupation by an enemy, the bureaucratic machinery will normally continue to function just as it has for the previous legal government.

The question is always who controls the existing bureaucratic machinery. And such control is possible only in a very limited degree to persons who are not technical specialists. Generally speaking, the trained permanent official is more likely to get his way in the long run than his nominal superior, the Cabinet minister, who is not a specialist.

Though by no means alone, the capitalistic system has undeniably played a major role in the development of bureaucracy. Indeed, without it capitalistic production could not continue and any rational type of socialism would have simply to take it over and increase its importance. Its development, largely under capitalistic auspices, has created an urgent need for stable, strict, intensive, and calculable administration. It is this need which gives bureaucracy a crucial role in our society as the central element in any kind of large-scale administration. Only by reversion in every field—political, religious, economic, etc.—to small-scale organization would it be possible to any considerable extent to escape its influence. On the one hand, capitalism in its modern stages of development strongly tends to foster the development of bureaucracy, though both capitalism and bureaucracy have arisen from many different historical sources. Conversely, capitalism is the most rational economic basis for bureaucratic administration and enables it to develop in the most rational form, especially because, from a fiscal point of view, it supplies the necessary money resources.

Along with these fiscal conditions of efficient bureaucratic administration, there are certain extremely important conditions in the fields of communication and transportation. The precision of its functioning requires the services of the railway, the telegraph, and the telephone, and becomes increasingly dependent on them. A socialistic form of organization would not alter this fact. It would be a question whether in a socialistic system it would be possible to provide conditions for carrying out as stringent bureaucratic organization as has been possible in a capitalistic order. For socialism would, in fact, require a still higher degree of formal bureaucratization than capitalism. If this should prove not to be possible, it would demonstrate the existence of another of those fundamental elements of irrationality in social systems—a conflict between formal and substantive rationality of the sort which sociology so often encounters.

Bureaucratic administration means fundamentally the exercise of control on the basis of knowledge. This is the feature of it which makes it specifically rational. This consists on the one hand in technical knowledge which, by itself, is sufficient to ensure it a position of extraordinary power. But in addition to this, bureaucratic organizations, or the holders of power who make use of them, have the tendency to increase their power still further by the knowledge growing out of experience in the service. For they acquire through the conduct of office a special knowledge of facts and have available a store of documentary material peculiar to themselves. While not peculiar to bureaucratic organizations, the concept of 'official secrets' is certainly typical of them. It stands in relation to technical knowledge in somewhat the same position as commercial secrets do to technological training. It is a product of the striving for power.

Bureaucracy is superior in knowledge, including both technical knowledge and knowledge of the concrete fact within its own sphere of interest, which is usually confined to the interests of a private business—a capitalistic enterprise. The capitalistic entrepreneur is, in our society, the only type who has been able to maintain at least relative immunity from subjection to the control of rational bureaucratic knowledge. All the rest of the population have tended to be organized in large-scale corporate groups which are inevitably subject to bureaucratic control. This is as inevitable as the dominance of precision machinery in the mass production of goods.

The following are the principal more general social consequences of bureaucratic control:—

(1) The tendency to 'levelling' in the interest of the broadest possible basis of recruitment in terms of technical competence.

(2) The tendency to plutocracy growing out of the interest in the greatest possible length of technical training. To-day this often lasts up to the age of thirty.

(3) The dominance of a spirit of formalistic impersonality, *'Sine ira et studio,'* without hatred or passion, and hence without affection or enthusiasm. The dominant norms are concepts of straightforward duty without regard to personal considerations. Everyone is subject to formal equality of treatment; that is, everyone in the same empirical situation. This is the spirit in which the ideal official conducts his office.

The development of bureaucracy greatly favours the levelling of social classes and this can be shown historically to be the normal tendency. Conversely, every process of social levelling creates a favourable situation for the development of bureaucracy; for it tends to eliminate class privileges, which include the appropriation of means of administration and the appropriation of authority as well as the occupation of offices on an honorary basis or as an avocation by virtue of wealth. This combination everywhere inevitably foreshadows the development of mass democracy, which will be discussed in another connexion.

The 'spirit' of rational bureaucracy has normally the following general characteristics:

(1) Formalism, which is promoted by all the interests which are concerned with the security of their own personal situation, whatever this may consist in. Otherwise the door would be open to arbitrariness and hence formalism is the line of least resistance.

(2) There is another tendency, which is apparently in contradiction to the above, a contradiction which is in part genuine. It is the tendency of officials to treat their official function from what is substantively a utilitarian point of view in the interest of the welfare of those under their authority. But this utilitarian tendency is generally expressed in the enactment of corresponding regulatory measures which themselves have a formal character and tend to be treated in a formalistic spirit.[21] This tendency to substantive rationality is supported by all those subject

[21] This will be further discussed in the Sociology of Law.

to authority who are not included in the class mentioned above as interested in the security of advantages already controlled. The problems which open up at this point belong in the theory of 'democracy.'

III. TRADITIONAL AUTHORITY

6: TRADITIONAL AUTHORITY

A system of imperative co-ordination will be called 'traditional' if legitimacy is claimed for it and believed in on the basis of the sanctity of the order and the attendant powers of control as they have been handed down from the past, 'have always existed.' The person or persons exercising authority are designated according to traditionally transmitted rules. The object of obedience is the personal authority of the individual which he enjoys by virtue of his traditional status. The organized group exercising authority is, in the simplest case, primarily based on relations of personal loyalty, cultivated through a common process of education. The person exercising authority is not a 'superior,' but a personal 'chief.' [22]

His administrative staff does not consist primarily of officials, but of personal retainers.[23] Those subject to authority are not 'members' of an association, but are either his traditional 'comrades' or his 'subjects.' What determines the relations of the administrative staff to the chief is not the impersonal obligation of office, but personal loyalty to the chief.

Obedience is not owed to enacted rules, but to the person who occupies a position of authority by tradition or who has been chosen for such a position on a traditional basis. His commands are legitimized in one of two ways: (a) partly in terms of traditions which themselves directly determine the content of the command and the objects and extent of authority. In so far as this is true, to overstep the traditional limitations would endanger his traditional status by undermining acceptance of his legitimacy. (b) In part, it is a matter of the chief's free personal decision, in that tradition leaves a certain sphere open for this. This sphere of traditional prerogative rests primarily on the fact that the obligations of obedience on the basis of personal loyalty are essentially unlimited.[24]

[22] *Herr.*

[23] *Diener.*

[24] This does not seem to be a very happy formulation of the essential point. It is not necessary that the authority of a person in such a position, such as the head of a household, should be unlimited. It is rather that its extent is unspecified. It is generally limited by

There is thus a double sphere: on the one hand, of action which is bound to specific tradition; on the other hand, of that which is free of any specific rules.

In the latter sphere, the chief is free to confer 'grace' on the basis of his personal pleasure or displeasure, his personal likes and dislikes, quite arbitrarily, particularly in return for gifts which often become a source of regular income. So far as his action follows principles at all, these are principles of substantive ethical common sense, of justice, or of utilitarian expediency. They are not, however, as in the case of legal authority, formal principles. The exercise of authority is normally oriented to the question of what the chief and his administrative staff will normally permit, in view of the traditional obedience of the subjects and what will or will not arouse their resistance. When resistance occurs, it is directed against the person of the chief or of a member of his staff. The accusation is that he has failed to observe the traditional limits of his authority. Opposition is not directed against the system as such.

It is impossible in the pure type of traditional authority for law or administrative rules to be deliberately created by legislation. What is actually new is thus claimed to have always been in force but only recently to have become known through the wisdom of the promulgator. The only documents which can play a part in the orientation of legal administration are the documents of tradition; namely, precedents.

7: TRADITIONAL AUTHORITY—(*Continued*)

A traditional chief exercises authority with or without an administrative staff. The typical administrative staff is recruited from one or more of the following sources:

(a) From persons who are already related to the chief by traditional ties of personal loyalty. This will be called 'patrimonial' recruitment. Such persons may be kinsmen, slaves, dependents who are officers of the household, clients, coloni, or freedmen.

(b) It may be recruited from other sources on an 'extra-patrimonial' basis. This category includes people in a relation of purely personal loyalty, such as all sorts of 'favourites,' people standing in a relation of fealty to their chief—'vassals'—and, finally, those who have of their own free will entered into a relation of personal loyalty as officials.

higher obligations, but the burden of proof rests upon the person on whom an obligation is laid that there is such a conflicting higher obligation.—ED.

In traditionalistic organizations, it is very common for the most important posts to be filled with members of a ruling family or clan.

In patrimonial administrations, it is common for slaves or freedmen to rise even to the highest positions. It has not been uncommon even for Grand Viziers to have been at one time slaves.

The typical household officials have been the following: the senechal, the marshal (once in charge of horses), the chamberlain, the carver, the steward, who was the head of the service personnel and possibly even of the vassals. These are to be found everywhere in Europe. In the Orient, in addition, the head eunuch, who was in charge of the harem, has been particularly important. In the African kingdoms, the executioner is often included. Universally, the body physician, the astrologer, and various others have been common.

In China and in Egypt, the principal source of recruitment for patrimonial officials lay in the clientele of the king. Armies of coloni have been known throughout the Orient and were typical of the Roman nobility. Even in modern times, in the Mohammedan world, armies of slaves have existed.

The regime of 'favourites' is characteristic of every patrimonial system and has often been the occasion for 'traditionalistic' revolutions.

The status of 'vassal' will be dealt with separately.

Bureaucracy has first developed in patrimonial states with a body of officials recruited from extra-patrimonial sources; but, as will be shown presently, these 'officials' have originally been personal followers of their chief.

In the pure type of traditional authority, the following features of a bureaucratic administrative staff are absent: (a) a clearly defined sphere of competence subject to impersonal rules, (b) a rational ordering of relations of superiority and inferiority, (c) a regular system of appointment and promotion on the basis of free contract, (d) technical training as a regular requirement, (e) fixed salaries, in the type case paid in money.

In place of a well-defined impersonal sphere of competence, there is a shifting series of tasks and powers commissioned and granted by a chief through his arbitrary decision of the moment. They then tend to become permanent and are often traditionally stereotyped. An important influence is exerted by competition for sources of income and advantage which are at the disposal of the persons acting on behalf of the chief or of the chief himself. It is often in the first instance through these interests that definite functional spheres are first marked off and, with them, genuine administrative organs.

In the first instance, those with permanent functions are household officials of the chief. Their functions outside the administration of the household itself are often in fields of activity which bear a relatively superficial analogy to their household function, or even which have originated in a completely arbitrary act of the chief, and have later become traditionally stereotyped. In addition to household officers, there have existed primarily only persons with *ad hoc* specific commissions.

The absence of clear spheres of competence is clearly evident from a perusal of the list of the titles of officials in any of the Ancient Oriental states. With rare exceptions, it is impossible to associate with these titles a set of functions rationally delimited in the modern Western sense which has remained stable over a considerable period.

The process of defining permanent functions in terms of competition among and compromise between interests seeking favours, income, and other forms of advantage is especially clearly evident in the Middle Ages. This phenomenon has had very important consequences. The interests in fees of the powerful Royal courts and of the powerful legal profession in England was largely responsible, partly for breaking the influence of Roman and Canon law, partly for limiting it. Existing irrational divisions of official functions have frequently in all periods been stereotyped by the existence of an established set of rights to fees and perquisites.

In contrast to the rational hierarchy of authority in the bureaucratic system, the question who shall decide a matter—which of his officials or the chief himself—or who shall deal with complaints, is, in a traditional regime, treated in one of two ways. (1) Traditionally, on the basis of the authority of particular received legal norms or precedents. (2) Entirely on the basis of the arbitrary decision of the chief. Whenever he intervenes personally, all others give way to him.

In Germanic law, apart from the traditionalistic system of adherence to precedent, there is a principle which is derived from the arbitrary power of the political chief; namely, that in the presence of the chief himself the jurisdiction of any court is suspended. This principle has the same source as the *jus avocandi,* in the arbitrary grace of a monarch and its modern derivative, chamber justice. A court rendering judgment in terms of precedents was in the Middle Ages very often the agency which declared and interpreted the law and was thus the principal source from which the law of a locality was taken.

As opposed to the bureaucratic system of free appointment, household officials and favourites are very often recruited on a purely patrimonial basis from among the slaves or serfs of the chief. If, on the other hand, the recruitment has been extra-patrimonial, they have tended to be holders of benefices which he has granted as an act of grace without being bound by any formal rules. A fundamental change in this situation is first brought about by the rise of free vassals and the filling of offices by a contract of fealty. Since, however, such relations of fealty have been by no means primarily determined by considerations of objective function, this has not altered the situation with respect to definite spheres of competence or clearly determined hierarchical relationships. Except under certain circumstances when the administrative staff is organized on a basis of praebends, there is such a thing as 'promotion' only according to the arbitrary grace of the chief.

Rational technical training as a basic qualification for office is scarcely to be found at all among household officials or the favourites of a chief. Where there is even a beginning of technical training for appointees, regardless of what it consists in, this fact everywhere makes for a fundamental change in the development of administrative practice.

For many offices a certain amount of empirical training has been necessary from very early times. This is particularly true of the 'art' of reading and writing which was originally truly an art with a high scarcity value. This has often, most strikingly in China, had a decisive influence on the whole development of culture through the mode of life of persons with a literary education. Among other things, it has eliminated the recruiting of officials from intra-patrimonial sources and has thus limited the power of the chief by making him dependent on a definite social group.

In place of regular salaries, household officials and favourites are usually supported and equipped in the household of the chief and from his personal stores. Generally, their exclusion from the lord's own table means the creation of benefices, at first usually benefices in kind. It is easy for these to become traditionally stereotyped in amount and kind. Along with the elements supported by benefices or in place of them, there are various agencies commissioned by the lord outside his own household, as well as various fees which are due him. The latter are often collected without any regular rate or scale, being agreed upon from case to case with those seeking favours.[25]

[25] The concept of 'benefices' will be taken up presently.

7A: GERONTOCRACY, PATRIARCHALISM, AND PATRIMONIALISM

1. The most primitive types of traditional authority are the cases where a personal administrative staff of the chief is absent. These are 'gerontocracy' and 'patriarchalism.'

The term 'gerontocracy' is applied to a situation where so far as imperative control is exercised in the group at all it is in the hands of 'elders'—which originally was understood literally as the eldest in actual years, who are the most familiar with the sacred traditions of a group. This is common in groups which are not primarily of an economic or kinship character. 'Patriarchalism' is the situation where, within a group, which is usually organized on both an economic and a kinship basis, as a household, authority is exercised by a particular individual who is designated by a definite rule of inheritance. It is not uncommon for gerontocracy and patriarchalism to be found side by side. The decisive characteristic of both is the conception which is held by those subject to the authority of either type that this authority, though its exercise is a private prerogative of the person or persons involved, is in fact pre-eminently an authority on behalf of the group as a whole. It must, therefore, be exercised in the interests of the members and is thus not freely appropriated by the incumbent. In order that this shall be maintained, it is crucial that in both these cases there is a complete absence of an administrative staff over which the individual in authority has personal control. He is hence still to a large extent dependent on the willingness of the group members to respect his authority, since he has no machinery to enforce it. Those subject to authority are hence still members [26] of the group and not 'subjects.' But their membership exists by tradition and not by virtue of legislation or a deliberate act of adherence. Obedience is owed to the person of the chief, not to any established rule. But it is owed to the chief only by virtue of his traditional status. He is thus on his part strictly bound by tradition.

The different types of gerontocracy will be discussed later. Primary patriarchalism is related to it in that the authority of the patriarch carries strict obligations to obedience only within his own household. Apart from this, as in the case of the Arabian Sheik, it has only an exemplary character, similar to charismatic authority. He is able to influence people only by example, by advice, or by other non-compulsory means.

[26] *Genossen.*

2. With the development of a purely personal administrative staff, especially a military force under the control of the chief, traditional authority tends to develop into 'patrimonialism.' Where absolute authority is maximized, it may be called 'Sultanism.'

The 'members' are now treated as 'subjects.' An authority of the chief which was previously treated principally as exercised on behalf of the members, now becomes his personal authority, which he appropriates in the same way as he would any ordinary object of possession. He is also entitled to exploit it, in principle, like any economic advantage —to sell it, to pledge it as security, or to divide it by inheritance. The primary external support of patrimonial authority is a staff of slaves, coloni, or conscripted subjects, or, in order to enlist its members' self-interest in opposition to the subjects as far as possible, of mercenary bodyguards and armies. By the use of these instruments of force the chief tends to broaden the range of his arbitrary power which is free of traditional restrictions and to put himself in a position to grant grace and favours at the expense of the traditional limitations typical of patriarchal and gerontocratic structures. Where authority is primarily oriented to tradition but in its exercise makes the claim of full personal powers, it will be called 'patrimonial' authority. Where patrimonial authority lays primary stress on the sphere of arbitrary will free of traditional limitations, it will be called 'Sultanism.' The transition is definitely continuous. Both are distinguished from primary patriarchalism by the presence of a personal administrative staff.

Sometimes even Sultanism appears superficially to be completely bound by tradition, but this is never in fact the case. The non-traditional element is not, however, rationalized in impersonal terms, but consists only in an extreme development of the sphere of arbitrary will and grace. It is this which distinguishes it from every form of rational authority.

3. When, in a system of patrimonial authority, particular powers and the corresponding economic advantages have become appropriated, this will be called 'decentralized' [27] authority. As in all similar cases [28] appropriation may take the following forms:

Appropriation may be carried out by an organized group or by a cate-

[27] *Ständische Herrschaft.* The term *Stand* with its derivatives is perhaps the most troublesome single term in Weber's text. It refers to a social group the members of which occupy a relatively well-defined common status, particularly with reference to social stratification, though this reference is not always important. In addition to common status, there is the

[28] See chap. ii, sec. 19.

gory of persons distinguished by particular characteristics. It may, on the other hand, be carried out by individuals, for life, on a hereditary basis, or as free property.

Decentralized authority thus involves, on the one hand, limitations on the chief's power of free selection of his administrative staff because positions or governing powers have been appropriated. Thus they may be limited to the members of a corporate group or of a group occupying a particular social status.

In addition, on the other hand, there may be appropriation by the individual members of the administrative staff. This may involve appropriation of positions, which will generally include that of the economic advantages associated with them, appropriation of the non-human means of administration, and appropriation of governing powers.

Those holding an appropriated status may have originated historically from the members of an administrative staff which was not previously an independent class. Or, before the appropriation, they may not have belonged to the staff.

Where governing powers are appropriated by members of an independent group, the costs of administration are met from the incumbent's own means, which are not distinguishable from his personal property. Persons exercising military command or members of this type of army provide their own equipment and may even recruit units of the army on their own responsibility. It is also possible that the provision of means of administration and of the administrative staff can be made the object of a profit-making enterprise which exploits access to payments from the stores or the treasury of the chief. This was the principal mode of organization of the mercenary armies in the sixteenth and seventeenth centuries in Europe. Where appropriation by independent groups is complete, all the powers of government are divided between the chief and the different branches of the administrative staff, each on the basis of his own personal rights. It is also, however, possible for these rights to

---

further criterion that the members of a *Stand* have a common mode of life and usually more or less well-defined code of behaviour. There is no English term which even approaches adequacy in rendering this concept. Hence it has been necessary to attempt to describe what Weber meant in whatever terms the particular context has indicated. In the present case it is the appropriation of authority on the part of the members of the administrative staff, in such a way that their position becomes independent of the arbitrary will of their chief, which is decisive. This particular aspect is brought out by describing it as 'decentralized authority.' It should not, however, be forgotten that in describing it as he does, Weber implies that this group not only has a distinctive status in the organization of authority, but also in other respects.—ED.

be regulated by special decrees of the chief or special compromises with the holders of appropriated rights. The first type is illustrated by the court offices of a realm when they have become appropriated as fiefs; the second, by landlords who, by virtue of their privileged position or by usurpation, have appropriated powers of government. The former is apt to be merely a legalization of the latter.

Appropriation by an individual may rest on leasing, on pledging as security, on sale, or on privileges—which may in turn be personal, hereditary, or freely appropriated—may be unconditional, or may be subject to performance of certain functions. Such a privilege may be purchased in return for services or granted for compliance with the chief's authority, or it may constitute merely the formal recognition of actual usurpation of powers.

Appropriation by an organized group or by those occupying a particular social status is usually a consequence of a compromise between the chief and his administrative staff or between him and an organized social group. It may leave the chief relatively free in his selection of individuals, or it may lay down rigid rules for the selection of incumbents.

Appropriation, finally, may rest on a process of education or apprenticeships. It will be necessary to devote a special discussion to this case.

1. In the cases of gerontocracy and patriarchalism, so far as there are clear ideas on the subject at all, the means of administration are generally appropriated by the corporate group as a whole or by the household of the individual who carries out the governing functions. The administrative functions are performed 'on behalf' of the group as a whole. Appropriation by the chief personally is a phenomenon of patrimonialism. It may vary enormously in degree to the extreme cases of a claim to full proprietorship of the land [29] and to the status of master over subjects treated as slaves. Appropriation by particular social groups generally means the appropriation of at least a part of the means of administration by the members of the administrative staff. In the case of pure patrimonialism, there is complete separation of the functionary from the means of carrying out his function. But exactly the opposite is true of decentralized patrimonialism. The person exercising governing powers has personal control of the means of administration—if not all, at least of an important part of them. This was true of the feudal knight, who provided his own equipment, and of the count, who by virtue of holding his fief took the court fees and other perquisites for himself and met his

[29] *Bodenregal.*

obligations to his superior lord from his own means, in which these appropriated sources of income over which he had full control were included. Similarly, the Indian *jagirdar,* who provided and equipped a military unit from the proceeds of his tax benefices, was in complete possession of the means of administration. On the other hand, a colonel who recruited a mercenary regiment on his own account, but received certain payments from the royal exchequer and paid his deficit either by curtailing the service or from booty or requisitions, was only partly in possession of the means of administration and was subject to certain regulations. On the other hand, the Pharaoh, who organized armies of slaves or coloni, put his clients in command of them, and clothed, fed, and equipped them from his own storehouses, was acting as a patrimonial chief in full personal control of the means of administration. It is not always the formal mode of organization which is most decisive. The Mamelukes were formally slaves recruited by the purchases of their owner. In fact, however, they monopolized the powers of government as completely as any feudal class has ever monopolized fiefs.

There are examples of land appropriated in fief by a closed corporate group without any individual appropriation. This occurs where the land is granted to individuals quite freely by chiefs so long as they are members of the group, as well as subject to regulations specifying qualifications. Thus, military or possibly ritual qualifications have been required of the candidates, whereas, on the other hand, once these are given, close blood relations have had priority. The situation is similar in the case of artisans attached to a court or to guilds or of peasants whose services have been attached for military or administrative purposes.

2. Appropriation by lease, especially tax farming, by pledging as security, or by sale, have been found in the Western World, but also in the Orient and in India. In Antiquity, it was not uncommon for priesthoods to be sold at auction. In the case of leasing, the aim has been partly a practical financial one to meet stringencies caused especially by the costs of war. It has partly, also, been a matter of the technique of financing, to insure a stable money income available for budgetary uses. Pledging as security and sale have generally arisen from financial necessities. This is true of the Papal States as well as others. Appropriation by pledging played a significant role in France as late as the eighteenth century in filling judicial posts in the *Parlements.* The appropriation of officers' commissions by regulated purchase continued in the British army well into the nineteenth century. Privileges, as a sanction of usurpation, as a

reward, or as an incentive for political services, were common in the European Middle Ages, as well as elsewhere.

8: Modes of Support of the Patrimonial Retainer

The patrimonial retainer may receive his support in any of the following ways: (a) By maintenance at the table and in the household of his chief; (b) by allowances from the stores of goods or money of his chief, usually primarily allowances in kind; (c) by rights of use of land in return for services; (d) by the appropriation of property income, fees, or taxes; (e) by fiefs.

So far as in an amount or within a scope which is traditionally stereotyped, they are granted to individuals and thereby appropriated, but not made hereditary, the forms (b) to (d), inclusive, will be called 'benefices.' When an administrative staff, according to its fundamental principle of organization, is supported in this form, it will be said to be based on 'praebends.' In such a situation it is possible to maintain a system of promotion on a basis of seniority or of particular objectively determined achievements. And it is also possible to require a certain social status as a criterion of eligibility and to make use of the corresponding sense of honour of a distinctive social group.

A set of appropriated governing powers will be called a 'fief' if it is granted primarily to particular qualified individuals by a contract and if the reciprocal rights and duties involved are primarily oriented to conventional standards of the honour, particularly in a military connexion, of a distinctive social group. The situation where an administrative staff exists which is primarily supported by fiefs, will be called 'feudalism.'

The transition between fiefs and military benefices is so gradual that at times they are almost indistinguishable.[80]

In cases (d) and (e), sometimes also in (c), the individual who has appropriated governing powers pays the cost of his administrative function, and possibly also of equipment, from the proceeds of his benefice or fief. In that case his own position of authority over the subject may take on a patrimonial character and thus become hereditary, and capable of division by inheritance.

1. The earliest form of support for royal retainers, household officials,

[80] This will be further discussed below in chap. iv.

priests and other types of patrimonial followers has been their participation at the table and in the household of the chief or their support by allowances arbitrarily paid out from the stores. The 'men's house,' which is the oldest form of professional military organization and will have to be dealt with below, very often has the character of communistic consumption. Separation from the table of the chief or of the temple or cathedral and the substitution of allowances or the use of land for this direct mode of support has by no means always been regarded with approval. It has, however, been the usual consequence of the establishment of independent families. Allowances in kind granted to temple priests and officials who have left the chief's household constituted the original form of support of officials throughout the Near East and have also existed in China, India, and to a large extent in the Western World. The use of land in return for military services is found throughout the Orient from very ancient times and also in Medieval Germany as a means of providing for household officials, officers of the court and other functionaries. The sources of income of the Turkish *spahis,* of the Japanese *samurai,* and of various other types of Oriental retainers and knights are, in the present terminology, 'benefices' and not 'fiefs,' as will be pointed out later. In some cases they have been derived from the rents of certain land; in others, from the tax income of certain districts. In the latter case, they have not necessarily been combined with appropriation of governmental powers in the same district; but this has, however, been the general tendency. The concept of the fief can be further developed only in relation to that of the state. Its object may be land under a patrimonial system, or it may be any one of various kinds of claims to property income and fees.

2. The appropriation of property income and rights to fees and the proceeds of taxes in the form of benefices and fiefs of all sorts is widely distributed. It became an independent form of organization in a highly developed fashion in India in particular. The usual arrangement was the granting of rights to these sources of income in return for the provision of military contingents and the payment of administrative costs.

9: DECENTRALIZED PATRIMONIAL AUTHORITY

In patrimonial systems generally, and particularly in those of the decentralized type, all governmental authority and the corresponding economic rights tend to be treated as privately appropriated economic advantages. This does not, of course, mean that they cannot be qualitatively differentiated. This is true particularly in that some of them are appropriated in a form subject to special regulations. Furthermore, the appropriation of judicial and military powers tends to be treated as a legal basis for a privileged class position of those appropriating them, as compared to the appropriation of purely economic advantages having to do with the income from domains, from taxes, or other sources. Within the latter category, again, there tends to be a differentiation of those which are primarily patrimonial from those which are primarily extra-patrimonial or fiscal in the mode of appropriation. For the present terminological purposes the decisive fact is that, regardless of content, governing powers and the associated advantages are treated as private rights.

Von Below [31] is quite right in emphasizing strongly that it was especially the appropriation of judicial authority which was made the basis of special treatment and a source of privileged class status. Indeed it is not possible to prove that the medieval political organization had either a purely patrimonial or a purely feudal character. Nevertheless, so far as judicial authority and other rights of a purely political origin are treated as private rights, it is for present purposes terminologically correct to speak of patrimonial authority. This concept itself, as is well known, has been most consistently developed by Haller in his *Restauration der Staatswissenschaften*. Historically there has never been a purely patrimonial state in the sense of one corresponding perfectly to the ideal type.

Where traditional authority is decentralized through the appropriation of governing powers by privileged social groups, this may become a formal case of the separation of powers when organized groups of the members of such a privileged class participate in political or administrative decisions by a process of compromise with their chief.

The subjects of such compromises may be rules or concrete administrative decisions or measures regulating the administrative process. The members of such groups may possibly exercise imperative control on their own authority and by means of their own administrative staff.

I. Under certain circumstances groups, such as peasants, which do not enjoy a privileged social position, may be included. This does not, however, alter the concept. For the decisive point is the fact that the members of the privileged group exercise independent rights. If all kinds of socially

[31] *Der Deutsche Staat des Mittelalters.*

privileged groups were absent, the case would obviously belong under another type.

2. This type has been fully developed only in the Western World. Both its peculiar organization in more detail and the reasons for its development in that case will be discussed separately below.[32]

3. The possession of his own administrative staff by a member of such a privileged group has been unusual. The exercise of independent governing authority on his part is still more exceptional.

9A. The Relations of Traditional Authority and the Economic Order

The primary effect of traditional authority on modes of economic activity is usually in a very general way to strengthen traditional attitudes. This is most conspicuous in gerontocratic and purely patriarchal situations since those exercising authority are not in possession of any distinct administrative machinery which is not available to the other members of the group. Thus they are, in upholding their own legitimacy, most strongly dependent on the safeguarding of tradition in every respect.

1. Beyond this, the consequences for the economic order are in the first instance a function of the mode in which the group exercising imperative authority is financed. In this respect, patrimonialism is open to a wide variety of different possibilities. The following, however, are particularly important.

(a) An *oikos* maintained by the chief where needs are met on a liturgical basis wholly or primarily in kind in the form of contributions of goods and compulsory services. In this case, economic relationships tend to be strictly bound to tradition. The development of markets is obstructed, the use of money is primarily oriented to consumption, and the development of capitalism is impossible.

(b) Provision by the services of socially privileged groups has very similar effects. Though not necessarily to the same extent, the development of markets is also limited in this case by the fact that ownership exists in kind, is pre-empted on a non-monetary basis, and purchasing power correspondingly reduced. Furthermore, the productive capacity

---

[32] This appears to refer to another of the unfinished parts of Weber's projected work. No systematic discussion of the subject is included in his text. Certain phases of it are, however, discussed in part iii, chaps. vii and viii of *Wirtschaft und Gesellschaft* which are not included in the present translation.—ED.

of individual economic units is to a large extent pre-empted for the needs of the governing group.

(c) Finally, it is possible for patrimonialism to be organized on a monopolistic basis of meeting its needs, partly by profit-making enterprise, partly by fees, and partly by taxes. In this case, the development of markets is, according to the type of monopolies involved, more or less seriously limited by irrational factors. The important openings for profit are in the hands of the chief and the members of his administrative staff. In so far as productive enterprises are directly administered by the governing group itself, the development of capitalism is thereby directly obstructed. If, on the other hand, there is tax farming, leasing or sale of offices, and provision for armies and administration on a capitalistic basis for fiscal reasons, there is an opening for capitalistic development; but it is diverted in the direction of political orientation.[33]

Even where it is carried out in money terms, the financing of patrimonialism and even more of Sultanism tends to have irrational consequences for the following reasons:—

(1) The obligations placed on sources of direct taxation tend both in amount and in kind to remain bound to tradition. At the same time there is complete freedom—and hence arbitrariness—in the determination of fees and of newly imposed obligations, and in the organization of monopolies. This element of arbitrariness is at least claimed as a right. It is, however, historically effective to a widely varying extent.

(2) Two fundamental bases of the rationalization of economic activity are entirely lacking; namely, a basis for the calculability of obligations and of the extent of freedom which will be allowed to private acquisitive activity.

(3) It is, however, possible that in individual cases patrimonial fiscal policy can, by systematic attention to the prosperity of its sources of taxation and by the rational organization of monopolies, have a rationalizing effect. This, however, is structurally fortuitous and is dependent on specific historical circumstances, some of which have, however, existed in the Western World.

Where the groups appropriating governing powers are formally organized,[34] fiscal policy typically tends to be a result of compromise. This results in making the burdens relatively predictable and in eliminating or at least sharply limiting the arbitrary powers of the chief to impose

---

[33] See chap. ii, sec. 31.
[34] By *Ständische Gewaltenteilung*.

new burdens and, above all, to create monopolies. Whether the resulting concrete fiscal policy tends to promote or to limit rational economic activity depends largely on the type of group occupying the predominant position of power, above all, whether it is a feudal or a patrician [35] class.

The dominance of a feudal class tends, because the structure of feudalized powers of government is normally predominantly patrimonial, to set rigid limits to the freedom of acquisitive activity and the development of markets. It may even involve deliberate attempts to suppress them to protect the power of the feudal group. The predominance of a patrician class may have the opposite effect.

1. What has been said above must suffice for the present. It will be necessary to return to these questions repeatedly in different connexions.

2. The *oikos* has been found in ancient Egypt and in India. Provision by socially privileged groups is found in large parts of the Hellenistic world, in the late Roman Empire, in China, in India, and to some extent in Russia and the Mohammedan states. The monopolistic type under direct control of the regime is illustrated by the Egypt of the Ptolemies, to some extent by the Byzantine Empire, and in a different way by the regime of the Stuarts in England. The other type of monopolistic organization, which has been favourable to politically oriented capitalism, has been most highly developed in the patrimonial states of the Western World in the period of 'enlightened despotism.' The system organized by Colbert is the best-known example.

3. It is not only the financial policy of most patrimonial regimes which tends to restrict the development of rational economic activity, but above all the general character of its administrative practices. This is true in the following respects:

(a) Traditionalism places serious obstacles in the way of formally rational regulations, which can be depended upon to remain stable and hence are calculable in their economic implications and exploitability.

(b) A staff of officials with formal technical training is typically absent. The fact that such a class developed in the patrimonial states of the Western World is, as will be shown, accounted for by a set of very peculiar conditions. These were present only in this particular case and developed for the most part out of sources wholly different from the general structure of patrimonialism.

[35] 'Patrician' is here used not in the Roman sense, but in that of the privileged commercial classes of the Free Cities of the German Empire, such as the Hanseatic cities.—ED.

(c) There is a wide scope for actual arbitrariness and the expression of purely personal whims on the part of the chief and the members of his administrative staff. The opening for bribery and corruption, which is simply a matter of the disorganization of an unregulated system of fees, would be the least serious effect of this if it remained a constant quantity, because then it would become calculable in practice. But it tends to be a matter which is settled from case to case with every individual official and is thus highly variable. If offices are leased, the incumbent is put in a position where it is to his immediate interest to get back the capital he has invested by any available means of extortion, however irrational.

(d) Running through patriarchalism and patrimonialism generally, there is an inherent tendency to substantive regulation of economic activity. This is derived from the character of the claim to legitimacy and the corresponding interest in the contentment of the subjects. Its effect is to break down the type of formal rationality which is oriented to a formally technical legal order. This type of influence is conspicuous, indeed decisive, in the case of the type of patrimonialism organized on a hierocratic basis. In the case of pure Sultanism, on the other hand, it is fiscal arbitrariness which is likely to be most important.

For all these reasons, under the dominance of a patrimonial regime only certain types of capitalism are able to develop. It leaves room for a certain amount of capitalistic mercantile trade, for capitalistic organization of tax farming, and the sale and lease of offices, for the provision of supplies for the state, the financing of wars and, under certain circumstances, capitalistic plantations and other colonial enterprises. All these forms are indigenous to patrimonial regimes and often reach a very high level of development. This is not, however, true of the type of profit-making enterprise with heavy investments in fixed capital and a rational organization of free labour which is oriented to the market purchases of private consumers. This is altogether too sensitive to all sorts of irrationalities in the administration of justice, in other forms of administrative practice, and in taxation. For these upset the basis of calculability.

The situation is fundamentally different only in cases where a patrimonial ruler, in the interest of his own power and financial provision, develops a rational system of administration with technically specialized officials. For this to happen, it is necessary in the first place that technical training should be available. Secondly, there must be a sufficiently powerful incentive to embark on such a policy. This is notably supplied by sharp competition between a plurality of patrimonial powers within the same cultural area. Finally, a very special factor is necessary, namely, the participation of urban communes as a financial support in the competition of the patrimonial units.

1. The principal forerunners of the modern, specifically Western form of capitalism are to be found in the organized urban communes of Europe with their particular type of relatively rational administration. Its primary development took place from the sixteenth to the eighteenth centuries within the framework of the class structure and political organization of Holland and England, which were distinguished by the unusual power and preponderance of the economic interests of the bourgeois classes. The secondary limitations based on fiscal and utilitarian motives, which were introduced into the purely patrimonial or largely feudal states of the Continent, have in common with the Stuart system of monopolistic industry the fact that they do not stand in the main line of continuity with the later autonomous capitalistic development. This is true in spite of the fact that particular measures of agricultural and industrial policy—so far as and because they were oriented to English, Dutch, and later to French, models—played a very important part in creating some of the essential conditions for this later development. All this will be discussed further on.

2. In certain fields the patrimonial states of the Middle Ages developed a type of formally rational administrative staff which consisted especially of persons with legal training both in the civil and the canon law, and which differed fundamentally from the corresponding administrative staffs in political bodies of any other time or place. It will be necessary later to inquire more fully into the sources of this development and into its significance. For the present it is not possible to go beyond the very general observations introduced above.

IV. CHARISMATIC AUTHORITY

10: The Principal Characteristics of Charismatic Authority and Its Relation to Forms of Communal Organization

The term 'charisma' will be applied to a certain quality of an individual personality by virtue of which he is set apart from ordinary men and treated as endowed with supernatural, superhuman, or at least specifically exceptional powers or qualities. These are such as are not accessible to the ordinary person, but are regarded as of divine origin or as exemplary, and on the basis of them the individual concerned is treated as a leader. In primitive circumstances this peculiar kind of deference is paid to prophets, to people with a reputation for therapeutic or legal wisdom, to leaders in the hunt, and heroes in war. It is very often thought of as resting on magical powers. How the quality in question would be ultimately judged from any ethical, aesthetic, or other such point of view is naturally entirely indifferent for purposes of definition. What is alone important is how the individual is actually regarded by those subject to charismatic authority, by his 'followers' or 'disciples.'

For present purposes it will be necessary to treat a variety of different types as being endowed with charisma in this sense. It includes the state of a 'berserker' whose spells of maniac passion have, apparently wrongly, sometimes been attributed to the use of drugs. In Medieval Byzantium a group of people endowed with this type of charismatic war-like passion were maintained as a kind of weapon. It includes the 'shaman,' the kind of magician who in the pure type is subject to epileptoid seizures as a means of falling into trances. Another type is that of Joseph Smith, the founder of Mormonism, who, however, cannot be classified in this way with absolute certainty since there is a possibility that he was a very sophisticated type of deliberate swindler. Finally it includes the type of intellectual, such as Kurt Eisner,[36] who is carried away with his own demagogic success. Sociological analysis, which must abstain from value judgments, will treat all these on the same level as the men who, according to conventional judgments, are the 'greatest' heroes, prophets, and saviours.

1. It is recognition on the part of those subject to authority which is decisive for the validity of charisma. This is freely given and guaranteed by what is held to be a 'sign' or proof,[37] originally always a miracle, and consists in devotion to the corresponding revelation, hero worship, or absolute trust in the leader. But where charisma is genuine, it is not this which is the basis of the claim to legitimacy. This basis lies rather in the conception that it is the *duty* of those who have been called to a charismatic mission to recognize its quality and to act accordingly. Psychologically this 'recognition' is a matter of complete personal devotion to the possessor of the quality, arising out of enthusiasm, or of despair and hope.

No prophet has ever regarded his quality as dependent on the attitudes

---

[36] The leader of the communistic experiment in Bavaria in 1919.—ED.

[37] *Bewährung.*

of the masses toward him. No elective king or military leader has ever treated those who have resisted him or tried to ignore him otherwise than as delinquent in duty. Failure to take part in a military expedition under such leader, even though recruitment is formally voluntary, has universally been met with disdain.

2. If proof of his charismatic qualification fails him for long, the leader endowed with charisma tends to think his god or his magical or heroic powers have deserted him. If he is for long unsuccessful, above all if his leadership fails to benefit his followers, it is likely that his charismatic authority will disappear. This is the genuine charismatic meaning of the 'gift of grace.' [38]

Even the old Germanic kings were sometimes rejected with scorn. Similar phenomena are very common among so-called 'primitive' peoples. In China the charismatic quality of the monarch, which was transmitted unchanged by heredity, was upheld so rigidly that any misfortune whatever, not only defeats in war, but drought, floods, or astronomical phenomena which were considered unlucky, forced him to do public penance and might even force his abdication. If such things occurred, it was a sign that he did not possess the requisite charismatic virtue, he was thus not a legitimate 'Son of Heaven.'

3. The corporate group which is subject to charismatic authority is based on an emotional form of communal relationship.[39] The administrative staff of a charismatic leader does not consist of 'officials'; at least its members are not technically trained. It is not chosen on the basis of social privilege nor from the point of view of domestic or personal dependency. It is rather chosen in terms of the charismatic qualities of its members. The prophet has his disciples; the war lord his selected henchmen; the leader, generally, his followers. There is no such thing as 'appointment' or 'dismissal,' no career, no promotion. There is only a 'call' at the instance of the leader on the basis of the charismatic qualification of those he summons. There is no hierarchy; the leader merely intervenes in general or in individual cases when he considers the members of his staff inadequate to a task with which they have been entrusted. There is no such thing as a definite sphere of authority and of competence, and no appropriation of official powers on the basis of social privileges. There may, however, be territorial or functional limits to charismatic powers and to the individual's 'mission.' There is no such thing as a salary or a

[38] *Gottesgnadentum.*
[39] Weber uses the term *Gemeinde,* which is not directly translatable.—ED.

benefice. Disciples or followers tend to live primarily in a communistic relationship with their leader on means which have been provided by voluntary gift. There are no established administrative organs. In their place are agents who have been provided with charismatic authority by their chief or who possess charisma of their own. There is no system of formal rules, of abstract legal principles, and hence no process of judicial decision oriented to them. But equally there is no legal wisdom oriented to judicial precedent. Formally concrete judgments are newly created from case to case and are originally regarded as divine judgments and revelations. From a substantive point of view, every charismatic authority would have to subscribe to the proposition, 'It is written . . . , but I say unto you. . .'[40] The genuine prophet, like the genuine military leader and every true leader in this sense, preaches, creates, or demands *new* obligations. In the pure type of charisma, these are imposed on the authority of revolution by oracles, or of the leader's own will, and are recognized by the members of the religious, military, or party group, because they come from such a source. Recognition is a duty. When such an authority comes into conflict with the competing authority of another who also claims charismatic sanction, the only recourse is to some kind of a contest, by magical means or even an actual physical battle of the leaders. In principle, only one side can be in the right in such a conflict; the other must be guilty of a wrong which has to be expiated.

Charismatic authority is thus specifically outside the realm of everyday routine and the profane sphere.[41] In this respect, it is sharply opposed both to rational, and particularly bureaucratic, authority, and to traditional authority, whether in its patriarchal, patrimonial, or any other form. Both rational and traditional authority are specifically forms of everyday routine control of action; while the charismatic type is the direct antithesis of this. Bureaucratic authority is specifically rational in the sense of being bound to intellectually analysable rules; while charismatic authority is specifically irrational in the sense of being foreign to all rules. Traditional authority is bound to the precedents handed down from the past and to this extent is also oriented to rules. Within the

[40] Something contrary to what was written, as Jesus said in opposition to the Scribes and Pharisees.—ED.

[41] Weber used the antithesis of *Charisma* and *Alltag* in two senses. On the one hand, of the extraordinary and temporary as opposed to the everyday and routine; on the other hand, the sacred as opposed to the profane. See the editor's *Structure of Social Action*, ch. xvii.—ED.

sphere of its claims, charismatic authority repudiates the past, and is in this sense a specifically revolutionary force. It recognizes no appropriation of positions of power by virtue of the possession of property, either on the part of a chief or of socially privileged groups. The only basis of legitimacy for it is personal charisma, so long as it is proved; that is, as long as it receives recognition and is able to satisfy the followers or disciples. But this lasts only so long as the belief in its charismatic inspiration remains.

The above is scarcely in need of further discussion. What has been said applies to the position of authority of such elected monarchs as Napoleon, with his use of the plebiscite. It applies to the 'rule of genius,' which has elevated people of humble origin to thrones and high military commands, just as much as it applies to religious prophets or war heroes.

4. Pure charisma is specifically foreign to economic considerations. Whenever it appears, it constitutes a 'call' in the most emphatic sense of the word, a 'mission' or a 'spiritual duty.' In the pure type, it disdains and repudiates economic exploitation of the gifts of grace as a source of income, though, to be sure, this often remains more an ideal than a fact. It is not that charisma always means the renunciation of property or even of acquisition, as under certain circumstances prophets and their disciples do. The heroic warrior and his followers actively seek 'booty'; the elective ruler or the charismatic party leader requires the material means of power. The former in addition requires a brilliant display of his authority to bolster his prestige. What is despised, so long as the genuinely charismatic type is adhered to, is traditional or rational everyday economizing, the attainment of a regular income by continuous economic activity devoted to this end. Support by gifts, sometimes on a grand scale involving foundations, even by bribery and grand-scale honoraria, or by begging, constitute the strictly voluntary type of support. On the other hand, 'booty,' or coercion, whether by force or by other means, is the other typical form of charismatic provision for needs. From the point of view of rational economic activity, charisma is a typical anti-economic force. It repudiates any sort of involvement in the everyday routine world. It can only tolerate, with an attitude of complete emotional indifference, irregular, unsystematic, acquisitive acts. In that it relieves the recipient of economic concerns, dependence on property income can be the economic basis of a charismatic mode of life for some groups; but that is not usually acceptable for the normal charismatic 'revolutionary.'

The fact that incumbency of church office has been forbidden to the Jesuits is a rationalized application of this principle of discipleship. The fact that all the 'virtuosi' of asceticism, the mendicant orders, and fighters for a faith belong in this category, is quite clear. Almost all prophets have been supported by voluntary gifts. The well-known saying of St. Paul, 'If a man does not work, neither shall he eat,' was directed against the swarm of charismatic missionaries. It obviously has nothing to do with a positive valuation of economic activity for its own sake, but only lays it down as a duty of each individual somehow to provide for his own support. This because he realized that the purely charismatic parable of the lilies of the field was not capable of literal application, but at best 'taking no thought for the morrow' could be hoped for. On the other hand, in such a case as primarily an artistic type of charismatic discipleship, it is conceivable that insulation from economic struggle should mean limitation of those who were really eligible to the 'economically independent'; that is, to persons living on income from property. This has been true of the circle of Stefan George, at least in its primary intentions.

5. In traditionally stereotyped periods, charisma is the greatest revolutionary force. The equally revolutionary force of 'reason' works from without by altering the situations of action, and hence its problems finally in this way changing men's attitudes toward them; or it intellectualizes the individual. Charisma, on the other hand, may involve a subjective or internal reorientation born out of suffering, conflicts, or enthusiasm. It may then result in a radical alteration of the central system of attitudes and directions of action with a completely new orientation of all attitudes toward the different problems and structures of the 'world.' [42] In prerationalistic periods, tradition and charisma between them have almost exhausted the whole of the orientation of action.

V. THE ROUTINIZATION OF CHARISMA

11: The Routinization of Charisma and Its Consequences

In its pure form charismatic authority has a character specifically foreign to everyday routine structures. The social relationships directly

---

[42] Weber here uses *Welt* in quotation marks, indicating that it refers to its meaning in what is primarily a religious context. It is the sphere of 'worldly' things and interests as distinguished from transcendental religious interests.—ED.

involved are strictly personal, based on the validity and practice of charismatic personal qualities. If this is not to remain a purely transitory phenomenon, but to take on the character of a permanent relationship forming a stable community of disciples or a band of followers or a party organization or any sort of political or hierocratic organization, it is necessary for the character of charismatic authority to become radically changed. Indeed, in its pure form charismatic authority may be said to exist only in the process of originating. It cannot remain stable, but becomes either traditionalized or rationalized, or a combination of both.

The following are the principal motives underlying this transformation: (a) The ideal and also the material interests of the followers in the continuation and the continual reactivation of the community, (b) the still stronger ideal and also stronger material interests of the members of the administrative staff, the disciples or other followers of the charismatic leader in continuing their relationship. Not only this, but they have an interest in continuing it in such a way that both from an ideal and a material point of view, their own status is put on a stable everyday basis. This means, above all, making it possible to participate in normal family relationships or at least to enjoy a secure social position in place of the kind of discipleship which is cut off from ordinary worldly connexions, notably in the family and in economic relationships.

These interests generally become conspicuously evident with the disappearance of the personal charismatic leader and with the problem of succession, which inevitably arises. The way in which this problem is met—if it is met at all and the charismatic group continues to exist—is of crucial importance for the character of the subsequent social relationships. The following are the principal possible types of solution:—

(a) The search for a new charismatic leader on the basis of criteria of the qualities which will fit him for the position of authority. This is to be found in a relatively pure type in the process of choice of a new Dalai Lama. It consists in the search for a child with characteristics which are interpreted to mean that he is a reincarnation of the Buddha. This is very similar to the choice of the new Bull of Apis.

In this case the legitimacy of the new charismatic leader is bound to certain distinguishing characteristics; thus, to rules with respect to which a tradition arises. The result is a process of traditionalization in favour of which the purely personal character of leadership is eliminated.

(b) By revelation manifested in oracles, lots, divine judgments, or other techniques of selection. In this case the legitimacy of the new leader is dependent on the legitimacy of the technique of his selection. This involves a form of iegalization. It is said that at times the *Schofetim* of Israel had this character. Saul is said to have been chosen by the old war oracle.

(c) By the designation on the part of the original charismatic leader of his own successor and his recognition on the part of the followers. This is a very common form. Originally, the Roman magistracies were filled entirely in this way. The system survived most clearly into later times in the appointment of 'dictators' and in the institution of the 'interrex.' In this case legitimacy is acquired through the act of designation.

(d) Designation of a successor by the charismatically qualified administrative staff and his recognition by the community. In its typical form this process should quite definitely not be interpreted as 'election' or 'nomination' or anything of the sort. It is not a matter of free selection, but of one which is strictly bound to objective duty. It is not to be determined merely by majority vote, but is a question of arriving at the correct designation, the designation of the right person who is truly endowed with charisma. It is quite possible that the minority and not the majority should be right in such a case. Unanimity is often required. It is obligatory to acknowledge a mistake and persistence in error is a serious offence. Making a wrong choice is a genuine wrong requiring expiation. Originally it was a magical offence.

Nevertheless, in such a case it is easy for legitimacy to take on the character of an acquired right which is justified by standards of the correctness of the process by which the position was acquired, for the most part, by its having been acquired in accordance with certain formalities, such as coronation. This was the original meaning of the coronation of bishops and kings in the Western World by the clergy or the nobility with the 'consent' of the community. There are numerous analogous phenomena all over the world. The fact that this is the origin of the modern conception of 'election' raises problems which will have to be gone into later.

(e) By the conception that charisma is a quality transmitted by heredity; thus that it is participated in by the kinsmen of its bearer, particularly by his closest relatives. This is the case of hereditary charisma. The order of hereditary succession in such a case need not be the same as that which is in force for appropriated rights, but may differ from it. It is also sometimes necessary to select the proper heir within the kinship group by some of the methods just spoken of; thus in certain Negro states brothers have had to fight for the succession. In China, succession had to take place in such a way that the relation of the living group to the ancestral spirits was not disturbed. The rule either of seniority or of designation by the followers has been very common in the Orient. Hence, in the house of Osman, it has been obligatory to eliminate all other possible candidates.

Only in Medieval Europe and in Japan universally, elsewhere only sporadically, has the principle of primogeniture, as governing the inheritance of authority, become clearly established. This has greatly facilitated the consolidation of political groups in that it has eliminated struggle between a plurality of candidates from the same charismatic family.

In the case of hereditary charisma, recognition is no longer paid to the charismatic qualities of the individual, but to the legitimacy of the position he has acquired by hereditary succession. This may lead in the direction either of traditionalization or of legalization. The concept of 'divine right' is fundamentally altered and now comes to mean authority by virtue of a personal right which is not dependent on the recognition of those subject to authority. Personal charisma may be totally absent. Hereditary monarchy is a conspicuous illustration. In Asia there have been very numerous hereditary priesthoods; also, frequently, the hereditary charisma of kinship groups has been treated as a criterion of social rank and of eligibility for fiefs and benefices.

(f) The concept that charisma may be transmitted by ritual means from one bearer to another or may be created in a new person. The concept was originally magical. It involves a dissociation of charisma from a particular individual, making it an objective, transferrable entity. In particular, it may become the charisma of office. In this case the belief in legitimacy is no longer directed to the individual, but to the acquired qualities and to the effectiveness of the ritual acts. The most important example is the transmission of priestly charisma by anointing, consecration, or the laying on of hands; and of royal authority, by anointing and by coronation. The *caracter indelibilis* thus acquired means that the charismatic qualities and powers of the office are emancipated from the personal qualities of the priest. For precisely this reason, this has, from the Donatist and the Montanist heresies down to the Puritan revolution, been the subject of continual conflicts. The 'hireling' of the Quakers is the preacher endowed with the charisma of office.

12: The Routinization of Charisma and Its Consequences— (*Continued*)

Comcomitant with the routinization of charisma with a view to insuring adequate succession, go the interests in its routinization on the part of the administrative staff. It is only in the initial stages and so long as the charismatic leader acts in a way which is completely outside everyday social organization, that it is possible for his followers to live communistically in a community of faith and enthusiasm, on gifts, 'booty,' or sporadic acquisition. Only the members of the small group of enthusiastic disciples and followers are prepared to devote their lives purely idealistically to their call. The great majority of disciples and followers will in the long run 'make their living' out of their 'calling' in a material sense as well. Indeed, this must be the case if the movement is not to disintegrate.

Hence, the routinization of charisma also takes the form of the appropriation of powers of control and of economic advantages by the followers or disciples, and of regulation of the recruitment of these groups. This process of tradionalization or of legalization, according to whether rational legislation is involved or not, may take any one of a number of typical forms.

1. The original basis of recruitment is personal charisma. With routinization, the followers or disciples may set up norms for recruitment, in particular involving training or tests of eligibility. Charisma can only be 'awakened' and 'tested'; it cannot be 'learned' or 'taught.' All types of magical asceticism, as practiced by magicians and heroes, and all novitiates, belong in this category. These are means of closing the group which constitutes the administrative staff.[43]

Only the proved novice is allowed to exercise authority. A genuine charismatic leader is in a position to oppose this type of prerequisite for membership. His successor is not, at least if he is chosen by the administrative staff. This type is illustrated by the magical and warrior asceticism of the 'men's house' with initiation ceremonies and age groups. An individual who has not successfully gone through the initiation, remains a 'woman'; that is, is excluded from the charismatic group.

2. It is easy for charismatic norms to be transformed into those defin-

---

[43] On the charismatic type of education, see chap. iv. (No discussion of this subject is included in the fragment of chap. iv which Weber completed.—Ed.)

ing a traditional social status on a hereditary charismatic basis. If the leader is chosen on a hereditary basis, it is very easy for hereditary charisma to govern the selection of the administrative staff and even, perhaps, those followers without any position of authority. The term 'familistic state' [44] will be applied when a political body is organized strictly and completely in terms of this principle of hereditary charisma. In such a case, all appropriation of governing powers, of fiefs, benefices, and all sorts of economic advantages follow the same pattern. The result is that all powers and advantages of all sorts become traditionalized. The heads of families, who are traditional gerontocrats or patriarchs without personal charismatic legitimacy, regulate the exercise of these powers which cannot be taken away from their family. It is not the type of position he occupies which determines the rank of a man or of his family, but rather the hereditary charismatic rank of his family determines the position he will occupy. Japan, before the development of bureaucracy, was organized in this way. The same was undoubtedly true of China as well where, before the rationalization which took place in the territorial states, authority was in the hands of the 'old families.' Other types of examples are furnished by the caste system in India, and by Russia before the *Mjestnitschestvo* was introduced. Indeed, all hereditary social classes with established privileges belong in the same category.

3. The administrative staff may seek and achieve the creation and appropriation of individual positions and the corresponding economic advantages for its members. In that case, according to whether the tendency is to traditionalization or legalization, there will develop (a) benefices, (b) offices, or (c) fiefs. In the first case a praebendal organization will result; in the second, patrimonialism or bureaucracy; in the third, feudalism. These become appropriated in the place of the type of provision from gifts or booty without settled relation to the everyday economic structure.

Case (a), benefices, may consist in rights to the proceeds of begging, to payments in kind, or to the proceeds of money taxes, or finally, to the proceeds of fees. Any one of these may result from the regulation of provision by free gifts or by 'booty' in terms of a rational organization of finance. Regularized begging is found in Buddhism; benefices in kind, in the Chinese and Japanese 'rice rents'; support by money taxation has been the rule in all the rationalized conquering states. The last case is

---

[44] *Geschlechterstaat.*

common everywhere, especially on the part of priests and judges and, in India, even the military authorities.

Case (b), the transformation of the charismatic mission into an office, may have more of a patrimonial or more of a bureaucratic character. The former is much the more common; the latter is found principally in Mediterranean Antiquity and in the modern Western World. Elsewhere it is exceptional.

In case (c), only land may be appropriated as a fief, whereas the position as such retains its originally charismatic character. On the other hand, powers and authority may be fully appropriated as fiefs. It is difficult to distinguish the two cases. It is, however, rare that orientation to the charismatic character of the position disappears entirely; it did not do so in the Middle Ages.

12A: The Routinization of Charisma and Its Consequences— (Continued)

For charisma to be transformed into a permanent routine structure, it is necessary that its anti-economic character should be altered. It must be adapted to some form of fiscal organization to provide for the needs of the group and hence to the economic conditions necessary for raising taxes and contributions. When a charismatic movement develops in the direction of praebendal provision, the 'laity' become differentiated from the 'clergy';[45] that is, the participating members of the charismatic administrative staff which has now become routinized. These are the priests of the developing 'church.' Correspondingly, in a developing political body the vassals, the holders of benefices, or officials are differentiated from the 'tax payers.' The former, instead of being the 'followers' of the leader, become state officials or appointed party officials. This process is very conspicuous in Buddhism and in the Hindu sects. The same is true in all the states resulting from conquest which have become rationalized to form permanent structures; also of parties and other movements which have originally had a purely charismatic character. With the process of routinization the charismatic group tends to develop into one of the forms of everyday authority, particularly the patrimonial form in its decentralized variant or the bureaucratic. Its original peculiarities are apt to be retained in the charismatic standards of honour attendant on the social status acquired by heredity or the holding of office. This

---

[45] Derived from κλῆρος, meaning a 'share.' See the Sociology of Religion.

applies to all who participate in the process of appropriation, the chief himself and the members of his staff. It is thus a matter of the type of prestige enjoyed by ruling groups. A hereditary monarch by 'divine right' is not a simple patrimonial chief, patriarch, or sheik; a vassal is not a mere household retainer or official. Further details must be deferred to the analysis of social stratification.

As a rule the process of routinization is not free of conflict. In the early stages personal claims on the charisma of the chief are not easily forgotten and the conflict between the charisma of office or of hereditary status with personal charisma is a typical process in many historical situations.

1. The power of absolution—that is, the power to absolve from mortal sins—was held originally only by personal charismatic martyrs or ascetics, but became transformed into a power of the office of bishop or priest. This process was much slower in the Orient than in the Occident because in the latter case it was influenced by the Roman conception of office. Revolutions under a charismatic leader, directed against hereditary charismatic powers or the powers of office, are to be found in all types of corporate groups, from states to trade unions.[46] The more highly developed the interdependence of different economic units in a monetary economy, the greater the pressure of the everyday needs of the followers of the charismatic movement becomes. The effect of this is to strengthen the tendency to routinization, which is everywhere operative, and as a rule has rapidly won out. Charisma is a phenomenon typical of prophetic religious movements or of expansive political movements in their early stages. But as soon as the position of authority is well established, and above all as soon as control over large masses of people exists, it gives way to the forces of everyday routine.

2. One of the decisive motives underlying all cases of the routinization of charisma is naturally the striving for security. This means legitimization, on the one hand, of positions of authority and social prestige, on the other hand, of the economic advantages enjoyed by the followers and sympathizers of the leader. Another important motive, however, lies in the objective necessity of adaptation of the patterns of order and of the organization of the administrative staff to the normal, everyday needs and conditions of carrying on administration. In this connexion, in particular, there are always points at which traditions of administrative practice and of judicial decision can take hold; since these are needed

[46] This last is particularly conspicuous at the present time (1920).

both by the normal administrative staff and by those subject to its authority. It is further necessary that there should be some definite order introduced into the organization of the administrative staff itself. Finally, as will be discussed in detail below, it is necessary for the administrative staff and all its administrative practices to be adapted to everyday economic conditions. It is not possible for the costs of permanent, routine administration to be met by 'booty,' contributions, gifts, and hospitality, as is typical of the pure type of military and prophetic charisma.

3. The process of routinization is thus not by any means confined to the problem of succession and does not stop when this has been solved. On the contrary, the most fundamental problem is that of making a transition from a charismatic administrative staff, and the corresponding principles of administration, to one which is adapted to everyday conditions. The problem of succession, however, is crucial because through it occurs the routinization of the charismatic focus of the structure. In it, the character of the leader himself and of his claim to legitimacy is altered. This process involves peculiar and characteristic conceptions which are understandable only in this context and do not apply to the problem of transition to traditional or legal patterns of order and types of administrative organization. The most important of the modes of meeting the problem of succession are the charismatic designation of a successor and hereditary charisma.

4. As has already been noted, the most important historical example of designation by the charismatic leader of his own successor is Rome. For the *rex,* this arrangement is attested by tradition; while for the appointment of the 'dictator' and of the co-emperor and successor in the principate, it has existed in historical times. The way in which all the higher magistrates were invested with the *imperium* shows clearly that they also were designated as successors by the military commander, subject to recognition by the citizen army. The fact that candidates were examined by the magistrate in office and that originally they could be excluded on what were obviously arbitrary grounds shows clearly what was the nature of the development.

5. The most important examples of designation of a successor by the charismatic followers of the leader are to be found in the election of bishops, and particularly of the Pope, by the original system of designation by the clergy and recognition by the lay community. The investigations of U. Stutz have made it probable that, though it was later altered, the election of the German emperor was modelled on that of the bishops.

He was designated by a group of qualified princes and recognized by the 'people,' that is, those bearing arms. Similar arrangements are very common.

6. The classical case of the development of hereditary charisma is that of caste in India. All occupational qualifications, and in particular all the qualifications for positions of authority and power, have there come to be regarded as strictly bound to the inheritance of charisma. Eligibility for fiefs, involving governing powers, was limited to members of the royal kinship group, the fiefs being granted by the eldest of the group. All types of religious office, including the extraordinarily important and influential position of *guru,* the *directeur de l'âme,* were treated as bound to hereditary charismatic qualities. The same is true of all sorts of relations to traditional customers and of all positions in the village organization, such as priest, barber, laundryman, watchman, etc. The foundation of a sect always meant the development of a hereditary hierarchy, as was true also of Taoism in China. Also in the Japanese 'feudal' state, before the introduction of a patrimonial officialdom on the Chinese model, which then led to praebends and a new feudalization, social organization was based purely on hereditary charisma.

This kind of hereditary charismatic right to positions of authority has been developed in similar ways all over the world. Qualification by virtue of individual achievement has been replaced by qualification by birth. This is everywhere the basis of the development of hereditary aristocracies, in the Roman nobility, in the concept of the *stirps regia,* which Tacitus describes among the Germans, in the rules of eligibility to tournaments and monasteries in the late Middle Ages, and even in the genealogical research carried on on behalf of the parvenu aristocracy of the United States. Indeed, this is to be found everywhere where a differentiation of hereditary social classes has become established.

The following is the principal relation to economic conditions: The process of routinization of charisma is in very important respects identical with adaptation to the conditions of economic life, since this is one of the principal continually-operating forces in everyday life. Economic conditions in this connexion play a leading role and do not constitute merely a dependent variable. To a very large extent the transition to hereditary charisma or the charisma of office serves in this connexion as a means of legitimizing existing or recently acquired powers of control over economic goods. Along with the ideology of loyalty, which is certainly by no means unimportant, allegiance to hereditary monarchy in

particular is very strongly influenced by the consideration that all inherited property and all that which is legitimately acquired would be
endangered if subjective recognition of the sanctity of succession to the
throne were eliminated. It is hence by no means fortuitous that hereditary
monarchy is more acceptable to the propertied classes than, for instance,
to the proletariat.

Beyond this, it is not possible to say anything in general terms, which
would at the same time be substantial and valuable, on the relations of
the various possible modes of adaptation to the economic order. This
must be reserved to a special investigation. The development of a praebendal structure, of feudalism and the appropriation of all sorts of advantages on a hereditary charismatic basis, may in all cases have the same
stereotyping effect on the economic order if they develop from charismatic starting points as if they developed from patrimonial or bureaucratic origins. The immediate effect of charisma in economic as in other
connexions is usually strongly revolutionary; indeed, often destructive,
because it means new modes of orientation. But in case the process of
routinization leads in the direction of traditionalism, its ultimate effect
may be exactly the reverse.[47]

12B: FEUDALISM

The case noted above, under sec. 12, § 3—namely that of the Fief—
requires separate discussion. This is because a type of structure of authority may develop out of it, which is different both from patrimonialism
and from hereditary charisma and which has had very great historical
significance; namely, feudalism. The two genuine sub-types which will
be distinguished are the feudalism which is based on fiefs and that
based on benefices.[48] All other forms in which the use of land is granted
in exchange for military services really have a patrimonial character and
therefore will not be dealt with separately. The different kinds of benefices will not be distinguished until later, when they can be discussed
in detail.

A.—A fief involves the following elements:—

(1) The appropriation of powers and rights of exercising authority.
Appropriation as a fief may apply only to powers relevant within the

---

[47] The economics of charismatic revolutions will have to be discussed separately. It is
by no means the same in all cases.

[48] *Lehensfeudalismus* and *Pfründenfeudalismus.*

individual household or budgetary unit or it may be extended to include those belonging to the corporate group. The later type may be restricted to economic rights—that is, fiscal rights—or it may also include imperative control over the members of the group. Fiefs are granted in return for specific services. Normally they are primarily of a military character, but may also include administrative functions.

(2) The grant of the fief takes a very specific form. It is carried out on a basis which is purely personal for the lifetime of the lord and of the recipient of the fief, his vassal.

(3) The relationship is established by a contract, thus it is presupposed that the vassal is a free man.

(4) In the type of case which is here treated as the feudalism based on fiefs, the recipient is a person who carries on a specific social class tradition,[49] that of a 'knight.'

(5) The contract of fealty is not an ordinary business contract, but establishes a relation of personal solidarity which, though naturally unequal, involves reciprocal obligations of loyalty. These obligations are upheld by a social class honour of the knight and are clearly delimited.

It was pointed out above that the object of appropriation as a fief may be only the land, whereas the position as such retains its originally charismatic character. On the other hand, powers and authority may also, in addition to land, be appropriated. The transition tends to take place when fiefs are appropriated on hereditary basis subject only to the condition that each new vassal will pledge fealty to his lord and the existing vassals will do so to a new lord. It is further promoted by the ability of a feudal administrative staff to compel the granting of fiefs because all fiefs are treated as sources of support for the members of their class.

The first step, the transition to a hereditary basis, took place relatively early in the Middle Ages; the second, later in the course of its development. The struggles of kings and princes with their vassals were above all directed, though usually not explicitly, toward the elimination of this principle, since it made impossible the establishment and the command of a personal patrimonial administration on the part of the lord.

B.—This type of feudalism has never been historically realized in the completely pure type any more than has pure patrimonialism. But to

---

[49] *Ständische Lebensführung.*

the extent that it has been approximated, it has had the following principal consequences:—

(1) The authority of the chief is reduced to the likelihood that the vassals will voluntarily remain faithful to their oaths of fealty.

(2) The political corporate group is completely replaced by a system of relations of purely personal loyalty between the lord and his vassals and between these in turn and their own sub-vassals (sub-infeudation) and so on. Only a lord's own vassals are bound by fealty to him; whereas they in turn can claim the fealty of their own vassals, and so on.

(3) Only in the case of a 'felony' does the lord have a right to deprive his vassal of his fief, and the same in turn applies to the vassal in his relation to his own vassal. When such a case, however, arises, in enforcing his rights against a vassal who has broken the oath of fealty, the lord is dependent on the help of his other vassals or on the passivity of the sub-vassals of the guilty party. Either source of support can only be counted on when the relevant group recognizes that a felony has actually been committed. He cannot count on the non-interference of sub-vassals unless the higher lord has at least been able to secure recognition on their part of the principle that a struggle against an overlord is an exceptional state. Lords have always attempted to establish this principle but often without success.

(4) There is a hierarchy of social rank corresponding to the hierarchy of fiefs through the process of sub-infeudation. In the *Sachsenspiegel,* it is called the *Heerschilde.* This is not, however, a hierarchy of authority in the bureaucratic sense. For whether an order or a decision can be challenged and to what authority appeal can be made is in principle a matter for the royal court. It does not follow the hierarchy of feudal relationships. It is theoretically possible for the judicial authority to be granted as a fief to some associate of its legal possessor, but in practice this was not often the case.

(5) The elements in the population who do not hold fiefs involving some element of patrimonial or other political authority are 'subjects'; that is, they are patrimonial dependents. They are dependent on the holders of fiefs, on the one hand, in that their traditional status, particularly class status, determines or permits it, or on the other so far as the coercive power in the hands of the possessors of military fiefs compels it, since they are to a large extent defenceless. Just as the supreme lord is under obligation to grant land in fief, those who do not hold fiefs are always under the authority of a lord; the rule, *nulle terre sans sei-*

gneur, holds. The sole survival of the old immediate political power is the principle, which is almost always recognized, that political authority, particularly judicial authority, is turned over to the chief whenever he is personally present.

(6) Powers over the individual budgetary unit, including domains, slaves and serfs, the fiscal rights of the political group to the receipt of taxes and contributions, and specifically political powers of jurisdiction and compulsion to military service—thus powers over free men—are all objects of feudal grants in the same way. It is, however, usual for the strictly political powers to be subject to special regulation.[51]

It is usual for political powers to be fully appropriated in the same way as property rights in fief. There are, however, numerous transitional forms and irregularities. There is, nevertheless, one conspicuous uniformity, namely the existence of a class distinction between those enjoying only purely economic or fiscal rights and those with strictly political powers, notably judicial and military authority. Only the latter are political vassals.

It goes without saying that whenever this type of feudalism is highly developed, the status of supreme authority is precarious. This is because it is always very dependent on the voluntary obedience and hence the purely personal loyalty of the members of the administrative staff who, by virtue of the feudal structure, are themselves in possession of the means of administration. Hence, the struggle for power, which is always latent in authoritarian structures, comes to be chronic between a lord and his vassals. The ideal extent of feudal authority has never been effectively carried out in practice or remained effective on a permanent basis.

The feudal chief may attempt to meet this situation in one of the following ways:

(a) He may not rely on the purely personal loyalty of his vassals, but may attempt to secure his position by limiting or forbidding sub-infeudation.[52] In case it is merely limited, he may attempt to establish the principle that the fealty of a sub-vassal to his immediate lord is void in case

---

[51] In ancient China the granting of economic income in fiefs and of territorial authority were distinguished in name as well as in fact. The distinctions in name are not found in the European Middle Ages, but there were clear distinctions in class status and in numerous other particular points.

[52] This was common in Western feudalism, but often was initiated by the administrative staff in the interest of their own power. The same was true of the alliance of princes in China in 630 B.C.

of war against the higher lord. Or, if possible, the attempt is made to obligate the sub-vassal to direct fealty to him, the liege lord.

(b) The feudal chief may seek to implement his control of the administration of political powers in a variety of ways. He may grant all the subjects a right of appeal to him or his courts. He may station supervising agents at the courts of his political vassals. He may attempt to enforce a right to collect taxes from the subjects of all his vassals. He may appoint certain officials of the political vassals. Finally, he may attempt to enforce the principle that all political authority is forfeited to him in his personal presence or beyond that to any agent he designates and that he, as the supreme lord, is entitled to try any case in his own court at will.

It is possible for a supreme lord to attain and maintain his power against vassals, as well as against other types of holders of appropriated authority, only if he creates or re-creates an administrative staff under his personal control and organizes it in an appropriate manner. There are three main possibilities. (1) It may be a patrimonial bureaucracy. This was to a large extent what happened in the European Middle Ages and in Japan in the *Bakufu* of the *Shogun,* who exercised a very effective control over the feudal *Daimyos.* (2) It may be an extra-patrimonial staff recruited from a class with literary education. The principal examples are clerical officials, whether Christian, Brahman, Buddhist, Lamaist, or Mohammedan, or Humanists, such as the Confucian scholars in China.[53] (3) Or it may be a group of technically trained officials, particularly legal and military specialists. This was proposed in China in the eleventh century by Wang An Shi, but by that time it was directed against the classical scholars and not the feudal magnates. In the Western World, such a bureaucracy was recruited for civil administration from university-trained men. In the Church the primary training was in the Canon Law, in the State, the Roman Law. In England, it was the Common Law, which had, however, been rationalized under the influence of Roman modes of thought. In this development lie the seeds of the modern Western state. The development of military organization in the Western World took a somewhat different course. The feudal organization was first replaced by capitalistic military entrepreneurs, the *condottieri.* These structures were in turn appropriated by the territorial princes with the development of a rational administration of royal finance from

---

[53] On the peculiarities of such groups and their immense importance for cultural development, see chap. iv (not in completed part.—ED.).

the seventeenth century on. In England and France, it happened somewhat earlier.

This struggle of the feudal chief with his feudal administrative staff in the Western World, though not in Japan, largely coincided with his struggle against the power of corporately organized privileged groups.[54] In modern times it everywhere issued in the victory of the chief, and that meant of bureaucratic administration. This happened first in the Western World, then in Japan and in India, and perhaps also China, under the influence of foreign conquest. Along with special local power relationships, economic conditions have played a very important part in this process in the Western World. Above all, it was influenced by the rise of the bourgeois classes in the towns, which had an organization peculiar to Europe.[55] It was in addition aided by the competition for power by means of rational—that is, bureaucratic—administration among the different states. This led, from fiscal motives, to a crucially important alliance with capitalistic interests, as will be shown later.

12C. FEUDALISM BASED ON BENEFICES AND OTHER TYPES

Not every kind of 'feudalism' involves the fief in the Western sense. In addition, there are the following principal types:—

A.—The type where the place of the fief is taken by a benefice of fiscal significance. This was typical of the Mohammedan Near East and of India under the Moguls. On the other hand, Ancient Chinese feudalism before the time of Shi Huang Ti had at least in part a structure of fiefs, though benefices were also involved. Japanese feudalism also involved fiefs, but they were subject in the case of the *Daimyos* to a rather stringent control on the part of the supreme lord. But here, also, the fiefs of the Samurai and the Bake often originated in benefices granted to court officials, which then came to be appropriated.

The type of feudalism based on benefices exists when (1) it is a question of the appropriation of benefices which are valued and granted according to the income they yield, and where (2) appropriation is, in principle, though not always effectively, carried out on a personal basis in accordance with services, thus involving the possibility of promotion. This was, at least from the legal point of view, true of the benefices

---

[54] *Stände-Corporationen*. Notably ecclesiastical and professional (lawyers) and urban communes and guilds.

[55] Cf. Weber's study, *Die Stadt, Wirtschaft und Gesellschaft*, part ii, chap. viii.—ED.

held by the Turkish *spahis*. Finally and above all, (3) it does not involve primarily a free individual relation of personal fealty arising from a contract of personal loyalty with the lord as the basis of a particular fief. It is rather a matter primarily of fiscal considerations in the context of a system of financing which is otherwise patrimonial, often sultanistic. This is for the most part made evident by the fact that the sources of income are granted according to a regular system of registration.

Though not inevitable, it is very common for the fief to originate in a system of provision for the needs of the political group on the basis of a purely natural economy and in terms of personal obligations. The obligations to personal services and to military services are primary. The principal motive is, in place of an inadequate military force lacking in training, and of economic inadequacy, above all, for the independent provision of satisfactory equipment, to organize a well-trained and equipped army of knights who are bound to their chief by personal honour. The type of feudalism based on benefices, on the other hand, usually originates in a process of transformation of the organization of finance on a money basis. It involves a reversion to financing in kind. The following are the principal reasons leading to such a policy:—

(a) The transfer of the risk involved in fluctuating income to an entrepreneur; that is, a sort of tax farming. Rights to such income may be transferred in return for undertaking to supply certain particular army contingents, such as cavalry, sometimes war chariots, armoured troops, supply trains, or artillery, for a patrimonial army. This was common in the Chinese Middle Ages. Quotas for the army in each of the different categories were established for a particular territorial area.

Either in addition to this or alone, fiefs may be established as a means of meeting the costs of civil administration and of securing tax payments for the royal treasury. This was common in India.

In return for these various services, in the first instance to enable those who undertook them to meet their obligations, there has been involved a process of appropriation of governmental power in varying degrees and respects. Such appropriation has usually been for a limited period and subject to repurchase. But when means to do this have been lacking, it has often in fact been definitive. Those who hold such definitively appropriated powers then become, at the very least, landlords, as opposed to mere landowners, and often come into the possession of extensive governing powers in the political organization.

This process has been typical above all of India. It is the source of the powers over land of the *Zamindars,* the *Jagirdars,* and the *Tuluḳdars.* It is also found in a large part of the Near East as C. H. Becker has clearly shown—he was the first to understand the difference from the European fief. The primary basis lies in the leasing of taxes. As a secondary consequence, it developed into a system of landlordism. The Rumanian Bojars were also tax farmers who on this basis appropriated governing authority. They are the descendants of the most heterogeneous society the world has ever seen, of Jews, Germans, Greeks, and various other elements.

(b) Inability to pay the contingents of a patrimonial army may lead to an usurpation of the sources of taxation on their part, which is subsequently legalized. The result is that appropriation of the land and of the subjects is carried out by the officers and members of the army.

This was true of the famous Khans of the empire of the Caliphs. It was the source or the model for all forms of Oriental appropriation, including the Mameluke army, which was formally composed of slaves. It is by no means inevitable that this should lead to systematic registration as a basis for the granting of benefices. But this is a readily available course and has often actually been followed out. It is not possible yet to discuss how far the 'fiefs' of the Turkish *spahis* were genuine fiefs or whether they were closer to benefices. From a legal point of view, promotion according to achievement was possible.

It is clear that the two types of feudalism are connected by gradual imperceptible transitions and that it is seldom possible to classify cases with complete definiteness under one category or the other. Furthermore, the type of feudalism based on benefices is closely related to a purely praebendal organization, and there are also gradual transitions in this direction.

B.—If terminological rigour is somewhat relaxed, there may, in addition to the fief resting on a free contract with the lord and the feudal benefice, be said to be two other principal types of 'feudalism.'

(1) The so-called 'Polis' feudalism, resting on a real or fictitious 'synoikism' of landlords. These enjoy equal rights in the conduct of a purely military mode of life with high standards of class honour. Its economic basis is the 'cleros,' a plot of land which is appropriated by qualified persons on a personal basis and passed on by individual hereditary succession. It is cultivated by the services of unfree persons, control over whom is

a criterion of class status and forms the basis of provision of military equipment. This type is found only in Greece, in fully developed form, only in Sparta, and originated out of the 'men's house.' It has been called 'feudalism' because of the set of conventions regulating class honour and of the element of chivalry in the mode of life of a group of landlords. This is hardly legitimate usage. In Rome the term *'fundus'* corresponds to the Greek *'cleros.'* There is, however, no information available about the organization of the *curia,* which may have corresponded to the Greek *'andreion,'* the 'men's house.' We do not know how far it was similar to the Greek.

The term 'feudal' is often used in a very broad sense to designate all military classes, institutions and conventions which involve any sort of military class privileges. This usage will be avoided here as entirely too vague.

(2) The second doubtful type is called feudalism for the opposite reason. The fief is present but, on the one hand, is not acquired by a free contract of personal solidarity either with a lord or with equals, but is bestowed by the order of a patrimonial chief. On the other hand, it may not be administered in the spirit of a chivalrous mode of life involving high prestige. Finally, both criteria may be absent. Thus there may be fiefs held by a chivalrous group who, however, are dependent; or, conversely, fiefs may be freely acquired but their holders are not subject to a code of chivalry. Finally, fiefs may be granted to clients, coloni, or slaves who are employed as fighting forces. All these cases will be treated here as benefices.

The case of a dependent chivalrous class is illustrated by the Samurai of Japan. Freely recruited soldiers without a chivalrous code are known to the Orient; this was probably the origin of the Ptolemaic military organization. When the hereditary appropriation of land has led further to the appropriation of the military function as such, the end result is a typical liturgical organization of the state. The third type, the use of unfree military forces, is typical of the warrior caste of Ancient Egypt, of the Mamelukes of Medieval Egypt, and of various other unfree Oriental and Chinese military classes. These have not always been granted rights in land, but such an arrangement is common.

In such cases, it is not correct to speak of 'feudalism,' but rather of military classes, which, at least from a formal point of view, occupy a negatively privileged position. They will be discussed in Chapter IV.

13: COMBINATIONS OF THE DIFFERENT TYPES OF AUTHORITY

The above discussion makes it quite evident that imperatively co-ordinated groups, which belong only to one or another of these pure types, are very exceptional. Furthermore, in relation to legal and traditional authority especially, certain important types, such as the collegial form and some aspects of the feudal, have either not been discussed at all or have been barely suggested. In general, it should be kept clearly in mind that the basis of every system of authority, and correspondingly of every kind of willingness to obey, is a *belief,* a belief by virtue of which persons exercising authority are lent prestige. The composition of this belief is seldom altogether simple. In the case of 'legal authority,' it is never purely legal. The belief in legality comes to be established and habitual, and this means it is partly traditional. Violation of the tradition may even be fatal to it. Furthermore, it has a charismatic element, at least in the negative sense that persistent and striking lack of success may be sufficient to ruin any government, to undermine its prestige, and to prepare the way for charismatic revolution. For monarchies, hence, it is dangerous to lose wars since that makes it appear that their charisma is no longer genuine. For republics, on the other hand, striking victories may be dangerous in that they put the victorious general in a favourable position for making charismatic claims.

Communal groups [56] approximating the purely traditional type have certainly existed. But they have never been stable indefinitely and, as is also true of bureaucratic authority, have seldom been without a head who had a personally charismatic status by heredity or office. Under certain circumstances, the charismatic chief can be different from the traditional one. Sometimes everyday economic needs have been met under the leadership of traditional authorities; whereas certain exceptional ones, like hunting and the quest of 'booty' in war, have had charismatic leadership. The idea of the possibility of 'legislation' is also relatively ancient, though for the most part it has been legitimized by oracles. Above all, however, whenever the recruitment of an administrative staff is drawn from extra-patrimonial sources, the result is a type of official which can be differentiated from those of legal bureaucracies only in terms of the ultimate basis of their authority and not in terms of formal status.

[56] *Gemeinschaften.*

Similarly, entirely pure charismatic authority, including the hereditary charismatic type, etc., is rare. It is not impossible, as in the case of Napoleon, for the strictest type of bureaucracy to issue directly from a charismatic movement; or, if not that, all sorts of praebendal and feudal types of organization. Hence, the kind of terminology and classification set forth above has in no sense the aim—indeed, it could not have it—to be exhaustive or to confine the whole of historical reality in a rigid scheme. Its usefulness is derived from the fact that in a given case it is possible to distinguish what aspects of a given organized group can legitimately be identified as falling under or approximating to one or another of these categories. For certain purposes this is unquestionably an important advantage.

For all types of authority the fact of the existence and continual functioning of an administrative staff is vital. For the habit of obedience cannot be maintained without organized activity directed to the application and enforcement of the order. It is, indeed, the existence of such activity which is usually meant by the term 'organization.' For this to exist in turn, it is essential that there should be an adequate degree of the solidarity of interests, both on the ideal and material levels, of the members of the administrative staff with their chief. It is fundamental in understanding the relation of the chief to these members that, so far as this solidarity exists, the chief is stronger than any individual member but is weaker than the members taken together. It is, however, by no means necessary for the members of an administrative staff to enter into any deliberate agreement in order to obstruct or even consciously oppose their chief so successfully that the leadership of the chief becomes impotent. Similarly, any individual who sets out to break up a system of imperative control must, if he is going to take over the position of power, build up an administrative staff of his own, unless he is in a position to count on the connivance and co-operation of the existing staff against their previous leader.

Solidarity of interest with a chief is maximized at the point where both the legitimacy of the status of the members and the provision for their economic needs is dependent on the chief retaining his position. For any given individual, the possibility of escaping this solidarity varies greatly according to the structure. It is most difficult where there is complete separation from the means of administration, thus in purely traditional patriarchal structures, under pure patrimonialism and in bureaucratic organizations resting on formal rules. It is easiest where fiefs or bene-fices have been appropriated by socially privileged groups.

It is most important, finally, to realize that historical reality involves a continuous, though for the most part latent, conflict between chiefs and their administrative staffs for appropriation and expropriation in rela-tion to one another. For the development of culture as a whole, it has been crucial in what way this struggle has worked out and what has been the character of the class of officials dependent upon him which has helped the chief win out in his struggle against the feudal classes or other groups enjoying appropriated powers. In different cases it has been a ritually trained type of educated class, the clergy, purely secular clients, household officials, legally trained persons, technically specialized finan-cial officials, or private individuals without official status.[57]

One of the reasons why the character of these struggles and of their outcome has been so important, not only to the history of administra-tion as such, but to that of culture generally, is that the type of educa-tion has been determined by them and with it the modes in which dif-ferent social strata have been subject to different types of educational influence.

1. Both the extent and the way in which the members of an admin-istrative staff are bound to their chief will vary greatly according to whether they receive salaries, opportunities for profit, allowances, or fiefs. It is, however, a factor common to all of these that anything which endangers the legitimacy of the chief who has granted and who guaran-tees them, tends at the same time to endanger the legitimacy of these forms of income and the positions of power and prestige in the social system which go with membership in the administrative staff. This is one of the reasons why legitimacy, which is often so much neglected in analysing such phenomena, plays a crucially important role.

2. The history of the dissolution of the older system of legitimate authority in Germany during and immediately after the World War is instructive in this connexion. The War, on the one hand, went far to break down the authority of tradition; and the German defeat involved a tremendous loss of prestige for the government. These factors com-bined with systematic habituation to illegal behaviour, undermined the

---

[57] *Honoratioren.* There is no good English equivalent term. It refers to persons per-forming functions and exercising authority who do not depend on the position as a major source of income and generally enjoy an independent status in the social struc-ture.—Ed.

amenability to discipline both in the army and in industry and thus prepared the way for the overthrow of the older authority. At the same time, the way in which the old administrative staff continued to function and the way in which its system of order was simply taken over by the new supreme authorities, is a striking example of the extent to which, under rationalized bureaucratic conditions, the individual member of such a staff is inescapably bound to his technical function. As it has been noted above, this fact is by no means adequately explained by the private economic interests of the members—their concern for their jobs, salaries, and pensions—although it goes without saying that these considerations were not unimportant to the great majority of officials. In addition to this, however, the disinterested ideological factor has been crucial. For the breakdown of administrative organization would, under such conditions, have meant a breakdown of the provision of the whole population, including, of course, the officials themselves, with even the most elementary necessities of life. Hence an appeal was made to the sense of duty of officials, and this was successful. Indeed the objective necessity of this attitude has been recognized even by the previous holders of power and their sympathizers.

3. In the course of the present revolution in Germany, a new administrative staff came into being in the Soviets of workers and soldiers. In the first place it was necessary to develop a technique of organizing these new staffs. Furthermore, their development was closely dependent on the War, notably the possession of weapons by the revolutionary element. Without this factor the revolution would not have been possible at all.[58] It was only by the rise of charismatic leaders against the legal authorities and by the development around them of groups of charismatic followers, that it was possible to take power away from the old authorities. It was furthermore only through the maintenance of the old bureaucratic organization that power once achieved could be retained. Previous to this situation every revolution which has been attempted under modern conditions has failed completely because of the indispensability of trained officials and of the lack of its own organized staff. The conditions under which previous revolutions have succeeded have been altogether different.[59]

[58] This and its historical analogies will be discussed further below.

[59] See below, the chapter on the theory of revolutions. (This projected chapter was apparently never written and no systematic account of revolutions is available either in *Wirtschaft und Gesellschaft* or elsewhere in Weber's published works.—ED.)

4. The overthrow of authority on the initiative of the administrative staff has occurred in the past under a wide variety of conditions. Some form of organization of the members of the staff has always been a necessary prerequisite. According to the circumstances, it might have more the character of a conspiracy or more that of a general solidarity with corresponding organization. The latter is, under the conditions to which the modern official is subject, peculiarly difficult; but as the Russian case has shown, it is not altogether impossible. As a general rule, however, such types of organization do not go further than the kind which is open to workers through the ordinary procedure of the strike.

5. The patrimonial character of a body of officials is above all manifested in the fact that admission involves a relation of personal dependency. In the Carolingian system, one became a *puer regis,* under the Angevins, a *familiaris.* Survivals of this have persisted for a very long time.

VI. THE TRANSFORMATION OF CHARISMA IN AN ANTI-AUTHORITARIAN DIRECTION

14: The Transformation of Charisma in an Anti-Authoritarian Direction

A charismatic principle which originally was primarily directed to the legitimization of authority may be subject to interpretation or development in an anti-authoritarian direction. This is true because the validity of charismatic authority rests entirely on recognition by those subject to it, conditioned as this is by 'proof' of its genuineness. This is true in spite of the fact that this recognition of a charismatically qualified, and hence legitimate, person is treated as a duty. When the organization of the corporate group undergoes a process of progressive rationalization, it is readily possible that, instead of recognition being treated as a consequence of legitimacy, it is treated as the basis of legitimacy. Legitimacy, that is, becomes 'democratic.' Thus, for instance, designation of a successor by an administrative staff may be treated as 'election' in advance; while designation by the predecessor is 'nomination'; whereas the recognition by the group becomes the true 'election.' The leader whose legitimacy rested on his personal charisma then becomes leader by the grace of those who follow him since the latter are formally free to elect and elevate to power as they please and even to depose. For the loss of charisma and its proof involves the loss of genuine legitimacy. The chief now becomes the freely elected leader.

Correspondingly, the recognition of charismatic decrees and judicial decisions on the part of the community shifts to the doctrine that the group has a right to enact, recognize, or repeal laws, according to their own free will, both in general and for an individual case. Under genuinely charismatic authority, on the other hand, it is, to be sure, true that conflicts over the correct law may actually be decided by a vote of the group. But this takes place under the pressure of the feeling that there can be only *one* correct decision and it is a matter of duty to arrive at this. The most important transitional type is the legitimization of authority by plebiscite. The commonest examples are to be found in the party leaders of the modern state. But it is always present in cases where the chief feels himself to be acting on behalf of the masses and where his recognition is based on this. Both the Napoleons are classical examples, in spite of the fact that legitimization by plebiscite took place only after the seizure of power by force. In the case of the second Napoleon, it was confirmed on this basis after a severe loss of prestige. Regardless of how its real value as an expression of the popular will may be regarded, the plebiscite has been formally the specific means of establishing the legitimacy of authority on the basis of the free confidence of those subject to authority, even though it be only formal or possibly a fiction.

Once the elective principle has been applied to the chief by a process of reinterpretation of charisma, it may be extended to the administrative staff. Elective officials whose legitimacy is derived from the confidence of those subject to their authority and to recall if confidence ceases to exist, are typical of certain types of democracies, for instance, the United States. They are not 'bureaucratic' types. Because they have an independent source of legitimacy, they are not strongly integrated in a hierarchical order. To a large extent their 'promotion' is not influenced by their superiors and, correspondingly, their functions are not controlled. There are analogies in other cases where several charismatic structures, which are qualitatively heterogeneous, exist side by side, as in the relations of the Dalai Lama and the Taschi Lama. An administrative structure organized in this way is, from a technical point of view, a greatly inferior 'instrument of precision' as compared with the bureaucratic type consisting of appointed officials.

1. The use of the plebiscite as a means of legitimizing leadership on a democratic basis is the most conspicuous type in which democracy is

combined with an important role of leadership. In its fundamental significance it is a type of charismatic authority in which the authoritarian element is concealed, because the traditional position of the leader is held to be dependent on the will of those over whom he exercises authority and to be legitimized only by this will. In actual fact the leader, in this case the demagogue, is able to influence action by virtue of the devotion and trust his political followers have in him personally. In the first instance his power is only a power over those recruited to his following, but in case, with their aid, he is able to attain positions of wider authority it may extend to the political group as a whole. The type is best illustrated by the 'dictators' who have emerged in the revolutions of the ancient world and of modern times. Examples are: the Greek Aisymnetes and the tyrants and demagogues; in Rome the Gracchi and their successors; in the Italian city states the *Capitani del popolo;* and certain types of political leaders in the German cities such as emerged in the democratic dictatorship of Zürich. In modern states the best examples are the dictatorship of Cromwell, and the leaders of the French Revolution and of the First and Second Empire. Wherever attempts have been made to legitimize this kind of exercise of power legitimacy has been sought in recognition by the sovereign people through a plebiscite. The leader's personal administrative staff is recruited in a charismatic form usually from able people of humble origin. In Cromwell's case, religious qualifications were taken into account. In that of Robespierre along with personal dependability also certain 'ethical' qualities. Napoleon was concerned only with personal ability and adaptability to the needs of his imperial 'rule of genius.'

At the height of revolutionary dictatorship the position of a member of the administrative staff tends to be that of a person entrusted with a specific *ad hoc* task subject to recall. This was true of the role of the agents of the 'Committee of Public Safety.' When a certain kind of communal 'dictators' have been swept into power by the reform movements in American cities the tendency has been to grant them freedom to appoint their own staff. Thus both traditional legitimacy and formal legality tend to be equally ignored by the revolutionary dictator. The tendency of patriarchal authorities, in the administration of justice and in their other functions, has been to act in accordance with substantive ideas of justice, with utilitarian considerations and in terms of reasons of state. These tendencies are paralleled by the revolutionary tribunals and by the substantive postulates of justice of the radical democracy of

Antiquity and of modern socialism.[60] The process of routinization of revolutionary charisma then brings with it changes similar to those brought about by the corresponding process in other respects. Thus the development of a professional army in England is derived from the principle of free choice in the participation in religious struggles in the days of Cromwell. Similarly, the French system of administration by prefects is derived from the charismatic administration of the revolutionary democratic dictatorship.

2. The introduction of elected officials always involves a radical alteration in the position of the charismatic leader. He becomes the 'servant' of those under his authority. There is no place for such a type in a technically rational bureaucratic organization. He is not appointed by his superiors and the possibility of promotion is not dependent on their judgment. On the contrary, his position is derived from the favour of the persons whose action he controls. Hence he is likely to be little interested in the prompt and strict observance of discipline which would be likely to win the favour of superiors. The tendency is rather for electoral positions to become autocephalous spheres of authority. It is in general not possible to attain a high level of technical administrative efficiency with an elected staff of officials. This is illustrated by a comparison of the elected officials in the individual states in the United States with the appointed officials of the Federal Government. It is similarly shown by comparing the elected communal officials with the administration of the reform mayors with their own appointed staffs. It is necessary to distinguish the type of democracy where positions of authority are legitimized by plebiscite from that which attempts to dispense with leadership altogether. The latter type is characterized by the attempt to reduce to a minimum the control of some men over others.

It is characteristic of the democracy which makes room for leadership[61] that there should in general be a highly emotional type of devotion to and trust in the leader. This accounts for a tendency to favour the type of individual who is most spectacular, who promises the most, or who employs the most effective propaganda measures in the competition for leadership. This is a natural basis for the utopian component which is found in all revolutions. It also indicates the limitations on the level of rationality which, in the modern world, this type of administration can attain. Even in America it has not *always* come up to expectations.

[60] This will be further discussed in the Sociology of Law.
[61] *Führerdemokratie.*

The following are the principal relations to the economic order:

1. The anti-authoritarian direction of the transformation of charisma normally leads into the path of rationality. If a ruler is dependent on recognition by plebiscite he will usually attempt to support his regime by an organization of officials which functions promptly and efficiently. He will attempt to consolidate the loyalty of those he governs either by winning glory and honour in war or by promoting their material welfare, or under certain circumstances, by attempting to combine both. Success in these will be regarded as proof of the charisma. His first aim will be the destruction of traditional, feudal patrimonial, and other types of authoritarian powers and privileges. His second main aim will have to be to create economic interests which are bound up with his regime as the source of their legitimacy. So far as, in pursuing these policies, he makes use of the formalization and legalization of law he may contribute greatly to the formal rationalization of economic activity.

2. On the other hand, plebiscitary regimes can easily act so as to weaken the formal rationality of economic activity so far as their interests in legitimacy, being dependent on the faith and devotion of the masses, forces them to impose substantive ideas of justice in the economic sphere. This will result in an administration of justice emancipated from formal procedures, and in all sorts of rationing and control of both production and consumption which breaks down the formal character of the judicial process and of administration. This tendency will be dominant so far as the leader is a 'social dictator.' It is a tendency which is by no means confined to the modern socialist type. When it is and when it is not 'socialistic' in the modern sense and what are the consequences cannot yet be discussed.

3. The presence of elective officials is a source of disturbance to formally rational economic life. This is true in the first place because such officials are primarily elected according to party affiliations and not technical competence. Secondly, the risks of recall or of failure of re-election make it impossible to pursue a strictly objective course of decision and administration, without regard to such consequences. There is, however, one type of case where the unfavourable effects for the rationality of economic activity are not evident. This is true where there is a possibility of applying the economic and technical achievements of an old culture to new areas. In this case, the means of production are not yet appropriated and there is a sufficiently wide margin so that the almost inevitable cor-

ruption of elected officials can be taken account of as one of the cost factors, and large-scale profits still be attained.

The classical example of a favourable effect on economic rationality is to be found in the two Napoleonic regimes. Under Napoleon I the *Code Napoléon* introduced compulsory division of estates by inheritance and destroyed all the traditional authorities in French society. It is true that his regime created what almost amounted to fiefs for his deserving followers, and that the soldiers got almost everything, the citizen nothing. But this was compensated for by national glory and on the whole the small bourgeois were relatively well off. Under Napoleon III there was a conscious adoption of the motto of Louis Philippe 'enrichissez-vous.' Grand scale building was carried out but there was also the *Crédit Mobilier* affair with its well-known scandal.

The tendencies of 'social dictatorship' are classically illustrated by the Greek democracy of the Periclean age and of subsequent times. In Rome the jurors who tried a case were bound by the instructions of the Praetor, and decisions followed the formal law. But in the Greek Courts decisions were made in terms of substantive justice. In effect, this meant they were decided by sentimentality, flattery, demagogic invective, and humour. This can be clearly seen in the orations written by the Athenian rhetors. Analogous phenomena are found in Rome only in the case of such political trials as Cicero participated in.

The consequence was that the development of formal law and formal jurisprudence in the Roman sense became impossible. For the Heliaia was a 'people's court' directly comparable to the revolutionary tribunals of the French Revolution and of the Soviet phase of the post-war revolution in Germany. The jurisdiction of these lay tribunals was by no means confined to politically relevant cases. On the other hand, no revolutionary movement in England has ever interfered with the administration of justice except in cases of major political significance. It is true that there was a considerable arbitrary element in the decisions of the justices of the peace, but this applied only within a sphere which did not involve the interests of property. It was confined to police cases.

The United States of America is the classical example of the third type of influence. As late as the early 1900's the author inquired of American workers of English origin why they allowed themselves to be governed by party henchmen who were so often open to corruption. The answer was, in the first place, that in such a big country even though millions of dollars were stolen or embezzled there was still plenty left for everybody, and secondly, that these professional politicians were a group which even workers could treat with contempt whereas technical officials of the German type would as a group 'lord it over' the workers.

A more detailed discussion of relations to economic activity will have to be left for special treatment.[62]

VII. COLLEGIALITY AND THE SEPARATION OF POWERS

15: COLLEGIALITY AND THE SEPARATION OF POWERS

On either a traditional or a rational basis authority may be limited and controlled by certain specific means. The present concern is not with the limitations of authority as such, whether it is determined by tradition or by law. This has already been sufficiently discussed. Just now it is rather a question of specific social relationships and groups which have the function of limiting authority.

1. Patrimonial and feudal regimes generally have their authority limited by the privileges of social class groups. This type of limitation is most highly developed when there is a separation of powers on a class basis.[63] This situation has already been discussed.

2. A bureaucratic organization may be limited and indeed must be by agencies which act on their own authority alongside the bureaucratic hierarchy. This limitation is inherent in the legal type at its highest level of development because administrative action is restricted to what is in conformity with rules. Such limiting agencies have the following principal functions: (a) control and possibly a subsequent test of adherence to rules; (b) a monopoly of creation of the rules which govern the action of officials completely, or at least of those which define the limits of their independent authority; (c) above all a monopoly of the granting of the means which are necessary for the administrative function. These modes of limitation will be discussed separately below.[64]

3. It is possible for any type of authority to be deprived of its monocratic character, which binds it to a single person, by the principle of collegiality. This may, however, occur in a variety of ways with widely varying significance. The following are the principal types:—

(a) It may be that alongside the monocratic holders of governing

[62] As at so many other points, the development here referred to was apparently never completed. The fullest discussion of this point is to be found in the Sociology of Law.—Ed.

[63] *Ständische Gewaltenteilung.*

[64] See sec. 16.

powers there are other monocratic authorities which, by tradition or legislation, are in a position to delay or to veto acts of the first authority. The most important examples are the tribune, and originally the Ephor in Antiquity, the *Capitano del popolo* of the Middle Ages, and the Soviet of German workers and soldiers and its agents in the period from 9 November 1918, until the regular administrative organs were freed from the necessity of having their acts 'countersigned' by such agencies.

(b) The second type is precisely the opposite of this, namely the arrangement that the acts of an authority which is not monocratic must be carried out only after previous consultation and a vote. That is, their acts are subject to the rule that a plurality of individuals must co-operate for the act to be valid. This co-operation may follow the principle of unanimity or of decision by majority.

(c) In effect closely related to case (a) is that in which, in order to weaken monocratic power, a plurality of monocratic officials exists, each of whom has equal authority, without specification of function. In case a conflict arises over the same function, there must be a resort either to mechanical means such as lots, rotation, or oracles, or some controlling agency must intervene. In effect the tendency is for each member of the collegial body to have a power of veto over the others. The most important example is the collegiality of the Roman magistrates, such as the consuls and the praetors.

(d) A type which is closely related to case (b) is that in which, although there is an actually monocratic *primus inter pares,* his acts are normally subject to consultation with formally equal members, and disagreement in important matters may lead to breaking up the collegial body by resignation, thus endangering the position of the monocratic chief. The most important example is that of the position of the British Prime Minister in relation to his cabinet. This organization has, as is well known, changed greatly in the course of its history. The above formulation, however, is substantially correct for most cases in the period of cabinet government.

Advisory collegial bodies do not necessarily involve a weakening of the power of an autocratic chief but may well lead to a tempering of the exercise of authority in the direction of rationalization. It is, however, also possible that in effect they should gain the upper hand over the chief. This is particularly true if they are representative of well-established social classes. The following are the more important types:—

(e) The case noted above under (d) is closely related to that in which a body whose functions are formally only advisory is attached to a monocratic chief. Even though he is not formally bound to follow their advice but only to listen to it, the failure of his policies if this occurs may be attributed to neglect of this advice. The most important case is that of the Roman Senate as a body advisory to the magistrates. From this there developed an actual dominance over the magistrates, chiefly through the Senate's control of finance. The Senate was probably actually only an advisory body in the early days, but through the actual control of finance and still more through the fact that Senators and the formally elected magistrates belonged to the same social class, a situation developed in which the magistrates were in fact bound by the resolutions of the Senate. The formula '*Si eis placeret*,' in which the traditional lack of formal obligation was expressed, came to mean something analogous to 'if you please' accompanied by something like a command.

(f) A somewhat different type is found in the case where a collegial body is made up of individuals with specified functions. In such a case the preparation and presentation of a subject is assigned to the individual technical expert who is competent in that field or possibly to several experts, each in a different aspect of the field. Decisions, however, are taken by a vote of the body as a whole.

Most councils of state and similar bodies in the past have more or less closely approximated to this type. This was true of the English Privy Council in the period before the development of cabinet government. Though at times their power has been very great, they have never succeeded in expropriating monarchs. On the contrary, under certain circumstances the monarch has attempted to secure support in his council of state in order to free himself from the control of cabinets which were made up of party leaders. This attempt was made in England, but without success. This type is also an approximately correct description of the ministries or cabinets made up of specialized officials which hereditary monarchs or elective presidents of the American type have appointed for their own support.

(g) A collegial body, the members of which have specified functions, may be a purely advisory body. In this case it is open to the chief to accept or reject their recommendations, according to his own free decision. This situation is favourable to a high development of the specialization of functions. A good example is the Prussian organization under

Frederick William I. This type is always favourable to consolidating the power of the chief.

(h) The direct antithesis of rationally specialized collegiality is a traditional collegial body consisting of 'elders.' Their collegial function is primarily to guarantee that the law which is applied is really authentically traditional. Sometimes such bodies have a veto power as a means of upholding the genuine tradition against untraditional legislation. The 'Gerousia' which were found in many of the Greek city states are good examples. The Areopagus in Athens and the Patres in Rome held such a veto power. The latter, however, belong primarily in type (1).

(i) One way of weakening the power of supreme authorities is by applying the collegial principle to the highest authority whether the supremacy be formal or substantive. Several variations of this type are found, resembling the types already discussed in the above paragraph. The powers of individual members of such bodies may be assumed in rotation or may be distributed on a permanent basis. Such bodies are collegial so long as there is a formal requirement that legitimate acts require the participation of all the members. One of the most important examples is the Swiss Federal Council, the members of which do not have clearly defined specialized functions, while to some extent the principle of rotation is involved. Another type of example is found in the revolutionary councils of 'People's Commissars' in Russia, Hungary, and for a short time in Germany. In the past such bodies as the 'Council of Eleven' in Venice and the Colleges of *Anzianen,* belong in this category.

A great many cases of collegiality in patrimonial or feudal organizations belong in one or another of the following types:—

(i) They are cases of the distribution of power between socially established groups, which may consist in collegial organization of an administrative staff, the members of which have a privileged social position, or of those who have appropriated certain rights.

(ii) They may, secondly, be cases of collegial organization of patrimonial officials which the chief has organized in order to counterbalance the power of organized privileged groups. This is often the position of the councils of state discussed above under (f).

(iii) Thirdly, they may be cases of advisory bodies or sometimes bodies with executive authority over which the chief presides or the meetings of which he attends or from which at least he receives reports. Such bodies are generally made up either of technical experts or of persons of high social prestige or both. In view of the increasingly specialized considerations involved in the functions of government he may hope, through the advice of such bodies, to attain a level of information sufficiently above pure dilettantism so that an intelligent personal decision is possible.

In cases of the third type the chief is naturally interested in having heterogeneous and even opposed elements represented, whether this heterogeneity is one of technical opinions or of interest. This is because, on the one hand, he is concerned with the widest possible range of information, and on the other with being in a position to play the opposing interests off against each other.

In the second type, on the contrary, the chief is often, though not always, concerned with uniformity of opinions and attitudes. This is a main source of the 'solidary' ministries and cabinets in so-called 'Constitutional states' or others with an effective separation of powers. In the first case the collegial body which represents the appropriated interests will naturally lay stress on uniformity of opinion and solidarity. It is not, however, always possible to attain this, since every kind of appropriation through social privilege creates conflicting interests.

The first of these types is illustrated by the assemblies of estates and the assemblies of vassals which preceded them, and have been found frequently not only in Europe but elsewhere—for instance in China. The second type is well illustrated by the administrative organs which were formed in the early stages of the development of modern monarchy and were of a thoroughly collegial character. Though not exclusively, they were primarily, composed of legal and financial experts. The third type is illustrated by the councils of state of the earlier modern Western monarchies and is also found in other parts of the world. As late as the eighteenth century it was not unknown for an Archbishop to have a seat in the English cabinet. It is typical of these bodies that they have been composed of a mixture of socially prominent persons and of specialized officials.

(j) Where there is a conflict of interests of socially established groups it may work out to the advantage of a chief through a process of negotiation and struggle with the various groups. For organizations which are composed of delegated representatives of conflicting interests, whether their basis be in ideal causes, in power, or in economic advantage, may at least in external form be collegial bodies. What goes on within the body is then a process of adjustment of these conflicts of interest by compromise.

This type is present in a crude form wherever there is a separation of powers, as between socially established groups, in such a way that decisions can only be arrived at by a compromise between the privileged groups. A more highly rationalized form is built up when the delegated members of the collegial bodies are selected in terms of their permanent social or class status, or in terms of the specific interests they represent. In such a body, unless its character is radically changed, action cannot result from a 'vote' in the ordinary sense but is the outcome of a compromise which is either negotiated among the interests themselves or is imposed by the chiefs after the case for each of the groups involved has been considered.

The peculiar structure of the state based on socially privileged groups [65] will be discussed more in detail below. The above formulation applies to such situations as arose through the separation of the bodies representing different social groups. Thus in England the House of Lords was separated from the House of Commons, while the Church did not participate in Parliament at all but had its separate 'Convocations.' In France, the division came to be that of the nobility, the clergy, and the third estate, while in Germany there were various more complex divisions. These divisions made it necessary to arrive at decisions by a process of compromise, first within one estate and then between estates. The decisions were then generally submitted to the King as recommendations which he was not necessarily bound to follow. To-day there has been a revival of a somewhat similar theory of representation by occupational groups. The advocates of this proposal for the most part fail to see that even under these conditions it would not be possible to arrive at genuine agreement but that compromise would be inevitable. In so far as free workers' councils were the bodies concerned, the tendency would be for questions to be settled in terms of the relative economic power of different groups, and not by spontaneous agreement.

(k) A related case is that where collegial bodies which decide things by vote have been formed out of a plurality or organized groups which were previously autocephalous and autonomous. In such cases a right to a voice in decision is appropriated by the leaders or the delegates of the component groups. Examples are found in the representation of the phylae, the phratries, and the clans in the governing bodies of ancient city states, in the Medieval federation of tribes in the time of the *Consules,* in the Mercandanza of the guilds, in the delegates of the craft

[65] *Ständestaat.*

unions to the executive council of a federation of trade unions, in the federal council or senate in federal states and finally in the distribution of appointments to cabinet posts in coalition ministries. This last case is particularly clear in the case of Switzerland, where posts are distributed in proportion to the number of votes for each party.

(l) A rather special case is that of the collegial character of elected parliamentary bodies which is hence in need of separate treatment. Its composition rests on one of two bases. It is either based on leadership, in which case the particular members constitute the following of leaders, or it is composed of collegial party groups without subordination to a specific leader. To understand this it is necessary to discuss the structure of parties.

Except in the case of the monocratic type of collegiality where there is mutual veto, collegiality almost inevitably involves obstacles to precise, clear, and above all, rapid decision. In certain irrational forms it also places obstacles in the way of technical experts, but in introducing specialized officials monarchs have often found this consequence not altogether unwelcome. With the progressive increase in the necessity for rapid decision and action, however, these obstacles have been increasingly overcome. Generally speaking, where collegial bodies have had executive authority the tendency has been for the position of the leading member to become substantively and even formally pre-eminent. This is true of the positions of the Bishop and the Pope in the church and of the Prime Minister in cabinets. Any interest in reviving the principle of collegiality in actual executive functions is usually derived from the interest in weakening the power of persons in authority. This, in turn, is derived from mistrust and jealousy of monocratic leadership, not so much on the part of those subject to authority, who are more likely to demand a 'leader,' as on the part of the members of the administrative staff. This is not only or even primarily true of negatively privileged groups but is, on the contrary, typical of those enjoying positive privileges. Collegiality is in no sense specifically 'democratic.' Where privileged groups have had to protect their privileges against those who were excluded from them they have always attempted to prevent the rise of monocratic power. Indeed, they have had to do so because such a power could always base itself on the support of the underprivileged. Thus, while on the one hand they have tended to enforce strict equality within the privileged group they have tended to set up and maintain collegial bodies to supervise or even to take over power.

This was one important factor in the position of the Ephors in Sparta, of the council in Venice, and of the Senate in Rome before the time of the Gracchi and in the time of Sulla. It happened repeatedly in England in the eighteenth century, in Berne and the other Swiss cantons, in the Medieval towns with their collegial councils, and in the Mercadanza which represented the merchant guilds rather than the craft guilds. These last bodies very easily came to be controlled by the nobility.

Collegiality favours greater thoroughness in the weighing of administrative decisions. Apart from the considerations already discussed, where this is more important than precision and rapidity, collegiality tends to be resorted to even to-day. Furthermore, it divides personal responsibility, indeed in the larger bodies this disappears almost entirely, whereas in monocratic organizations it is perfectly clear without question where responsibility lies. Large-scale tasks which require quick and consistent solutions tend in general, for good technical reasons, to fall into the hands of monocratic 'dictators,' in whom all responsibility is concentrated.

It is impossible for either the internal or the foreign policy of great states to be strongly and consistently carried out on a collegial basis. The dictatorship of the proletariat for the purpose of carrying out the socialization of a society requires an individual 'dictator' with the confidence of the masses. The 'masses' as such are not necessarily adverse to this but the people holding power in Parliaments, parties, or, what makes very little difference, in 'Soviets,' cannot put up with such a dictator. This type has emerged only in Russia through the help of military force and supported by the interests of the peasants in the solidary maintenance of their newly acquired control of the land.

Finally, a few remarks may be made which partly summarize and partly supplement what has already been said. From a historical point of view, collegiality has had two principal kinds of significance. On the one hand it has involved a plurality of incumbents of the same office, or a number of persons in offices whose spheres of authority were directly competing, each with a mutual power of veto. This is primarily a matter of a technical separation of powers in order to minimize authority. The most conspicuous instance of this type of collegiality is that of the Roman magistrates. Their most important significance lay in the fact that every official act was subject to intercession by a magistrate with equal authority, thus greatly limiting the power of any one magistrate. But the magistracy remained an individual office merely multiplied in several copies.

The second main type has been that involving collegial decision. In such cases an administrative act is only legitimate when it has been produced by the co-operation of a plurality of people according to the principle of unanimity or of majority. This is the type of collegiality which is dominant in modern times; though not unknown in Antiquity, it is not characteristic of that civilization. It may involve collegiality in the supreme command and so in the direct exercise of authority, only in subordinate functions, or, finally, in bodies with an advisory function.

Collegiality in the supreme authority may be derived from the following considerations:—

(a) Its basis may lie in the fact that the governing authority has arisen from the combination of a plurality of previously autocephalous groups and that each of these demands its share of power. This was true of the 'synoikism' of the ancient city states with their councils organized on the basis of clans, phratries, and phylae. It was true of the Medieval towns with a council representing the important noble families, and of the Medieval guild federations, in the guild merchant with its council of representatives of the component guilds. It is also found in the bodies representing the component states in modern federal states and in the collegial structure of the ministries which have been built up by party coalitions. Collegiality in this case is a particular case of the representation of social or territorial groups.

(b) It may, secondly, be based on the absence of a leader. This may in turn result from mutual jealousy among those competing for leadership or from the attempt to prevent any individual from attaining undue power. It has appeared in most revolutions from a combination of these factors, in such forms as a council of officers or even soldiers of revolutionary troops or the Committee of Public Safety or the Councils of People's Commissars. In normal times of peace it has almost always been the last motive, antipathy to the individual 'strong man, which has underlain the establishment of collegial bodies. This has been true of Switzerland and of the new constitution of Baden. In the last case it was the socialists who most strongly manifested this antipathy; for fear of such centralized powers they sacrificed the strict unification which was an absolutely essential condition of successful socialization. The most decisive influence in this was the attitude of party officials in trade unions, local communities, and party headquarters, all of whom were suspicious of the powers of leadership.

(c) The third basis lies in the independent social position of the elements primarily available for positions of power and of the social groups monopolizing these positions. In this case collegiality is the product of an aristocratic regime. Every socially privileged class fears the type of leader who seeks support in the emotional devotion of the masses just as much as the type of democracy without leaders fears the rise of 'demagogues.' The senatorial regime in Rome, various attempts to rule through closed councils, and the Venetian and similar constitutions all belong in this category.

(d) The fourth basis may lie in the attempt of monarchs to counteract increasing expropriation at the hands of a technically trained bureaucracy. In the modern Western state, the modern type of administrative organization was first introduced at the top with the establishment of collegial bodies. This was similar to what happened to the patrimonial states of the Orient, in China, Persia, the Empire of the Caliphs, and in the Ottoman Empire, all of which served as models for Europe. A monarch is not only afraid of the power of particular individuals but hopes above all to be in a position, in the votes and counter-votes of a collegial body, to hold the balance himself. Furthermore, since he tends to become more and more of a dilettante he can also hope in this way to have a better comprehension of the details of administration than if he abdicated in favour of individual officials. Generally speaking the functions of the highest bodies have been a mixture of advisory and executive elements. It is only in the field of finance, where arbitrariness has particularly irrational consequences, that, as in the reform of the Emperor Maximilian, the power of the monarch was surrendered to specialized officials at an early stage. In this case there were powerful factors forcing the monarch to give way.

(e) Another basis lies in the need to reconcile the points of view of different technical specialists and divergent interests, whether material or personal, by collegial discussion, that is to make compromise possible. This has been particularly true in the organization of community affairs, which have on the one hand involved highly technical problems which could be appraised in local terms, and on the other hand have tended to rest heavily on the compromise of material interests. This has been true at least so long as the masses have put up with control by the classes privileged through property and education. The collegiality of ministries rests, from a technical point of view, on a similar basis. In Russia and to a less extent in Imperial Germany, however, it has not been possible to attain effective solidarity between the different parts of the government. The result has been bitter conflict between the different agencies.

The basis in cases (a), (c), and (d) is purely historical. Bureaucratic authority in the modern world has, wherever it has developed in large-scale associations such as states or metropolitan cities, everywhere led to a weakening of the role of collegiality in effective control. Collegiality unavoidably obstructs the promptness of decision, the consistency of policy, the clear responsibility of the individual, and ruthlessness to outsiders in combination with the maintenance of discipline within the group. Hence for these and certain other economic and technical reasons in all large states which are involved in world politics, where collegiality has been retained at all, it has been weakened in favour of the prominent position of the political leader, such as the Prime Minister. A similar process has taken place in almost all of the large patrimonial organizations, particularly those which have been strictly Sultanistic. There has again and again been the need for a leading personality such as the Grand Vizier in addition to the monarch, unless a regime of favourites has provided a substitute. One person must carry the responsibility, but from a legal point of view the monarch himself could not do this.

Collegiality as employed in agencies acting under the direction of higher authorities has been primarily intended to promote objectivity and integrity and to this end to limit the power of individuals. As in respect to the highest authority it has almost everywhere, for the same reasons, given way to the technical superiority of monocratic organizations. This process is illustrated by the fate of the 'governments' in Prussia.

Finally, in purely advisory bodies, collegiality has existed at all times and will probably always continue to exist. It has played a very important part historically. This has been particularly true in cases where the power structure was such that 'advice' submitted to a magistrate or a monarch was for practical purposes binding. In the present discussion it is not necessary to carry the analysis further.

The type of collegiality under discussion here is always collegiality in the exercise of imperative control. It is thus a matter of bodies which either themselves hold authority or which influence the authorities directly through their advice. The behaviour of assemblies representing social groups and of parliamentary bodies will be taken up later.[66]

[66] See below, part x of this chapter, pp. 416 ff.

From a historical point of view it is in terms of collegiality that the concept of an 'administrative organ'[67] first came to be fully developed. This is because collegial organization has always involved a separation of the sphere of office of the members from their private affairs, of the staff of officials serving the administrative body as such from those responsible to the members as private individuals and finally of the means of administration from personal property. It is thus by no means fortuitous that the history of modern administration in the Western World begins with the development of collegial bodies composed of technical specialists. This has also been true of every permanent organization of patrimonial, feudal, or other types of traditional political structures though in a different way. The monarchs of the Western World have been subject to a gradual process of political expropriation which has been made possible by the fact that in their increasing dilettantism they could not be a match for collegial bodies of officials, the members of which were capable of acting harmoniously. If officials had been merely individual appointees, the obligation of personal obedience would have made it far more difficult to maintain consistent opposition to the irrational arbitrary will of the monarch. When it became evident that a transition to the rule of technical bureaucracy was inevitable, the monarch has regularly attempted to extend the system of advisory collegial bodies in the form of councils of state, in order to maintain his supremacy in spite of his lack of technical competence by playing off the internal dissensions of these bodies against each other. It was only after rational technical bureaucracy had come to be finally and irrevocably supreme that a need has been felt, particularly in relation to parliaments, for solidarity of the highest collegial bodies under monocratic direction through a prime minister. With this latest development the general tendency of monocracy, and hence bureaucracy, in the organization of administration has become definitively victorious.

1. The significance of collegiality in the early stages of the development of modern administration is particularly evident in the struggle which the financial bodies, which the Emperor Maximilian was forced to create to meet the emergencies of the Turkish invasions, carried on against his tendency to go over the heads of his officials and to issue orders and pledge securities for loans in accordance with every momentary whim. It was in the sphere of finance that the expropriation of the

[67] *Behörde.*

monarch began, for it was here in the first place that he lacked technical competence. This development occurred first in the Italian city states with their commercially organized system of accounting, then in the Burgundian and French Kingdoms, in the German territorial states, and independently of these in the Norman state of Sicily and in England. In the Near East the Divans played a similar role, as did the Yamen in China and the Bakufu in Japan. In these cases, however, no rationally trained group of technically competent officials was available, and it was necessary to resort to the empirical knowledge of 'experienced' officials. This accounts for the fact that a rationally bureaucratic system did not result. In Rome a somewhat similar role was played by the Senate.

2. The role of collegiality in promoting the separation of the private household from the sphere of office is somewhat similar to that played by the large-scale voluntary trading companies in the separation of the household and the profit-making enterprise on the one hand, of personal property and capital on the other.

16: The Functionally Specific Separation of Powers

It is further possible for imperative powers to be limited by a functionally specific separation of powers. This means entrusting different individuals with specifically differentiated 'functions' and the corresponding powers. In the strictly legal type as in the constitutional separation of powers these functions are rationally determined. It follows that in questions which involve two or more authorities it is only by means of a compromise between them that legitimate measures can be taken.

1. Functionally specific separation of powers differs from that based on socially independent groups in that powers are divided in terms of their functionally objective character. This involves some kind of 'constitution' which need not, however, be formally enacted or written. The organization is such either that different types of measures have to be undertaken by different authorities or that the same type involves the co-operation by informal compromise of a plurality of agencies. It is not merely spheres of competence which are separated in this case but also the ultimate rights to imperative control.

2. The functionally specific separation of powers is not wholly a modern Western phenomenon. The separation of an independent political

authority from an equally independent religious authority instead of either Caesaropapism or theocracy belongs in this category. Similarly, there is a certain sense in which the specified spheres of competence of the different Roman magistracies may be thought of as a kind of 'separation of powers.' The same is true of the specialized charismata of lamaist Buddhism. In China the Confucian Hanlin Academy and the 'censors' had a position which, in relation to the Emperor, was largely independent. In most patrimonial states as well as in the Roman Principate it has been usual for the administration of justice and the civil aspect of finance to be separated from the military establishment, at least in the lower reaches. But in these cases the concept of separation of powers loses all precision. It is best to restrict its application to the supreme authority itself. If this restriction is accepted then the rational formally enacted constitutional form of the separation of powers is entirely a modern phenomenon. Even in a non-parliamentary state, if it is constitutional, a budget can be put through only by a process of compromise between the legal authorities, such as the crown, and one or more legislative chambers.

Historically, the separation of powers in Europe developed out of the old system of estates. Its theoretical basis for England was first worked out by Montesquieu and then by Burke. Further back the separation of powers began in the process of appropriation of governing powers and of the means of administration by privileged groups. Another important factor lay in the increasing financial needs of the monarchs, both the recurring needs arising from the social and economic organization and the exceptional ones of war time. They could not be met without the consent of privileged groups, though funds were often supplied on the initiative of the latter. In this situation it was necessary for the estates to reach a compromise, which was the historical origin of compromises over the budget and over legislation. The latter phenomena do not, however, belong in the context of the separation of powers as between privileged social groups but to the constitutional type.

3. The constitutional separation of powers is a specifically unstable structure. What determines the actual power structure is the answer to the question what would happen if a constitutionally necessary compromise, such as that over the budget, were not arrived at. An English king who attempted to rule without a budget to-day would risk his

crown, whereas in pre-revolutionary Germany a Prussian king would not, for under the German system the position of the dynasty was dominant.

17: The Relations of the Political Separation of Powers to the Economic Situation

1. Collegiality of legal bodies with rationally defined functions may be favourable to objectivity and the absence of personal influences in their administrative actions. In this case, in spite of the negative influence of imperfect precision of function, the general effect is likely to be favourable to the rationality of economic activity. On the other hand, the very large capitalistic interests of the present day, like those of the past, are apt, in political life—in parties and in all other connections that are important to them—to prefer a monocratic type of organization. For monocracy is, from their point of view, more 'discrete.' The monocratic chief is more open to personal influence and is more easily swayed, thus making it more readily possible to influence the administration of justice and other governmental activity in favour of such powerful interests. If German experience is to be trusted this preference is justified.

Conversely, the type of collegiality involving mutual veto powers or that in which collegial bodies have arisen out of the irrational appropriation or power of a traditional administrative staff may have irrational consequences. The type of collegiality of financial bodies which was found in the early stages of the development of technical bureaucracy has on the whole certainly been favourable to the formal rationalization of economic activity.

In the United States the monocratic 'party boss' has, much more than the official party organs which are often collegial, favoured the interests from which party funds are derived. Precisely for this reason he is indispensable. In Germany large sections of so-called 'heavy industry' have favoured the power of the bureaucracy rather than the collegial parliamentary groups. The reason is in both cases the same.

2. Like every form of appropriation, the separation of powers creates established spheres of authority which, though they may not yet be rational, still involve an element of calculability. Hence in the functioning of the political system the separation of powers is generally favourable to the formal rationalization of economic activity. Movements which, like the Soviet type, the French Convention, and the Committee on Pub-

lic Safety, aim to abolish the separation of powers, are definitely concerned with a more or less rational reorganization of economic life in substantive terms. They are, accordingly, unfavourable to formal rationalization.[68]

VIII. PARTIES

18: THE CONCEPT OF PARTIES AND THEIR FEATURES

The term 'party' will be employed to designate an associative type of social relationship, membership in which rests on formally free recruitment. The end to which its activity is devoted is to secure power within a corporate group for its leaders in order to attain ideal or material advantages for its active members. These advantages may consist in the realization of certain objective policies or the attainment of personal advantages or both. Parties may have an ephemeral character or may be organized with a view to permanent activity. They may appear in all types of corporate groups and may themselves be organized in any one of a large variety of forms. They may consist of the following of a charismatic leader, of traditional retainers, or of rational adherents, that is, persons adhering from motives of expediency or of attachment to absolute values. They may be oriented primarily to personal interests or to objective policies. In practice, they may be officially or merely in fact solely concerned with the attainment of power for their leaders and with securing positions in the administrative staff for their own members. They may, on the other hand, predominantly and consciously act in the interests of a social group or a class or of certain objective policies or of abstract principles. The attainment of positions in the administrative staff for their members is, however, almost always a secondary aim and objective programmes are not infrequently merely a means of persuading outsiders to participate.

By definition a party can exist only *within* a corporate group, in order to influence its policy or gain control of it. Federations of party groups which cut across several corporate bodies are, however, possible and not uncommon.

A party may employ any one of the conceivable means of gaining power. In cases where the government of the corporate body is determined by a formally free ballot and legislation is enacted by vote they are primarily organizations for the attraction of votes. Where voting

[68] All further detail must be reserved to the specialized parts of this work.

takes a course in accord with legitimate expectations they are legal parties. The existence of legal parties, because of the fact that their basis is fundamentally one of voluntary adherence, always means that politics becomes a matter of the play of interests. It should, however, be noted that in this context, 'interests' is by no means necessarily primarily an economic category. In the first instance, it is a matter of political interests which rest either on the ideological basis or on an interest in power as such.

The following elements are primarily involved in party activities:

(a) Party leaders and their staffs, who are apt to play the dominant role.

(b) Active party members who for the most part merely have the function of acclamation of their leaders. Under certain circumstances, however, they may exercise some forms of control, participate in discussion, voice complaints, or even initiate revolutions within the party.

(c) The inactive masses of electors or voters, who are merely objects whose votes are sought at election time. Their attitudes are important only as an object of orientation for the soliciting of the party organization, where there are actual struggles with other parties for power.

(d) Contributors to party funds who usually, though not always, remain behind the scenes.

Apart from formally organized legal parties in formal legal corporate groups, there are the following principal types:

(a) Charismatic parties arising from disagreement over the charismatic quality of the leader or over the question of who, in charismatic terms, is to be recognized as the correct leader. They arise through a process of schism.

(b) Traditionalistic parties arising from controversy over the way in which the chief exercises his traditional authority in the sphere of his arbitrary will and grace. They arise in the form of movements to obstruct innovations or in open revolt against them.

(c) Parties organized about questions of faith.[69] These are usually, though not necessarily, identical with (a). They arise out of disagreement over the content of doctrines or declarations of faith. They take the form of heresies, which are to be found even in rational parties such as the socialist.

(d) Appropriation parties arising from conflict with the chief and his administrative staff over the filling of positions in the administrative staff.

---

[69] *Glaubensparteien.*

This type is very often, though by no means necessarily, identical with (b).

In their form of organization, parties may conform to the same types as any other corporate groups. They may thus be charismatically oriented by devotion to the leader, with the plebiscite as an expression of confidence. They may be traditional with adherence based on the social prestige of the chief or of an eminent neighbour, or they may be rational with adherence to a leader and staff set up by a 'constitutional process' of election. These differences may apply both to the basis of obedience of the members, and of the administrative staff. Further elaboration must be reserved to the Sociology of the State.[70]

It is of crucial importance for the economic aspect of the distribution of power and for the determination of party policy by what method the party activities are financed. Among the possibilities are small contributions from the masses of members and sympathizers, large contributions from disinterested sympathizers with its cause, what directly or indirectly amounts to purchase on the part of interested parties or taxation either of elements under obligation to the party, including its members, or of its defeated opponents. It is not, however, possible to discuss these problems further at this point.

1. As has been pointed out, parties can exist by definition only within a corporate group, whether political or other, and only when there is a struggle for control of the main group. Within a party there may be and very often are sub-parties, for example, as ephemeral structures they are typical in the nomination campaigns of the presidential candidates of the American parties. On a permanent basis an example is the 'young liberals' in Germany. Parties which extend to a number of different corporate units are illustrated by the Guelfs and Ghibellines in Italy in the thirteenth century and by the modern socialists.

2. The criterion of formally voluntary solicitation and adherence in terms of the rules of the corporate group within which the party exists is treated here as the crucial point. It involves a distinction of crucial sociological significance from all organized groups which are prescribed and controlled by the central corporate body. Even where the order of the main corporate group takes notice of the existence of parties, as in

---

[70] There is no section of *Wirtschaft und Gesellschaft* under this title, and apparently none was ever written. More of the material appropriate to such a discussion is in part iii, *Typen der Herrschaft*, than in any other part of the work. There is, however, no extended discussion of parties.—ED.

the United States and in the German system of proportional representation, the difference remains. It remains even if an attempt is made to regulate their constitution. When a party becomes a closed group which is incorporated by law into the administrative staff as was true of the Guelfs in the Florentine statutes of the thirteenth century, it ceases to be a party and becomes a part of the structure of the political group itself.

3. In a genuinely charismatic imperatively co-ordinated group, parties are necessarily schismatic sects. Their conflict is essentially over questions of faith and, as such, is not subject to final solution. The situation in a strictly patriarchal body may be somewhat similar. Both these types of parties, at least in the pure form, are radically different from parties in the modern sense. In the usual type of hereditary monarchy and of political organization with traditionally privileged groups, it is common for groups of retainers, composed of pretenders to fiefs and offices, to rally around a pretender to the throne. Personal followings are also common in such cases as the aristocratic city states which are governed by unpaid office holders. They are, however, also prominent in many democracies. The modern type of party does not arise except in the legal state with a representative constitution. It will be further analysed in the Sociology of the State.

4. The classic example of parties in the modern state organized primarily around patronage are the two great American parties of the last generation. Parties primarily oriented to objective policies and systems of value have been the older type of conservatism in Germany, nineteenth century Liberalism, the middle-class Democratic parties, later the Social Democrats, and the Centre Party. In all, except the last, there has been a very prominent element of class interest. Since the Centre has attained the principal points of its original programme it has become very largely a pure patronage party. In all these types, even those which are most purely an expression of class interests, the interests, both ideal and material, which both the party leaders themselves and the members of the party organization have, in power, office, and remuneration always play an important part, along with other factors. There is a tendency for the interests of the electorate to be taken into account only so far as their neglect would endanger electoral prospects. This fact is one of the sources of opposition to political parties as such.

5. The different forms which the organization of parties take will be dealt with separately in the proper place. One fact, however, is common to all these forms, namely, that there is a central group of individuals

who assume the active direction of party affairs, including the formulation of programmes and the selection of candidates. There is, secondly, a group of 'members' whose role is notably more passive, and, finally, the great mass of members of the larger corporate group whose role is only that of objects of solicitation by the various parties. Their function is to choose between the various candidates and programmes offered by the different parties. Given the voluntary character of party affiliation this structure is unavoidable. It is this which is meant by the statement that party activity is a matter of 'play of interests,' it being understood, as has already been stated, that it is political interests and not economic interests which are involved. The role of interests in this sense is the second principal point of attack for the opposition to parties as such. In this respect there is a formal similarity between the party system and the system of capitalistic enterprise which rests on the exploitation of formally free labour.

6. The role in party finance of large-scale contributors [71] is by no means confined to the 'bourgeois' parties. Thus Paul Singer was such a contributor to the socialistic party, though to be sure from humanitarian motives which so far as is known were entirely disinterested. His whole position as chairman of the party rested on this fact. Furthermore the Russian revolution in its party structure in the Kerensky stage was partly financed by very large Moscow business interests. Other German parties on the 'right' have been financed by heavy industry, while the Centre party has often had large contributions from Catholic millionaires.

For reasons which are readily understandable, the subject of party finances, though one of the most important aspects of the party system, is the most difficult to secure adequate information about. It seems probable that in certain special cases a 'machine' has actually been 'bought.' Apart from the role of individual large contributors there is a fundamental alternative. On the one hand, as in the English system, the electoral candidate may carry the principal burden of campaign expenses, with the result that the candidates are selected on a plutocratic basis. On the other hand, the costs may be borne by the 'machine,' in which case the candidates become dependent on the party organization. Parties as permanent organizations have always varied between these two fundamental types, in the thirteenth century in Italy just as much as to-day. These facts should not be covered up by fine phrases. Of course, there are limits to the power of party finance. It can only exercise an influence in so far

[71] *Mäzenaten.*

as a 'market' exists, but as in the case of capitalistic enterprise, the power of the seller as compared with the consumer has been tremendously increased by the suggestive appeal of advertising. This is particularly true of 'radical' parties regardless of whether they are on the right or the left.

IX. TYPES OF GOVERNMENT OF CORPORATE GROUPS WHICH MINIMIZE IMPERATIVE POWERS; THE ROLE OF REPRESENTATION

19: ANTI-AUTHORITARIAN FORMS OF GOVERNMENT

Though a certain minimum of imperative powers in the execution of measures is unavoidable, certain corporate groups may attempt to reduce it as far as possible. This means that persons in authority are held obligated to act solely in accordance with the will of the members and in their service by virtue of the authority given by them. In small groups where all the members can be assembled at a single place, where they know each other and can be treated socially as equals this can be attained in a high degree. It has, however, been attempted in larger groups, notably the corporate cities and city states of the past and certain territorial groups.

The following are the principal technical means of attaining this end: (a) Short terms of office, if possible only running between two general meetings of the members; (b) Liability to recall at any time; (c) The principle of rotation or of selection by lot in filling offices so that every member takes a turn at some time. This makes it possible to avoid the position of power of technically trained persons or of those with long experience and command of official secrets; (d) A strictly defined mandate for the conduct of office laid down by the assembly of members. The sphere of competence is thus concretely defined and not of a general character; (e) A strict obligation to render an accounting to the general assembly; (f) The obligation to submit every unusual question which has not been foreseen to the assembly of members or to a committee representing them; (g) The distribution of powers between a large number of offices each with its own particular function; (h) The treatment of office as an avocation and not a full time occupation.

If the administrative staff is chosen by ballot, the process of election takes place in the assembly of members. Administration is primarily oral, with written records only so far as it is necessary to have a clear record of certain rights. All important measures are submitted to the assembly.

This type of administration in which the assembly of members is effective, and those closely related to it, will be called 'immediate democracy.'

1. The North American 'town' and the smaller Swiss Cantons such as Glarus, Schwyz, and Appenzell are all, on account of their size alone, on the borderline of applicability of immediate democracy. The Athenian democracy actually overstepped this boundary to an important extent, and the *parliamentum* of the Medieval Italian cities still more radically. Voluntary associations, guilds, scientific, academic, and athletic associations of all sorts often have this type of organization. It is, however, also applicable to the internal organization of aristocratic groups of people who are unwilling to allow any individual to hold authority over them.

2. In addition to the small scale of the group in numbers or territorial extent, or still better in both, as essential conditions of immediate democracy, is the absence of qualitative functions which can only be adequately handled by professional specialists. Where such a group of professional specialists is present, no matter how strongly the attempt is made to keep them in a dependent position, the seeds of bureaucratization are present. Above all, such persons can neither be appointed nor dismissed according to the procedures appropriate to immediate democracy.

3. Closely related to the rational forms of immediate democracy is the organization of the primitive types of gerontocratic or patriarchal groups. This is because those holding authority are expected to administer it in the 'service' of the members. There are two principal differences: governing powers are normally appropriated and action is strictly bound to tradition. Immediate democracy is either a form of organization of rational groups or may become a rational form. The transitional types will be discussed presently.

20: 'AMATEURS' OR 'NON-PROFESSIONAL' TYPES OF ADMINISTRATIVE PERSONNEL

The term 'amateur' [72] will be applied to persons with the following characteristics: (1) If by virtue of their economic situation they are able on a continuous basis to occupy positions of leadership or authority in a corporate group without remuneration or with a remuneration which

[72] *Honoratioren.*

is merely nominal. (2) If, regardless of the basis on which it rests, they occupy a position of social prestige such that in a formally democratic process there is a probability that the free or traditional expression of the confidence of the members will result in their election to office.

This type of 'amateur' status rests in its primary significance on the essential condition that the individual is able to live *for* politics without living *from* politics. He must hence be able to count on a certain level of provision from private sources. This condition is most likely to be met by receivers of property income of all sorts, such as landowners, slaveowners, and owners of cattle, real estate, or securities. Along with these, people with a regular occupation are in a favourable position if their occupation is such as to leave them free for political activity as an avocation. This is particularly true of persons whose occupational activity is seasonal, notably agriculture, of lawyers, who have an office staff to depend on, and certain others of the free professions. It is also to a large extent true of patrician merchants whose business is not continuously exacting. The most unfavourably situated are independent industrial entrepreneurs and industrial workers. Every type of immediate democracy has a tendency to shift to a form of government by this type of 'amateur.' From an ideal point of view this is because they are held to be especially well-qualified by experience and objectivity. From a material point of view this form of government is especially cheap, indeed, sometimes completely costless. Such a person is partly himself in possession of the means of administration or provides them out of his own private resources, while in part they are put at his disposal by the corporate group.

1. The role of social class status in determining amateur governing groups will be analysed later. The primary source of this status in all primitive societies is wealth. Possession of wealth alone is often sufficient to make a man a 'chief.' In addition to this, according to different circumstances, the attribution of hereditary charisma or the mere fact of birth may be more prominent than wealth as such.

2. In the American township the tendency has been to favour actual rotation on grounds of natural rights. As opposed to this the immediate democracy of the Swiss Cantons has been characterized by recurrence of the same names and still more families among the office holders. The fact that well-born people were considered more eligible in the Germanic communal groups and in the towns of northern Germany which were in part originally strictly democratic is one of the sources of the differen-

tiation from the masses of the *meliores,* and hence of the patriciate, who monopolized the city councils.

3. This type of government by amateurs is found in all kinds of corporate groups. It is, for instance, typical of political parties which are not highly bureaucratized. It always means an extensive rather than intensive type of administration. When there are very urgent economic or administrative needs for precise action, though it is free to the group as such, it is hence often very expensive for individual members.

Both immediate democracy and government by amateurs are technically inadequate, on the one hand in organizations beyond a certain limit of size, constituting more than a few thousand full-fledged members, or on the other hand, where functions are involved which require technical training or continuity of policy. If, in such a case, permanent technical officials are appointed alongside of shifting heads, actual power will normally tend to fall into the hands of the former, who do the real work, while the latter remain essentially dilettantes.

A typical example is to be found in the situation of the annually elected Rector of the German University who administers academic affairs as a sideline, as compared with the 'syndics,' or under certain circumstances even the government officials in the ministries of education. Only an autonomous university President with a long term of office like the American type would, apart from very exceptional cases, be in a position to create a genuinely independent self-government of a university which went beyond phrase-making and expressions of self-importance. In Germany, however, both the vanity of academic faculties and the interests of the state bureaucracy in their own power stand in the way of any such development. Varying according to particular circumstances similar situations are to be found everywhere.

It is further possible for immediate democracy and government by amateurs to exist in their genuine forms only so long as parties which contend with each other and attempt to appropriate office do not develop on a permanent basis. As soon as such parties develop, the leaders of the parties and their administrative staffs constitute an imperatively co-ordinated structure, which will be introduced into the structure of the group as such by the victorious party, however it attains power. This is true regardless of the formal retention of the previous organization. Indeed, this is a relatively common process by which such types of organization are broken up.

X. REPRESENTATION

21: The Principal Forms and Characteristics of Representation

The primary fact underlying representation is that the action of certain members of a group, the 'representatives,' is binding on the others or is looked upon as legitimate so that its result must be accepted by them.[73] In the organization of authority in corporate groups, however, representation takes a variety of typical forms.

1. Appropriated representation. In this case the chief or a member of the administrative staff holds appropriated rights of representation. In this form it is very ancient and is found in all kinds of patriarchal and charismatic groups. The power of representation has a traditionally limited scope. This category covers the sheiks of clans and chiefs of tribes, the headmen of castes in India, hereditary priests of sects, the patel of the Indian village, the *Obermärker,* hereditary monarchs, and all sorts of similar patriarchal or patrimonial heads of corporate groups. Authority to conclude contractual agreements and to agree on binding rules governing their relations is found permitted to the elders of neighbouring tribes in what are otherwise exceedingly primitive conditions, as in Australia.

2. Closely related to appropriated representation is that on a basis of socially independent grouping.[74] This does not constitute representation so far as it is a matter primarily of representing and enforcing their own appropriated rights or privileges. It may, however, have a representative character and be recognized as such, so far as the effect of the decisions of such bodies as estates extends beyond the personal holders of privileges to the unprivileged groups. This may not be confined to the immediate dependents of the members of the class in question but may include others who are not in the socially privileged class. These others are regularly bound by the action of the privileged group, whether this is merely taken for granted or a representative authority is explicitly claimed. This is true of all feudal courts and assemblies of privileged estates, and includes the *Stände* of the late Middle Ages in Germany and of more recent times. In Antiquity and in non-European areas this institution occurs only sporadically and has not been a universal stage of development.

[73] See above chap. i, sec. 11.
[74] *Ständische Repräsentation.*

3. The radical antithesis of this is 'instructed' representation. In this case elected representatives or representatives chosen by rotation or lot or in any other manner exercise powers of representation which are strictly limited by an imperative mandate and a right of recall, the exercise of which is subject to the consent of those represented. This type of 'representative' is, in effect, an agent of those he represents. The imperative mandate has had for a very long time a place in the most various types of groups. For instance, the elected representatives of the communes in France were almost always bound by the *cahiers des doléances*. At the present time this type of representation is particularly prominent in the Soviet type of republican organization where it serves as a substitute for immediate democracy, since the latter is impossible in a mass organization. Instructed mandates are certainly to be found in all sorts of organizations outside the Western World, both in the Middle Ages and in modern times, but nowhere else have they been of great historical significance.

4. Free representation. The representative, who is generally elected though he may actually or formally be subject to rotation, is not bound by instruction but is in a position to make his own decisions. He is obligated only to express his own genuine conviction, and not to promote the interests of those who have elected him.

Free representation in this sense is not uncommonly an unavoidable consequence of the incompleteness or absence of instructions, but in other cases it is the deliberate object of choice. In so far as this is true, the representative, by virtue of his election, exercises authority over the electors and is not merely their agent. The most prominent example of this type is modern parliamentary representation. It shares with legal authority the general tendency to impersonality, the obligation to conform to abstract norms, political or ethical.

As a feature of the representative bodies of modern political organization of parliaments, the function of this type of representation is not understandable apart from the voluntary intervention of parties. It is the party groups which present candidates and programmes to the politically passive citizens. They also, by the process of compromise and balloting within the parliament, create the norms which govern the administrative process. They subject the administration to control, support it by their confidence, or overthrow it by withdrawal of confidence whenever, by virtue of commanding a majority of votes, they are in a position to do this.

The party leader and the administrative staff which is appointed by him, consisting of ministers, secretaries of state, and sometimes under-secretaries, constitute the political administration of the state, that is, their position is dependent upon the electoral success of their party, and an electoral defeat forces their resignation. Where party government is fully developed they are imposed on the formal head of the state, the monarch, by the party composition of the parliament. The monarch is expropriated from the actual governing power and his role is limited to two things. On the one hand by negotiation with the parties, he selects the effective head, and formally legitimizes his position by appointment. On the other hand, he acts as an agency for legalizing the measures of the party chief who at the time is in power.

The 'cabinet' of ministers, that is the executive committee of the majority party, may be organized in a monocratic or a more collegial form. The latter is unavoidable in coalition cabinets, whereas the former is more precise in its functioning. The cabinet protects itself from the attacks of its followers who seek office and its opponents by the usual means, by monopolizing official secrets, and maintaining solidarity against all outsiders. Unless there is an effective separation of powers, this system involves the complete appropriation of all powers by the party organization in control at the time. Not only the top positions but often many of the lower offices become benefices of the party followers. This may be called parliamentary cabinet government.[75]

Where the appropriation of power by the party government is not complete but the monarch or a corresponding elected president enjoys independent power especially in appointments to office, including military officers, there is a 'constitutional' government. This is particularly likely to be found where there is a formal separation of powers. A special case is that where an elective presidency is combined with a representative parliament.

It is also possible for the government of a parliamentary organization to be chosen by a process of election of the executive authorities or the chief executive by the parliament, which would be a purely representative form of government.

[75] The facts are in many respects best presented in the brilliantly polemical attack on the system by W. Hasbach which has erroneously been called a 'political description.' The author in his own essay, *Parlament und Regierung im neugeordneten Deutschland,* has been careful to emphasize that it is a polemical work which has arisen out of the particular situation of the time.

The governing powers of representative bodies may be both limited and legitimized where direct canvassing of the masses of members of the groups is permitted through the referendum.

1. It is not representation as such but free representation in conjunction with the presence of parliamentary bodies which is peculiar to the modern Western World. Only relatively small beginnings are to be found in Antiquity and elsewhere in such forms as assemblies of delegates in the confederations of city states. But in principle the members of these bodies were usually bound by instructions.

2. The abolition of imperative mandates has been very strongly influenced by the positions of the monarchs. The French kings regularly demanded that the delegates to the Estates General should be elected on a basis which left them free to vote for the recommendations of the king. If they had been bound by imperative mandates, the king's policy would have been seriously obstructed. In the English Parliament, as will be pointed out below, both the composition and the procedure of the body led to the same result. It is connected with this fact that right up to the Reform Bill of 1867, the members of Parliament regarded themselves as a specially privileged group. This is shown clearly by the rigorous exclusion of publicity as late as the middle of the eighteenth century. Heavy penalties were laid upon newspapers which reported the transactions of Parliament. The theory came to be that the parliamentary deputy was 'a representative' of the people as a whole and that hence he was not bound by any specific mandates, was not an 'agent' but a person in authority. This theory was already well developed in the literature before it received its present connotation in the French Revolution.

3. It is not possible at this point to analyse in detail the process by which the English king and certain others following his example came to be gradually expropriated by the unofficial cabinet system which represented only party groups. This seems at first sight to be a very peculiar development in spite of the universal importance of its consequences. But in view of the fact that bureaucracy was relatively undeveloped in England, it is by no means so 'fortuitous' as has often been claimed. It is also impossible to analyse the peculiar American system of functional separation of powers combined with electoral representation and the place in it of the referendum which is essentially an expression of mistrust of corrupt legislative bodies. Also Swiss democracy, and the related forms of purely representative democracy which have recently appeared in some of the German states, will have to be left aside for the present. The purpose

of the above discussion was only to outline a few of the most important types.

4. So-called 'constitutional monarchy,' which is above all characterized by appropriation of the power of patronage including the appointment of ministers and of military commanders by the monarch, may concretely come to be very similar to a purely parliamentary regime of the English type. Conversely, the latter by no means necessarily excludes a politically gifted monarch like Edward VII from effective participation in political affairs. He need not be a mere figurehead.

5. Groups governed by representative bodies are by no means necessarily 'democratic' in the sense that all their members have equal rights. Quite the contrary, it can be shown that the classic soil for the growth of parliamentary government has tended to be an aristocratic or plutocratic society. This was true of England.

The relations of the different forms of representation to the economic order are highly complex and will have to be analyzed separately later on. For the present primary purposes only the following general remarks will be made:

1. One factor in the development of free representation was the undermining of the economic basis of the older estates. This made it possible for persons with demagogic gifts to pursue their own inclinations without reference to their social position. The source of this undermining process was the development of modern capitalism.

2. Calculability and reliability in the functioning of the legal order and the administrative system is vital to rational capitalism. This need led the middle classes to attempt to impose checks on patrimonial monarchs and the feudal nobility by means of a collegial body in which the middle classes had a decisive voice, which controlled administration and finance and could exercise an important influence on changes in the legal order.

3. At the time when this transition was taking place, the proletariat had not reached a stage of development which enabled it to become an important political factor which could endanger the position of the bourgeoisie. Furthermore, there was no hesitation in eliminating any threat to the power of the propertied classes by means of property qualifications for the franchise.

4. The formal rationalization of the economic order and the state, which was favourable to capitalistic development, could be strongly

promoted by parliaments. Furthermore, it seemed relatively easy to secure influence on party organizations.

5. The development of demagogy in the activities of the existing parties was a function of the extension of the franchise. Two main factors have tended to make monarchs and ministers everywhere favourable to universal suffrage, namely, the necessity for the support of the propertyless classes in foreign conflict and the hope, which has proved to be unjustified, that, as compared to the bourgeoisie, they would be a conservative influence.

6. Parliaments have tended to function smoothly as long as their composition was drawn predominantly from the classes of wealth and culture, that is, as they were composed of political 'amateurs.' Established social status rather than class interests as such underlay the party structure. The conflicts tended to be only those between different forms of wealth, but with the rise of class parties to power, especially the proletarian parties, the situation of parliaments has changed radically. Another important factor in the change has been the bureaucratization of party organizations, with its specifically plebiscitary character. The member of parliament thereby ceases to be in a position of authority over the electors and becomes merely an agent of the leaders of the party organization. This will have to be discussed more in detail elsewhere.

22: Representation by the Agents of Interest Groups

A fifth type of representation is that by the agents of interest groups. This term will be applied to the type of representative body where the selection of members is not a matter of free choice without regard to occupational, social, or class status, but where the body consists of persons who are chosen on the basis of their occupations or their social or class status, each group in the social system being represented by persons of its own sort. At the present time the tendency of this type is to representation on an occupational basis.

This kind of representation may, however, have a very different significance, according to certain possible variations within it. In the first place, it will differ widely according to the specific occupations, social groups and classes which are involved, and, secondly, according to whether direct balloting or compromise is the means of settling differences. In the first connection its significance will vary greatly according to the numerical proportions of the different categories. It is possible for such a system to be radically revolutionary or extremely conservative in its character. In every case it is a product of the development of powerful parties representing class interests.

It is, at least, the theory that this type of representation weakens the dominance of the play of party interests in politics, though, if experience so far is conclusive, it does not eliminate it. It is also theoretically possible that the role of campaign funds can be lessened, but it is doubtful to what degree this is true. Representative bodies of this type tend to be unfavourable to individual leaders. The professional representative of an interest group can only be a person who devotes his whole time to this function. In classes without independent means the function hence devolves on the paid secretaries of the organized interest groups.

1. Representation where compromise has provided the means of settling differences is characteristic of all the older historical bodies of 'estates.' To-day it is dominant in the trade unions and everywhere where negotiation between the various advisory and executive authorities is the order of the day. It is impossible to assign a numerical value to the 'importance' of an occupational group. Above all the interests of the masses of workers on the one hand and of the increasingly smaller number of entrepreneurs, who are likely both to be particularly well informed and to have strong personal interests, somehow have to be taken account of regardless of numbers. These interests are often highly antagonistic, hence voting by units which are made up of elements which in social and class status are highly heterogeneous, is exceedingly artificial. The ballot as a basis of final decision is characteristic of settling the conflicts and expressing the compromise of parties. It is not, however, characteristic of the estates.

2. The ballot is adequate in social groups where the representation consists of elements of roughly equal social status. Thus the so-called Soviets are made up only of workers. The prototype is the Mercadanza of the time of the conflict between guilds. It was composed of delegates of the individual guilds who decided matters by majority vote. It was, however, in fact in danger of secession if certain particularly powerful guilds were out-voted. Even the participation of 'white-collar workers' in Soviets raises problems. It has been usual to put mechanical limits to their share of votes. If representatives of peasants and craftsmen are admitted, the situation becomes still more complicated, and if the so-called 'higher' professions and business interests are brought in, it is impossible for questions to be decided by ballot. If such a body is organ-

ized in terms of equal representation of workers and employers, the tendency is for 'yellow' unions to support the employers and certain types of employers to support the workers. The result is that the elements which are most lacking in class loyalty have the most decisive influence.

But even purely proletarian 'Soviets' would in settled times be subject to the development of sharp antagonism between different groups of workers, which would probably paralyze the Soviets in effect. In any case, however, it would open the door for adroit politics in playing the different interests off against each other. This is the reason why the bureaucratic elements have been so friendly to the idea. The same thing would be likely to happen as between representatives of peasants and of industrial workers. Indeed any attempt to organize such representative bodies otherwise than on a strictly revolutionary basis comes down in the last analysis only to another opportunity for electoral manipulation in different forms.

3. The probability of the development of representation on an occupational basis is by no means low. In times of the stabilization of technical and economical development it is particularly high, but in spite of this it does not follow that 'partisanship' will be greatly reduced. Unless there is reason to believe that it will be reduced, it is obvious that occupational representative bodies will fail to eliminate parties. On the contrary, as can be clearly seen at the present time, all the way from the 'works councils' to the Federal Economic Council in Germany, a great mass of new benefices for loyal party henchmen are being created and made use of. Politics is penetrating into the economic order at the same time that economic interests are entering into politics. There are a number of different possible value attitudes toward this situation, but this does not alter the facts.

Genuine parliamentary representation with the voluntary play of interests in the political sphere, the corresponding plebiscitary party organization with its consequences, and the modern idea of rational representation by interest groups, are all peculiar to the modern Western World. None of these is understandable apart from the peculiar Western development of social stratification and class structure. Even in the Middle Ages the seeds of these phenomena were present in the Western World but only there. It is only in the Western World that 'cities' in the peculiar corporate sense 'estates' (*rex et regnum*), 'bourgeois,' and 'proletarians' have existed.

IV. Social Stratification and Class Structure

I. CONCEPTS

1: THE CONCEPTS OF CLASS AND CLASS STATUS

THE term 'class status'[1] will be applied to the typical probability that a given state of (a) provision with goods, (b) external conditions of life, and (c) subjective satisfaction or frustration will be possessed by an individual or a group. These probabilities define class status in so far as they are dependent on the kind and extent of control or lack of it which the individual has over goods or services and existing possibilities of their exploitation for the attainment of income or receipts within a given economic order.

A 'class' is any group of persons occupying the same class status. The following types of classes may be distinguished: (a) A class is a 'property class' when class status for its members is primarily determined by the differentiation of property holdings; (b) a class is an 'acquisition class' when the class situation of its members is primarily determined by their opportunity for the exploitation of services on the market; (c) the 'social class' structure is composed of the plurality of class statuses between which an interchange of individuals on a personal basis or in the course of generations is readily possible and typically observable. On the basis of any of the three types of class status, associative relationships between those sharing the same class interests, namely, corporate class organizations may develop. This need not, however, necessarily happen. The concepts of class and class status as such designate only the fact of identity or similarity in the typical situation in which a given individual and many others find their interests defined. In principle control over

[1] Weber uses the term 'class' (*Klasse*) in a special sense, which is defined in this paragraph and which, in particular, he contrasts with *Stand*. There seems no other alternative translation of *Klasse*, but it should be kept in mind that it is being used in a special sense.—ED.

424

different combinations of consumers goods, means of production, investments, capital funds or marketable abilities constitute class statuses which are different with each variation and combination. Only persons who are completely unskilled, without property and dependent on employment without regular occupation, are in a strictly identical class status. Transitions from one class status to another vary greatly in fluidity and in the ease with which an individual can enter the class. Hence the unity of 'social' classes is highly relative and variable.

The primary significance of a positively privileged property class lies in the following facts: (i) Its members may be able to monopolize the purchase of high-priced consumers goods. (ii) They may control the opportunities of pursuing a systematic monopoly policy in the sale of economic goods. (iii) They may monopolize opportunities for the accumulation of property through unconsumed surpluses. (iv) They may monopolize opportunities to accumulate capital by saving, hence, the possibility of investing property in loans and the related possibility of control over executive positions in business. (v) They may monopolize the privileges of socially advantageous kinds of education so far as these involve expenditures.

Positively privileged property classes typically live from property income. This may be derived from property rights in human beings, as with slaveowners, in land, in mining property, in fixed equipment such as plant and apparatus, in ships, and as creditors in loan relationships. Loans may consist of domestic animals, grain, or money. Finally they may live on income from securities.

Class interests which are negatively privileged with respect to property belong typically to one of the following types: (a) They are themselves objects of ownership, that is they are unfree. (b) They are 'outcasts' that is 'proletarians' in the sense meant in Antiquity. (c) They are debtor classes and, (d) the 'poor.'

In between stand the 'middle' classes. This term includes groups who have all sorts of property, or of marketable abilities through training, who are in a position to draw their support from these sources. Some of them may be 'acquisition' classes. Entrepreneurs are in this category by virtue of essentially positive privileges; proletarians, by virtue of negative privileges. But many types such as peasants, craftsmen, and officials do not fall in this category. The differentiation of classes on the basis of property alone is not 'dynamic,' that is, it does not necessarily result in class struggles or class revolutions. It is not uncommon for very strongly privileged property classes such as slaveowners, to exist side by side with such far less privileged groups as peasants or even outcasts without any class struggle. There may even be ties of solidarity between privileged property classes and unfree elements. However, such conflicts as that between land owners and outcast elements or between creditors and debtors, the latter often being a question of urban patricians as opposed to either rural peasants or urban craftsmen, may lead to revolutionary conflict. Even this, however, need not necessarily aim at radical changes in economic organization. It may, on the contrary, be concerned in the first instance only with a redistribution of wealth. These may be called 'property revolutions.'

A classic example of the lack of class antagonism has been the relation of the 'poor white trash,' originally those not owning slaves, to the planters in the Southern States of the United States. The 'poor whites' have often been much more hostile to the Negro than the planters who have frequently had a large element of patriarchal sentiment. The conflict of outcast against the property classes, of creditors and debtors, and of landowners and outcasts are best illustrated in the history of Antiquity.

2: THE SIGNIFICANCE OF ACQUISITION CLASSES

The primary significance of a positively privileged acquisition class is to be found in two directions. On the one hand it is generally possible to go far toward attaining a monopoly of the management of productive enterprises in favour of the members of the class and their business interests. On the other hand, such a class tends to insure the security of its economic position by exercising influence on the economic policy of political bodies and other groups.

The members of positively privileged acquisition classes are typically entrepreneurs. The following are the most important types: merchants, shipowners, industrial and agricultural entrepreneurs, bankers and financiers. Under certain circumstances two other types are also members of such classes, namely, members of the 'liberal' professions with a privileged position by virtue of their abilities or training, and workers with special skills commanding a monopolistic position, regardless of how far they are hereditary or the result of training.

Acquisition classes in a negatively privileged situation are workers of the various principal types. They may be roughly classified as skilled, semi-skilled and unskilled.

In this connexion as well as the above, independent peasants and craftsmen are to be treated as belonging to the 'middle classes.' This category often includes in addition officials, whether they are in public or private employment, the liberal professions, and workers with exceptional monopolistic assets or positions.

Examples of 'social classes' are (a) the 'working' class as a whole. It approaches this type the more completely mechanized the productive process becomes. (b) The 'lower middle' classes.[2] (c) The 'intelligentsia' without independent property and the persons whose social position is primarily dependent on technical training such as engineers, commercial and other officials, and civil servants. These groups may differ greatly among themselves, in particular according to costs of training. (d) The classes occupying a privileged position through property and education.

The unfinished concluding section of Karl Marx's *Kapital* was evidently intended to deal with the problem of the class unity of the proletariat, which he held existed in spite of the high degree of qualitative differentiation. A decisive factor is the increase in the importance of semi-skilled workers who have been trained in a relatively short time directly on the machines themselves, at the expense of the older type of 'skilled' labour and also of unskilled. However, even this type of skill may often have a monopolistic aspect. Weavers are said to attain the highest level of productivity only after five years' experience.

At an earlier period every worker could be said to have been primarily interested in becoming an independent small bourgeois, but the possibility of realizing this goal is becoming progressively smaller. From one generation to another the most readily available path to advancement both for skilled and semi-skilled workers is into the class of technically trained individuals. In the most highly privileged classes, at least over the period of more than one generation, it is coming more and more to be true that money is overwhelmingly decisive. Through the banks and corporate enterprises members of the lower middle class and the salaried groups have certain opportunities to rise into the privileged class.

Organized activity of class groups is favoured by the following circumstances: (a) the possibility of concentrating on opponents where the immediate conflict of interests is vital. Thus workers organize against

---

[2] Like the French 'petite bourgeoisie,' the German term *Kleinbürgertum* has a somewhat more specific meaning than the English 'lower-middle class.' It refers particularly to economically independent elements not employed in large-scale organizations. The typical example are the small shopkeeper and the proprietor of a small handicraft workshop.—ED.

management and not against security holders who are the ones who really draw income without working. Similarly peasants are not apt to organize against landlords. (b) The existence of a class status which is typically similar for large masses of people. (c) The technical possibility of being easily brought together. This is particularly true where large numbers work together in a small area, as in the modern factory. (d) Leadership directed to readily understandable goals. Such goals are very generally imposed or at least are interpreted by persons, such as intelligentsia, who do not belong to the class in question.

3: SOCIAL STRATA AND THEIR STATUS

The term of 'social status' [8] will be applied to a typically effective claim to positive or negative privilege with respect to social prestige so far as it rests on one or more of the following bases: (a) mode of living, (b) a formal process of education which may consist in empirical or rational training and the acquisition of the corresponding modes of life, or (c) on the prestige of birth, or of an occupation.

The primary practical manifestations of status with respect to social stratification are conubium, commensality, and often monopolistic appropriation of privileged economic opportunities and also prohibition of certain modes of acquisition. Finally, there are conventions or traditions of other types attached to a social status.

Stratificatory status may be based on class status directly or related to it in complex ways. It is not, however, determined by this alone. Property and managerial positions are not as such sufficient to lend their holder a certain social status, though they may well lead to its acquisition. Similarly, poverty is not as such a disqualification for high social status though again it may influence it.

Conversely, social status may partly or even wholly determine class status, without, however, being identical with it. The class status of an officer, a civil servant, and a student as determined by their income may be widely different while their social status remains the same, because they adhere to the same mode of life in all relevant respects as a result of their common education.

A social *'stratum' stand* is a plurality of individuals who, within a

[8] *Ständische Lage.* The difficulties of translating the term *Stand* have already been commented upon (see page 347, note 27).—ED.

larger group, enjoy a particular kind and level of prestige by virtue of their position and possibly also claim certain special monopolies.

The following are the most important sources of the development of distinct strata: (a) The most important is by the development of a peculiar style of life including, particularly, the type of occupation pursued. (b) The second basis is hereditary charisma arising from the successful claim to a position of prestige by virtue of birth. (c) The third is the appropriation of political or hierocratic authority as a monopoly by socially distinct groups.

The development of hereditary strata is usually a form of the hereditary appropriation of privileges by an organized group or by individual qualified persons. Every well-established case of appropriation of opportunities and abilities, especially of exercising imperative powers, has a tendency to lead to the development of distinct strata. Conversely, the development of strata has a tendency in turn to lead to the monopolistic appropriation of governing powers and of the corresponding economic advantages.

Acquisition classes are favoured by an economic system oriented to market situations, whereas social strata develop and subsist most readily where economic organization is of a monopolistic and liturgical character and where the economic needs of corporate groups are met on a feudal or patrimonial basis. The type of class which is most closely related to a stratum is the 'social' class, while the 'acquisition' class is the farthest removed. Property classes often constitute the nucleus of a stratum.

Every society where strata play a prominent part is controlled to a large extent by conventional rules of conduct. It thus creates economically irrational conditions of consumption and hinders the development of free markets by monopolistic appropriation and by restricting free disposal of the individual's own economic ability. This will have to be discussed further elsewhere.[4]

[4] This chapter breaks off at this point but is obviously incomplete. There is, however, no other part of Weber's published work in which the subject is systematically developed, although aspects of it are treated in different connexions at many points.—ED.

Index

A

Abel, Theodore, 89 n.
Accounting, capital, 34, 35, 36, 50, 51, 181, 191 ff., 199, 267 ff.
Acquisitiveness, 81, 253
  ethical sanction of, 33
  orientation of economic activity, 34, 35
  vs. profit-making, 201
Action
  as individual behaviour, 101
  four types of, 13, 14
  task of sciences of, 94
  voluntaristic theory of, 12
Administration, *see* Bureaucracy
'Affect,' 14, 17, 27, 92, 115
Aisymnetes, 131, 388
Alltag, 266 n., 361 n.
  see also Charisma
Amateurs, role of in administration, 413 ff.
Anomie, 71
Animals, social organization among, 104
'Appropriation,' *see* Property
Aristotle, 187 n.
'Ascetic Protestantism,' 79, 80, 81
Association, *see* Corporate group
'Atomism, type,' 15
Ausseralltäglichkeit, 64
Authority, 22, 56 ff., 152 ff.
  combinations of different types, 382-6
  charismatic, 64 ff., 358-63
  legal, 329-41
  legitimate, three types of, 328 ff.
  traditional, 59 ff., 341-58
  types of, 57 ff., 324 ff.
Autocephaly vs. heterocephaly, 148
Autonomy vs. heteronomy, 148

B

Bank, definition of, 272
Becker, C. H., 380
von Below, G., 353
von Benedek, L., 111

'Benefice,' 63, 312, 335, 345, 351, 368 ff., 378 ff.
von Böhm-Bawerk, E., 165 n., 165
le Bon, G., 113
Bucher, Karl, 201 n., 219 n., 235 n., 253 n.
Buchmanism, 71
Budgetary unit, 43, 187, 198, 231, 267
  vs. profit-making enterprise, 199 ff.
Bureaucracy, 39, 54, 58, 73
  character of, 329-41
Burke, Edmund, 405

C

Calculability, 193, 316, 337, 355, 357, 420
Calculation
  in kind, 202 ff.
  rational vs. speculative, 272
'Calling,' concept of, 33, 52, 81, 214
Cannon, W. B., 103 n.
Capital
  goods, 267 ff.
  market, 196
  role of, 191 ff.
Capitalism
  character of modern, 279 ff.
  genesis of in Western world, 6
  modern order as, 78 ff.
  politically oriented, 280
  rationalization of activity in, 32
  'spirit' of, 33, 81 n.
  stages in development, 258
  types of, 51-2
  see also Profit-making
Cartel, 209, 215, 253, 274, 275, 313
Catholic Church, 66
  as bureaucracy, 334
Causal relationships, 11, 97 n., 99, 100, 317
Change, institutional, 24
Charisma, 106 n., 265, 328
  authority, 64 ff.
  movements, 71 ff.
  routinization of, 363-73

Charisma (Cont.)
transformation in anti-authoritarian direction, 386-92
see also Alltag
'Chartal,' *see* Money
China, 63, 83, 166 n., 167, 178, 179, 218, 232, 245, 255, 259, 260, 261, 263, 274, 279, 281, 282, 284, 285, 286, 301, 306, 310, 311, 313, 314, 317, 343, 345, 352, 356, 360, 366, 368, 369, 372, 376 n., 377, 378, 379, 381, 396, 401, 404, 405
Christian Science, 71 n.
Church, concept of, 152, 154, 156, 369
Class structure, 424 ff.
Closure of theoretical systems, 8
Collegiality, 392-407
Commenda, 196, 270
Commerce, concept and principal forms, 268 ff.
Communism, 72
see also Socialism
'Company of equals' pattern, 60 n.
Comparative method, 32, 78, 83
Competence, technical, 59 n.
see also Specialization of function
Conflict, concept of, 132
Consumption unit, 193 ff.
Contract, system of, 170-71
Contractual relationships, 163
feudal vs. modern, 64
Convention, definition of, 127
Convergence, in development of theory of action, 7
Corporate group
concept of and types, 145
economic, types of, 171
influence of economic factors on, 318
political and religious, 154
types of association, 151
types of order in, 148
Credit, 179
Cromwell, 388, 389
Cults, religious, 71
Cultural lag, theory of, 71
Custom, definition of, 121

D

Dalai Lama, 364, 387
Democracy, 73, 74
Dilthey, W., 9
Division of labour
social aspects of, 228 ff.
types of economic, 218 ff.

Division of labour (Cont.)
types of technical, 225 ff.
Duelling, 125 n.
Durkheim, E., 7, 53, 71 n., 76

E

Economic action
concept of, 158
institutional structure of, 31
motives of, 319
rational modes of orientation, 34
traditional vs. rational orientation of, 166
see also Motivation, economic
Economic development, stages of, 223
Economic theory, 31, 96, 111, 189, 193, 199, 201, 215
Egypt, 167, 203, 217, 218, 231, 235, 244, 260, 267, 313, 314, 343, 350, 356, 381
Eisner, Kurt, 359
Empiricism, 10
Ends, ultimate, 14, 91, 185
Equilibrium of a system, 15
'Ergasterion,' 243, 257
Error, 92
Escherich, K., 105 n.
Ethics, 129
Evidenz, 90 n.
see also Meaning, interpretation of
Exchange, 169, 170
media of, 173 ff.
see also Money

F

Factors in a system, 11
Factory, 223, 243, 264
Fads, 71
Father Divine, 71 n.
Feudalism, 43, 45, 83, 351, 356, 373-81
Feudalization, process of, 218
Fichte, J., 217
'Fief,' 63, 351, 368, 373 ff.
'Financing,' definition of, 274
effects on private economic activity, 315 ff.
Fontenoy, battle of, 133
Force, use of, 56, 159
as economically irrational, 53
in military structures, 53
Freud, 27 n.
Friedrich, C. J., 206 n.
Friendship, 75
Functional analysis, 18-24, 103, 107
see also Equilibrium of a system
'Fundamentalist reaction,' 72

G

Gay, E. F., 223 n.
Gemeinschaft, 43, 70
General categories, 10
George, Stefan, 363
Germany
  National Socialist, 47
  inflation in, 49
Gerontocracy, 62, 346 ff.
Gerth, H., 72 n.
von Gierke, O., 150 n.
Goldhamer, H., 57 n.
Goldstein, Kurt, 19 n.
Goods, definition of, 165
Götte, 105
von Gottl, F., 88, 162 n., 163 n.
Greece, 235, 243, 244, 260, 261, 315, 318,
  356, 395, 397, 399
Gresham's Law, 98, 107
Guillebaud, W. C., 142 n.

H

von Haller, K. L., 353
Hanseatic town, 243
Hasbach, W., 418 n.
Heterocephaly vs. autocephaly, 148
Heteronomy vs. autonomy, 148
Hitler, 74, 85
Hollin, 328

I

Ideal type, 4, 12, 13 ff., 15, 89 n., 92,
  108 n., 110
Ideas, role of, 6, 123 n., 299 n.
Ideas, religious
  relation to economic activity, 30
von Ihering, R., 122 n., 127 n.
Imputation, problem of, 205
Imperative co-ordination, types of, 152,
  324 ff.
India, 83, 142, 143, 230, 232, 233, 239,
  259, 260, 261, 263, 266, 306, 310, 311,
  314, 315, 317, 350, 352, 356, 368, 369,
  372, 378, 380, 416
Insecurity, psychological, 70
Instability, social, 30, 31, 32, 39, 40, 44,
  68, 84
Instincts, 26
  see also Psychology
Integration of total social systems, 17
Interessenlage, 121 n.
Interest, 198
  definition of, 195
  role of, 299 n.

Irrationality, 15, 17, 92
  substantive, 248-9

J

Jaspers, Karl, 88
Jesuits, 363
Jesus, 361 n.
Jews, 138

K

Kant, 8, 9
Kerensky, 411
Kinship, 75
Knapp, G. F., 49, 174 n., 176, 177, 273,
  282, 283, 286 n., 287 n., 288 n., 293 n.,
  299-309
Knies, Karl, 4, 6 n., 10 n., 13
Knight, F. H., 3 n., 272 n.

L

Labour
  definition of, 219
  expropriation of workers, 246 ff.
  free, 42, 235
  medieval, 220
  modern movement, 208
  productivity of, 261 ff.
  slave, 43, 46, 236
  types of communal organization of, 265
Language, 104 n., 138
Lassalle, F., 149
Law, definition of, 127
Legitimacy of a social order, 57
  bases of, 130 ff., 324 ff.
  concept of, 124
  types of, 126
Leitner, F., 195 n.
Lenin, 216
Leonardo, 228
Liefmann, Robert, 162 n., 323 n.
Lippincott, B. E., 194 n.
Liturgies, 231, 252, 257, 261, 265, 312, 318
Lytric policy, see Money

M

Magic, 82
Malinowski, B., 53
Managerial functions, 219, 248
  property in, 245 ff.
Marriage, 75
Marathon, battle of, 98
Market
  competition, 193

Market (Cont.)
  definition of, 181
  economy, 194, 212 ff.
  freedom, 36, 42, 49
  relationship, principal forms of, 254 ff.
  system, 35
Marx, Karl, 6, 55, 78, 79, 81, 216, 427
Meaning
  complex of, 99; see also Sinnzusammenhang
  interpretation of, 90
Meaningful action, 90
  ideal type of, 112
  see also Subjective point of view, Verstehen, Understanding
Meaningful categories, 93
Means-end schema, 93 n.
Medicine, modern, lack of magic in, 82
Methodology, of social science, 6, 8 ff.
Meyer, Eduard, 98
Middle Ages, 172, 178, 190, 208, 226, 232,
  233, 234, 236, 238, 240, 242, 244, 250,
  261, 263, 282, 288 n., 313, 314, 317,
  344, 351, 366, 369, 372, 374, 376 n.,
  377, 393, 397, 400, 416, 417, 423
von Mises, L., 211 n.
Misplaced concreteness, fallacy of, 26, 103 n.
  see also Reification
von Moltke, 111
Money, 173
  'chartal' form, 174, 178, 291
  consequences of use, 179
  different kinds of, 280 ff.
  formal and material value of, 292 ff.
  'lytric' policy, 282, 287, 294, 295, 297
  paper, 291 ff.
  role of, 33 ff.
Money economy
  formal and substantive rationality in,
  211 ff.
Monetary policy
  methods and aims of, 294 ff.
Monetary system, 40 n., 49
  of modern state, 280 ff.
Montesquieu, 405
Motivation
  economic, 35, 52, 319
  understanding of, 95
Motives, 22
  definition of, 98

N

Napoleon, 387, 388, 391
National Socialism, 71, 72, 74, 85
  see also Germany

'Natural economy,' concept of, 202 ff.
Neurath, O., 207, 208, 211 n., 215
Newbury, Jack of, 264
Non-logical action, Pareto's category of, 16

O

'Objective possibility,' concept of, 149 n.
Occupation, concept of, 250 ff.
Occupational structure, types of, 250 ff.
  see also 'Calling,' Specialization of function, Competence, technical
Oertmann, K., 122 n.
'Office,' 50, 58, 59 n., 68, 330 ff., 332 n., 368
  see also Bureaucracy
Oppenheimer, F., 160, 208 n.
Organism, see Functional analysis
Organization, definition of, 221

P

Pareto, V., 7, 16, 323 n.
Pariah group, 239
Particularistic patterns, 75
  see also Universalism, ethical
Parties, 74, 407-12
Patriarchalism, 62, 346 ff.
Patrimonialism, 62, 346 ff.
Payment, means of, 173 ff.
  see also Money
Planned economy, 37-9, 212 ff., 320
  accounting method in, 205
  see also Socialism
Plechanov, G., 216
Plenge, J., 279 n.
Political authority, 49
Political bodies
  anti-authoritarian forms of, 412-13
  financing of, 310 ff.
  significance of for the economic order,
  309 ff.
  see also Corporate group, political
Political system, British, 57, 73
Power, 152
Powers, separation of, 392-407
'Praebend,' definition of, 351
Preuss, H., 150 n.
Price system, competitive
  functions of, 40 ff.
Probability, 99, 118, 119, 126, 146, 326
Producers' co-operatives, 45
Profane, see Alltag
Professions, the, 54
  learned, 251
  medical, 59 n.

Profit-making, 34, 35
  concept and types, 191 ff.
  enterprise, definition of, 197
  enterprise vs. budgetary unit, 199
  principal capitalistic modes of, 278 ff.
Proof, logic of, 11
Property
  as a system, 40 ff., 163 n.
  in jobs, 236 ff.
  in land, 240 ff.
  in managerial functions, 245 ff.
  in non-human means of production, 238 ff.
  modern system of, 173
  principal forms of, 254 ff.
Protestant Ethic, the, 214 n.
Psychoanalysis, 92 n., 115 n.
Psychological insecurity, 70
Psychology, 22, 25-6
  and sociology, 108
  clinical, 70
Putting-out system, 222, 230, 233, 268

R

Rational action, 12, 15 ff., 27
  ideal type of, 92
Rationality, formal vs. substantive, 35 ff., 50-1, 185, 207, 209
  conditions of maximum, 248, 275 ff.
  in money economy, 211 ff.
  opposition between, 215
Rationality
  of capitalism, 80
  of money accounting, 186
Rationalization, process of, 18, 123
Rational-legal authority, 57 ff.
Reification, 18, 103 n., 118
  see also Misplaced concreteness, fallacy of
Representation, 143
  by interest groups, 421
  forms and characteristics of, 416 ff.
Resentment, 69
Responsibility, 143
Restriction of output, 236
Revolution, 385 n.
Rickert, H., 9, 88, 107 n.
Robertson, H. M., 79 n., 81 n.
Robespierre, 388
Rodbertus, K., 201 n., 231 n., 231
Roethlisberger, F. J., 70 n., 137 n., 263 n.
Roles
  functional specificity and diffuseness, 75, 82 ff.
  occupational, 54

Roles (Cont.)
  specialization of, 33, 80, 81
  segregation of, 69, 75
Romantic love, 75
Rome, 67, 68, 207, 235, 241, 243, 260, 274, 277, 279, 314, 315, 343, 356, 365, 370, 371, 372, 388, 393, 394, 395, 399, 401, 404, 405
Roscher, W., 6 n., 10 n.
Routine activity, see Alltag

S

Sacred, concept of, 76
  see also Charisma
Salamis, battle of, 98
Schäffle, A., 102 n.
Schär, E., 195 n.
von Schelting, A., 13 n., 89 n., 98 n., 109 n.
Schmoller, C., 223
Schönberg, 223
Sciences, 'natural' vs. 'social and cultural,' 8, 9
Sect, 152, 157
Self-interest, 35, 52
  and the institutional order, 53
Serfdom, 234
Services, definition of, 165
Simmel, G., 88, 97 n.
Singer, Paul, 411
Sinnzusammenhang, 26, 95 n.
  see also Meaning, complex of
Sismondi, F., 207
Slavery, 234, 268, 276 ff.
Smith, Joseph, 359
Social action
  definition of, 88, 112
  modes of orientation, 120
  types of, 115
Social relationships
  'associative,' 136
  'communal,' 136
  concept of, 118
  open and closed, 139
  solidary, types of, 136
  types of, 14
Social stratification, 251, 424 ff.
Social system, structure of, 14, 15
Socialism, 37, 164, 185, 194 n., 207, 286, 309, 319, 338, 339, 389, 390, 399, 408, 409, 410, 411
  guild, 216 n., 216
  Kathedersozialisten, 208
  Russian, 216
Sociology
  definition of, 88

Sociology (Cont.)
    science of, 7
    science of and history, 109
    task of comparative, 97
Sociological generalizations, 100
Sohm, R., 328
Sombart, W., 207
Spann, O., 18 n., 106
Spengler, O., 84
Spoils system, 74
    see also Parties
Specialization of function, 225 ff., 228, 261
St. Paul, 363
Stammler, R., 5, 6 n., 88, 122 n., 126 n., 127
Stand, definition of, 347 n.
State, modern definition of, 156
State, rational-legal, 33
Stinnes combine, 229 n.
Stratification, social, 251, 424 ff.
Structional-functional analysis, 24
    see also Functional analysis
Subjective point of view, 9, 18, 22
    see also Meaningful categories, Verstehen
'Sultanism,' 62, 347
Sumner, W. G., 121 n.

T

Tarde, G., 114
Taxation, 50, 312, 313
Tax farming, 201
Tawney, R. H., 3 n.
Taylor system, 205, 261
'Technique,' see Technology
Technology, 160
Tension, in human action, 32, 35, 39, 46 n.,
    53, 69, 80
    see also Instability, social
Theory, role of in empirical science, 23
Timasheff, N. S., 152 n.
Tönnies, F., 88, 127 n., 136 n.
Traditional action, 14, 47, 116
Traditional authority, 59 ff.
'Type generalization,' 108 n.

U

Ultimate ends, see Ends, ultimate
'Understanding,' 87, 94-6
    see also Verstehen

Unions, trade, 46 n., 236
    leaders of, 70
United States, political system of, 74
Universalism, ethical, 33
    in capitalism, 80, 82 ff.
    see also Particularistic patterns
Urban communes, 358
Usage, definition of, 121
Utility, concept of, 158, 164
Utopianism, 56, 60 n., 84

V

Value, concept of, 158
Value-attitudes, 52
Variation, institutional, 31, 52, 54
Veblen, Thorstein, 40 n.
Vedda, 166
Verband, 56 ff., 70, 145 n.
    see also Corporate groups
Verfügungsgewalt, 163
Vergemeinschaftung, 136 n.
    see also Social relationship, 'communal'
Vergesellschaftung, 136 n.
    see also Social relationship, 'associative'
Verstehen, 9, 10, 18, 87 n.
    aktuel and erklärend, 94 n.
    see also 'Understanding'

W

War economy, 209
Weber, Alfred, 206 n.
Weber, Marianne, 4 n.
Weber, Max
    biography, 4
    political interests, 5
    intellectual career, 5
Weigelin, E., 122 n., 127 n.
Weisman, A., 105
Wertbeziehung, 109 n.
Wertrationalität, 14, 115 n., 116, 130 n.
Whitehead, A. N., 103 n.

Z

Zionists, 138
Zweckrationalität, 14, 115 n.